Careers in International Affairs

Careers in International Affairs

Ninth Edition

Laura E. Cressey

Barrett J. Helmer

Jennifer E. Steffensen

Editors

Edmund A. Walsh School of Foreign Service
Georgetown University
Georgetown University Press / Washington, DC

Library of Congress Cataloging-in-Publication Data
Careers in international affairs / Laura E. Cressey, Barrett J. Helmer, and Jennifer E. Steffensen, editors. — Ninth Edition.
p. cm.
Includes bibliographical references and index.
ISBN 978-1-62616-075-0 (pbk. : alk. paper)
1. International relations—Vocational guidance—United States.
2. International economic relations—Vocational guidance—United States. I. Cressey, Laura E. II. Helmer, Barrett J. III. Steffensen, Jennifer E.
JZ1238.U6C37 2014
327.023'73—dc23
2013039859

♾ This book is printed on acid-free paper meeting the requirements of the American National Standard for Permanence in Paper for Printed Library Materials.

15 14 13   9 8 7 6 5 4 3 2 First printing

The following UN Photos by Isaac Billy appear on the front cover: center image of water shortage in Malakal, South Sudan; and lower left image of Peacekeepers in Juba, South Sudan.

Contents

PART II: THE INTERNATIONAL JOB MARKET: TYPES OF EMPLOYERS

PART III: DIRECTORY OF ORGANIZATIONS
∙∙∙

Barrett J. Helmer and Jennifer E. Steffensen

Preface

··

his book is intended to assist those seeking a career in the international affairs community. From my position as a career and internship coordinator at Georgetown University's Master's of Science in Foreign Service (MSFS) program, and my coeditors' positions as graduate students in the MSFS program, much of the content of the book is written with undergraduate and graduate students in mind. But we hope that young professionals, those seeking a career change, and those at an even earlier place in their academic pursuits will also find value in the discussion of the different sectors and organizations in which one can find challenging and enriching internationally focused positions and careers.

Ironically, I used an earlier edition of this book while I was in college and was trying to figure out where to go to graduate school and how to make sense of all the government agencies involved in national security issues. Admittedly, I focused on only one section of the book—the US government and, to some extent, international organizations—given my firm desire to work for the federal government. But my career path to date, which began at the State Department working primarily on nonproliferation issues and then meandered to consulting and to Georgetown, is one that I could not have predicted while thumbing through the pages of this book. Yet I have since discovered that careers spanning the public, private, and nonprofit sectors are more frequent than not. In perusing this book I hope that you recognize that which I often try to convey to my graduate students: Opportunities in a particular field or function do not exist just in one organization, or even in one sector, but usually exist across multiple organizations and sectors. Taking my original focus of nonproliferation, for example, I could have found opportunities in the US government (e.g., in the State, Defense, Commerce, and Energy departments; the intelligence community, the Treasury Department, the Office of Management and Budget, and the US Congress); in the private sector, with any number of consulting firms and government contractors; in international organizations (in the United Nations, the International Atomic Energy Agency, and the Organization for the Prohibition of Chemical Weapons); and in numerous nonprofits, think tanks, and universities. It is extremely easy—and common, as I have repeatedly witnessed—for a person to focus his or her job search on attaining the one perfect job at one specific organization. Hopefully, what you will take away from this book is that it is advisable (and perhaps even essential) to broaden your perspective and be as inclusive as possible in your search for a career in international affairs.

Since the last edition of this book was published in 2008, the international landscape has changed dramatically. Economic and fiscal crises have profoundly affected not just the banking and finance industry but also international business and government. People who are graduating from law school are finding it more difficult to land a plum position in a law firm, meaning that increasing numbers wander into other professions, including public policy and international affairs. For example, in the last several years there has been a dramatic increase in the number of applicants with JDs seeking Presidential Management Fellowships with the US government. The proliferation of social and new media has also altered how we interact with others, how we inform ourselves, and how we pursue job opportunities. We have updated elements of this book to try to reflect some of these changes. In particular, in part II, which discusses different types of employers, we have

- included a chapter on the media, and a discussion of social media also occurs in several places throughout the book.
- expanded the coverage of international development issues, in keeping with the growth of the sector. As such, we have also added an essay in the US government chapter examining government-sponsored development organizations; expanded the nongovernmental organization (NGO) chapter to include a more complete discussion of the different types of NGOs; included an essay on development consulting in the consulting chapter; and added an essay on the international financial institutions in the international organizations chapter.
- incorporated essays on management, risk, development, and business consulting to reflect the diverse nature of the consulting sector.
- broadened the chapter on international business in order to examine opportunities in multinational businesses, entrepreneurship, government contracting, and government relations and lobbying.

As in past editions, this book contains a directory of organizations. These listings are no longer located at the back of each chapter, but are now incorporated in a single directory at the back of the book, which constitutes part III. We have included more than 250 employers spanning all the sectors. This list has been updated from the last edition to reflect changes in the marketplace (including mergers and acquisitions) and to include those organizations that Georgetown's School of Foreign Service Graduate Career Development Center, as well as career centers in other institutions that belong to the Association of Professional Schools in International Affairs, have noted employ our graduates. This directory is by no means all-inclusive, but instead is intended to provide you with a sample of organizations in each of the disciplines that may be attractive to international affairs professionals. With information about these organizations easily accessible on the internet, we are providing you with each organization's website, the location of its headquarters, and a brief description of its work.

Understanding yourself, your strengths, and your goals and interests is a large part of the career puzzle, for if you do not know what you want, it is hard for people to help you succeed. Chapter 1 thus delves into establishing the knowledge and skills that will help you explore yourself and the international affairs field, and serve as the basis for your successful career. Chapter 2 tackles issues with which I have seen students grapple repeatedly, in particular crafting an effective cover letter, using new media to help build a personal brand that is an extension of one's resume, and effective networking and interviewing techniques.

This book would not exist without the wonderful contributions from our MSFS alumni and friends around the world. Their observations, experiences, and advice have been crafted to give you insights into the wide variety of opportunities around the globe. In many cases they have blazed new trails, served as excellent role models, and become valuable mentors to the members of our MSFS community. The essays offer you an in-depth look into particular sectors, and the new "Notes from the Field" pieces provide you with a more detailed look at the everyday life and the career paths of our alumni throughout the public, private, and nonprofit sectors. Our alums are so important to the success of the MSFS program, and we applaud their successes as they continue to inspire new generations of students and professionals.

I am honored to have had the opportunity to work with my wonderful coeditors Barrett J. Helmer and Jennifer E. Steffensen on this book, the first edition of which was published in 1967. Barrett and Jennifer are newly minted MSFS alums, having graduated in May 2013. Their tireless work and unending humor during their two years in the MSFS program were an inspiration, and without them this project would never have come to fruition.

I would also like to thank Maria Pinto Carland for passing the *Careers in International Affairs* torch to us. She edited the last four editions of this publication and was an invaluable resource and an endless source of support and encouragement. In addition to Maria we were incredibly lucky to have the support of so many talented members of the Georgetown community. Our thanks to Casey Dlott, MSFS 2013, who was essential at crunch time, assisting in writing and compiling the organization summaries. Many thanks to Tiffany Li, Amy Liu, Connor Lock, and Lily Wang, all Georgetown undergraduates, who helped us assemble the more than 250 organizations you will find in part III. The MSFS leadership team during the writing of the book—Director Anthony Arend, Associate Director Eleanor Monte Jones, and concentration chairs Ross Harrison, Mark Lagon, and Michael Morfit—provided us with excellent advice and unflagging support. Finally, we would like to thank Lisa Keathley and Anne Steen of the Georgetown School of Foreign Service Graduate Career Development Center for contributing essays to the book and sharing their expertise and experience with us.

Laura E. Cressey

PART I

Strategies

CHAPTER 1

Preparing for Your Career

Education, Coursework, and Internships

Laura E. Cressey

Laura E. Cressey, at the time of writing, was the internship and career coordinator for the Master's of Science in Foreign Service (MSFS) program in the School of Foreign Service at Georgetown University. Before joining the university in 2008, she was an associate at Booz Allen Hamilton and deputy director of the Office of Chemical Biological and Missile Nonproliferation in the Bureau of Nonproliferation at the Department of State. She joined the Department of State as a Presidential Management Fellow in 1992. She is a graduate of MSFS, and received a bachelor's degree in international relations and history from Tufts University.

Careers today look very different from those of our parents and grandparents. Whether due to the economic climate or changing society, it is no longer typical for the average employee to stay with the same organization for the duration of his or her career. Significant retirement packages and pensions do not command company loyalty, as they once did. In the international affairs field this means that individuals are frequently in movement and transition. There is no normal career path and no normal career progression; career paths are frequently less linear and more likely to meander through different organizations and even different sectors. Individuals are as likely to move between organizations in a particular sector (e.g., among US government agencies) as they are between sectors (e.g., from an agency in the public sector to a consulting firm in the private sector to a nonprofit organization).

Take the career path of David Weiss, the author of the "International Development and Humanitarian Assistance NGOs" essay in chapter 5 of this book. David began his career in the US government, working for the Peace Corps, the US Foreign Service, and the US trade representative, and he then moved to the private sector where he worked for a global law firm. After thirteen years in the private sector he moved to the nonprofit sector

3

and currently is the president and CEO of Global Communities (formerly CHF International), an international nonprofit organization that works with communities to bring about sustainable social, economic, and environmental changes. Likewise, Nicole Bibbins Sedaca, who has a piece in chapter 9 on universities, research institutes, and think tanks, has also moved seamlessly between the public and nonprofit sectors while pursuing a career in democracy, human rights, and security work.

The benefit of this fluidity for those entering the international affairs field is that job opportunities lie not just in the well-traveled traditional paths but also throughout various organizations and sectors. As Nicole Melcher explains in her essay in chapter 3 on the US government, those seeking international jobs with federal employers would do well to look beyond the State and Defense departments and to consider departments such as Commerce, Energy, and Treasury. Those interested in working on development issues also have more options than ever before. As the development-related essays mention, the increased presence of the public sector in the development field and the rise of public–private partnerships has diversified the job opportunities for those seeking to enter the field. Likewise, as Barrett Helmer points out in the "Private-Sector Changes since 2008" essay in chapter 7, those interested in entering the business world have more options than ever before to work not just in traditional business positions but also in the area of corporate social responsibility.

So what does this all mean for someone seeking to enter the international affairs field? The good news is that with the loss of the traditional career path comes the loss of the traditional education path. You are no longer expected to check specific boxes in preparation for your career. Instead, students with undergraduate and graduate degrees in a wide variety of disciplines, from international relations and economics, to public health and energy, are marketable in this sector. Moreover, just as there is no one "must have" college or graduate degree, there are no one or two "must have" internships or professional experiences. You are encouraged instead to develop skills and expertise that can span across sectors and make you a valuable, productive, and innovative employee no matter where your career may take you. In this chapter we examine key elements for you to think about while preparing for your career: your education, overseas experience, and fellowships. This essay provides a framework for considering these elements and discusses the value of internships in preparing for your international affairs career.

Your Education

Choosing an undergraduate and graduate school and program is a complicated process dependent on many factors, which Barrett Helmer addresses in his "Considering Graduate School" essay below in this chapter. Of course, the process would be a bit simpler if, from day one of your freshman year in college, you knew exactly what degree you wanted to pursue and what career you wanted to have. But we all know that this is hardly ever the case. As you progress throughout your education, new classes may open up your mind to new opportunities, new courses of study, and different career paths. Embrace these situations! However, as you explore new ideas and paths, keep in mind that there are some skills that employers will seek and that will make you marketable across the spectrum of international affairs career paths. These include:

- a thorough understanding of international relations theory and practice, and knowledge of the history of patterns in international relations;
- a firm grasp of economics—preferably both macro and micro—and an ability to apply these concepts to international policy issues;
- comprehension of finance and trade, and comfort with quantitative analysis;
- proficiency in a second language;
- time spent living, studying, or working abroad;
- excellent analytic skills;
- the ability to effectively communicate complex ideas both orally and in writing;
- a capacity to work independently, and in team situations, in both leadership and subordinate positions;
- skillful time management; and
- demonstrated intellectual curiosity, imagination, drive, and creativity.

You can develop many of these skills in the classroom. But you should also look outside the classroom—such as in student groups, campus activities, internships, and community events—for opportunities to sharpen your skills. Select courses that develop and encourage your intellectual curiosity; take on challenging classes, projects, and internships that help you improve your time management skills; and seek opportunities through classwork or student groups to refine your public speaking and writing abilities. And though you can delve deeply into specific subjects, and specialize in certain academic areas, understand that employers appreciate well-rounded, diverse individuals with demonstrated curiosity, drive, and passion. Intensive specialization in a region or an issue can be valuable, but it should not be gained at the expense of the essential knowledge necessary to effectively operate in the broader international sphere. Those with the ability to look at issues from a variety of perspectives and incorporate multidisciplinary ideas in international policy, development, and business analysis and prescriptions will be more successful.

Papers and projects can be valuable in building your experience in an issue area, especially if you are lacking professional expertise. When given a choice on papers or research projects, be strategic and choose topics that are relevant to your career field. Or write articles for your school's newspaper or international affairs journals. These can be excellent additions to your résumé and can give you material on which to draw in interviews and networking sessions.

Internships

For those seeking to enter the international affairs field, gaining experience to make yourself marketable can seem like a catch-22: You need a job to get relevant experience, but you cannot get a job without relevant experience. If you are not planning to take a gap year before undergraduate school, or to take some time to work between undergraduate and graduate school, or if you are changing careers, then internships are an excellent way of gaining this experience. Internships allow you to explore your options and to "try on" different jobs and organizations to see if they suit you. Internships are also excellent ways to learn about a specific field, to get to know the players, to expand your network, and to learn from others who may be in the sorts of positions and careers that you are considering. Luckily, as mentioned above, there are no one or two specific internships that you should have if you want to become an international affairs professional, which allows you a certain freedom to pursue opportunities that appeal to you. You should choose internships in areas that you want to learn about but also for organizations that allow you to gain experience and demonstrate responsibility.

When looking for or deciding between internships, among the things you should consider are the following:

- What are your responsibilities? Will you be able to write, brief superiors, conduct research, perform analysis, or take responsibility for a task? The more responsibility you have, the more valuable the internship can be. If you are considering having several internships (e.g., while in graduate school), you should try to ensure that you have different responsibilities at the internships so that the experience reflected on your résumé is not one-dimensional (e.g., you do not want to have four internships where you only performed research, unless you ultimately want a career in research).
- Who will you be working for and with? Are they well known or well respected in their field? Could they serve as good role models or as a mentor? Do they have a reputation for helping employees just starting in their career? This is not to say that you should only work

for well-known people, but pay attention to the reputation of the organization and its principals.

- What network of people will you be exposed to? Will you be working alone, or will you be exposed to a broad network of people in your field of choice? Although working independently can be very valuable and can demonstrate your initiative and drive, internships can be very useful in expanding your network and in your job search.

- Does the internship expose you to a different aspect of the business? If you are interested in international trade, for example, you could seek an internship with the Office of the US Trade Representative, the House of Representatives Energy and Commerce Committee, a multinational import-export firm, or a business council (Jonathan Huneke and John Murphy write about their experiences in the "Careers in Lobbying and Advocacy" section of chapter 7, on business), each of which would provide you with a different perspective on the issues and challenges involved in international trade policy. Demonstrating various skills and responsibilities on your résumé as well as an understanding of the different perspectives of issues that you are interested in can be very valuable.

- Is the internship a strategic choice? Some internships involve heavy administrative work assisting a senior official of an organization, which can be attractive based on the access to that official and potential payoffs down the line. As Anna Tunkel notes in the business consulting section of chapter 8, her internship with the CEO of APCO Worldwide led to a full-time position with the firm. She is now a vice president responsible for managing several global accounts. Not all internships provide such payoffs, and you should accept the position with your eyes open; but the potential plus side can be substantial.

Admittedly, not all internships are the same: Some are paid, but many are not; some involve travel; some enable you to bear witness to historic events; and some allow you to publish. Still other internships may be a total bust because they do not live up to their billing or your expectations; because the supervisor is ineffective or ignores you; or because your work is entirely clerical. But these bad experiences can be just as useful as the good ones. Although you may not get a job out of the internship, it may instead help inform your decision making about where you *do not* want to work or what career path you *do not* want to follow or, equally important, what sort of manager you *do not* want to be. These experiences can teach you valuable lessons about effective and ineffective leadership styles. And they can offer you an opportunity to advocate for yourself and seek out responsibilities when they are not provided to you. The bottom line is that the internship experience is what you make of it. Be proactive, energetic, and eager to contribute as well as to learn from your experience.

Achieving Your Goal

With careful selection, your coursework, educational experiences, and internships together can provide you with the necessary background, experience, and expertise to put you in a prime position to achieve your career goals. With the dissolution of the traditional international affairs career path, networking should be an essential element of your job search strategy. This will enable you to better understand the range of available opportunities, to gain information about the backgrounds and qualities that employers seek in prospective employees, and make connections with people who may be able to help you break into the international affairs field.

Overseas Experience
....
Jennifer E. Steffensen

Jennifer E. Steffensen is a 2013 graduate of the MSFS program in the School of Foreign Service at Georgetown University and currently a Presidential Management Fellow with the US Department of State. Before attending graduate school, she worked in China as a marketing and admissions coordinator at the British School of Nanjing and as a broadcast journalist with China Radio International in Beijing. While in graduate school, she interned at the US Embassy in Singapore and the Office of the US Trade Representative in Washington. She graduated cum laude from the College of William and Mary with a BA in history.
....

We live in a globalized world with shrinking borders. Advances in information, communications, and transportation technology have increased the speed at which goods, money, and ideas circumnavigate the globe. Protests in Tunisia can spark uprisings in Libya, Egypt, and Syria. A student in South Korea can receive English lessons from a teacher in the Philippines. Products are no longer simply "made in America" or even "made in China"; they are made in the world, through complex global supply chains that cross national boundaries and complicate concepts such as outsourcing and exporting. Likewise, security and economic challenges—from the European sovereign debt crisis to international terrorism and climate change—have become transnational challenges that require international coordination and global cooperation. Although the sovereign nation still reigns supreme, the changing role of international organizations, and changing norms such as the responsibility to protect, will test the Westphalian system in the decades to come.

Such characterizations are undoubtedly simplifications. Globalization has been taking place for centuries not decades, and other trends such as growing regionalism and interstate conflicts are equally important subjects for students of international affairs. Still, globalization is occurring at an unprecedented rate. International travel and communications have never been faster or cheaper. Indeed, to many, it feels as if the world is spinning faster and faster.

In this changing environment the value of international experience has grown more important. Those who seek to survive in an increasingly complex, interconnected world must develop the foreign language skills, cross-cultural competencies, and flexibility to compete with global talent and to tackle complex international challenges. Thus, it is not surprising that students today are familiar with fervent calls from parents, policymakers, and university presidents urging them to study abroad, work overseas, follow the international news, and become comfortable with diversity. As the now-former assistant secretary of state for educational and cultural affairs, Ann Stock, described it, "Young people who study abroad gain the global skills necessary to create solutions to twenty-first-century challenges."

Many American students have responded to the call. According to a study by the Center for Strategic and International Studies, one in four Americans expects to live, study, or work overseas in their lifetime. Rates of study abroad for American students have tripled over the past twenty years. A record 6.4 million Americans studied or worked abroad in 2011, according to estimates by the US Department of State.

For international policymakers, practitioners, and business leaders, this is encouraging news. Creating a globally minded citizenry with international experience and cross-cultural competencies is critical to tackling the economic, security, environmental, and humanitarian challenges of this century. Yet the influx of young people seeking to gain international experience has also created new challenges. As a growing number of job candidates add international experience to their résumés, employers are looking for longer and more substantive overseas experience to set apart talented candidates. Indeed, for students interested in international development work, field experience and foreign language skills are critical. Some recruiters at competitive firms indicate that professional-level foreign language fluency in one or more languages is sometimes used as a simple parameter by which to narrow down the applicant pool, even when these language skills are not essential to the job itself. The UN requires five years of international work experience in addition to high-level proficiency in one UN working language (English or French). Even in jobs where a set number of years of international work experience may not be directly stated, the applicant with the more substantive overseas work experience will have the competitive edge. A one-month volunteer stint in Honduras may be a transformative personal experience that is well worth pursuing, but a recruiter would be more impressed by a candidate with several years' work experience in a Latin American country and fluency in Portuguese and Spanish. During difficult economic times, the burden on the applicant becomes higher as a scarcity of jobs creates a market more favorable to recruiters than job seekers.

On the positive side, students also have more resources and infrastructure available to help them find work, volunteer, and internship opportunities overseas. A growing study abroad industry has created an increasing array of options and programs that students can tailor to their specific needs. The prudent student thus should research a variety of options before selecting the one that best matches their interests and goals. For instance, a student should decide if they prefer to study abroad through a study abroad assistance program, such as the Council on International Educational Exchange, a program run by their home university, or direct enrollment with a foreign university. Different programs provide different levels of support, resources, and opportunities, and of course come with different price tags, so it is important research the options fully. On the issue of cost, many governments, universities, and nonprofits provide scholarships, grants, and fellowships to make overseas study a more affordable option for motivated and talented students. Just a few examples of US government programs include the Critical Language Scholarship, the Boren Fellowship, and the Fulbright Scholarship, which is available to US citizens as well as foreign nationals. The Institute of International Education also maintains an extensive database of scholarships, fellowships, and grants for all levels of postsecondary US study across a range of academic areas. There are also businesses, study abroad programs, and websites (e.g., www.gooverseas.com and www.goabroad.com) that help students access information on work and volunteer opportunities abroad.

For students, overseas experience can be critical to getting started and advancing in one's career. Whether you aspire to work in international business, diplomacy, advocacy, or development, learning how to work with people from different countries and within different cultures, appreciating the local context of another country, and maintaining relationships with key contacts in your field or industry will have an impact on your success at every stage of your career. If professional motives are not enough, there are also many personal reasons to pursue overseas experience. For many people, the adventure of exploring a new country and culture, the challenge of adaptation, and the joy of forging international friendships can be key motivations to travel or work abroad. Indeed, time spent abroad can lead to profound personal growth as well as lasting relationships. In my own experience the time I spent working in China was a transformative experience. Not only did I improve my language abilities and understanding of the Chinese culture but I also became a more independent, flexible, resourceful, and culturally aware person. And I emerged with a more nuanced perspective on my own country and its role in the world.

Yet living overseas can also be an emotional roller-coaster ride, especially in the beginning, as one is faced with many new challenges on a daily basis. After moving to Nanjing I quickly discovered that working in China, even for a *British* school in China, came with a steep learning curve. First, I realized that in all my years of classroom language study, I had never learned business Mandarin. Although I knew how to discuss China's environmental problems, I did not know how to politely answer the telephone. I had to learn basic phone etiquette and much new vocabulary. Second, I learned that bargaining for goods was a requirement not only for my personal shopping but also for business transactions. Everything was negotiable, and price did not equal quality. Simple tasks such as printing brochures involved day-long excursions to smoky factories, where my colleague and I performed quality control to ensure that the final product met our standards. Indeed, my first year working in China was exhausting. Not only was I adjusting to a new job and new physical environment (and new germs), but everyday tasks, such as learning how to pay my utility bills and use the washing machine, required much more energy and patience than they would in the United States.

Many people who have lived or studied overseas share similar experiences. However, despite all the extra headaches and inevitable mistakes, those who spend time abroad often feel that the benefits outweigh the costs. On a personal level I have made lasting friendships from my time overseas. On a professional level I now appreciate the advantage that international experience brings on the job market. Many employers view past performance as a strong indicator of future behavior. If you can build a track record of working or studying overseas successfully, it will give you credibility when applying for future overseas assignments.

At Georgetown University's MSFS program, nearly 100 percent of students enter the program with overseas experience. My classmates have worked for business councils in Asia, think tanks in Europe, media outlets in the Middle East, the Peace Corps in Africa, and banks in Latin America. Each of my classmates brings to our program a wealth of international academic, professional, and personal experiences that enrich our conversations in the classrooms and corridors and help us to better understand the world.

If you are a student or a young professional interested in working in international affairs, my best career advice to you is to go out into the world with flexibility and an open mind. Pick a country or follow a passion. Research and apply for scholarships, grants, and fellowships to fund your overseas volunteer and study experiences. If you have already graduated, then consider applying for jobs overseas. Overseas experience will change the way

Notes from the Field

Gaining Overseas Experience and Preparing for Graduate School through the Peace Corps

Michael Brannagan

My vision after college was to join the MSFS program at Georgetown, and eventually, to live and work overseas. To gain experience working internationally, and to further explore my interests, I joined the Peace Corps, where I spent two years living in the Amazon Rainforest in Suriname, working on projects ranging from a food security assessment with the Red Cross to local business consulting and several activities with the village school.

Living in a small village in the jungle, any impact I had required humility and taking time to learn the needs of my community, in addition to the culture and language. At the request of one of my local friends, I started a weekly radio program in the Ndjuka language on small business economics. I found that the abstract concepts that I wanted to teach had little meaning for the oral-based Ndjuka culture. To communicate in a relevant way, I used narratives of daily life to convey economic ideas: a woman's reluctance to buy acai berries because cassava was unavailable demonstrated that the two foods are complementary goods; periods of mango scarcity and abundance illustrated the law of diminishing returns and introduced marginal analysis. As a result of the program, people in the region began discussing economic ideas, and this opened up more opportunities for me to serve the village. The Peace Corps prepared me for graduate school and beyond by teaching me to navigate intercultural waters, to apply local habits to global knowledge, and to thrive in challenging physical and mental conditions.

While the Peace Corps prepared me for Georgetown, graduate studies at MSFS opened up a world of options for international work in nearly any sector and geography. From the world of development in the Peace Corps, I took internships during graduate school with the Department of State at the US Embassy in Ethiopia and with the Treasury Department covering Latin America. Upon graduation I joined the British bank HSBC in Hong Kong, where I am currently working on the strategy team. Service in the Peace Corps provided me with the knowledge and character that I would need for MSFS and beyond.

you view the world. It can also give you the skills, experience, and insight to help you make it a better place.

Considering Graduate School

....

Barrett J. Helmer

Barrett J. Helmer does business intelligence and risk analysis for a global investment bank. His professional experience and interests rest at the intersection of foreign investment and the risk considerations of emerging markets, primarily Latin America. Barret has lived and worked in Chile and Colombia. Before his international craeer, Barret worked at the law firm Skadden and began his professional career at Fortune *maganize in New York City. Barret holds a Master of Science in Foreign Service from Georgetown University and graduated with a degree in journalism from the University of Colorado at Boulder. He is fluent in Spanish.*

....

There are plenty of reasons to attend graduate school: academic knowledge, lifetime access to a network of trusted classmates and university alumni, career advancement, and increased earnings potential. The list is long and will be unique to each individual. Though these benefits are not created equal at all programs and across all graduate degrees, they are often magnified and apparent at top master's programs in business, law, and international affairs. For the purpose of this internationally focused book, "graduate school" in this chapter refers to programs in international affairs. In some cases, due to similar academic components and because many students will consider different graduate programs, MBA and JD degrees are given pointed attention. As is discussed in the following pages, considering and deciding to attend graduate school is a rewarding venture that bestows unique rewards, yet it is also an endeavor that must be done through a lens that places paramount value on your interests and long-term goals professional goals.

Before beginning the process of applying to graduate school, you need to decide if you want a graduate degree in the first place. In an increasingly competitive global environment and economy, it may seem like a clear decision and "must have" credential. That said, you should consider various factors in detail to truly know if graduate school is for you: Why are you considering graduate school? For a career change? To be competitive for more prestigious or interesting jobs? For advancement in a current job or organization? To make more money? Is it a graduate degree a mandatory credential for a certain field of work? Are you driven by pure academic interest? Does being back on a college campus offer refuge from a tough economy? Is the window for graduate school closing due to other life commitments, like family? For most readers, the answer will likely be based on an individually unique combination of these factors.

You are in a prime position to consider graduate school if you have worked for a few years following college, and especially if you are increasingly drawn to jobs that list a graduate degree as a requisite. In some instances students enter graduate school directly from undergraduate study, though this is more common in the humanities, social sciences, and medical fields. If you are considering a graduate degree in international affairs or business, you would do well to spend a few years in the professional world before starting graduate school, as this work history allows you to learn more about your interests and gain experience.

Most international affairs gradate schools (and especially those giving MBAs) recommend that students work in a professional environment for at least a few years before applying, because few newly minted college graduates, even those from top undergraduate universities, have gained enough pertinent professional experience. Graduate admissions officers will agree with this statement, even those representing graduate programs that have a handful of young students who are outliers in their graduate school class. Tara Campbell, director of admissions for Georgetown's MSFS program, explains: "We look for at least a few years of increasingly responsible professional experience. Very few students are admitted right from undergrad. Those admitted without substantive professional experience are the exception, not the rule." Even for those students who have impressive, top-firm undergraduate summer internships on their résumés, there is no substitute for real-world work experience.

If you need more professional experience, there are various steps to take, the first of which is to pursue additional responsibilities and projects in your current position. If that does not offer increased challenges, as a shrewd and career-focused individual you should be willing, after investing appropriate time in your current position, to pursue a new job. You are ultimately responsible for your career path and how it can make for a competitive graduate school application and overall career, so candidly assessing your professional growth and its congruency with your aspirations is good practice. This is not to say that you should have a new job every six months, but you must evaluate your objectives and be on the lookout for new challenges if your current endeavors become inconsistent with your ultimate goals. When advancing your own career and gaining related experience, you are exploring your interests and professional goals, which will ultimately make graduate school, if you decide to attend, a more professionally rewarding and personally meaningful experience.

Once you decide you want to attend graduate school—for whatever individual reasons are motivating you—you should then focus on which graduate degrees to pursue. In past decades this decision was made with the understanding that graduate schools were highly focused on their core academic focus. For example, an MBA has always understandably been focused on business fundamentals, whereas traditional international affairs degrees have focused on foreign policy, diplomacy, or international relations theory. But to the benefit of the prospective graduate student, these degree programs have evolved to incorporate various fields of study while still maintaining their academic core. For example, numerous international MBAs and master of international business programs offer a business core but are taught with international case studies and tend to lead students to international pursuits. In international affairs, top degrees have grown to include unique specializations that allow students to broaden their study. In Georgetown's MSFS program, for example, you can chose between a concentration in international relations and security, international development, or international business while still taking core courses in international relations. The beauty of the evolution of many top graduate programs is that they have taken into account globalization and the need to incorporate various skill sets while maintaining their fundamental offerings.

Even with the convergence of coursework in some programs mentioned above, it remains important to pursue a specific graduate degree for its fundamental academic field. In essence, you go to law school to study law, just as an international affairs degree educates you in international affairs. With this factor kept in mind, how do you know which graduate degree is for you? You need to develop a clear view of what you want from a graduate program, an understanding of the financial costs of graduate school, and a plan to ensure that graduate school helps pave the way to achieve future goals. As you consider various graduate degrees, this is again why it is important to work for a few years, because your professional interests will likely evolve in the years following college.

My career started in New York City in magazine publishing, led me to a law firm in Washington, and finally brought me to a start-up educational services firm in Santiago. This eclectic mix of experiences let me evaluate different industries before finally giving me a firm grasp of my professional goals and personal passions. With this clarity, I realized what I wanted from work and life, and therefore understood what credentials and specific graduate education I would need to achieve these goals, I focused on several international affairs and dual MBA–international affairs degrees before deciding on Georgetown's professionally focused MSFS program.

A unique combination of factors brought me to MSFS, just as your ideal program will be determined by your own objectives, background, and interests; there is no one "must attend" graduate program in any academic field, because no program is the same and prospective graduate students value and look for different things. What I was looking for was an international affairs program accredited by the Association of Professional Schools of

International Affairs (for business schools, the equivalent is the Association to Advance Collegiate Schools of Business) in a career-focused US city like Washington that offered networking and a solid overall university reputation, and included a flexible curriculum that allowed me to take courses in business, security, diplomacy, and Latin American studies.

The variety of courses available allowed me to focus my own interests while still taking skill-intensive core courses such as international trade, international finance, statistics, globalization, and international relations theory. Just as an MBA student takes necessary courses like accounting and corporate finance, these required international affairs courses provide knowledge that employers expect students to have, and are also necessary for further success during graduate school. Additionally, as someone who has spent time abroad on the personal and professional levels, MSFS's sizable international student population and international alumni base appealed to me because I knew that having an international career after graduation was one of my top goals.

Of note is that at the writing of this essay, the Georgetown University Edmund A. Walsh School of Foreign Service is ranked as the number one international affairs graduate school in the United States, according to the January–February 2012 edition of *Foreign Policy* magazine. Although this speaks to the courses, professors, administration, and student body, basing a graduate school search on rankings alone is shortsighted. At no point in my graduate school research, application process, and ultimate decision on where to study did top rankings play the key factor. To be fair, rankings are important to the degree that they reflect overall quality and network, but setting your sights on a graduate program simply due to its ranking should not be the top motivator to pursue acceptance. Instead of trying to be accepted to a program due to its assumed benefit or prestige, you should scrutinize the program's ability to meet your professional objectives and academic interests. For example, if you are highly focused on Asia, then it may make sense to consider a program with high-quality Asia-focused courses and professors. Or if you want to intern for the State or Treasury departments during the school year, that would require being in Washington. Are you set on a career in the UN? Do you love econometrics? There are programs whose curriculum and alumni base are more in line with such ventures, again depending on what your final career goals may be. The ultimate decision about where to put your efforts will vary for every individual and should be your compass to bring you to your ideal graduate program.

Once an academic field has been selected and you have decided on a group of potential programs to which to apply, you will need to consider each program-specific application component, such as your Graduate Record Examination (GRE) score, required undergraduate grade point average, personal essays, and recommendations. Although all these elements are important in their own regard, standardized tests represent a crucial and highly competitive portion of any successful graduate school application. These exams, though time intensive and stressful, must be reasonably mastered in order to achieve a solid score and offer you a realistic chance at acceptance to a top graduate program. For the GRE or Graduate Management Admission Test, to apply to a top MBA or master's program and/or to make up for less-than-stellar undergraduate grades, you should start studying long before the exam, consider a tutor or test preparation course, and be prepared to take the test more than once before applying.

As mentioned above, you should gauge programs based your interests and fit with the program but also with a realistic assessment of your grade point average and exam scores. For example, if you did not take undergraduate grades as seriously as possible, you may require an excellent standardized test score, sizable professional experience, and stellar recommendations to make up for such a reality. Conversely, if you rank in the 99th percentile of the quantitative section of GRE but only have six months of work experience, you should consider spending more time in the workforce and make sure your admissions essays are excellent. Overall, the point is for you to know your strengths and weaknesses when formulating a plan of attack for your graduate school application.

For those considering international affairs programs, significant international experience is a must-have credential. I can say from my first-hand view of the students in the MSFS program that substantial time spent living and working abroad is mandatory among a pool of competitive applicants. My classmates include Fulbright scholars, journalists, teachers, consultants, bankers, workers at nongovernmental organizations, business executives, current and former military, and diplomats; all these individuals have spent sizable time abroad doing various interesting and challenging things. Although international travel is rewarding, you should use trips and personal travel as a springboard to build interest in more long-term and demanding international ventures. For example, two weeks in Buenos Aires will not make you an expert on Argentine fiscal policy, but it may plant the seed for further interest in Latin America and make you want to pursue future study focused on international finance and economics. It is crucial to nourish such inclinations and start to pursue legitimate overseas experience, such as work, education, and volunteering. These further exploits make for robust personal and professional achievement, which is essential for narrowing the pool of potential graduate programs and making you a top candidate.

Given the high cost of graduate school, it should be regarded as an investment in yourself and your earning potential. According to the Georgetown University Center on Education and the Workforce, from 2010 to 2012, those with a master's degree earned a median amount of nearly 24 percent more than those with a bachelor's degree alone. Over the long term, this shows that graduate education is an investment that tends to pay off. There is ample research to bolster this assessment, even after the 2008 financial crash and related backlash that cast some doubt upon the value of some graduate degrees. Despite these positive data, you should keep in mind that not all graduate degrees and programs are the same, and your career path is what you make of it, even with a graduate degree to your credit.

Despite the long-term financial incentive, you should be realistic about the financial cost of graduate school. Higher education of any kind is expensive, and government-sponsored loans are more costly than before. Total student loan debt is higher than credit card and auto loan debt in the United States, according to a 2012 study by the Federal Reserve Bank of New York. For most full-time graduate programs, you will be out of work and without employee benefits for nearly two years, so that is an important consideration when deciding if you need to stay employed during graduate school. If financial concerns are significant, an option is to look for a part-time or evening program, again understanding that your individual needs must align with what a program offers. Doing extensive research on scholarships and fellowships is also a prudent option, but it is unlikely that those earnings would completely offset the entire cost of graduate school.

I write this essay as I near the end of my graduate school degree program, and I have put my faith in my program, coursework, and myself to make graduate school pay off and help me achieve my long-term goals. Regardless of a program's reputation, you must do the work, network for professional opportunities, and keep focused on your goals in order for your investment to be realized. It would be inadvisable to go to graduate school out of boredom or as a dilettante, so considering graduate school requires you to be honest about what you want from a degree, which programs to pursue, and how your degree will aid you in achieving your long-term goals. Until you can answer these questions, continue to seek new experiences to further understand your interests and career goals.

Considering a Fellowship

Maryam Henson

Maryam Henson is the director of corporate and foundation relations in the Office of Advancement at Georgetown University, where she works to secure foundation and corporate funding for faculty research and university programs. From 2008 to 2012, she served as the associate director of the Office of Fellowships, Awards, and Research at Georgetown. A lifelong Hoya, she received her bachelor of science degree from the School of Foreign Service, and her JD from the Georgetown Law Center.

A fellowship is a sponsored grant opportunity that funds the recipient to pursue an education or internship-based program. You will often hear the terms "scholarship" and "fellowship" used interchangeably. Generally, in the field of fellowships advising, the term "fellowship" includes scholarship opportunities and refers more specifically to nationally competitive grant applications. Well-known fellowships of which you may have heard include the Rhodes Scholarship, the Fulbright Program, the Truman Scholarship, and the Pickering Fellowship. This essay explores the question of whether pursuing a fellowship is a good fit for your stage of academic or professional development, and examines ways to prepare for these highly competitive opportunities.

Reasons to Pursue a Fellowship

In challenging economic times more people apply for fellowship opportunities but fewer opportunities typically are available because of cuts in government funding and ongoing financial challenges at private institutions. Pursuing a fellowship requires a sustained time commitment to put together a proposal; winning a fellowship depends on a strong fit between the candidate, his or her qualifications and goals, and the mission of the fellowship-granting organization. Each grant-making organization is looking for a very specific person. Almost all foundations are looking to support candidates who can demonstrate commitment to a cause, can demonstrate transformative leadership abilities, have a record of original research, and can communicate effectively in speaking and writing.

Fellowships can provide significant personal and professional benefits. The application itself provides an important training process in writing, editing, rewriting, interviewing, embracing competition, and often dealing with disappointment. These are important skills to master in any profession. The application process often forces the individual to answer self-reflective questions about personal motivations, qualifications, strengths, weaknesses, and ambition. Applying for a fellowship requires personal honesty.

The fellowship experience itself offers several other advantages:

- Fellowships provide an opportunity for *experiential learning*. This may take place in an academic environment or in an internship / work environment. They allow the recipient to gain experience in a field while in a learning position that allows for mistakes. This kind of training and development in a professional setting is valuable for building a skill set, receiving mentoring, networking, and gaining in-depth expertise in an area of study or practice. One compelling form of experiential learning might be one that takes place abroad. Several government and many private fellowships offer the opportunity to study, teach, or work abroad—a kind of on-the-ground learning that is difficult to emulate in a United States–based environment.

- *Compensation* is often considered an advantage and somewhat of a disappointment with fellowship opportunities. Although you will not be compensated as generously as you might be in a full-time job, most likely you will be better compensated than you would be working as a graduate or undergraduate student on a stipend. For example, academic fellowships often cover the full cost of tuition in addition to a small living stipend; internship-based and experiential fellowships often cover the cost of living and a small stipend; and many international fellowships cover the cost of travel to the host country at the start of the grant, and of returning from the country once the grant is over. The reality is that though the fellowship will greatly ease your financial burden for this kind of academic, professional, and networking opportunity, nowadays you may have to cover anything beyond necessities with your own savings.

- Finally, fellowships can convey *significant prestige*. This is a double-edged sword. Having a prestigious fellowship on your résumé can open doors and help you stand out in any applicant pool. Prestige can certainly be part of the reason to pursue a fellowship opportunity; but it cannot, and should not, be the sole reason. I have seen many students spend a significant amount of time trying to make their activities and background fit a prestigious fellowship for which they are not well matched. To ensure that this does not happen to you, read profiles of past winners and try to connect with them via e-mail, Facebook, or LinkedIn. Do your experience and level of expertise match theirs? What is their personality, what is the personality of their fellowship cohort, and is personality important to the grant-making foundation? Be realistic and honest about your qualifications and fit. If your school offers it, seek a fellowship adviser's opinion (many universities work with current students and alumni). Applicants who pursue fellowships primarily for the prestige of the name are often very transparent to interview committees, which tend to resent this approach. If the grant's status is your primary motivation in seeking it, the experience is likely to be a frustrating one.

When to Consider Pursuing a Fellowship

If a fellowship opportunity and the experience it offers fit into your academic, professional, and personal goals, then you should consider pursuing it, as long as you meet the fellowship's guidelines (e.g., academic performance, experience, skill set, age). Many applicants pursue fellowship opportunities at a period of life change—after graduation from college or graduate school, when they are looking for a change of career or jobs, or when they are looking to gain or improve a set of proficiencies. These are all good times to look into fellowships; however, the reality is that what may be good timing for you may not make sense for the fellowship committee. It is up to you to make the case to the fellowship committee that you are the right person, with the strengths they are seeking, at the right time, for this opportunity.

It is important to pay attention to eligibility guidelines and to research opportunities well in advance of completing your application. Many fellowships are available only to students in a particular year at a university. Others are available only to students who already have a bachelor's or graduate degree. Do your research about a year in advance of when you would consider applying and read the guidelines thoroughly.

Let me illustrate with the Fulbright US Student Program as an example. The application process for the Fulbright takes about a year from the time of submitting your application until you arrive in the host country; so if you applied in October 2013, you would not be abroad until September or October 2014. Many schools have an earlier deadline for applying through the university (at Georgetown that would be September 2013), which means that in this example you should have been working on your application, and securing your language evaluations and recommendations, throughout the summer of 2013. Because a Fulbright requires that you have a bachelor's degree *by the time the grant begins*, you should begin working on your application in the summer between your junior and senior years of college if you want to go abroad the year after you graduate. You do not need your bachelor's degree in order to apply, but you do need it in order to begin the grant (but note that some countries clearly state that they prefer graduate student applications). The bottom line: Read the instructions closely and plan accordingly.

Creating a Successful Application

Anyone interested in applying for a fellowship should begin by closely examining the grant program as described by the organization offering the fellowship, and through the words and achievements of past winners. One repeated theme you might notice is that fellowships reward significant past achievement in the area in which they are interested. In some ways fellowships gain their luster from the achievements of those awarded the grant. They are accomplishment oriented, not aspiration oriented. A successful fellowship applicant, like a successful job applicant, can show a history of achievement or skills that makes them well qualified for the opportunity.

For most fellowship applications you will be asked to provide letters of recommendation, a proposal or statement, and your résumé. *Letters of recommendation* are the most important part of your application. They are independent evaluations of your skills and personality from experienced experts in the field. Choose your recommenders carefully. Spend time developing relationships with faculty members and work supervisors. Fellowship committees expect substantial letters that are about two pages long. They should address your background and skills in detail from the perspective and experience of the recommender. The recommender should connect these skills to qualities desired by the fellowship. You can help the recommender by providing him or her with a brief description of the fellowship, a draft of your proposal, your transcript, and a copy of your résumé. It is polite practice to ask for a letter—preferably in person—at least a month in advance of a deadline. For academic fellowships you will be expected to provide primarily academic recommendations. For internship-type fellowships, letters from job supervisors may be more important. For especially prestigious fellowships, the titles of your recommenders matter. (For example, a letter from a full professor counts more than one from an associate or assistant professor because a full professor has many more years of experience, publications, and expertise in the field.) For professional recommendations you should get a letter from the person with the highest-ranking title. It is common practice, for example, if you worked in a senator's office for the person who immediately supervised you to write the letter, and for their supervisor, perhaps the chief of staff or even the senator, to sign the letter.

The *proposal*, or *statement*, is the meat of your application. At most you might be allotted two pages or 1,000 words. Succinct, clear writing is key. Be clear upfront about the field, discipline, or idea in which you are grounding your project. This is not the time for clichéd writing or to use obtuse sentences. Reread every sentence you write. Are there unnecessary words? Could someone else have written the same sentence? If so, discard it. If you are asked to submit a personal statement in addition to a project proposal, it is important that your writing be genuine without being overly emotional or professionally inappropriate. Seek input from past fellowship winners or from experts who advise on fellowship writing. The kind of academic writing that works for college papers, or the kind of emotional writing that worked for your college essay, will not read well in a fellowship context. Good grant writing makes clear your goals, skills, and motivation, and helps the reader understand why you would be a good investment for their organization. Finally, your proposal is not an elaborated résumé. Do not list your accomplishments or courses—if the reader can find such an item somewhere else in the application, for example in your résumé or transcript, you are wasting precious space listing the unnecessary.

Your *résumé* helps the reader understand your background, experience, skills, and accomplishments in an immediately accessible and easily understood format. A fellowship résumé is usually expected to be more elaborate than a job application résumé. Unlike the standard one-page job résumé, the fellowship résumé can be up to two pages long. Like a job résumé, the fellowship résumé should be targeted to the opportunity you wish to pursue. A strong résumé is well edited and uncluttered. Similar to the proposal, you must be comfortable with discarding unnecessary information in order to produce a strong statement of your experience.

Fellowships are not simply study abroad or internship programs. Each award is a prize that is given to an individual with extraordinary achievement, intense passion, and deep intellectual curiosity—and who has already made that passion and curiosity bear fruit. As such, fellowships are not easily won. They require time, energy, and determination; but as outlined above, there are things you can do now to begin preparing for an opportunity that could change your life.

CHAPTER 2

Marketing Yourself

Résumés and Cover Letters

Lisa A. Keathley

Lisa A. Keathley was assistant dean and director of the Graduate Career Development Center for the Edmund A. Walsh School of Foreign Service at Georgetown University from 2005 to 2013. She coached, advised, and helped devise career strategies for graduate students seeking opportunities in a range of disciplines, from finance and trade to international development to homeland security and intelligence. Before coming to Georgetown, she was a distinguished executive in residence at the Trachtenberg School of Public Policy and Public Administration at George Washington University. She was also a senior executive with the Voice of America and the US Information Agency. She received a master of international public policy degree from the Paul H. Nitze School of Advanced International Studies at Johns Hopkins University and a BA in communications from the University of Michigan.

The two traditional primary tools for marketing yourself to potential employers are the résumé and cover letter. They help employers and contacts understand your qualifications and skills, and—depending on how you structure them—your motivations for applying to an organization. This chapter discusses ways to make the most of both of these tools, based on feedback received from employers and observations made while I directed the Graduate Career Development Center at Georgetown's School of Foreign Service.

Your Résumé

The job application process undoubtedly will continue to change as social media evolve and influence the hiring process. More jobs will be posted via social media, and applicants will have to seek jobs and/or be found for jobs via social media. However, a résumé will still be standard in many industries as the best way candidates can market themselves to an employer. In writing a résumé, think of it as a billboard with only a few seconds to deliver your message. In fact, you should assume that an employer will spend no more than 20 seconds scanning your résumé. What do you want a prospective employer to know? Are you an effective researcher? Do you have foreign language skills and experience overseas? Have you managed projects or had your work published? Have you taken courses or given presentations on a topic that would be of interest to an employer? What skills, experiences, and *results* can you cite that will set you apart in a sea of ten, twenty, or a hundred résumés? Your résumé is your marketing piece that should represent your brand.

Your résumé should be focused and targeted for the job for which you are applying. In any job search, applicants often have multiple targeted résumés for particular types of employers and job listings. Résumés can differ in the skills and experience they emphasize, depending on the needs of the employer and the specifics of the job listing. For example, if the first requirement on the job listing for which you are applying is "research," and you have experience doing research with a previous employer, include that as one of your top bullets to show that you are a clear match for that job.

How long should your résumé be —one page or two? The answer to this question will vary depending on the industry. Because most recruiters or employers will receive hundreds of résumés for each job they post, expecting them to read more than one page is unrealistic. In one page, applicants can generally tell the employer what the employer needs to know. However, if you have a significant amount of professional experience that is *relevant* to a prospective employer, use two full pages to demonstrate your accomplishments. Keep in mind that employers will turn to the second page only if they have been captivated by what they read on the first page. In certain industries, a two-page résumé is the norm, so educate yourself on what is expected where you are applying. One possibility is to include a summary statement at the top of the résumé. This would include a brief list of the highlights of your qualifications and give an employer a synopsis of your professional background at a glance. Note that the US federal résumé and a curriculum vitae may be several pages long.

Your Narrative

Start writing a résumé by thinking about your narrative. In just a few seconds, what do you want to communicate to an employer or recruiter? This will vary depending on how much experience you have in an industry or field. For example, if you have held jobs or internships or taken classes in nuclear nonproliferation, it is relatively easy to offer a narrative that supports your interest in a job in that field. If you do not have much experience, but you have taken courses and written papers on the subject, that could contribute to your narrative. If you do not have any background in nuclear nonproliferation but have language or research skills that could be useful in that field, those points can help build a narrative. As you write papers, blog, make presentations, take additional classes, or gain internships or jobs in the field, you can use all these components to build a résumé that will stand out from competitors. Do not be afraid to draw on classwork and projects to help round out the experience on your résumé!

Organizing Your Résumé

It is critical to organize your résumé in a way that gives the reader a road map that is both easy to follow and attractive to view. Here are a few tips to make your résumé aesthetically pleasing:

1. *Use a standard font* because employers are used to seeing the more common fonts. Use only one font in the document because multiple fonts can be distracting. Reduce italicization for the same reason. However, bolding key institutions or employers can help the recruiter's eye move down the page and draw attention to important features of your résumé. Do not include distracting visuals—such as multiple colors, shading, or boxes—because they take away from the employer's ability to quickly locate your most relevant skills and experiences.
2. *White space is critical.* Leave some space at the top and bottom and on the side margins so the résumé can breathe. Too much information crammed to the edges of the margins will make the reader uncomfortable (and make reading the résumé a chore) and suggest you did not know what to cut.
3. *Use sectioning to indicate the different portions of your résumé.* Sections will include relevant employment, education, and key activities and distinctions. Lines can be used to separate the various sections.
4. *Use the left side of your résumé effectively.* In just a few seconds, the recruiter will scan down the left side, looking for key words that will be of interest—the name of your school and the places where you have worked, interned, or volunteered. Based on just a few seconds, the employer will decide whether to read further or to put you in the "no" pile. This is why you never want to put dates on the left side because this will be the first thing the employer sees. You do not want to call attention to the fact that you might have interned at an organization for only a few weeks. Instead, use the left side to note where you interned, which will be of more interest to the reader. Once an employer is interested in you based on this quick look, he or she will then focus on the details.

Your Contact Information
Your name and contact information should be at the top of your résumé. In the United States, this should include an email address and a telephone number where you can be reached. Thinking varies about including a home address. Privacy experts say to leave it off because résumés are most generally submitted electronically and are often forwarded beyond where you originally intended your résumé to go. Others say you should include it so the potential employer knows that you are local, and hiring you would require no relocation expenses. One compromise is to include your street address on your cover letter because the cover letter is only intended for a specific employer. Never include your social security number, age, or marital status on a US résumé.

Your Education versus Your Relevant Employment: Which Is First?
If you are a student, your education should be the first section, followed by your relevant employment, including internships and volunteer experiences. If you are working, you will want to place the relevant work experience at the top, followed by your education. If you are working and going to school, you can decide which is most important for the prospective employer. If you are changing careers and your education rather than experience is most relevant to the jobs to which you are applying, you may wish to lead with your education. If you are sending your résumé to an alumnus of your university, your schooling may be more important to place at the top because that is the connection you share.

The Education Section
Begin the education section of your résumé with the most recent degree you are pursuing or have earned. On the left, list the academic institution and follow with degree level, concentration, or major. Put the month and year of completion and location with city and state on the right. List additional degrees, training, and study in reverse chronological order, starting with the most recent experience and working backward. If you have achieved academic honors, such as Phi Beta Kappa or cum laude or above, include this information because it indicates that you are or were a good student. Your grade point average and standardized test scores are normally included on résumés for consulting, international business, and finance.

Pertinent coursework, consulting or capstone projects, special training, a relevant thesis, or course-related research briefs can be listed under education. These elements can add depth to a résumé for a candidate with little work experience. List only courses that directly relate to the type of job, company, and/or employment sector where you are applying. The education section can also include your experiences studying abroad. Include the overseas institution where you studied, what you studied, the location of your study, and the dates you were overseas. If you earned your degree in another country, you can say, "degree equivalent to US bachelor of science in engineering," for example.

The Employment or Experience Section

Employers consider your experience—paid or unpaid—as an integral part of your résumé. You have several options in naming this section. "Employment" is the most common. If you have been employed in multiple jobs or internships in multiple sectors, you may want to highlight only the relevant jobs and call this section "Relevant Employment." If you have not worked very much but have volunteered or held unpaid positions, you may call this section "Experience."

In your employment section, you want to highlight your experiences, skills, and results using bullets and key action verbs. Never describe your experiences in paragraph form in a résumé. Paragraphs take too long to read and can often hide the key actions, experiences, and results. One of the reasons potential employers put résumés in the "no" pile is that the text is too dense. Just as an outline is faster to read than a full text, bullet points are faster to read than paragraphs.

List each employer where you worked and the position you held in the organization and do so in reverse chronological order, with the most recent employer given first. Whether it was a paid position or a volunteer experience, use bullet points to describe your main activities. Bullet points should begin with action verbs, highlighting your skills, accomplishments, and results, not your duties. Telling the story with numbers or percentages always gets the recruiter's attention.

Whenever possible, describe your accomplishments with statements that reflect problems, actions, and results—which are called PAR statements. Employers are looking for candidates with a proven record of accomplishments and results. As you craft your bullets, consider these kinds of questions: Did you initiate a

> **Make your bullets effective:**
> - **P**roblems
> - **A**ctions
> - **R**esults

new procedure that saved your organization time or money? Did you build new relationships that resulted in new clients for your firm? Did your work result in the creation of a better system to help refugees or a new educational program in a poor region of a foreign country? Did you set up a volunteer organization that raised funds for a cause?

Let us look at an example of a badly crafted bullet that does not address the problem, only partially addresses the action, and does not address the results:

- *Wrote a grant proposal.*

Using the PAR technique, a good bullet would look like this:

- *Wrote a successful $300,000 grant proposal to address high illiteracy rates in Niger that led to the creation of a reading program for children in twenty-five schools in Niger's capital city, Niamey.*

The problem is high illiteracy rates in Niger. The action was writing the grant proposal. The result was the new reading program for children in twenty-five schools in Niamey.

Here is another common example:

- *Attended congressional hearings.*

A better bullet would read:

- *Attended fourteen congressional hearings on tax legislation and wrote notes and recommendations for Representative Smith's overburdened legal team.*

The problem was the overburdened legal team. The action was attending congressional hearings. The result was writing notes and recommendations to help the team.

Employers increasingly rely on key skill word searches to find the candidates they need. When you apply via a job board or to a company with a high volume of applications, your résumé might be reviewed first by an electronic keyword search. Research keywords in your industry to find out what must be included in your résumé in order to pass through the electronic gatekeeper.

The Distinctions/Activities Section

The last section of your résumé can often be as important as the education and employment sections. This section can be the place where you set yourself apart by indicating the attributes or experiences that make you unique and that do not necessarily fit into other parts of the résumé. The distinctions list can include:

- *Security clearance:* If you have a security clearance, include it on your résumé if that information is relevant to the job. If you do not have a clearance but are confident you can be successful during the security clearance process, you can include the term "clearable."
- *Language skills:* Applicants can rank themselves as native, fluent, proficient, reading proficient, possessing basic knowledge, or beginning in a particular language. Keep in mind that you may need to verify or demonstrate your skills at some point during the application process, so do not inflate your ability level.
- *Computer skills:* Most employers expect applicants to be proficient in Microsoft Office products and the internet. If the position description

requires these skills, indicate them on your résumé. You may also want to highlight any additional computer knowledge—such as Lexis-Nexis, STATA, SPSS, Dreamweaver, and Adobe Photoshop—and any social networking skills if they are relevant.

- *Global mindset*: You can include significant global travel or projects and community service conducted abroad in this section. Specific regional expertise worth emphasizing can be included here as well.
- *Research/publications/presentations*: Include this if you are applying for a research job, a job with a think tank, or any other position where in-depth knowledge of a particular subject would be of interest to the employer. If relevant, you may also want to highlight your public speaking and presentation skills.
- *Leadership activities*: If relevant, you may list a few of your extracurricular and community activities. By listing such activities, you can help an employer learn about your interests, motivations, and interpersonal skills that set you apart from other candidates.
- *Professional associations/affiliations*: Include these organizations only if they are of interest to the employer, or if you have held a leadership position in the organization.
- *Community/interests*: If relevant, you may highlight a hobby or passion that gives the employer insight into other dimensions of your life. Perhaps you are a marathon runner, rescue animals, or tutor underprivileged children. If so, list this information. If the employer shares the same interest, you will have an instant connection.
- *Citizenship:* Indicating citizenship is recommended when this information will prove helpful in landing the job.

The Federal Résumé

The federal résumé includes all the information the US federal government requires in an application for employment. It takes time to complete a federal résumé, so be sure to allot plenty of time to meet deadlines and supply high-quality documents. The federal résumé must include specific information, usually in a certain chronological format. It calls for you to list your employment, education, training, and skills. It is essential to tailor your résumé to each federal job announcement, because each one will likely require you to highlight different skills.

Final Résumé Tips

Here are some final résumé tips:

- *Proof your résumé.* Employers are looking for reasons to eliminate applicants from the candidate pool. An error or inconsistency on your résumé will ensure that you will be eliminated as a candidate. For example, if you use a period at the end of every bullet point, be consistent throughout the document. Likewise, if you use a comma before the "and" in a listing, make sure you do this throughout the résumé.

- *References* should be listed on a separate sheet of paper and *not* on your résumé. The reference name, title, and contact information should be provided when the employer requests this information, usually when you are further along in the interview process.
- *Be honest.* Do not risk embellishing your credentials to set yourself apart. Employers can verify information, so only include information that is accurate.

Cover Letters

A cover letter is your introduction to a prospective employer. When well written, it demonstrates that you have good writing and organizational skills. An effective cover letter provides insight into your qualifications, prior experience, and motivation for contacting the employer. It is often the only example of your writing that an employer will see before making a hiring decision, so you need to make it count.

Research the employer carefully when crafting your letter. Demonstrate that you appreciate and understand the organization's principal activities. Analyze the job description and figure out how your strengths and background can match the job's requirements. Do not simply restate what is on your résumé; instead, link the skills outlined on your résumé with the employment needs of the organization. Make the reader "see" why you would be a good fit by including real examples of your experiences and accomplishments. Tell stories that will be remembered, using key skill words that match the job description. The employer will no doubt have many other cover letters to read. Make yours stand out and be memorable by telling interesting stories that are relevant to the position and the organization. State your story in terms of the actions you took to address a problem and the results you achieved.

If the job description is vague, read what else the employer says on its website. If teamwork is something you see on the website as one of the employer's values, cite an example of your teamwork skills in your cover letter. If community service is a value, outline an achievement in this area. If the website and job description are both vague, try to find contacts you may know in the organization to get a feel for what the employer values.

Whenever possible, you should address the letter to a specific person. If you do not know whom to address or are unclear about the contact's gender, call the organization and find out. When the contact is unknown, ask for the name and title of the person in charge of the division to which you are sending the letter. The name of the addressee is preceded by an appropriate title, such as Mr., Ms., or Dr.

You should write a new cover letter for each position for which you are applying. An employer can easily detect a canned letter. If you use elements of one cover letter in another letter, make sure to include the correct company name and job title. When you are writing many cover letters at the same time, it is easy to make a mistake and address the letter to the wrong firm or the wrong person.

Content

Limit cover letters to one page. If your letter does not fit on one page, do not shrink the font; edit the text. Keep it simple and to the point in three or four paragraphs. The first and last paragraphs are your introduction and your closing, and the paragraphs in between will highlight your match to the position, focusing on the elements of your background that show the employer your fit for the job. It is useful to consider the letter in more detail, paragraph by paragraph.

First paragraph: State the area in the organization or the specific position for which you are applying. Do not make the reader guess why you are writing. Are you looking for a specific summer internship, or are you inquiring about future employment possibilities? If you are applying on the recommendation of a particular individual, mention his or her name. Briefly describe how your skills and background match the position or company. This will give the reader a preview of the rest of the letter and encourage him or her to read further.

Second paragraph: Tell why you are interested in the employer or the type of work the employer does. Employers want to hire people who *want* to work for them. Demonstrate that you know enough about the employer or the position by relating relevant background that explains why you are a good match. If you are a student, the second paragraph might focus on your academic experiences. Do not waste the reader's time by repeating information that is already on the résumé (e.g., "I am a student at University X and will graduate in May"). Instead, use the vocabulary from the job description to highlight your skills, experiences, and/or knowledge by giving specific examples. In doing so, present a coherent story—showing how your coursework, a capstone project, and relevant papers and presentations have prepared you for the position you are seeking.

Third paragraph: In this paragraph, you may want to focus on your prior employment, volunteer experiences, and/or internships and cite examples from these experiences. If the job requires research, tell how you used your research skills at another company to help write a successful proposal. If presentation skills are required, relate how you updated the CEO on a weekly basis. If project management is a key skill, tell about a successful project you initiated and how it generated income for your organization. The second and third paragraphs can be switched if your work/internship experiences are more relevant than your academic background.

Concluding paragraph: This paragraph should be one or two sentences, reaffirming your interest and motivation and restating how your skills make you a strong fit for the employer or for the specific job/internship. Thank the employer for his or her consideration and tell how you plan to follow up.

Reminder Checklist

✓ Address your letter to a specific individual whenever possible.

✓ Make sure the names of your contacts and of the organization are spelled correctly.

✓ If you do not know the gender of the addressee, call the organization to find out.

✓ Personalize each letter and connect your skills to the job description, using key skill words.

✓ If you do use the same letter to apply to different organizations (not recommended), be very careful in cutting and pasting so you do not address the letter to the wrong person or the wrong company. Avoid the tone of a recycled or form letter.

✓ Address what you will *bring* to the employer, but also mention what you hope to *get* out of the experience.

✓ Do not repeat information directly from your resume in your cover letter. Highlight two to three key experiences most relevant to the position and expand upon them in more detail. Words tell but stories "sell" and will be remembered in a sea of cover letters from other applicants.

✓ Express your motivation to work in the organization where you are applying. Employers want to hire interested and committed candidates.

✓ Be concise and to the point. Show you are an effective writer. Treat the cover letter as a writing sample.

✓ Run spell check and grammar check. Then check again!

✓ Read your letter *out loud* to detect awkward phrasing or repetition of words and phrases.

✓ If English is not your first language, you may wish to ask a native speaker to check for correct usage.

✓ Save a copy! Reread your letter before you go to your interview so you can remember what you said!

Style and Layout

Your style is your own, but you should have a businesslike tone and write in the active voice. For example, it is better to say "I initiated and completed" than "I was responsible for initiating and completing." Use straightforward language (e.g., "as we discussed" not "as per our conversation"). Verb contractions—such as "don't," "I've," and "it's"—are not appropriate in a business letter.

Follow the conventional layout for a business letter. Use the same font and header as your résumé so your cover letter and résumé are clearly part of the same application package. Use traditional fonts such as Times New Roman for both the résumé and cover letter. More exotic or scripted fonts are distracting. The salutation, such as "Dear Ms. Jones," is usually concluded with a colon on business letters versus a comma on personal letters. Use the complimentary close—"Sincerely"—followed by a comma and your typed signature underneath. Remember to sign your name if you are sending a hard copy of your letter.

Spelling and grammar must be perfect. Use your word processor's spell check and grammar check functions to make sure, and then check again. One tip is to read your letter backward to detect transposed letters or typos. Your eye is more likely to catch errors this way.

Your Personal Narrative and Online Social Media Presence

Anne M. Steen and Nicolette Pizzitola

Anne M. Steen has more than twenty years of career development and coaching experience working with undergraduates, graduate students, alumni, and professionals at all levels. For the past six years, she has developed and implemented the career management initiatives for the Graduate Career Development Center in the Edmund A. Walsh School of Foreign Service at Georgetown University. As the current director, she works directly with the eight graduate programs and alumni in the School of Foreign Service. She is a certified career management coach, federal job search coach, and federal résumé coach. She received a master's degree from the University of Virginia in counselor education and a bachelor's degree in economics from the University of Mary Washington.

Nicolette Pizzitola is the founder and chief executive officer of Compass Point Associates, a coaching and consulting firm providing services ranging from career management strategies for individuals, executives, and entrepreneurs to talent management and leadership coaching within organizations. A frequent speaker on career management, identity, and social media, she also teaches career management strategies at the George Washington University School of Business and is a career consultant at the F. David Fowler Career Center. She received a bachelor's degree in political science from George Washington University.

Whether you are looking for an internship or your first job after college, are transitioning into a new field, or are seeking career advancement where you are currently employed, a solid social media strategy can enhance your professional image, strengthen your current relationships, facilitate networking beyond your current sphere of influence, and provide access to information and opportunities. However, for many people, using social media for job search and career management feels a bit foreign. Even those with LinkedIn profiles worry about using the medium effectively and appropriately. And though many use various social platforms—from Facebook and Twitter to Instagram, Flickr, and Pinterest—most do not associate these engagements with their professional lives. But with a little planning and effort, anyone can develop a coherent and appropriate strategy to leverage social media in their job search and career management endeavors.

Start with a Plan

Although you do not have to be on all networks to have an impact, LinkedIn is a must for professionals. The site is your first means of establishing professional context and connection. If you are interested in working abroad, there are country- and region-specific sites for certain countries that are worth looking into, yet LinkedIn's global network includes more than 60 million users in 150 industries, from more than 2 million companies. In fact, more than 63 percent of LinkedIn's users are outside the United States.

Although many people use Facebook and Twitter for purely personal social interaction, such thinking dismisses the most meaningful connections to friends and family. Having a plan to ensure that these networks accurately convey your professional aspirations, contributions, and explorations opens a whole world of opportunities.

Understanding your professional expectations for each platform will help you decide how to present yourself, build your network, and structure your engagement. For each network, consider how you want to be perceived, with whom you will connect, what the appropriate level of engagement is, and what you hope to achieve. Your participation will define how you are received. Networking is a two-way street; foster connections within your network—studies have shown that "bridging ties" are often a predictor of success over time.

Know Your Audience

With your plan in hand, it is time to do some research. Check out the organizations for which you want to work and the professionals you consider mentors. Research what networks the organizations and their employees are utilizing and how they are using them.

It is important to note that your audience can take various forms. We typically include those working or who have worked in the field, as well as targeted agencies, associations, and companies. However, in fields where hiring is often done by niche recruiters, consultants, and consulting firms, your audience is significantly larger than you assume. In addition, anyone who experiences you online (e.g., by reading your blog or a blog post, seeing your Facebook status, or reading your published work) is your audience.

Limiting your network to the singular dimension of the job search results in diminishing returns over time. Your network is a vital part of your professional life. It is a dynamic and ever-changing organism that requires care and attention. Waiting until you need a job to build or activate your network is a rookie mistake. Professional connections offer the ability to exchange information, best practices, opportunities, experiences, and expertise. Through them you can find mentorship, camaraderie, industry perspective, and access to information, as well as contribute yourself—if you take the time to build and maintain your network.

Develop and Manage Your Digital Presence

Your online activity establishes your digital "first impression" and sets a tone for your interaction. Search functions on various platforms are becoming more robust, resulting in everything from your "likes" on Facebook to the handles you follow on Twitter to the groups you join on LinkedIn combining to create an image of you. Your job is to make sure that this image is an accurate reflection of you and your professional contribution. *It is wise to make sure that a random political posting, off-color comment, or compromising photo does not take away from your otherwise well-polished presence.*

Employers and recruiters routinely use Google and search

> **Managing Your Online Presence:**
>
> - Your privacy settings on Facebook and other platforms have an impact on how your personal pictures and videos are shared and thus how they show up in search results.
>
> - Set a Google Alert and platform-specific notifications to keep abreast of your social mentions and tags.

LinkedIn for potential candidates. An active and up-to-date LinkedIn profile will often be on the first page of Google search results. Your own blog, Facebook pages, and Twitter profiles often follow. Comments on blogs, published works, videos and pictures, and even individual tweets can all enter coveted top spots in your Google results page depending on the number of views and sharing popularity. Although you want to be thoughtful about what you share, your personal activities and comments provide a fuller picture of who you are and how you spend your time. Recruiters are looking for a sense of a candidate's personality. Yes, they want to know you can do the work, but they also want to be sure you fit their culture and how you will contribute to the office environment.

LinkedIn. LinkedIn, the leading professional career site, is a powerful and evolving tool that allows you to move beyond the page of your résumé. Seventy percent of jobs are found through networking. To enable this site to work for you, first and foremost, your profile should be current, relevant, and 100 percent complete. This means returning to your profile regularly to update it. Your professional headline, summary, and skills sections need as much attention as your work history. To make sure you are searchable, use keywords that make you stand out in your industry. Your descriptions might differ from your standard résumé to include words and phrases that a recruiter or employer would use to search for a qualified candidate.

As you develop your strategy, you should secure recommendations and build your connections with peers, coworkers, and industry contacts. You should reach out on LinkedIn to new contacts immediately following meetings, conferences, and networking events. Make sure to personalize your connection request to include a reference point—using the prepopulated form is simply lazy, and reduces the chances both that your request will be accepted and you will be remembered.

LinkedIn Tips

Industry publications, company mission statements, and job descriptions are good sources of keywords.

Check out LinkedIn.com/alumni to reconnect with former college pals, and to reach out to alums in industry, companies, or jobs you are targeting.

To better understand how to use new functions, search LinkedIn Help: http://help.linkedin.com/.

Check out "Managing Account Settings" regularly to keep privacy and visibility settings up to date. Claim your custom URL, and link to your LinkedIn profile on your email, blogs, and other online profiles.

Next, join alumni, industry, and company groups. These groups will afford you access to thought leaders and allow you to share information with your peers and receive it from them. The key here is engagement. Select groups wisely, and contribute to the conversation. If your company is hiring, let your peers know. Contribute to group discussions, post relevant updates, and share articles and events that your industry colleagues may find interesting. Following key industry organizations and target employers will help keep you up to date on news, hiring, promotions, and key data that you can use in networking and interviewing. Before industry events, meetings, or interviews, use LinkedIn to research companies and contacts. And do not forget the status update—it is a quick way to share good news, wins, new employment, change of jobs, company and industry news, or simply a good article or useful tip.

Use LinkedIn to search for jobs based on your interests and to look for connections with target companies. Check out the backgrounds of current employees, or see what companies past employees later joined. The jobs section recommends potential jobs based on the data you have on your profile, as well as opportunities connected to your current network.

Facebook. Facebook has always been a social space, but with OpenGraph the possibilities for job search are expanding rapidly. OpenGraph allows users to conduct searches based on likes, connections, about data, and other shared information. OpenGraph can assist you in searches for friends of friends working at the State Department, or friends in your college network who have traveled to Egypt. In addition, the data you share can help people find you. For instance, recruiters could search for Georgetown School of Foreign Service graduates who have worked or interned at Deloitte. Shape up your profile to include your study and professional references, and make sure that your privacy settings are secure.

It might be wise to use your Timeline to look through your likes to consider if anything is in poor taste or might misrepresent you. Often, we "like" something that seems funny without considering how people who do not

---

Facebook Tips

Facebook changes privacy rules and introduces new features regularly. Take time to review privacy updates. Google "Facebook Privacy Updates"—look for credible sources and check out where you might be vulnerable.

Make sure your privacy settings require your approval before anyone can tag you in a photo. You will receive alerts when someone tags you in a photo and have the opportunity to approve or deny the tag.

know us might perceive them. Yes, this is your personal page, but potential employers and recruiters are making judgments about your professionalism based on what they find.

Even if you have adjusted your privacy settings so that you feel protected, the people closest to you can be your referrals into a job opportunity—if they know your interests and professional qualifications, and are sure a reference will reflect well on them. Everyone from distant family members to childhood friends, former coworkers, classmates, and their families all have connections and interests you may not know about—so make sure what they see about you on Facebook paints an accurate picture.

Twitter. Initially, Twitter may not come to mind as a job search tool; however, it is a fabulous resource that will enable you to learn from your peers, share information, build awareness of your professional expertise, and position yourself as a thought leader. Start by creating a Twitter handle that is professional—that is, it should also be short to allow more for content. Fill out your profile, and consider linking to your LinkedIn profile or blog. Next, start by following people and organizations in the industry in which you are interested, and start engaging. Create meaningful conversations—I have seen thought leaders and their followers debate new protocols for global emergencies, poignant conversations about breaking news, references to conference attendees and speakers, and even lively dialogue about current events. You can follow companies, hiring agents, and recruiters—look for job-related Twitter handles. You can also check out Twitter chats on hiring or for your target industry.

Twitter's open platform means there is a low barrier for entry—you can connect with people you do not know and develop a rapport. Best of all, it is the perfect blend of professional and personal—you can show both your expertise and your personality as you engage with people in your field of interest.

Tips for Twitter

Twitter is about being a resource—be engaging, not a braggart—do not be overly self-promotional or lurk without contributing.

With Twitter you can build lists of people to follow. Create lists of subsections of your network (university, industry, associations, media, conferences) to keep up with streams of information that are most interesting and useful.

Make sure you learn Twitter conventions and give attribution when you share others' material.

People follow and engage with others who are active and provide a resource. Twitter is a unique supplement to your résumé and LinkedIn profile—if you are tweeting, make sure recruiters can find you.

Connect and Engage

Once you have established your profiles and your presence, it is time to start connecting and engaging with organizations and individuals. LinkedIn connections are often formal and follow professional etiquette, such as asking for a connection or requesting an introduction. Keep in mind that any correspondence through LinkedIn should be professional. Do not use abbreviations or informal phrases. A quick query through LinkedIn is an online representation of your professionalism. As mentioned above, your connection requests should be personalized. Introduction requests should provide enough information so the intermediary can make your case for the connection, be clear about why you want to be introduced, and be aware that this email request may be forwarded to the connection.

On Facebook, liking, following, and tagging an individual, a personality, or an organization is much less formal; however, caution should be taken when friending coworkers, mentors, and potential employers. Although you want everyone to see the great work you are doing, you may not want your boss to see the pictures of last Thursday's party. It is possible to maintain separate lists, but it is easy to forget to limit access or mismanage these settings.

Twitter offers immediate access to professionals and thought leaders. You can follow, share information, and engage through industry-related Twitter chats—this is a powerful way to connect and impress recruiters, hiring managers, and executives. Look for chats in your industry or the industry you wish to join.

Keep abreast of new changes and features. One of the challenges with social media networks is the constant changes and added features that can often have an impact on your security and profile settings. Make a point to learn about these changes and understand how they affect your account security and profile privacy. While you are using these platforms to connect, the sites themselves are using you for their own business purposes. Know how they are using your data and where you can opt out. New features on popular platforms usually come by acquiring popular new platforms and apps. Facebook acquired Instagram, LinkedIn bought SlideShare, Twitter purchased We Are Hunted, and even Dropbox got in the mix, acquiring

> Rapportive is a great tool to use within Gmail—it shows you information about your contacts right inside your inbox.

Mailbox. Make sure to keep on top of the information, access, and permissions you have on your various platforms and applications.

Learn standard conventions and give attribution. Be sure to learn the conventions and nuances of each medium to avoid faux pas. For example:

- Personalize connection requests on LinkedIn.
- Only connect with people you know on LinkedIn.
- Use # (hashtags) on Twitter.
- On Facebook and Twitter use @(name) attribution when mentioning a person or organization.

To thine own self be true. Before engaging a new platform, starting a blog, Tumblr, or other outlet, think through your objective and resources. Although these activities will help you build your online presence, share your interests, keep up to date, meet contacts, and demonstrate your creativity, it is also vital to be sure that you maintain your engagement level and control your content. The quality and frequency of your posts reflect on your seriousness and involvement. If you are not going to keep up with a blog, the lack of activity can look like lack of initiative or follow-through. If you do not have time to keep up with regular blogging, at least you can research outlets for guest posts, comment on highly regarded blogs, share noteworthy information on existing platforms, and engage with industry experts, as shown in table 2.1.

Table 2.1 Social Media Can Help Your Chances or Derail Your Efforts: Be Sure That Your Carefully Crafted Web Presence Reinforces Your Professional Efforts

Discovery Leads to an Offer	Discovery Leads to No Offer
Good feel for personality	Provocative/inappropriate photos/information
Conveys professional image	
Background information supports professional qualifications	Evidence of drinking or drug use
	Lied about qualifications
Well-rounded; demonstrates wide range of interests	Bad-mouthed previous employer, coworkers, or clients
Demonstrates creativity	Confidential information about previous employer revealed
Other people post references about candidate	
Solid communication skills	Made discriminatory remarks related to race, gender, religion, or other
	Frequent misspellings and grammatical errors

Prepare for your interview. Social media and online resources are the perfect tools for interview preparation. Check LinkedIn to research an industry, organization, employees, your interviewer, and competitors. Company pages will have news updates, latest hires, and demographic information about employees, their education, skills, job listings, and more. On job posting pages, you may be able to identify the job poster, and if you have a connection, that too will be listed. Often the company and/or employees will have blogs, Twitter streams, or groups on LinkedIn or Facebook—all can provide insight, information, and background that can help you in the interview process.

Use your online activity to enhance your offline world. Your online networking should lead to real-world relationships. Vibrant networks are not built so that you can find a job. Successful networks are based on common interests—both personal and professional. Powerful networks are communities where you contribute *and* find resources.

Networking

Laura E. Cressey

"Networking": It is amazing what a visceral reaction this one word can elicit from people. Most dread the prospect of networking, in part because they imagine themselves reaching out to people they do not know, people who are well established in their careers, asking for advice, contacts, or a job. But in fact, networking is—at its basic level—about interacting with people and establishing relationships. It is about letting people know who you are and what you are interested in, and making connections. Although it is about marketing yourself, effective networking is also a two-way street—one in which you can help the other person as much as they can help you. Networking is an essential part of the job search. Because most people get jobs on the basis of face-to-face interviews, and most job announcements are not publicized or advertised far in advance, the more people you meet and see face-to-face, the greater the likelihood that you will be in the right place at the right time and land that internship or job. Statistics vary, but most fall within the range cited by the Harvard Business School, which notes that 65 to 85 percent of jobs are found through networking (see www.alumni .hbs.edu/careers/networking.html). However, networking does not stop when you have landed a job; in fact, networking is something that should continue throughout your career. It will, among other things, help broaden your circle of contacts in your profession, assist you in finding a mentor, and enhance your ability to collaborate among organizations. This essay seeks to help you think about who to reach out to and how to prepare to make these discussions useful for your career search, and as painless as possible.

What Is Networking?

We have all seen that person—the one who is almost desperately working the ballroom after a panel discussion, or the cocktail hour at an alumni event. He is feverishly collecting business cards from the "important" people in the room, barely listening to what they have to say as he pockets their card and scans the room over their shoulder for the next "big name." He checks out everyone's name tag, only stopping those he deems high level enough to help him get a job. He is the first one in line cornering the speaker after she steps away from the podium, telling her how much he admires her, that he would love to work in her organization, and—ignoring the growing line behind him—divulging all the information he can about the subject she just finished speaking about. This is not effective networking.

It is hard to recognize someone who is good at networking, because often you do not even know that is what they are doing. The best networkers are good listeners. They are truly interested in what you are doing and what you are working on, and they often introduce you to acquaintances involved in similar work. They gather information, but they also share much information. They build relationships *that last* with peers and colleagues who are both their senior and junior. They are the people to whom you turn when you are looking for someone in a specific sector or organization because they seem to know so many people.

The overwhelming questions for most people embarking on a new career is how to *start* this networking process. Students often wonder how to start networking without coming across as overbearing and rude, like the person in the example above. If you are new to the international affairs field and new to a certain geographical area, it can be daunting and overwhelming when you do not have many (or any) contacts, which is the primary reason why you cannot start networking when you start looking for a job. It is a much longer process, and the earlier you start the better. You do not want to be in the position of reaching out to people only when you need something.

Why Should You Network?

As mentioned above, networking can dramatically help improve your odds of landing a position in the field or organizations of your choice. But networking serves other purposes as well. Used properly, networking can

- provide insight into employment sectors and organizations;
- increase understanding about job functions, career ladders, and salaries, thus helping you set realistic goals and expectations;
- help develop effective job search strategies;
- inform you about internship and job opportunities;

- help uncover your professional strengths and weaknesses; and
- assist you in finding a mentor.

In other words, networking can make you a better informed about the career you are seeking, the positions that appeal to you, and the actual opportunities that exist.

Before You Network

It is imperative that you be fully prepared before you start meeting and talking with people. The quickest way to ensure that your networking efforts will fail is to be unprepared and unprofessional, appear ignorant about the sector in which you are interested and the person with whom you are speaking, and bumble your opening pitch. You want to convey that you are proactive, have done your homework, and are willing to pound the pavement. Above all, you want it to be readily apparent that you are not expecting someone to hand you the keys to their Rolodex or offer you a job on a silver platter. Any whiff of entitlement is a sure killer—including (and maybe even especially) with relatives and family acquaintances.

How do you make the best impression and start off on the right foot? Make sure you do your homework, not only on the sector in which you are interested and the person with whom you are talking but also on yourself. It is surprising how many people who cannot provide a coherent answer to the question "What are you interested in doing?" Be able to identify your skills and interests as they relate to the sector and organizations in which you are interested. Have a handful of accomplishments to which you can refer in conversations that are relevant, demonstrate your skills, and relate to the goals of the organizations for which you have worked. Make sure that you can talk coherently about what you want to do and how what you did before has led you to the place you are now.

What motivates and excites you? This question can be difficult to answer, and it is important not to fall into overly dramatic, emotional, or clichéd motivations. You should not talk about how you became interested in foreign affairs at the knees of your grandmother as she spoke about escaping the Nazis in World War II. Although those stories can be quite interesting, too often they come across as schmaltzy, and they can make the speaker seem shallow and so should be avoided. Instead, be prepared to talk about why you are interested in going from a career in investment banking to one in global health. Be able to discuss what led you to choose this particular graduate school and how you expect that degree to help you land the job you are seeking in an international financial institution. In thinking about how you will pitch yourself in a networking situation, you do not (and should not) need to narrow your sights to one or two specific jobs. Claiming that your goal after obtaining your master's degree is to get one of two action officer positions in counternarcotics and global threats in the Office of the Secretary of Defense may seem focused, but instead may backfire and make you seem rigid and inflexible. (A better approach would be to declare an interest in working in this area for the Defense, State, or Treasury departments, or possibly for the private sector.) At the same time you should not indicate your interest in so many areas and sectors that you come across as scattered and unfocused. Someone may not be able to readily understand, for example, why you are equally excited about and qualified for positions in cybersecurity, infant and child nutrition, and Asian economic security. The fear, of course, is that you will rule out an area where there are ample job opportunities. There is no denying that it is a delicate balance that you need to strike.

Taking some time to think through your motivations, skills, and goals will help you to put together a coherent pitch. You should have a solid two-minute pitch prepared (and rehearsed) that introduces yourself, briefly sets out your goals and objectives, and generally answers the questions "Tell me about yourself" or "Tell me why I should hire you." You can use this pitch in cocktail parties, in an elevator, during an interview, or anywhere you may meet someone who takes an interest in your career and career goals. It is a good idea to have a couple versions of varying lengths that you can use in different situations and with people of varying seniority.

Now that you have gotten your thoughts about yourself and your career goals in order, you should research the sectors and organizations for which you are interested in working or about which you would like to learn more. As with constructing your pitch, cast your net widely—do not focus on just one organization. Saying that you want to work for the Department of State because it handles international affairs demonstrates a limited understanding of the players in US foreign policy and unnecessarily cuts out a large number of interesting and rewarding positions in other parts of the US government. There is never just one organization that works on a specific issue. In the government or multilateral arena, there are always multiple agencies or international institutions that work on issues. If you are interested in working on counterterrorism, for instance, the Agriculture, Defense, Energy, Homeland Security, Justice, State, Transportation, and Treasury departments, not to mention the many agencies of the intelligence community, all have offices that deal with some aspect of the issue. The same can be said for the private and nonprofit sectors. The key is to try to think broadly and creatively. For instance, if you are interested in working on food security issues, you could organize your thinking as shown in table 2.2.

Once you have a notional list, even if it is not exhaustive, try to fill in the names of people in those organizations, or people who know people in those organizations. Use your full network of contacts, especially school alumni and professors, to help you fill in your chart. There is your starting point. As

Table 2.2 Think Broadly and Creatively about Sectors and Organizations

Option A: US Government Agencies	Option B: International Organizations/Financial Institutions	Option C: Nongovernmental Organizations
Food and Drug Administration	United Nations	CARE
	World Food Program	Global Harvest Institute
US Agency for International Development	World Bank	
	Inter-American Development Bank	Mercy Corps
Department of Commerce		
Department of State		

you talk with more people, your chart should expand, not only with names of individuals but also with additional organizations and "players" in your chosen field. You are now well on your way to expanding your network.

To Whom Should You Reach Out?

When considering whom to reach out to, think about all your resources and contacts. If you are in school, your network should include your classmates, your professors, and the career guidance staff. If you are in an internship or job, your colleagues and supervisors can be excellent resources. But beyond the obvious, useful connections also can be made anywhere and in unexpected places, such as at family events, at the gym, or on the bus or airplane. It may be helpful to make a chart or list of your personal network, and add to it as you meet people. Categories of possible contacts are given in figure 2.1.

Alumni networks are a resource that should not be overlooked or underestimated. You already have at least one thing in common with people who graduated from the same school you did. Generally, people are more likely to talk with and help those who share a similar background or experience, and an alumnus of your school is automatically going to have a basic understanding of your education and expertise. So why not start with them? Reach out to alums for informational interviews to learn about their career path after graduation, successful strategies they employed, and (if you are still in school) courses, internships, or extracurricular activities that were particularly useful in helping them land their job. Likewise, while you are in school, join academic and extracurricular clubs. These clubs can have

• Friends	• Contacts in professional organizations
• Parents of friends	
• Classmates	• Members of academic clubs
• Undergraduate and graduate school alumni	• Relatives
	• Friends of relatives
• Teachers/faculty	• Neighbors
• Current and former coworkers	• Social contacts
• Current and former supervisors	• Church/civic community contacts
• Advisers/coaches	
• Professional acquaintances	• Sorority/fraternity club members

Figure 2.1 Your Network

excellent connections with employers and professionals in the field, and they often host events to bring these people in to talk with students. For instance, at Georgetown University clubs have become recruiting mechanisms for employers in the consulting field. Participation in these events is an excellent way to launch your networking process.

Social networking sites like LinkedIn also are quite useful for building your contact list. Checking out the contacts of friends and colleagues can help broaden your universe and alert you to people with similar interests and backgrounds. LinkedIn is also an invaluable tool when researching potential contacts and interviewers, because you essentially have access to their résumés, and not just their biographical blurbs on organizational websites.

How Should You Reach Out?

You have done some serious thinking about who you are, your career goals, the sector in which you are interested, and the organizations and people to which you would like to reach out. Now it is time to get yourself out there and meet people. Many assume that people who are networking are looking for a job. Instead, take some pressure off the situation and off yourself, and meet and talk with people in order to find out more about the sector in which you are interested and various organizations. In other words, network to gain information. If during the course of your conversations, people let you know about internship or career opportunities, that is wonderful. But just as helpful is getting people to give you the names of other people with whom you can talk. This way, you are continually expanding your outreach and increasing your visibility.

Conferences and events. The best way to meet people in your field of interest is to attend conferences, lectures, speeches, and discussions in a variety of venues, such as universities, professional associations, and think tanks. During the question-and-answer period, after introducing yourself and thanking the speakers, ask a succinct question. Then after the session, go up to the speaker, thank him or her for their time and response to your question, ask a follow-up question if there is not a large line behind you, and then exchange business cards. Send a thank-you note or email to that person the next day. Include a question if you have one, or mention an interesting thing you learned from the session. You will be surprised how this small gesture can snowball and help you establish a rapport with people. Try to keep in touch—you never know where this could lead. Additionally, talk with the other people attending the event. You are in a room full of people who are interested in the same subject matter you are, so make the most of it. Most likely the only expert in the room is not just the one behind the podium. Talk with the people next to you, or standing in line around you.

Proactive reaching out. In addition to conferences and events, you need to reach out to people on the networking chart you developed to schedule a phone call or, preferably, a face-to-face meeting. I often refer to these meetings as informational interviews. Phone calls will do if you are not in the same city or general area. But if this is not an issue, a face-to-face meeting can be much more productive. One can establish a better rapport in person; it is easier to read the other person's responses and attitude, pick up on body language, and interpret silences while sitting across the table from them instead of just listening to their voice. Additionally, you are embarking on this process to gain information about people, organizations, and the sector in general. If you meet someone in his or her office, you have the chance to observe their workplace and the dynamic of the organization. Plus, in a perfect world, your contact may take the opportunity to introduce you to the people with whom he or she works, and you never know whom you are going to bump into while in the elevator. A more informal setting—such as grabbing a cup of coffee—is perfectly acceptable, and may at times be less intimidating for you (especially when you are just starting to get the hang of the networking thing), and could even result in your interlocutor being more frank and open because he or she is out of the office. The bottom line is, whenever possible, to schedule a meeting in person.

Email is a totally acceptable way to contact professionals, introduce yourself, and request a meeting (or phone call). When writing an email, however, treat it as a formal piece of communication. With networking, as with the formal job search, every word counts. With this email, you likely are constructing what will be the reader's first impression of you. The content of your message should reflect the time and care you bring to your job search, which in turn reflects on your level of professionalism. Even if you are contacting a friend of a friend, or a family acquaintance, put some time and thought into your message. You are requesting that the person take time out of his or her busy schedule to meet with you. Be respectful and appreciative of this.

Random meetings. Beyond lectures, events, and meetings you have initiated, you never know where you will meet people who could help you with your job search. It could happen in the airport, on the bus, at church, at a baseball game, or at your parent's house. Because these random meetings could happen just about anywhere, it is important to have your pitch prepared and on the tip of your tongue, ready to deploy at any time. Unfortunately, however, if you fail to read the situation correctly, these serendipitous meetings are worthless and, more important, could be harmful to your networking efforts. If you are enjoying drinks at a wedding, for instance, it is most likely not appropriate to engage the uncle of the bride in an in-depth discussion of the hiring prospects at his political risk company, even if it is one in which you are very interested. Instead, note that you are a graduate student trying to break into the political risk market and that his company, which has an excellent reputation, is one that you have researched extensively. Mention if you have spoken with anyone in the company, hand him your card (which you never leave home without), and tell him you would love to talk with him further in a more appropriate setting. Hopefully, he will see your potential, will appreciate your refraining from pitching him hard at a wedding, and will invite you to follow-up with him. Now would be the time for you to excuse yourself and write his name and any other details on the back of one of your cards. If he gave you his email address, send him a message that weekend. Mention in the email that you met at his niece's lovely wedding, you enjoyed talking with him, and would like to schedule a meeting or coffee with him to learn about his experience with J&T Political Risk, and get his reaction to your job search strategy.

Say, instead, that you meet someone in the seat next to you on a transatlantic flight. She is the chief executive officer of XYZ Development, one of a handful of international development organizations engaged in children's health issues that you have been targeting in your job search. The good news is that you have a captive audience; you have several hours to talk with and impress her. You can deploy a more lengthy pitch, and engage in a more detailed discussion of the development sector in general and the work of her firm in particular. The bad news is that you have a captive audience who could come to resent you keeping her from sleeping, doing work, reading, or just relaxing on the long flight. Again, it is important that you read both the situation and *her.* Is she engaged in the conversation and really listening to what you have to say? Is she making eye contact? Or are her eyes glazing over and is she shooting you halfhearted smiles while eyeing her book, turning her body away from you, or looking for the flight attendant? You do not want to overstay your welcome. Just because you have the good fortune to be sitting next to someone who is in a senior position in an organization where you would like to work does not mean that you should monopolize her time. You want to make a good impression, including appearing considerate of her time and space. Figuratively overstaying your welcome will get you nowhere.

Before the Meeting: Do Your Research

Now that you have started contacting people on your networking chart and set up some appointments, it is time to do your homework and prepare for your meetings. At this point, you should have already prepared your pitch (which you conceivably used in your phone calls or emails), and you likely know some basic information about the organization for which these people work. The key now is to make sure that you are as prepared as possible for the meetings.

First, how much do you know about the organization? You should be familiar with its general mission, of course, but also with its basic organizational structure, its management team, and some of its current projects. Has the organization been in the news lately? If so, for what? Has the organization's leadership recently proposed any major initiatives, such as expanding business into new markets? Knowing the answers to these questions will give you more information to draw upon in your conversation. It will also make you appear informed and interested. These days, with so much information literally at our fingertips, it is inexcusable not to do your homework. Second, know the person with whom you are meeting. Look him or her up on LinkedIn, or at least run a Google search. Know where the person went to school, and other jobs he or she has held. You may find that you have experiences in common, which can help break the ice or make for a more relaxed conversation. Just remember, when using the information in your meeting, you want to subtly work it into the conversation and not come across as a stalker.

During the Meeting: What Should You Talk About?

Often, people worry about what to say to others when they are networking. Understandably, they want to appear relaxed and want the conversation to flow and not feel stilted or as if they are following a script. The good news is that networking discussions should not be very long initially. A conversation over a cup of coffee could last 20 minutes. That is not a lot of time to fill if you get your contact talking about his or her experience and field. So instead of peppering him or her with a series of questions, it is helpful to start the process by getting the person to respond to your job strategy and then to open up about his or her experience. For example, you could begin a conversation along the following lines:

> I really appreciate you taking the time to meet with me. I am interested in pursuing a career in international security, specifically in counterterrorism. I have a background in international affairs, Middle Eastern studies, and economics, and I speak Arabic and French. I would like to learn more about the work of the State, Treasury, and the Defense departments, and how they interact. I understand that you have worked in the intelligence community, Treasury, and Defense. I would be very interested in hearing about your career progression and the decisions that led you to change positions I would also appreciate your opinion on my résumé and the leads I am pursuing.

You can continue the discussion by asking if there are particular organizations of which your contact thinks highly (and why), whether there were particular skills that he or she has (or courses he or she took) that helped propel him or her to where he or she is now, what experiences were rewarding, and what has frustrated him or her in his or her career. The idea is to get a feel for the jobs that your contact has had, to try to understand the players in the sector, and to help you set realistic expectations for your own career. It is also very useful to get opinions about your job search strategy: Are you reaching out to the right people and the right organizations, are you overlooking interesting places to work, and do you have the right combination of skills and experience for the types of jobs you are seeking? All this can be very useful information. One of your goals should be to leave each networking event or informational interview with one or two additional names of people. As stated above, this will help expand your network. If you are applying for a position in your contact's organization, make sure that you have done all the legwork you can before asking for his or her help. It is fine, and advisable, to meet with someone in an organization to which you are applying, but you do not want to be in a situation where you are asking your contact to shepherd your application when you have not even submitted it. That would come across as if you were expecting your contact to do your work for you, and that is never good.

After the Meeting

After each of your networking conversations, immediately send your contact a thank-you letter, either by email or the regular mail. The note can be short—a word of thanks and a mention of something useful that you learned during the conversation are all that is needed. This is a simple thing to do that takes virtually no time but can have a significant payoff: It demonstrates that you have good manners and common courtesy, and it also shows that you value the person's time and advice. And equally important, it can help the recipient remember you in a positive light. Speaking for myself, students who send me thank-you notes after meetings always stand out in my mind. By all means, send another note if you get an internship or a job because of the contacts you made through that person or because of his or her advice (frankly, you should send everyone with whom you meet a note to let them know where you landed). People like to know that they have been helpful, and this gives you another chance to keep this person in your network.

Networking often seems daunting; I have found it is the most feared piece of the career puzzle for the students I have advised. My advice is to just jump in. Have your first conversation with someone you know, whether it is a neighbor, classmate, or family member. Then make yourself reach out to someone you do not know. Schedule one appointment and then another. The more people you contact and the more conversations you have, the more relaxed you will be and the easier networking will become.

Interviewing

Anne M. Steen

Congratulations! You have been offered an interview. The interview is the "make or break" step that can keep you on the road to the job, or kick you off onto a side street. The information in this essay gives you some guidelines to follow as you prepare for the interview and make this job your job.

Just as in your favorite class or seminar, in the best interview you listen, you share what you know, you ask questions, you learn, and you strive to make a good impression. In your seminar everyone was at ease with themselves, comfortable with one another, glad to be there, familiar with the topic, and, ideally, interested and enthusiastic about the discussion. To translate this to an interview and help you project confidence and competence, you need to perform due diligence, practice, and demonstrate strong listening skills.

Types of Interviews

There are many types of interviews used to find the best candidate. Hiring managers often use different names for the interviews they conduct. Even though there are different names, the three most common types of interviews are listed in table 2.3.

Table 2.3 **Interview Types**

Behavior- or competency-based interview	This interview focuses on how you handled situations in the past to see how your previous behavior applies to the future position. These interviews often have questions that start with "Tell me about a time when . . ." or "Give me an example of . . .".
Case interview	The interview is usually one-on-one and centers around a business problem or exercise. A successful interview does not rest on a correct answer to the problem, but rather on how you go about solving the problem in a time-sensitive or pressured situation.
Traditional interview	Traditional interviews are usually based on the résumé or other materials provided in the application. The questions asked in these types of interviews tend to be more open-ended, such as "Tell me about your last job?"

Setting Up the Interview

Remember, *information is power.* The best way to prepare for your upcoming interview is not only to learn what type of interview is planned but also to learn more about the format, interview length, and number of participants. A little additional information can give you a big advantage on interview day and can help you feel more prepared and comfortable.

When you get the call or email to set up the interview, be ready to respectfully ask some questions about the interview logistics, format, and process. Remember that you are being assessed during every interaction you have with the employer. The challenge is to be professional and succinct. In some situations you will be given details about the process; in other situations you will be given very little information. When you talk with the human resources representative or hiring manager, try to ask questions about the upcoming interview such as:

1. Can you tell me the expected length of the interview?
2. Who will be conducting the interview? Will there be more than one interviewer?
3. Can I get the names and titles of the people with whom I will be interviewing?
4. What information or insight can you give me about the interview format? Will it be one-on-one? Panel? Group? Case-based?
5. Do I need to bring additional materials to the interview, such as a list of references or writing samples?

6. Could you please confirm the time and place of the interview and the office address?

When asking about who will be conducting the interview, keep in mind that some organizations may not have that information at the time. If you cannot get the details you need, let it go for the moment. Managing candidate interviews is like putting together a puzzle. The last pieces may not come together until just before the interview. Some organizations do not want you to know who will be conducting the interview until you walk into the room. Employers like to hear what you have to say in an interview, but they also like to see how you handle unexpected situations.

Finally, when inquiring about the details of an interview, be informed before you ask. Do not ask questions that can be answered by the company website. This is where your contacts at the organization come into play. When you let your contacts know when you apply for a job, they can give you internal details about the interview process. You want to look competent and informed every time you talk or meet with a prospective employer, so use your contact to do just that.

Interview Preparation

You want to demonstrate your passion for the job, company, and industry at every step of the process. One way to demonstrate your passion is through your preparation for the interview.

First things first—start with you. The first step is to take some time for personal assessment and reflection. Why did you apply for this position? What sets you apart from your competition? How can you add value to the work and mission of the organization? Where do you want your career to take you in two years? Five years? It is important for you to take out the job description and review it. How will you become successful in this job? The interview is not a time for you to talk through your career goals and skill set. It is a time for you to demonstrate to the prospective employer that you have the mindset and skill set to lead in the position.

Next: your documents. The second step is to take a hard look at your cover letter, your résumé, and the job description. What does your résumé say about you? What stories can you share to demonstrate your accomplishments and skills? Many interviews start with questions about your résumé. I also encourage you to pull out your transcript and review it. What relevant topics did you research and analyze in class? Look through your academic and work experience and find some stories and examples you can share that demonstrate your accomplishments. If you submitted a writing sample, be sure to reread it before the interview.

The card. Once you have thoroughly worked through the first and second steps, commit some statements or words to writing. Take a $3'' \times 5''$ index card and write down four or five skills, experiences, or statements that demonstrate what sets you apart from the competition. Writing things down helps you commit things to memory. It also helps to develop a level of fluency with these words or statements in your personal narrative. As you know from studying foreign languages, fluency comes with knowledge and practice. When you are asked a question, you want to be able to use these phrases or words in a fluent and genuine response. Although you have stated your skills and experience, you also need to provide details and examples in the interview; see figure 2.2.

Obviously, you cannot pull out this card in an interview. However, you should tuck it in your portfolio to read on the bus or subway as you prepare for the interview. Keep it in your portfolio during the interview. Once you have your card memorized, the words will be naturally roll off your tongue.

Research the company. Because information is power, research comparable and competing companies and organizations. Analyze the organization's website, look at its mission statement, and try to understand how its different units work together. Other sources of valuable information are newspapers, professional journals, and online sites such as LinkedIn. Read the paper and online news sources. You need to know why and when the organization was in the headlines. Follow the company on LinkedIn, and you will get regular news updates on your LinkedIn feed. Finally, use your internal contacts. Make time to get information from the players inside the organization. What

Hard skills that set you apart:	Soft skills that set you apart:
• Language proficiency	• Time management
• Regional expertise	• Initiative
• Quantitative skills	• Problem-solving skills
• Analytical skills	• Team player
• Writing skills	• Passion
• Communication—oral and written	• Shared values with the organization
• Field experience	
• Financial modeling	
• Direct experience in the field or industry	
• Active security clearance	

Figure 2.2 **Charting Your Skills**

should you expect in the interview? What challenges does the organization face? Where can your experience and skill set best add value to the mission and work of the department and company?

Prepare your answers. Some interview questions will focus on strengths and experience. If regional expertise is a strength of yours, you need to tell the employer how that expertise will add value to their work. Relevant details will provide context and help the interviewer see your strengths. Questions related to professional goals are difficult for some people to nail down. Your answer does not cement your career path in stone, but you need to show the employer you are committed to the industry and company. Whether you choose to stay two more years or leave for another opportunity is irrelevant. You need to demonstrate that at this moment, you are interested in a future in the company and field.

Behavior-based interview questions focus on how you handled situations in the past as a way to assess how you might approach similar situations in the future. These questions are often called behavior-based or competency-based questions. To answer these questions effectively, you want to look for past experiences that demonstrate your skills and abilities. As you practice these types of questions, review your résumé and look for stories and experiences to share.

To better frame your response, think in terms of *PAR—problem or project, action,* and *result,* as discussed above and as explained in table 2.4.

Nonverbal communication. It is also important to remember the nonverbal messages you send. Eye contact is critical throughout the interview because it signifies confidence and competence. Do not forget to smile; a warm smile can set the tone of the interview. As you answer interview questions, remember to smile from time to time. You want to demonstrate your

Table 2.4 Use the PAR Paradigm to Make Your Statements Effective

Problem or project	Describe the situation you were in or the task that you needed to accomplish. Be as specific as possible with relevant information. Be sure to give enough detail for the interviewer to understand, but not too much detail that they get lost. The situation can be from a previous job, volunteer experience, a class, or a relevant event.
Action *you* took	Describe the action *you* took and be sure to keep the focus on you. If you are discussing a group project, be sure to describe what *you* did, not the efforts of the team. Be careful not to talk about what you might do but rather highlight what you did.
Results	What happened? How did the event or situation end? What did you accomplish? There may be times you are asked to talk about a failure or mistake; we all make mistakes, but just be sure to highlight what you learned from the situation.

passion and interest in the topic. You also want to look comfortable. If you look scared, bored, or angry, your nonverbal communication is not in sync with your words. If you sit up straight, it is easier to breathe. The more you breathe, the more oxygen gets to your brain, and the faster your synapses fire!

Prepare questions to ask. It is also important to have questions ready to ask the interviewer. Usually, an interview will end with an opportunity for you to ask questions. Never let that opportunity slip away by saying "I do not have any questions at this time." This is an opportunity for you to demonstrate your knowledge of and interest in the organization. For instance, you could ask what major challenges the department is facing in the coming year (just do not ask about compensation or vacation time).

Practice, practice, practice. Once you have your thoughts organized, practice. Set up a mock interview in your career center, role-play with a roommate, or simply go through your answers with your computer video rolling and critique yourself. Through repetition you will acquire a level of fluency in your answers that will demonstrate your skills and abilities.

Walking through the Door

You are what you wear. First impressions matter, and as you get ready for your interview, pay attention to the details. Pay close attention to your personal appearance. Business attire is the norm; men should wear a suit and tie with professional (and polished) shoes, and women should wear a suit, jacket and skirt, or conservative dress. Jewelry should be minimal and not cause any distractions. Hair (including facial hair) should be well groomed. A watch is helpful because you do not want to be looking at your cell phone to check the time. Your smile makes a powerful first impression. Before you walk into the office make sure you have clean teeth and fresh breath. Some interview rooms are small and can get warm, making deodorant an essential part of your personal hygiene. Keep perfume and cologne to a minimum.

You should bring a nice folder or portfolio (including paper and a pen) with you. Inside the portfolio, have your index card, an extra copy of your résumé, and anything else you sent in with the application. If you have a list of references handy, you can bring that with you as well.

Be on time—and that means 15 minutes early. Map out a travel plan well before the morning of the interview. If you are taking a cab or public transportation, allow extra time because delays are a fact of life. If you are driving, work out the parking logistics when you set up the interview.

Before you walk into the office, get yourself organized. Put away your iPod and cell phone. If it is raining, shake the water off your raincoat and umbrella. You do not want to be remembered as the person who left a puddle in the reception area. When you walk in, introduce yourself to the person at the desk. Smile warmly and shake hands with the receptionist. Remember, you are being evaluated from the minute you walk into the office. Take a seat, and pull out your index card and think "PAR" for a minute before the interview begins.

Nailing the interview: Do not forget to listen. When you meet your interviewer(s), introduce yourself with a firm handshake, warm smile, and good eye contact. If you have a hard time remembering names, repeat the person's name as you are introduced: "Good morning, Ms. Jones, thank you for having me here today." Take your seat, keep the eye contact going, and get ready for the questions to roll. Remember, you have prepared for this, and this is your opportunity to shine.

Keep in mind that every conversation has two sides. One is the ability to speak; the other is the ability to listen. Keen listening skills can give you more insight and information that may help you in framing your response to a question.

Tips to help things move along. There are some strategies that you can use to help you stay confident during the interview. If you do not understand a question you have been asked, feel free to ask the interviewer to restate or reframe the question. It is better to ask for clarity than to start down a road that is off course. Have you ever finished answering a question and felt like the interviewer was not happy or connecting with your response? There is a simple tactic to deal with this situation: When you are finished responding, simply ask the interviewer if you answered the question. If you did, all is well. If you did not, the interviewer will provide you with more context, which allows you to circle back and provide a different answer. Do not hesitate to ask for a minute to think about an answer. If a question causes you to pause, let the interviewer know you are thinking. This tactic keeps you in control and gives you a minute to collect your thoughts.

When it is your turn to ask questions, be ready. You want to have anywhere from three to five questions ready. Try not to only ask simple questions about the hiring timeline. Be sure to ask questions that are relevant to the industry and company. A question may be related to an article you have read or to a current event in the world. Asking an employer questions about the organization shows interest and integrity. Remember, this is a part of the evaluation process. The questions you ask can set you apart from the competition.

As the interview wraps up, be sure to restate your interest in the position and thank the interviewer. Again, a firm handshake and eye contact are appropriate when ending a meeting or interview. Remember to stop by and thank the receptionist on your way out as well. Take a few minutes in the reception area to be sure you have everything you brought with you. There is nothing worse than coming back in the next day because you forgot your portfolio or gloves.

Following Up

Take time immediately after the interview to follow up with a written thank-you note. The note can be handwritten or an email message. You should use this note to recap a memorable part of the conversation or to talk about something that resonated with you during the interview. You can also insert a line illustrating why you are the person for the job. Remember that thank-you notes should be brief. And typos in a thank-you letter can kill your chances of an offer—even if you nailed the interview.

If you have not heard from the employer in two weeks, or within the time period mentioned, it is appropriate to email or call to follow up. Ask if there is any additional information you can supply to help them in their decision-making process. Some employers use the "don't call us, we'll call you" philosophy, but most expect follow-up from the candidates they have interviewed.

Once you receive the offer (or even if you do not), be sure to follow up with anyone in your network who helped you make it to the interview phase. This illustrates a level of professionalism many people do not demonstrate. Little details, such as a simple note updating your contacts, can go a long way to nurture and grow your network.

PART II

The International Job Market: Types of Employers

CHAPTER 3

The US Government

Working for the US government is often described as a passion—government servants dedicated to serving their country in a meaningful manner and making a difference for their fellow citizens. Whether one is interested in economic, political-military, human rights, international development, trade, or intelligence issues, international relations graduates can find relevant jobs and careers throughout the US government. The essays within this chapter examine the opportunities available throughout government, in the executive and legislative branches, the intelligence community, and in development agencies. The essays discuss careers in the civil service and examine life on Capitol Hill and as a Foreign Service officer. This chapter aims to help the reader think creatively about government service, and help him or her expand the job search to include the wide variety of agencies with international functions. Most of these agencies offer internships, which are an excellent way to break into the field and peek into the culture of the agency to help you determine if a government career is right for you. One can also obtain government experience through positions with government contractors and consulting firms, an option addressed in chapter 7 on business, and in chapter 8 on consulting.

Careers in Executive Branch Agencies

Nicole Melcher

At the time of writing, Nicole Melcher was director of the Office of China and Mongolia in the Global Markets Unit of the International Trade Administration at the US Department of Commerce. Before she joined the Office of China and Mongolia in 2007, she served as director of Commerce's Office of Japan for four years. She also served as acting deputy assistant secretary of commerce for Asia for six months in 2006–7. Before joining the Commerce Department, she worked for the Overseas Development Council (ODC), a think tank in Washington that focused on international development issues. She received a master's of science in foreign service (MSFS) degree from Georgetown University and a bachelor of arts degree from Williams College in Massachusetts. She spent two years in Japan after college teaching English conversation to Japanese businesspeople and to high school students. The views expressed in this essay are solely those of hers and do not reflect the official views of the US government.

· ·

In an increasingly small world, with nations, people, and economies more connected than ever before, I often find myself in the middle of the United States' economic diplomacy efforts, working with multiple agencies seeking to help US companies enter into and thrive in foreign markets. For those who are considering a career in international affairs, the realization that all things international do not reside exclusively at the Department of State or even at the Department of Defense (DOD) can come as a surprise. It might be even more of a shock to find out that nearly every US agency—no matter how domestic its mandate—has an international component and staff who focus on international issues. From the US Department of Agriculture to the Department of Energy (DOE) to the Department of the Treasury, international jobs can be found throughout the US government. Many agencies like the Department of Commerce, DOD, and State have regional or country offices as well as industry, sector, economic, and other "functional" offices. When searching for a job, look for opportunities not only in the regional offices but also in other functional offices because country experts often reside within those offices as well.

I began my career with the ODC. Immediately out of graduate school with an MSFS from Georgetown University, where I concentrated in international development and trade and studied Japanese, I was able to apply my MSFS interests to my job, which focused on promoting United States–Japan cooperation in international development. I had interned with ODC throughout my MSFS tenure and was fortunate to be offered a job after graduation. After nearly four years with the organization, I was ready to use the international trade skills that I had developed during my MSFS years to make the transition from trying to influence the US government from the outside to working within the US government on trade policy. While at a party, a friend of mine told me of a job opening in Commerce's Office of Japan (yes, that actually does happen!). I applied through the normal federal application process (which is now known as USAJOBS, www.usajobs.gov), and nearly six months later got the job. The process was admittedly rather lengthy (and extended most likely by hiring freezes at the time), but because I kept my job at ODC throughout the process, I could afford to be patient.

This position turned out to be my dream job, and thus enabled me to use all the skills I had developed in graduate school and to follow my main interests. I worked on United States–Japan trade issues, helping US companies overcome various market challenges in exporting to Japan, and over the next six years covered nearly every sector—including construction, energy, medical devices, pharmaceuticals, and transportation. I advanced in the office from a GS-9 (GS is short for General Service, the name of the federal pay system), eventually becoming the deputy director and ultimately the office director (GS-15). In 2007, after twelve years in the Japan Office, I moved to the Office of China and Mongolia as the office director, a Senior Executive Service position.

One of the things I like most about my job at the Commerce Department is that every day is interesting. The United States' trade relationships with both Japan and China are dynamic, and US companies constantly seek our assistance and expertise in helping them solve issues they confront while doing business in or trying to enter these Asian markets. From trying to open markets to US companies to seeking changes in Japanese regulations to ensuring fair contract bidding and award practices, the issues never stop and are always engaging. The problem-solving aspect of the job requires creativity and teamwork, which are the most rewarding elements of the job. We try to use all the resources available to us as a government—whether it is through Commerce, State, the Office of the US Trade Representative (USTR), or other US government agencies—to help solve the problems confronting US business. One such example involved my work in the Japan Office. A US company bid on a railroad project in Japan that was covered by the World Trade Organization's (WTO's) Government Procurement Agreement. The US company informed Commerce that the Japanese company had not followed the proper WTO procedures. It took nearly a year of Commerce lodging complaints with different Japanese authorities in order to persuade the railroad company to retender the project. A US company ultimately won the bid. Although it took a long time to resolve, this case became a model and served as an example for future Japanese procurements.

The Interagency Process

Perhaps one of the biggest surprises when I entered government was how much teamwork is involved in the day-to-day work of a government employee. No one person makes a decision; groups of people make decisions. Typically, a memo is drafted by action officers in the lead office and agency, and it is then reviewed by multiple offices and agencies with a stake in the issue. Almost every major decision involves input from multiple agencies—known collectively as the interagency process. It is not always necessary to reach a consensus on a position, but the senior official is going to want to know what the various agencies—or stakeholders—think about the issue up for decision. This is precisely because no issue is one-dimensional, and all stakeholder offices and agencies come to the table with different perspectives. Including these voices in the policymaking process ensures that US foreign policy takes into account all relevant factors, and no policy decision is made in a vacuum. As a result, much of the work done within government requires coordination among various offices in several US government agencies.

For instance, on China trade issues, we at Commerce work closely with USTR, and with the Agriculture, Energy, Justice, State, and Treasury departments, among many others. If an energy company comes to Commerce with a problem regarding gaining access to the Chinese market, we will bring several regional and functional offices from other US government agencies such as DOE, State, and USTR into the process and will brainstorm about possible solutions. This requires cooperative teamwork among the relevant US government agencies.

Understanding the nature of the interagency process is extremely useful for those who are seeking jobs in the US government. As it gets increasingly difficult to enter the government workforce, it is that much more important to cast a wide net when applying for jobs. Concentrating only on China-related vacancies within State, for example, will significantly lower your chances of getting into government. Armed with the knowledge that almost every agency with an interest in international affairs has not only a China desk but also functional desks with China experts, an applicant has a much better chance at getting his or her résumé read and a foot in the door.

Where Are the International Jobs within the US Government?

International jobs are literally everywhere in the US government. To make your job search effective, you should get to know the organization in which you are interested, as well as its interagency partners. Research the organizational charts of each agency, down to the office level. This will help you with your networking, and help you target searches on USAJOBS.

International jobs are typically found in both regional and functional (or issue-oriented) offices within US government agencies. For example, the State Department has regional bureaus (e.g., the Bureau of Near East Affairs and the Bureau of Africa Affairs) as well as functional bureaus (e.g., the Bureau of Political Military Affairs and Bureau of Energy Resources). Individuals with energy expertise in Turkey may be interested in jobs in the Energy Resources Bureau as well as the Near East Affairs Bureau. If you can speak Chinese and are interested in trade issues, you could consider the Office of China and Mongolia Affairs and the Office of Economic Policy (both in the Bureau of East Asian Affairs) at State, as well as offices within the Bureau of Economic and Business Affairs. You should also investigate offices within the Commerce Department. For example, all the following bureaus at Commerce do something on China, even if the word "China" is not in the office's name:

- International Trade Administration (Office of China and Mongolia; industry offices such as the Office of Health and Consumer Goods and the Office of Telecommunications and Electronic Commerce; as well as the Import Administration, which handles antidumping and countervailing duty issues);
- Bureau of Industry and Security (export controls);
- Economic and Statistics Administration;
- National Institute of Standards and Technology;
- National Oceanic and Atmospheric Administration; and
- Patent and Trademark Office.

Depending on your expertise, you could also investigate offices in departments such as Agriculture, DOD, DOE, Justice, Joint Chiefs of Staff, Labor, Overseas Private Investment Corporation, Trade and Development Agency, Treasury, and the US Agency for International Development (USAID).

Like State and USAID, Agriculture and Commerce also have their own foreign service corps—respectively, the Foreign Agriculture Service (FAS) and the US and Foreign Commercial Service (US&FCS). The FAS represents US agricultural interests overseas and works to build and improve foreign market access for US food and agricultural products. The US&FCS has officers in US cities and around the world to help US companies enter or expand into foreign markets. Entry into the FAS and US&FCS is competitive. Both services require applicants to have advanced degrees in a related field and preferably some specialized experience—for example, in trade promotion.

Similar to the State Department's Foreign Service, FAS and US&FCS officers bid on overseas and domestic positions and rotate every three to four years. These officers work overseas in US embassies in the agricultural and commercial sections. However, these are not the only agencies with an overseas presence; multiple agencies such as DOD, DOE, Justice, and Treasury, among others, have officers working at US embassies. (In fact, at some posts overseas, employees from other agencies outnumber State employees.)

Joining the FAS and US&FCS:

- Complete an application on USAJOBS.
- Applicants are rated and rank ordered; highest-ranking applicants are invited to take the foreign service assessment, held once a year in Washington.
- The assessment consists of written, group, and oral examinations.
- Those who pass are placed on the Rank Order Register. Candidates who do not receive an offer within twenty-four months may reapply.

International jobs also exist within the Executive Office of the President, which is overseen by the White House chief of staff and includes the following entities:

- Council of Economic Advisers,
- Council on Environmental Quality,
- National Economic Council (NEC),
- National Security Council (NSC),
- Office of Management and Budget (OMB),
- Office of Science and Technology Policy (OSTP),
- USTR; and
- Office of the Vice President.

Several of these entities—including the NSC, NEC, OSTP, and USTR—have internationally focused positions. The NSC and NEC in particular are staffed by direct hires as well as officers temporarily loaned (commonly referred to as "on detail") from other agencies. Many of these are typically not entry-level positions. OMB oversees budget development and agency performance, coordinates and reviews federal regulations and executive orders, and reviews and clears agency communication with Congress. OMB employs budget specialists, policy analysts, and legislative analysts.

The Skills Needed to Succeed in a Bureaucracy

Admittedly, working within a large bureaucracy is not for everyone. I do not think that the government deserves the reputation that some give it for being a bloated, cumbersome, ineffective bureaucracy. However, you definitely need certain character traits—such as patience and flexibility—to be able to operate well and succeed within the structure of a bureaucracy. It is my experience that with this in mind, you can advance new ideas and facilitate change just as you can in other sectors. To be competitive for government jobs, applicants need to demonstrate through their experience that they have these skills.

Perhaps one of the top abilities that managers seek when hiring employees are *strong writing skills*. The ability to communicate complex ideas coherently and concisely is invaluable. Every time an official has a meeting—whether it is an interagency meeting, a meeting on Capitol Hill, or a negotiation with a visiting delegation—a briefing paper must be produced with background information and talking points for the official's use in the meeting. You need to be able to discuss complex issues in a limited amount of space—sometimes only a paragraph. If you are given only three talking points for your assistant secretary to use to discuss human rights abuses, you need to be able to convey the US position concisely and coherently. You also need to be able to accept comments on your writing. As discussed above, no one person works on an issue. Multiple people will read and comment on your writing. If you are protective and proprietary about what you write, and unwilling to accept comments and criticism, you will have a hard time succeeding in government.

Verbal communication skills are also extremely important. As with writing skills, you need to be able to communicate complex ideas in a short amount of time. Getting bogged down in the details at the expense of core ideas will not serve you well. Imagine having two minutes to brief your boss before she enters a meeting with the Senate Foreign Relations Committee on an Iran sanctions issue. You need to be able to brief her on the key points of the State Department's position and its response to congressional concerns without getting wrapped up in unnecessary details.

The ability to *work well with people* is key to a successful career in the US government. There is such a team atmosphere that you need to be able to work with people and deal with conflict calmly. Being *unflappable* in the face of tight deadlines and conflict will also serve you well.

Each job vacancy also will have specific skills that the recruiter is seeking in applicants. These can include foreign language skills, international experience, or knowledge of a particular sector or issue. Whether you possess these skills is also a good indicator of whether you will *like* working in a bureaucracy. If you like working by yourself in your office writing scholarly papers, then you are most likely not going to like working in the government at a desk job where you must deal with people every day while supporting senior officials.

Applying for Government Positions

Job announcements for US government positions are posted on USAJOBS. Applicants can search jobs by agency, grade level, and location, and they elect to receive email alerts for new job vacancies that fit the applicant's criteria.

Résumés play an integral part in the federal job application process. A federal résumé looks very different from a typical résumé, and should not be limited to one page, as is often the practice in other sectors. A federal résumé should not only be tailored to the general position but also should include information that specifically addresses the points listed in the job announcement, such as in the sections describing duties, qualifications required, and how you will be evaluated.

When an application is submitted through USAJOBS, the agency's human resources department evaluates each application (and résumé) against the position requirements to determine whether the applicant meets the minimum requirements. Applications deemed to meet the qualifications are then forwarded to the hiring office, which decides which applicants to interview. Because the human resources officials reviewing applications check specifically to see which applicants best meet the job requirements, it is essential to be specific and make very clear that you meet the job requirements. (This advice, of course, applies only in cases where it is true that you meet the job requirements. Never lie on an application.) Remember, these officials may be reviewing hundreds of job applications so it may be helpful to use boldface type or all capital letters to highlight key words or phrases. USAJOBS allows applicants to upload a résumé or use Résumé Builder to construct the résumé. Though it may take longer, use the Résumé Builder option, because some agencies cannot search uploaded résumés. Additionally, failure to include any of the required supporting documents, such as transcripts or questionnaires, can result in your application being deemed ineligible. You also are required to meet the deadline in the announcement—no extensions!

Sometimes job vacancy announcements can be vague. Use your networking skills to find out more about the vacancy announcement: What are the real responsibilities of the position? Are there any nuances to the kinds of experience the office is seeking? And so on. Most important, you must tailor each résumé to the specific job announcement to ensure that you capture the knowledge, skills, and experience the hiring office is seeking.

It is also important to apply to the correct level of job. Vacancy announcements are very clear in outlining the required level of education and experience. Applying for something too senior is a waste of time because you will immediately be deemed ineligible by the initial human resources review. Understand the GS pay scales, too. Additional experience or degrees may enable you to negotiate a higher step level within the pay grade.

In 2012, the Office of Personnel Management instituted the Pathways Program, which seeks to rationalize the internship and job entry process for students and recent graduates. The Pathways Program consists of:

- *Internship Program*, for students enrolled in high school, college, graduate school, and trade schools;
- *Recent Graduates Program,* for individuals not more than two years out of graduation from college, graduate school, or trade school; and
- *Presidential Management Fellows Program*, for individuals with an advanced degree (master's or professional degree).

Internships

Internships are an invaluable way to get relevant experience within the US government, and to sample government life to help you determine if it is for you. You can also get a feel for an agency's culture through an internship. Working at DOD is very different from working at Commerce, State, or DOE, for example. Work hours, emphasis on work/life balance, and mix

Table 3.1 US Government General Schedule Pay Scales

Grade	Step 1	Step 2	Step 3	Step 4	Step 5	Step 6	Step 7	Step 8	Step 9	Step 10	Within-Grade Increase
1	$17,803	$18,398	$18,990	$19,579	$20,171	$20,519	$21,104	$21,694	$21,717	$22,269	Varies
2	20,017	20,493	21,155	21,717	21,961	22,607	23,253	23,899	24,545	25,191	Varies
3	21,840	22,568	23,296	24,024	24,752	25,480	26,208	26,936	27,664	28,392	728
4	24,518	25,335	26,152	26,969	27,786	28,603	29,420	30,237	31,054	31,871	817
5	27,431	28,345	29,259	30,173	31,087	32,001	32,915	33,829	34,743	35,657	914
6	30,577	31,596	32,615	33,634	34,653	35,672	36,691	37,710	38,729	39,748	1,019
7	33,979	35,112	36,245	37,378	38,511	39,644	40,777	41,910	43,043	44,176	1,133
8	37,631	38,885	40,139	41,393	42,647	43,901	45,155	46,409	47,663	48,917	1,254
9	41,563	42,948	44,333	45,718	47,103	48,488	49,873	51,258	52,643	54,028	1,385
10	45,771	47,297	48,823	50,349	51,875	53,401	54,927	56,453	57,979	59,505	1,526
11	50,287	51,963	53,639	55,315	56,991	58,667	60,343	62,019	63,695	65,371	1,676
12	60,274	62,283	64,292	66,301	68,310	70,319	72,328	74,337	76,346	78,355	2,009
13	71,674	74,063	76,452	78,841	81,230	83,619	86,008	88,397	90,786	93,175	2,389
14	84,697	87,520	90,343	93,166	95,989	98,812	101,635	104,458	107,281	110,104	2,823
15	99,628	102,949	106,270	109,591	112,912	116,233	119,554	122,875	126,196	129,517	3,321

Source: "Salary Table 2011–GS, Rates Frozen at 2010 Levels, Effective January 2011, Annual Rates by Grade and Step," http://www.opm.gov /policy-data-oversight/pay-leave/salaries-wages/2011/general-schedule/gs.pdf.

Notes from the Field

The Department of Energy

Rhiannon Davis, MSFS 2006

At approximately 4 pm one Tuesday afternoon, a senior leader in my organization decided he needed to make a call to his counterpart in Latin America. He wanted to discuss the outcomes of an upcoming bilateral dialogue. Immediately, I got on the phone to notify that country's ambassador in Washington, arrange a time with the staff of the senior counterpart overseas, contract interpreter services through the US Department of State, and request updates from internal staff for the briefing memorandum I would write later that evening. All of this was to be secured for a call that likely would take place the following day.

My job as an international advisor in the Office of American Affairs at the US Department of Energy provides me the opportunity to interface with a variety of US and foreign government interlocutors to advance US international energy policy. Often, I am called on to do this at an accelerated pace. I also interact with the private sector and civil society to ensure a comprehensive approach to complex energy policy issues. As such, my position leans heavily on crisp, diplomatic, and collegial communication skills, and an ability to keep track of both the forest and the trees. This is in addition to the valuable skills I learned at Georgetown University, including

(Continued on page 73)

in personnel types (e.g., civil service, foreign service, and military) can vary widely between agencies and can result in a very different feel between departments.

US government internships during the school year and the summer are quite common. Most agencies offer internships, and you can apply for an overseas internship at an embassy through State, Commerce, or Agriculture. As mentioned above, the Office of Personnel Management's Pathways Program provides for student internships. You should consult USAJOBS and agency websites for details and application deadlines. Be aware that agencies requiring security clearances will have long application lead times.

Things to Consider When Weighing Job Opportunities

A career within the US government can (and should) be a fulfilling and rewarding path. There are countless career opportunities available within the US government for those who are interested in working on international

critical research and analysis and the art of the two-page memo. My foreign language skills also come in handy in communicating with counterparts overseas and researching key issues relevant to my work.

In the example above, I was responsible for everything from confirming the right telephone number for the call, to sitting down with the principal to go over talking points and messaging for the discussion. The former required an attention to detail that has always been a part of my skill set. The latter, briefing senior leadership concisely and with authority, required an expertise in the subject matter and a confidence in policy development that I began to cultivate as an MSFS student.

My position at the Department of Energy involves international travel and participation in delegation visits, US-government-supported trade missions, and other conferences. I may support the participation of a department principal in one of these visits or be in the position of representing my agency and, at times, the US government position on a particular issue. Energy is a topic that is basic to the functioning of the planet. It also cuts across the commercial, technical, political, and economic development spheres, both domestically and globally. As a result, I have a great deal of respect for the role my agency plays and the importance of being deliberate and thoughtful about the things I contribute to this far-reaching discussion.

I have been interested in international business and policy issues focused on Latin America since undergraduate school. Through coursework at Georgetown and internships during my time as student, I was able to hone in on a keen interest in the energy sector as a path for my career in international affairs.

issues. Here are some things to consider when contemplating entering the US government:

- *Potential for job growth.* Is there the potential for promotion within the position you are considering, or within the office or agency in general? I had the good fortune to be able to progress, develop, and be promoted within Commerce. Although there are rules regarding promotions within the GS schedule (you must have a certain amount of time within grade before you can be promoted to the next grade), rates of promotion do differ among agencies. It is useful to generally be aware of the policies within the agency you are considering.
- *Student loan repayment.* The US government has a program to help employees repay federally insured student loans. Each agency sets up its own student loan repayment plan and has the discretion to implement it as it sees fit. In some agencies, some bureaus or offices are allowed to use this benefit but others may not be, so ask about it before

The Presidential Management Fellows Program

The Presidential Management Fellows (PMF) program (formerly known as the Presidential Management Internship program) is considered to be the US government's premier program for developing young leaders, and one of the best ways to obtain an entry-level position in the federal government. The program is a two-year paid fellowship that provides individuals with leadership training and opportunities to rotate to different offices and agencies within the US government. Fellows are typically hired at a GS-9 level, are promoted to GS-11 after one year, and then, after another year, can convert to a full-time equivalent position at the GS-12 level. Students may negotiate different starting salaries (either step or grade levels), based on education and experience. Fellows receive government benefits, including health care.

The more than three-decade-old program has changed over the years, but the mission has remained constant: attract the brightest entry-level advanced degree candidates dedicated to public service, expose them to different government agencies, provide leadership training, and encourage a career in government. The program is open to candidates who are finishing graduate degrees in all disciplines, from accounting to veterinary science. Candidates must pass a rigorous written and oral exam. Once candidates pass both exams, they are selected as PMF finalists and can "shop" for jobs within the government. Finalists are not guaranteed positions, and they have one year from the date of selection to obtain a PMF appointment. Any necessary security clearances must be processed during this year.

Over the years, competition for PMF appointments has become increasingly fierce. According to FAQs on the PMF website (www.pmf.org), "The number of applicants has been approximately 9,000 annually, and the number of Finalists has been approximately 750." In 2013 there were approximately

(Continued on page 75)

accepting a job if this factor is important for you. The best time to ask may be after you are offered the job and before you decide if you will accept it. With the rising costs of higher education, this could be a significant factor when weighing your career options. Become familiar with the policies of the agencies you are considering.

- *Private sector/public sector.* There is no one way to enter the US government. Although many find jobs right after graduation, others, such as myself, work in the nonprofit or private sectors in the United States or abroad before entering government. There are advantages to all paths. Developing marketable skills outside government—for example, in nongovernmental organizations (NGOs), think tanks, consulting firms, trade associations, or industry—can give you an edge when applying for jobs. One can also work for a company on a government contract, which could place you in a government office

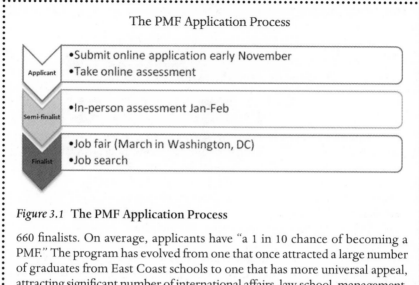

The PMF Application Process

Applicant
•Submit online application early November
•Take online assessment

Semi-finalist
•In-person assessment Jan-Feb

Finalist
•Job fair (March in Washington, DC)
•Job search

Figure 3.1 **The PMF Application Process**

660 finalists. On average, applicants have "a 1 in 10 chance of becoming a PMF." The program has evolved from one that once attracted a large number of graduates from East Coast schools to one that has more universal appeal, attracting significant number of international affairs, law school, management, public health, public policy, and technology graduates from across the country. The examination process is blind to experience, major, and school, with the résumé only factoring in to the final agency selection process.

The ability to rotate to different offices and agencies within the US government is arguably one of the most attractive components of the PMF program. It gives the individual insight into other organizations and processes—such as budgetary, congressional, or procurement—helps expand his or her professional network, and increases understanding of the US government bureaucracy and policymaking process.

Source: Presidential Management Fellows Program website, www.pmf.gov.

as a contractor working side by side with federal employees. Alternatively, many people start their careers within government and later transition to the private or nonprofit sectors (and even back again).

Most important, take advantage of your alumni network. Alumni want to help other alumni and to share their experiences. But many alums also are very busy with jobs they love. Do not hesitate to contact alums and ask for informational interviews, and do not be shy about following up if they do not respond immediately. They may have days where they receive five hundred emails in three hours and accidentally miss yours or intend to respond but get interrupted and simply forget. Reaching out to alums a second or third time does not offend them—rather, it gives them a second chance to meet and talk to a fellow alum. This is something they like to do. I wish you the best of luck in finding a job you enjoy!

Notes from the Field

The Presidential Management Fellowship
Karen Courington, MSFS 2010

Jumping out of airplanes with the army's Golden Knights. Evaluating antiretroviral treatment clinics in Namibia. Riding underway in a navy fast-attack submarine. These encounters are just a few of the incredible opportunities I have been afforded as part of the Presidential Management Fellowship (PMF) program. In my two years as a fellow in the Office of the Secretary of Defense, I have taken part in the national security policy process through strategy development, operational planning, budget analysis, monitoring and evaluation, and policy implementation.

The PMF affords recent graduates the opportunity to "choose your own adventure" in a unique exploration of government through rotations, training, and mentorship. The fellowship provides unparalleled access and exposure, bringing you to the center of the policy arena and to the most pressing policy problems of our time. For students interested in a public service career, the PMF is an excellent introduction.

From reviewing the Executive Order establishing a no-fly zone in Libya, to conducting budget analysis in support of debt negotiations, my PMF experience has come at a challenging time for government. As resources decline and our government faces critical decisions on spending priorities, I became motivated to focus on budget issues. I selected rotations at the Office of Management and Budget and the Senate Appropriations Subcommittee on Defense, in addition to rotations in the Office of the Secretary of Defense (Policy), US Embassy in Namibia, and the immediate Office of the Deputy Secretary of Defense. The congressional appropriations process has been a uniquely rewarding and challenging part of my PMF experience. With the spotlight on the defense budget, our subcommittee's decisions will have significant impact for years to come.

The people with whom I have worked have been the highlight of the fellowship. For those interested in the PMF, keep in mind as you select agencies and offices that the team you work with will be the most important aspect of the job. In seeking out rotations, spin the globe, pick a spot, and make it happen. Select a problem you've been wanting to research and delve into it. Focus on the core mission of an organization, as the skills you develop will be broadly applicable. Most of all, do not be afraid to think big!

Careers in the US Foreign Service

Lisa Kubiske

Lisa Kubiske was appointed US ambassador to Honduras in September 2011. She has also served as deputy chief of the US missions in Brazil and the Dominican Republic. Her earlier assignments include service as Western Hemisphere economics director at the State Department; officer in the State Department's Operations Center and Secretariat Staff; investment director and negotiator at the USTR; chief of the Economic-Political Section at the US Consulate General in Hong Kong; and additional work in Shanghai and in Mexico City. She was given the State Department's highest honor, the Valor Award, for her coordination of US search teams following the major Mexican earthquakes of September 1985. She has earned other awards as well, including a Superior Honor Award for her work as deputy chief of mission in Santo Domingo and, most recently, Superior Honor awards for her participation in the public outreach campaign on behalf of the United States–Peru Free Trade Agreement and her efforts on behalf of United States–Brazil biofuels cooperation. She received a bachelor's degree from Brandeis University and an MSFS from Georgetown University. The views expressed in this essay are solely hers and do not reflect the official views of the US government.

US diplomats are on the challenging front line of efforts to ensure peace, prosperity, and safety for America and US citizens abroad. I have to say, in all honesty, that each day I get a sense of pride in what the US government can and does offer to the rest of the world, ranging from assistance after a natural disaster to ensuring that American businesses get a fair opportunity in the global marketplace to defending and protecting human rights. At home, our work has a direct impact on America's social and economic well-being by expanding international trade. The US Foreign Service helps create jobs at home. This is public service at its very best. If I had to live my life over, I would still choose to be a US diplomat.

Getting into the Foreign Service

The first step to enter the Foreign Service is a competitive exam. In written and oral exams, candidates demonstrate their knowledge of US society, culture, economy, history, government, political systems, and the Constitution; world history and geography; and world political and social issues, basic mathematics and statistics, computer usage, principles of management, interpersonal communication and basic economic principles, and proper English usage.

Once past the written and oral exams, candidates face medical and security clearances and a final suitability review. After that, the candidate waits for a call from the State Department with a job offer.

Being a Foreign Service Officer

Foreign policy is not developed nor carried out in a vacuum. Much of the raw data necessary to formulate policy comes from Foreign Service officers (FSOs) in the field. Overseas, FSOs engage foreign government officials, private-sector leaders, representatives of international organizations, and average people to get an accurate picture of the political, economic, and social situation of each country.

A good portion of a Foreign Service career is spent overseas, often in places with difficult living conditions. Despite occasional inconveniences, few express regrets. There is a drive and a passion for their work that most FSOs feel—which I share—as we tackle our assignments.

The Foreign Service is broken into five basic career tracks: consular, economic, political, management, and public diplomacy. The *consular* track provides services to American citizens who need help overseas. The issues range from reissuing stolen or lost passports to helping with adoptions, or visiting US citizens in jail. Consular officers adjudicate visas and combat visa fraud. This is the section with the most contact with the American people and with large sections of host country populations. A consular officer is part social worker, part anthropologist, part detective, and part best friend to an American in need.

An officer in the *economic* track works to understand international economic conditions and use that information to strengthen the US and global economy. A good economic officer looks at how social pressures and political decisions affect the economic well-being of a country and the economic relationship with the United States and neighboring countries. This FSO actively works to advance US economic priorities in the host nation, promote US exports, and level the playing field for US businesses.

A *political* track officer analyzes the social and political conditions in a country, and advocates with the host government to advance US policies. Political officers look at how the local government interacts with its people and vice versa. They analyze how decisions strengthen or weaken democratic governance and improve or degrade human rights. They advocate for human rights for all.

The *management* track focuses on making sure that everyone working for the State Department in Washington and for all agencies working in embassies and consulates have the resources necessary to carry out their jobs. They also work directly with host governments to ensure that treaties and agreements that affect embassy operations are respected. Without them there would be no leases for embassy annexes, housing for officers, or building permits negotiated with foreign ministries. They also oversee health and retirement benefits for embassies' local employees and buy equipment and services.

Finally, the officers in the *public diplomacy* track have the job of sharing US culture with, and explaining US views to, overseas audiences. They coordinate exchange programs, bring US cultural activities to host countries, arrange for American speakers on a wide variety of topics to visit, and generally do all they can to make sure that the US message of peace, prosperity, democracy, and security is given a fair hearing.

Because of the high demand for visas and services for overseas Americans worldwide, all FSOs have one and sometimes two consular assignments in the first four years. Working in the consular section provides new FSOs with valuable opportunities to build management skills and meet the ordinary citizens of the host country.

Officers need to specialize in two geographic areas and to master two foreign languages if they hope eventually to enter the senior ranks of the Foreign Service. And there will be some service in hardship posts. Although there are rules about what is and is not a hardship posting, just how hard that posting feels depends on the officer. I served in Shanghai just as China was opening to the world. At the time, the city lacked many things we take

---

Eligibility Requirements for the Foreign Service Officers Exam

Applicants must be:

- Citizens of the United States.
- At least twenty years old on the day they submit their registration package.
- No older than fifty-nine years on the date they submit their registration package.
- At least twenty-one years of age to be appointed as a Foreign Service officer. Appointment as a Foreign Service officer must occur before an applicant reaches the age of sixty.
- Available for worldwide assignment, including assignments at posts where health, living conditions, or medical support may be rudimentary, or in danger zones where family members are not allowed.

No specific education level or proficiency in a foreign language is required for applicants.

Source: Guide to the Foreign Service Officer Selection Process, http://careers.state .gov.

for granted at home and, with the heavy surveillance by Chinese security forces, it was considered a medium hardship post. But I very much enjoyed my work there, and my family and I had many interesting excursions in China. It was difficult, but still rewarding.

Let us face it; this operation is called the Foreign Service for a reason. There are limits on how much time you can spend in Washington. Conversely, the State Department's rules also limit how much time an officer can serve overseas. Like most rules, there is room for flexibility. There are as many different opinions about the path to the top as there are FSOs. The top leadership comes from all career tracks, from different geographic areas of responsibility, and from many different backgrounds.

My Experience

My work in the Foreign Service has reflected the needs of the Foreign Service, my interests, and the opportunities that have come my way. I have been able to see history in the making, represent my country, and contribute in ways that I hope have made the world a better place.

Like many of my colleagues, I started Foreign Service life adjudicating visas (in my case, in Mexico City). As an economic officer, I was curious about the economic situation of the immigrant visa applicants I saw each day. A survey I conducted of the applicants yielded information of great interest to academicians, policymakers, and what was then called the Immigration and Naturalization Service.

Later, after the city suffered a terrible earthquake, I helped with the US post-quake efforts and ended up coordinating an international search and rescue effort. Honestly, helping to save people's lives was the single most rewarding thing I have ever done. An added benefit was learning how to work in a crisis, which has served me well for all subsequent assignments. The State Department rewarded my earthquake efforts with its highest award.

From Mexico I returned to Washington to serve in the State Department's round-the-clock Operations Center and then as a member of the Secretariat staff. In the Operations Center, I was part of a team that took calls from posts overseas when crises happened and helped senior officials reach each other quickly. In the Secretariat, I organized travel for the secretary of state (then George Shultz) and sometimes traveled with him. These jobs gave me a terrific overview of how the State Department works overseas and in Washington.

As an economic officer, I wanted to work on China issues. In Washington, I was on the China "desk." During that tour, I worked with many executive branch agencies on export control questions. One large issue at the time was how the US government should react to China's plans to launch a United

States–made communications satellite. In the end, the satellite was launched from China. As a result, billions of people in India and China could receive direct satellite TV programming for the first time.

In Shanghai, as a midlevel economic officer, I reported on the fast-paced economic reforms occurring, provided US negotiators information that helped guide talks with China over its entry into the WTO, and assisted a steady stream of US companies interested in doing business in the Shanghai area. Later, as a more senior officer in Hong Kong, I headed a combined economic and political section that tracked Hong Kong's evolving relationship with the mainland. After September 11, 2001, I worked with the head of a global organization, the Financial Action Task Force, on recommended international guidelines for tracking terrorism finance.

The State Department also loans its officers to cities, states, Congress, and other federal agencies, as well to universities. I spent two years at the USTR, co-leading negotiations of bilateral investment treaties and leading the US delegation for the investment portions of multilateral treaties. The investment work yielded real jobs in the United States and abroad.

Before starting my current job as ambassador, I served as the deputy chief of mission (DCM) in the Dominican Republic and Brazil. Although the ambassador is the "face" of the United States and the personal representative of the president to the host country, it is the job of the DCM to make sure that the embassy is working as a team to support the ambassador. In military parlance, a DCM is the executive officer of the embassy and handles its day-to-day operations.

Now, as ambassador, I work with an embassy team that not only includes my State Department colleagues but also representatives from a wide range of other US government agencies. Our joint mission—under my leadership—is to implement the policy set by the president and to provide information and advice to Washington about our relationship with Honduras.

Each day is different. I meet with Hondurans of all ranks and travel throughout the country to highlight and advance US programs. One day, I might check on how our security assistance to Honduras is being implemented, speak with the leaders of a chamber of commerce, give remarks on climate change, meet with farmers who received support from our development programs, and then have dinner with colleagues. Another day, I might have internal embassy meetings, then speak to a school group, meet with a Honduran leader on women's issues, and later in the day discuss with Honduran government officials ideas about how best to use newly raised tax revenues. Or I might meet with leaders who defend human rights and work to strengthen Honduras's public institutions, and then have a private coffee with the widow or mother of a family member killed in a violent crime. And so on.

The Foreign Service Officer Selection Process

To register for the Foreign Service Officer Test, applicants first complete an online application form that asks them to provide basic factual information about their education and work histories. The registration package takes approximately one to two hours to complete. Registrants should fully educate themselves about the five Foreign Service career tracks: consular, economic, management, political, and public diplomacy. Applicants will be required to select their career track when they register for the exam. Applicants will not have the opportunity to change career tracks after they submit their online registrations, so careful thought should be given to making this decision.

The Foreign Service Officer Test is administered at hundreds of commercial test centers throughout the United States and at locations abroad. The test lasts approximately three hours and draws upon a candidate's writing skills, general background, experience and education, and measures knowledge of English expression and other subjects basic to the functions of Foreign Service officers. The test includes three multiple-choice sections—general job knowledge, English expression, and a biographic information section that measures skills and abilities such as integrity, problem solving, and cultural sensitivity—and at least one 30-minute essay.

Candidates who have achieved the minimum score on both the multiple choice and essay tests receive instructions for completing *personal narratives*, which must be submitted prior to the deadline in order to advance to the QEP stage of the selection process. The personal narratives consist of six short essays about the skills, knowledge, and abilities they would bring to the Foreign Service. The questions seek a great deal of information in a limited space (200 words per question).

The *Qualifications Evaluation Panel (QEP)* reviews the work and education portions of the application form, the personal narratives, and the FSO/essay results to select those candidates qualified to be invited to the Oral Assessment.

The invitation to the full-day *Oral Assessment* process is based on anticipated hiring needs and budget. Assessments are conducted in Washington and in a limited number of other major cities in the United States. The assessment center exercises are based on the thirteen dimensions identified as essential elements of Foreign Service jobs. The oral assessment tests the abilities and personal characteristics considered necessary to perform that work. All candidates are advised at the end of the assessment day if they are eligible to continue their candidacy.

(Continued on page 83)

Candidates who are successful in the oral assessments have several additional selection steps before they can be offered appointments as Foreign Service officer career candidates, pending tenure. Each candidate must receive *medical and security clearances* and pass a *final suitability review*. Applicants must be available for worldwide assignment, including assignments at posts where health, living conditions, or medical support may be rudimentary, or in danger zones where family members are not allowed. Therefore, each candidate must meet medical fitness standards which are, of necessity, often more rigorous than those of other professions. Prior to being appointed to the Foreign Service, candidates must have a thorough medical examination and receive an unlimited medical clearance for assignment worldwide. A comprehensive security background investigation, conducted by the US Department of State in cooperation with other federal, state, and local agencies, provides information necessary to determine a candidate's suitability for appointment to the Foreign Service and for a top-secret security clearance.

When the security clearance process is completed, the Board of Examiners convenes a *Final Review Panel*. The panel assesses all of the information related to the applicant to determine suitability for appointment for the Foreign Service.

Candidates who pass the oral assessment and who have successfully passed the security background investigation, the medical clearance and the final suitability review process are placed on rank-ordered career track hiring registers (based on the career tracks chosen by the candidates). Appointments to entry-level positions are made from the five registers. If a candidate declines two job offers, that candidate is removed from the register. Candidates with veterans points and/or a demonstrated proficiency in a foreign language can earn bonus points and improve their rank order positions on the hiring lists.

Placement on the Register does not guarantee an appointment as a Foreign Service officer, for the number of appointments depends on the needs of the Foreign Service. Your rank order on the Register is dynamic. People with higher scores will be placed above you, regardless of when they are placed on the Register. Likewise, you will be placed above candidates with lower scores, regardless of how long they have been on the Register. Your name may stay on the Register for a maximum of eighteen months. After that, your name will be removed.

Sources: Guide to the Foreign Service Officer Selection Process, http://careers.state.gov/uploads/f7/33/f7332b47ed70772afdb35003f8735a66/3-0_FSO_Reg Guide_Nov152012.pdf, and http://careers.state.gov/officer/selection-process #nogo.

Notes from the Field

The US Foreign Service

Robin Dunnigan, MSFS 1992

It was an unusually humid day even for Hanoi; I felt sweat drenching my blouse and it was only 8 am. I was running late for a meeting downtown and there were no cabs in sight so I hopped onto a "xe om," a moped taxi that was a little risky (especially in a skirt) but could get me there in time. I had to laugh at the image of myself—riding through Hanoi traffic in a soaked blouse sidesaddle on the back of a moped hanging on to my Vietnamese driver for dear life—not the image I had once envisioned of life as a government "bureaucrat."

That day I was meeting a group of representatives from some of the United States' largest information technology companies, who were concerned about new internet laws being considered by the Vietnamese government. As deputy economic counselor at the US Embassy, I was responsible for bilateral trade and investment issues, a job I absolutely loved. Vietnam's economy was growing despite the global turndown, creating new opportunities for US exports. A typical day in Hanoi might include discussing the business climate with the local American Chamber of Commerce, meeting with Vietnam's Trade Ministry to encourage reforms that would provide US companies a more level playing field, or traveling throughout Asia to participate in ongoing regional free trade agreement negotiations.

(Continued on page 85)

Is This Career for You?

Living abroad presents many opportunities and challenges, both personal and professional. I can only say from my personal experience that if you are intellectually curious and have a high degree of flexibility, fortitude, energy, and ability to adapt to new and changing situations, and also have a strong interest in public service, this may be the job for you.

Let me be straightforward: when assigned overseas, FSOs are essentially always on call. And, as with so many other important jobs, there is always more work than time. Still, we understand there must be a balance between professional and family obligations. In general, officers are given the time they need to take care of personal or family events.

Speaking of families, the whole family—officer, spouse, and children—needs to decide if moving every two to four years is acceptable. Likewise, the spouse or partner needs to consider if his or her career can be adjusted

US–Vietnamese relations were at an all-time high, and every member of the US Embassy felt we were contributing to an important, long-term partnership.

I became a Foreign Service officer in the Department of State in 1992, soon after graduating from Georgetown's Master's of Science in Foreign Service (MSFS) program, and have loved (just about!) every minute of the last twenty years. I have served at US missions around the world, including in Vietnam, Chile, Turkey, Cuba, and El Salvador. As an economic officer, I have focused on promoting US trade and investment, but have also worked on political and consular issues. I have left every assignment even more convinced that diplomacy matters.

The Foreign Service has provided me a challenging and satisfying professional life, but has also afforded me and my family extraordinary opportunities and adventures. My husband is also a Foreign Service officer, and we have raised our two children mostly overseas. The four of us have shared the splendor of Machu Picchu at sunrise, kayaked along brilliant blue glaciers in Patagonia, crawled over the magnificent ruins of Ephesus in Turkey, biked through the rice fields of Vietnam's most remote villages, and snorkeled with exotic fish in Bali. Our children have worked in orphanages in the developing world, attended international schools with kids from fifty-five different countries, and learned to love the music, food, and people in every place they have lived.

Is it all roses? Of course not! My husband and I face the challenges of working parents everywhere, and the frequent moving required by the Foreign Service can certainly be stressful. But my husband and I—and our children—would not trade the life we have for any other.

to living overseas or if a career change is required. (My husband shifted his career after my Mexico City tour to one that more easily fits into living abroad.) The opportunities given to Foreign Service children are beyond description. My two sons grew up and studied in Taiwan, Shanghai, Hong Kong, and the Dominican Republic. They have visited me in Brazil and now Honduras during their college years. They, like many other Foreign Service children we know, revel in the adventure of seeing new places. Living abroad has also made them more knowledgeable about global affairs and ready for an interconnected world.

Single FSOs face different challenges, not the least of which is the possibility that someone in a host country may initially be interested in you because of your job or American passport. All officers must be able to distinguish between an opportunist and someone interested in you sincerely for your personality. There are numerous opportunities to meet with other single diplomats overseas. In almost every location where I have served there has been an informal—and sometimes formal—group of single diplomats organized to put together happy hours and excursions.

I have been happy with my Foreign Service career. I have to say that I never anticipated becoming an ambassador. To be sure, during my time in the Foreign Service, I have looked for opportunities to advance my career, but I have also looked for jobs and locations that would be fun and interesting to explore. And so far, I have no regrets.

Careers on Capitol Hill

Brent Woolfork

Brent Woolfork, a 2008 graduate of Georgetown University's MSFS program, is a Democratic senior professional staff member on the House Foreign Affairs Committee. He previously worked for Senator Bill Nelson of Florida as a legislative and administrative aide and spent time at the Treasury Department, Booz Allen Hamilton, and the Center for Strategic and International Studies. He earned a bachelor's degree in international relations from Rollins College in Winter Park, Florida. The views expressed in this essay are solely his and do not reflect the official views of the US government.

The halls of Congress are where politics, policy, and personality reside and at times collide. It is no wonder that the cast of actors in Congress calls upon a diverse, talented, and dedicated group of Americans. Today's world is a complex landscape filled with numerous challenges that require people with a range of expertise in international finance, energy, security, or health. These public servants advise members of Congress on how to shape, cajole, or coerce changes in US foreign policy.

The Congressional Role in Foreign Policy

The US Congress is integral to the formulation and implementation of US foreign policy. The members of the House of Representatives and Senate influence foreign policy in three basic ways:

1. authorization of new or modification of existing policies or programs,
2. appropriations, and
3. oversight.

Constitutionally, Congress has the responsibility to "regulate Commerce with foreign Nations" and is tasked with giving federal agencies the money they need to operate their programs and policies for each fiscal year. In 1948, for example, President Harry Truman would not have been able to move forward with a plan to rebuild Europe's economy if the Republican-controlled Congress had not passed the Economic Cooperation Act. That law, now known as the Marshall Plan, provided more than $12 billion in assistance to postwar Europe and helped garner decades of economic growth and relative peace on the continent. In more recent history Congress was integral in the response to the September 2001 terrorist attacks, in ratcheting up sanctions on the Iranian regime, and in funding military operations in Iraq and Afghanistan.

Congressional Staff Structure

Congressional staff can be generally divided into two categories: personal office staff and committee staff. Each representative or senator has a personal staff that is responsible for managing policy, formulating press strategies, and handling administrative functions. Every personal office has at least one person who is responsible for covering international relations. Legislative correspondents (LCs), who are responsible for responding to constituents' inquiries, are considered entry-level staff members among the legislative staff. Legislative assistants (LAs) follow international developments, prepare meeting memos, draft speeches, and meet with constituents, essentially acting act as national security advisers. Most LAs will also cover other issues, such as homeland security, veterans' affairs, and the environment, depending on a member's committee assignments and personal interests. The office staff is typically rounded out by communications directors and press assistants, who advise the member on press strategy, draft press releases, and respond to media inquiries.

Congressional staff also populate committees on both the House and Senate sides of the Hill. The House Foreign Affairs Committee and the Senate Foreign Relations Committee are the primary, but not the only, committees that deal with international relations. In the House, for instance, the Ways and Means Committee has jurisdiction over trade and the Financial Services Committee is responsible for covering the international financial institutions (e.g., the World Bank and International Monetary Fund). Both houses have intelligence committees that have authority over the seventeen federal intelligence agencies. These committees are called authorizing committees because they modify or create additional authorities for the agencies in their jurisdiction.

The other type of committee with which to be familiar are the two appropriations committees (the House Committee on Appropriations and the Senate Committee on Appropriations) that provide the funding for departments and agencies. Both committees have a State, Foreign Operations Subcommittee that has jurisdiction over the Department of State, USAID, and other international affairs agencies.

> ## Selected Committees of the US Congress with International Affairs–Related Jurisdiction
>
> - House Committee on Foreign Affairs
> - House Committee on Ways and Means (Subcommittee on Trade)
> - House Committee on Financial Services (Subcommittee on International Monetary Policy and Trade)
> - House Permanent Select Committee on Intelligence
> - Senate Committee on Foreign Relations
> - Senate Committee on Finance (Subcommittee on International Trade, Customs, and Global Competitiveness)
> - Senate Select Committee on Intelligence

Committee staff, referred to as professional staff members, are Congress's policy experts. Each committee has a separate Republican and Democratic staff composed of regional and functional staff members. In covering Afghanistan, for example, the foreign affairs committees will have a regional staff member who is an expert on the history and politics of Afghanistan but also functional experts who are knowledgeable about defense and security practices and who apply that expertise to military and police issues in Afghanistan. Staff members are responsible for keeping up to date in their responsibility areas by meeting regularly with State Department staff members, other agency officials, and NGOs.

Professional staff members often draft legislation and are also responsible for getting it through Congress. In 2009, for example, the House was considering legislation to regulate pollution from greenhouse gas emissions. The bill was under the primary jurisdiction of the House Energy and Commerce Committee but also fell under the responsibilities of a number of other panels. I, along with professional staff members on the Energy and Commerce Committee, was responsible for drafting the international provisions to assist developing countries in adapting to climate change, lowering greenhouse emissions, and developing forestry programs. We worked successfully with a variety of interest groups to prevent the provisions from being stripped out of the bill. The legislation passed the House but unfortunately failed to move in the Senate. Although the bill did not pass, our work had positive effects on international climate negotiations at the time by demonstrating that the United States was seriously working to address the issue.

Professional staff members are also responsible for preparing for hearings. For instance, when we hold our annual budget hearing and invite the

Congressional Resources

The Congressional Research Service (CRS) and the Government Accountability Office (GAO) both provide useful services to Congress and should not be overlooked in the job search.

CRS, Congress's in-house think tank, is staffed by nonpartisan experts who provide policy and legal analyses to congressional members and committees. GAO is an independent, nonpartisan agency that works for Congress. Often referred to as the "government watchdog," it holds the federal government accountable by examining its programs and projects.

In many cases, staffers with both these organizations have covered and worked in their area of study for decades. While researching a foreign assistance program during the 1990s, I found out to my good fortune that the CRS person assigned to my request actually ran the program over a decade before! Both organizations offer summer internships for students, although CRS prefers interns to be in graduate school.

secretary of state to testify, my colleagues and I are responsible for preparing the committee chairman, ranking member (i.e., the top minority party member), and committee members for the hearing. We draft background memos and talking points, and suggest questions for members to pose to the witnesses.

Professional staff members typically tend to have postgraduate degrees and to be older and have more work experience than personal office staff. I know one staff member who covered the Middle East at the State Department and then went to a think tank before coming to the Committee on Foreign Affairs. Another colleague worked in a personal House office before leaving for graduate school, and then returned to the Hill to work for the Committee.

One characteristic that can surprise individuals who are used to working in large organizations is Congress's relatively flat hierarchical structure. Clearing positions requires less coordination than one needs when trying to get approval on a new policy position in a large agency. In order to get your senator to approve a new bill, you would only need the approval of your legislative director, chief of staff, and perhaps the communications director. In other words, staff members can enjoy regular access and interaction with their member of Congress.

Finding a Job on the Hill

If you are considering a position on the Hill, keep the following points in mind:

- *First, know yourself.* Congress is a highly political place, so you need to decide if you are a Republican or Democrat, even if you are aiming for a committee position. Despite what the case may have been in the past, politics does not stop at the water's edge, and it does play a role in the national security debate. Political overtones can permeate national security discussions, although they may not be as strident as debates on social issues or taxation. Although you do not necessarily need to agree with every position in the party platform, you also do not want to work long hours for a member with whom you greatly disagree.
- *Second, do your homework.* Before applying to an office or requesting an informational interview, job seekers should understand the makeup of a member's district, such as whether they have a large Indian diaspora community that would cause the member to be interested in US–Indian relations. You also should understand a member's political leanings—liberal, conservative, or moderate—and positions on policy. Today, a lot of information can be found on a member's website. If not, internet and news searches should reveal valuable information. By being prepared, you will demonstrate to offices that you understand not only policy but also know the political forces that influence every member's actions and policies.
- *Third, demonstrate that you are a strong communicator.* Offices want people who can speak and write well because you will need to regularly talk with constituents, write decision memos, and brief a member.
- *Fourth, reach out to your own hometown representative or senator.* Even if a job is not available in that office, you can arrange an informational interview. That person can then be an advocate who can connect you with other offices and recommend you for positions. Often, positions may not be publicly advertised. Even if you do not know anyone in those offices, use your network to try to establish a link. Check with your family and friends for a name. Although you can always cold-call an office, a personal contact or recommendation can go a long way in easing the job search.

When I began my search for my first Hill job—an entry-level staff assistant position—I did not know anyone in Congress. But my supervisor at the time had just met the deputy director of the House Foreign Affairs Committee at a conference. I arranged an informational meeting with him and, as a result, he connected me with staff members from the Florida congressional delegation. One of these connections was Senator Bill Nelson's chief of staff. I ended up working in Senator Nelson's office for several years as a staff assistant and then as an LC. This succession of events is common on the Hill and the way that many people find jobs.

Work/Life Balance

Each personal and committee office has its own rhythms and characteristics that dictate work hours, workload, and personal time. Throughout most of my career, the basic office hours have been 9 am to 6 pm. However, it is usual to stay later to finish a request from the member or to prepare for upcoming meetings. In my experience, typically staff leave work around 7 pm. Such a schedule can make it more predictable to drop off kids at school and attend to other personal responsibilities.

In some offices staff remain in their office if their member is still in the office. This can lead to long nights, particularly when there are many votes on amendments to appropriations bills in what are colloquially called "vote-a-ramas." The pervasiveness of smart phones also means that staff members are never really off duty; they can literally be on call in the case of an unexpected international event or a congressman's pressing question.

As in many jobs, congressional rhythms oscillate between slower and faster periods. The spring tends to be busy because that is when Congress receives and holds hearings on the president's budget request. Summers, particularly during the last session of a Congress, tend to be busy because appropriations bills need to be passed and there is a realization that the year is almost over. Election years, particularly in the fall, tend to be much slower as members return to their districts or states more regularly to garner their constituents' votes.

Aside from the rewarding work, one of the benefits of working in Congress is the recess period. The congressional calendar is broken up into periods of being in session and being in recess. During the session, members are expected to be in Washington to undertake the duties of Congress (e.g., drafting legislation, voting). Recess is a time when members are not required to be present and often return to their home districts, allowing the pace on the Hill to slow down. Staff may find this an ideal time to catch up on long-term projects that take a back seat to more immediate tasks when Congress is in session.

It is particularly important when considering a job on the Hill to keep in mind that your job stability is directly tied to a member's reelection every two or six years *or*—if you are working on a committee—to which party controls the House or Senate. If your party loses the majority, for example, you could lose your job because minority staff sizes are much smaller than the majority staff. This uncertainty every two years can be unsettling.

Notes from the Field

The Senate Foreign Relations Committee

Mary deBree, MSFS 2012

Before coming to MSFS, I had a mix of political and international affairs experience. Having worked for Hillary Clinton and subsequently with the International Rescue Committee abroad and later as a Fulbright scholar in Vietnam, I knew I wanted to work at the nexus of foreign policy and politics. I also wanted experience on the Hill. The fall of my second year at MSFS, I began interning with the Senate Foreign Relations Committee. I decided to stay on with the Committee during my second semester and was offered a job in the late spring before graduation.

My current position on the Foreign Relations Committee is supporting the chief of staff and chief counsel on Committee activities, initiatives, and priorities. On a day-to-day and practical level this means I research and edit reports, schedule hearings, liaise with other Senate offices and staff, organize briefings at staff and member level, review and edit memos for the Chairman, and manage the office and twenty-five-person staff. Among the many issues and developments I have covered, I have been fortunate enough to work on both the Law of the Sea Treaty and the Convention on the Rights of Persons with Disabilities, the secretary of state nomination process, and post-Benghazi hearings and response. Working for Senator John Kerry provided me invaluable insight on the process and priorities in US foreign policy. Likewise, I believe that my previous experience has helped me contribute meaningfully and have a positive impact.

In addition to all of this, I have had the opportunity to work with and learn from other staff on the Foreign Relations Committee. The staff is made of a diverse mix of people with experience on all sides—field, intelligence, government, nonprofits, private sector, etc. The Committee obviously works closely with the State Department, the Department of Defense, the US Agency for International Development, the Department of the Treasury, and other sectors of the government. In our daily activity, we are constantly in contact with constituent groups, civic organizations, nonprofits, intergovernmental organizations, and various other actors in order to carry out our oversight responsibilities.

Working on the Hill provides broad perspective and valuable experience to help shape policy. Having Hill experience adds real legislative and process knowledge, legitimacy, and insight to how Congress functions. I will add a fair warning that you cannot expect to be working on the sexiest foreign policy issues every day. You may spend a whole day trying to get a resolution passed to commemorate the 80th birthday of a high-ranking Thai official. However, you will also have days where you get to work on issues like diplomatic security, attend hearings on North Korea, write memos on an unfolding crisis abroad, or see Aung Sang Suu Kyi awarded the Congressional Medal of Freedom.

Persistence Is Key

Just as in other fields, persistence is the key to attaining a job in Congress. Congressional positions are extremely competitive, but cultivating and maintaining contacts is the key to a successful search. If you are able to make it to the Hill, I hope you find it as rewarding as I have.

Careers in Development Agencies

Taylor Stager

Taylor Stager joined USAID in 2005. Currently the Budget and Finance Team leader in the Office of US Foreign Disaster Assistance (OFDA), she has also held information specialist and disaster operations specialist positions within OFDA focusing on Chad and Sudan. She received an MSFS from Georgetown University and a bachelor's of science in journalism from Northwestern University. The views expressed in this essay are solely hers and do not reflect the official views of the US government.

Development work attracts those who have the audacity to believe they can help solve major global challenges. In a recent USAID Town Hall meeting, USAID administrator Rajiv Shah reminded employees that it takes a certain boldness to walk into work every day and think, "Today I am going to help end hunger for millions of people," or "I am going to help end the HIV/AIDS crisis."

Development work within the US government attracts those who believe they can help alleviate poverty and improve conditions globally but also want to serve the United States. Working for a government agency on development issues provides the opportunity to shape priorities, develop broad policies, allocate funding for programs, and influence key decision makers on issues of critical national and global importance. US development experts are on the front lines in areas of foreign policy importance, working directly with partners on the ground to advance shared goals and ideals. Due to their in-depth practical knowledge of the countries they serve, US development experts can also play a key role in informing foreign policy throughout the federal government, including the State Department, the White House, and Congress.

US development professionals represent the best ideals of the American people. Their titles are ordinary, but they work in extraordinary contexts. They are doctors, engineers, accountants, governance advisers, humanitarians, and agriculture specialists. They are experts in water systems, solar energy, mobile banking, and grassroots community building. They are supported by logisticians, security officers, travel specialists, contracting officers, and human resources specialists. And they rely on skilled writers, photographers, Web designers, and social media officers to help communicate a message of partnership to populations around the globe. Whatever your expertise, if you have the audacity to believe that you can use your skills and talents to solve major global development problems, there is a place for you in the government's development community.

USAID

USAID is the premier international development agency within the US federal government and worldwide. In 1961 Congress created USAID through the Foreign Assistance Act to further America's national interests by expanding democracy, improving governance, supporting the growth of free markets, and helping people recover from crises and disasters. Today USAID works in more than a hundred countries worldwide:

- promoting good governance, democracy, and human rights;
- improving global health by combating maternal and child mortality and deadly diseases such as HIV/AIDS, tuberculosis, and malaria;
- advancing food security and agriculture by addressing the root causes of poverty and hunger;
- improving environmental sustainability and helping countries adapt to a changing environment;
- furthering education and literacy, especially among girls and young women;
- helping societies prevent and recover from conflicts; and
- providing humanitarian assistance following disasters.

USAID is an independent agency that reports to the secretary of state and takes overall foreign policy direction from the State Department. USAID is headquartered in the heart of Washington and is organized into geographic bureaus that coordinate assistance within particular regions, and functional bureaus that coordinate particular types of assistance across geographic regions. Overseas, formal USAID offices are known as missions. USAID missions coordinate all USAID assistance in a given country. Mission staff liaise with host government officials, NGOs, and civil society groups. In countries where security does not permit a robust presence or where USAID does not support a large amount of assistance, USAID staff may be collocated in US embassies.

USAID carries out its mission by funding a wide range of organizations to implement programs. Staff play a key role in setting goals for USAID programs, developing a strategy to achieve those goals, designing effective programs, and identifying capable implementing partners. USAID forms partnerships with implementing organizations through grants, cooperative agreements, and contracts that lay out goals, indicators, expected program costs, and other terms and conditions. USAID funding recipients include NGOs, international organizations and UN agencies, contractors, small businesses, academic institutions, and other federal agencies.

Foreign Service

When most people hear the term "Foreign Service," the State Department's diplomatic corps typically comes to mind. Many people are surprised to learn that USAID has its own Foreign Service of development and management professionals who staff USAID missions around the world, as well as some postings in Washington. Unlike State Department officers, who focus on overall US foreign policy and diplomatic relations in a given country, USAID's FSOs focus on development assistance. They design, evaluate, and monitor programs in the countries where they serve. USAID's Foreign Service attracts professionals who enjoy technical, program-related work and forming partnerships with organizations to work toward shared goals and objectives. USAID staff work in the most challenging and insecure environments, amid poverty and conflict, so USAID's FSOs possess genuine curiosity and openness to other cultures and ways of addressing challenges. USAID Foreign Service tours are fixed in duration, varying from one to four years.

USAID's FSOs are not required to take an examination as part of the hiring process. USAID selects its FSOs through a competitive, multistep interview process that is advertised through USAID's website and through the federal government's job posting site, www.usajobs.gov. The most notable recent USAID Foreign Service hiring initiative, known as the Development Leadership Initiative (DLI), focused on increasing the number of FSOs. The DLI program brought entry- and mid-level professionals into USAID through a specially designed training and rotation program. The DLI program and similar past programs have been excellent ways for entry-level professionals to enter the agency and begin their US government development career.

Many successful DLI and USAID Foreign Service candidates have some experience working in developing countries with international NGOs, local organizations, businesses, or other federal agencies before joining USAID. An advanced degree is not required, but competitive candidates usually have a master's degree in a relevant field such as international affairs, development, public policy, public health, or engineering.

The Civil Service

USAID's civil servants primarily staff USAID headquarters and provide policy guidance, technical expertise, broader-level interagency coordination, and administrative support to enable USAID staff and programs to flourish worldwide. The USAID civil service is an attractive option for those who enjoy international development but who wish to live and work in Washington or whose personal situation precludes overseas living. USAID's civil servants work alongside FSOs throughout the agency, supporting its overseas work and coordinating with the rest of the government and the international development community. Depending on the specific position and requirements, civil servants may travel frequently overseas for short or extended assignments. Other civil servants perform functions that do not require travel. Unlike Foreign Service assignments, which are limited in duration, civil service assignments are usually open-ended, which may suit those who wish to have more control over how and when they make career moves.

USAID civil service jobs are advertised on the agency's website and through USAJOBS. Many civil service jobs are only open to those who are already USAID staff members or employees of other federal agencies, so for many people seeking to join USAID's civil service, the tricky part is building a competitive résumé to gain that first coveted position. Many competitive civil service applicants possess a master's degree as well as experience working in a similar capacity with another federal agency, an NGO, an academic institution, or in the private sector. It is essential that applicants complete the application fully and demonstrate that their knowledge and experience meet the specific criteria for the position as described in the job posting.

Personal Services Contractors
Personal services contracts are one of the least-known and -understood ways to join USAID, but they can be one of the best entry points for new employees. USAID uses personal services contracts to hire individuals that possess specific skills and experience that the agency requires for a finite period. Additionally, the agency can hire for new positions under a personal services contract very quickly, allowing it to be fast and flexible in fluid situations. These contracts usually include an initial period of performance of one or two years, and may be renewable for up to five years. USAID employees working under these contracts are considered employees of the agency but are not eligible for full US direct-hire employee benefits; instead, a limited benefits package is offered. Because the positions are finite in duration and have more limited benefits, these positions can be less attractive to some individuals. Others appreciate that working on a personal services contract allows them to switch positions whenever they wish, and offers them great flexibility in charting their own path. Working under a contract can be an excellent way to gain experience with the agency and establish professional connections within the agency.

One of the most challenging things for applicants to understand is that personal services contracts are competed for through a procurement process, rather than using a traditional job hiring process. The contracts are advertised through solicitations, with criteria for selection clearly defined and specific point values allotted to various parts of the application and interview process. A technical evaluation committee determines the scores for each applicant, and the applicant(s) with the highest point totals are offered a contract. This can be a rigid and less familiar process for applicants.

Institutional Contractors

Institutional contractors are another less understood way to work for or alongside USAID around the world. USAID contracts with private companies for the provision of some services, such as communications, accounting, travel, information technology support, and training. The employees of institutional contractors work alongside agency employees daily, sometimes onsite at USAID locations, to fulfill the agency's global mission. Therefore, working for a USAID institutional contractor can be an excellent way to gain experience with USAID's work and to establish professional connections within the agency. Individuals working for an institutional contractor often enjoy the benefits of working for a company, including a complete benefits package, along with the opportunity to contribute to solving some of the most complex global challenges of our time in cooperation with USAID. Applicants apply directly to the company, which conducts the hiring process in accordance with its own corporate policies.

Other Agencies

The State Department

The State Department's mission, broadly, is to advance freedom on behalf of the American people and the international community, and the department plays a key role in requesting, justifying, and shaping priorities for US foreign assistance, including the development funding implemented by USAID. The Office of US Foreign Assistance Resources ensures the strategic and effective allocation, management, and use of foreign assistance resources by coordinating the joint State–USAID budget request, and by monitoring and reporting on the expenditures of funds. In addition, numerous bureaus throughout State implement assistance programs in their relevant functional or regional area that may contribute to the development strategy within a given country. State programs may help to lay the foundation for development through improved security, governance, and the rule of law. In addition, State is one of the federal agencies that implements the President's Emergency Program for AIDS Relief, which aims to provide access to HIV / AIDS prevention, care, and treatment programs. Information on jobs at the State Department is available at www.state.gov.

Notes from the Field

USAID

Alexandra Riboul, MSFS 2002

I felt the ground beneath me shaking and knew immediately what was happening—an earthquake! I could have never imagined the events that unfolded afterwards. A few days later, it dawned on me that I had experienced one of the largest disasters of modern history—the 7.0 earthquake in Haiti on January 12, 2010. Chaos, destruction, loss, death, friendship, compassion, help—it is still difficult to find words to truly describe the days that followed the earthquake during which Haiti's capital and nearby cities shook for 35 interminable seconds. At the time of the earthquake, I had been living in the country for nearly a year, serving as a Foreign Service officer for USAID/Haiti. While I had worked responding to disasters prior to living in Haiti, I always arrived after the disaster had happened. The Haiti earthquake was the first time that I had lived through a disaster of such magnitude and destruction.

Prior to becoming a Foreign Service officer and living in Haiti, I worked as part of USAID teams responding to disasters in different parts of the world—from the tsunami in Sri Lanka in 2004, to the food crisis in Niger in 2005, and the earthquake in Peru in 2007. At that time, I worked as an Information Officer for USAID's Office of US Foreign Disaster Assistance. During my five years in that position, I gained tremendous experience in disaster relief and humanitarian assistance, and honed skills that became particularly valuable during USAID's response in Haiti. Some of those skills included condensing large amounts of information into concise and well-written reports, monitoring programs, managing projects, being flexible

(*Continued on page 99*)

The Millennium Challenge Corporation

The Millennium Challenge Corporation (MCC) is a newer player in US government development assistance and is a relatively small government agency. Congress created MCC in 2004 to be an independent foreign assistance agency that fuses aspects of private-sector management, such as governance by a board of directors, into a US government structure. MCC provides well-performing countries with large-scale grants to fund country-led solutions for reducing poverty through sustainable economic growth. MCC's grants complement other US and international development programs. Similar to the USAID workforce, MCC's workforce includes civil servants and personal

and adaptable, and responding to constant demands for information with very tight deadlines.

Following the earthquake, I had to adapt quickly to be effective in managing an extremely challenging and complex work environment. During the two months after the disaster, my role and responsibilities shifted as the needs in Haiti and within USAID changed. For a few weeks, I resumed my former role as an information officer providing real-time information on the post-earthquake situation to assist senior US government officials in determining appropriate disaster assistance resources. Later, I became a field officer, monitoring food and non-food disaster assistance and making recommendations about programs based on the needs on the ground. Using the skills and experience I had acquired, combined with my knowledge of Haitian Kreyol and the country, I organized teams of between three and five USAID staff to conduct humanitarian assessments in cities receiving and hosting displaced persons who fled earthquake-affected areas and that had received limited assistance at that point in the response. The information gathered by the teams during the assessments helped USAID make decisions about appropriate assistance needed in those areas.

When I started at USAID, I was not an expert on disaster relief, humanitarian assistance or international development. However, my bachelor's degree in political science with a concentration in international economic relations and my master's degree in international affairs gave me a solid foundation, helped me understand the complexities of international affairs, and encouraged me to think analytically and critically. Ten years later, I marvel at the variety of experiences that I have had in my career, places I have visited, and people I have met. The work is not always glamorous. Sometimes, it can be dangerous. And at times, it is bureaucratic. Nonetheless, a career with USAID and in international development is extremely rewarding because it is one of the few that allows you to see the world while helping to improve lives in the developing world.

services contractors. More information on these opportunities is available at www.mcc.gov.

Other Agencies

Many agencies with primarily domestic mandates have international programs to provide technical assistance overseas in their areas of expertise. The US Forest Service, the US Centers for Disease Control and Prevention, and the US Census Bureau are among numerous such agencies. These opportunities can be more challenging to identify because the international programs tend to be a small component of these agencies' larger domestic mandates. Applicants interested in such opportunities should spend time exploring individual agency websites as well as keeping appraised of opportunities through USAJOBS.

Challenges

Individuals who like to work independently and see immediate results may find government development work to be challenging. Long-term change requires collaboration and sustained effort. Change can be incremental, and thus almost unnoticeable day to day. The time required to see a program through from start to finish can be years or decades, and many professionals do not get to follow a program through its whole lifespan. Therefore, professionals need to be comfortable working on programs at various points in the program cycle, and they need to have an understanding of how their work contributes to long-term goals. Like the rest of the government, USAID is not immune to bureaucratic hassles and hurdles that can frustrate employees. Working within such a defined set of regulations, policies, and directives, with a wide range of partners and players, can be difficult for individuals who prefer more autonomy or flexibility.

Development work can be demanding. Extended travel, assignments to dangerous posts, long hours, and tight deadlines can take employees away from family and friends. USAID has made significant efforts to recognize the unusual stress its employees face and offers a comprehensive staff care program to support employees and their families in Washington and around the world. Development work can also be dangerous. Some of USAID's most critical work occurs in conflict and transitional contexts, or in locations where some people may seek to harm US citizens or interests. USAID's employees are educated about the risks of each location where they work and are trained in security awareness.

Rewards

The rewards of working in international development are meaningful and personal. For many, a genuine desire to serve others and contribute to real, tangible change in individual lives is one of the main attractions of development work. Development professionals know their efforts will help prevent children from dying, provide water or electricity or internet access to communities, allow girls to attend school, and give people the opportunity to have a say in their own futures.

Development professionals within the US government also find it rewarding to serve their country through government service. Development programs are an important component of US relations with many countries, and working on these programs is a significant way to advance the country's interests overseas. US government development professionals take seriously their stewardship of taxpayer dollars and their role in proudly representing the ideals of America abroad.

Of course, traveling the world and getting to interact with people from many cultures is a major reward of doing development work for the US government. Such development professionals have a curiosity and desire to learn and appreciate the customs and practices of other cultures. Development work occurs in some of the most far-flung and least-traveled places in the world, offering the opportunity to experience things few others ever do—and make a real and lasting impact. For many, serving the United States overseas doing development work is a dream job and a lifelong calling worth any headaches and road bumps that occur along the way.

Careers in Intelligence

David A. Gutschmit

David A. Gutschmit is an assistant adjunct professor teaching with the MSFS program at Georgetown University. He has thirty-two years of government experience in the foreign affairs and intelligence communities. He is currently assigned to the Office of the Director of National Intelligence. The views expressed in this essay are solely his and do not reflect the official views of the US government.

A Flawed Image

No profession has been more prone to stereotyping than that of the intelligence professional. Intelligence insiders remain wryly amused, if a bit perplexed, by the appeal and tenacity of the myths perpetuated by the fictional exploits of the likes of James Bond and Jason Bourne. Perhaps we even feel a touch of envy toward the superhuman physical prowess and maverick individualism of these characters as they slash and burn their way across the international landscape and through their own bureaucracies with equal talent and disdain. It is a compelling myth, harking back to the earliest epic tales of extraordinary individuals achieving the extraordinarily difficult against extraordinary odds. Even the more cerebral and much-acclaimed treatment of an actual, complex, and high-stakes operation of the US Central Intelligence Agency (CIA) in the movie *Argo* could not avoid the temptation of gratuitous and entirely fictional adrenalin-filled chase scenes. Perhaps these stereotypes perform a service in alerting interested potential applicants to the very existence of a career in intelligence. However, these dominant popular images of the intelligence professional do not do justice to the complexity or impact of the field. They certainly perpetuate a sense of exclusivity, perhaps discouraging the less supernaturally gifted from pursuing a career in the intelligence community (IC). This would be a pity. The most compelling realities of the intelligence profession are the breadth and criticality of the mission and vast diversity of talent needed by the IC to execute it.

With the killing of Osama bin Laden and the winding down of more than a decade of war in Afghanistan and Iraq, there is a natural inclination to perceive the world as a less dangerous place. Such a collective sigh of relief also followed the end of the Cold War. It was accompanied by a vigorous debate as to whether the United States still required an extensive foreign intelligence apparatus, among other instruments of national security. This was proven to be disastrously shortsighted by the terrorist attacks of September 11, 2001. One hopes that we will not go through a similar experience this time around. A robust intelligence apparatus is necessary not only to deal with existing challenges to US national security but also to anticipate future challenges. Even without Osama bin Laden, Iraq, and Afghanistan, the list of current challenges warranting major allocations of intelligence resources is daunting. These include the possible resurgence of al-Qaeda affiliates with capabilities to target US interests in Africa and the Middle East, the proliferation of nuclear weapons in Iran and North Korea, and the regional rivalry with China in Asia as US policymakers plan a renewed emphasis on the US role in the Pacific. And these are only the known challenges. The IC must remain sufficiently deep and agile to identify nascent threats before they break upon US national security.

Compelling Missions

The IC indeed occupies a unique role in the American government, with its mission spanning war and peace. Above all, the US IC exists to avoid strategic surprise at the hands of existential threats to the United States. Pearl Harbor and the unexpected onset of World War II in the Pacific is the most often-cited example of the consequences of failure to carry out this key mission. The 9/11 attacks, although arguably not strategic in scope and certainly not amounting to an existential threat, are often discussed in this vein as well. September 11 does constitute a shocking acknowledgment that future strategic surprises may not come from a finite list of state-based usual suspects. A virulent nonstate actor armed with weapons of mass destruction (WMD) might indeed rise to the level of strategic and existential. This realization forever widens the burden on the US IC on identifying both emerging terrorist threats and tracking the potential spread of WMD to nonstate actors.

The US IC also supports the United States' national security and foreign affairs policymaking apparatus. Specific priorities within this very broad mission are driven both by the deliberate agenda of the current administration and by the unanticipated challenges to which it may have to respond. In the current policy environment, efforts to stabilize the long-standing Israeli–Palestinian dispute represent a discretionary issue requiring intelligence support. The need to deal with the ongoing results of the Arab Spring uprisings and the agonizing, two-year-old civil war in Syria and continued instability in Egypt are examples of the latter requirement. The IC often underlines the need to be flexible enough to meet these unanticipated challenges as the requirement for global coverage.

Finally, the US IC provides an important pool of deep expertise across the full range of regional and functional challenges to US national security and foreign policy. This is a fascinating aspect of interacting with the US IC from the policymaking perspective. For example, the CIA's primary foreign collection arm, the National Clandestine Service (NCS), can bring to bear unique area knowledge and linguistic capability on short notice to meet a crisis at any corner of the globe. This is backed by the uncanny ability of the CIA's Directorate of Intelligence (DI) to produce on short notice one or more analysts with the deep academic background to put streetwise savvy of the NCS into full context for policymaking purposes. This combination has proven to be a powerful asset to policymakers, particularly in crisis situations. The complementary impact of this resource has grown in recent years as the NCS and DI have succeeded in breaking down the organizational and cultural barriers that historically inhibited this synergy. It is one of the most exciting aspects of working in today's CIA.

It is true that some of this long-term or deep expertise resides in other executive departments, such as State. However, two important distinctions validate the unique contribution of the IC in this regard. The first is the relatively shallow, politically driven turnover rate at the senior levels of the IC, with the vast majority of senior officials rising from within the ranks of the individual agencies themselves. This contrasts sharply with the prevalence of political appointees at the assistant secretary level and above at State and elsewhere. Although these individuals may possess considerable expertise, it may not be of a nature that complements the need to mobilize the expertise of the organization as a whole to support the policy process.

Second, non-IC elements of the executive are necessarily closely lashed up to the policy objectives of their principals. This speaks to the most important boundary between the US IC and the policy realm. The IC exists to inform the policymaking community, not to make policy. The long-term expertise of the US IC is most helpful to policymakers because it is insulated from the act of policymaking, and it is thus better positioned to fulfill its mandate to provide objective, fact-based intelligence. For the system to function correctly, both policymakers and intelligence professionals must remain constantly aware of this sometimes fine but always bright red line separating their two milieus.

A Constellation of Opportunities

In meeting its broad mandate of avoiding strategic surprise, supporting the policy process, and providing long-term expertise for the US government, the US IC as currently constituted consists of a constellation of seventeen agencies and organizations within the executive branch charged with carrying out various, and at times overlapping, aspects of this mandate:

- Office of the Director of National Intelligence (ODNI);
- CIA;
- Bureau of Intelligence and Research, Department of State (INR);
- Defense Intelligence Agency (DIA);
- National Security Agency (NSA);
- National Reconnaissance Office (NRO);
- National Geospatial-Intelligence Agency (NGA);
- Federal Bureau of Investigation (FBI);
- Army Intelligence;
- Navy Intelligence;
- Air force Intelligence;
- Marine Corps Intelligence;
- Department of Homeland Security (DHS);
- Treasury Department;
- Coast Guard;
- Energy Department; and
- Drug Enforcement Administration.

With the signing of the Intelligence Reform and Terrorism Prevention Act in December 2004, the director of national intelligence (DNI) emerged as the leader of the IC and the president's principal adviser on intelligence matters, functions previously held by the director of central intelligence. The ODNI drives collaboration and integration among the sixteen other elements of the community, in both a general and programmatic sense, as well as specifically in the areas of counterterrorism, counterintelligence, and counterproliferation. The ODNI directly oversees the operations of the National Counterterrorism Center; the National Counterintelligence Executive; and the National Counterproliferation Center, where personnel from throughout the community assess and analyze threats in these key arenas.

The CIA remains the IC's only independent intelligence agency combining both collection and analytical functions. The DI conducts all-source analysis on a global basis regarding geographic, transnational, and functional issues. The NCS has the mandate to collect intelligence from human sources overseas. It is the standard bearer within the IC of the human intelligence (HUMINT) discipline. Their primary mission is to recruit foreign nationals to serve as human sources, or assets, to provide the intelligence that is required by policymakers for national security and foreign policy purposes but that is unavailable to the government by more conventional means. Its cadre of core collectors serve abroad under a variety of covers, defining the role of field operatives in the American intelligence system. At the direction of the president, the CIA also undertakes covert action, attempting to influence political and military events overseas while concealing the hand of the US government. The CIA is the only element of the IC empowered to carry out this mission.

Three other national-level intelligence agencies remain subordinate to the Department of Defense. The NSA is the center of excellence for the key intelligence discipline of signals intelligence (SIGINT). NSA operates in a deeply classified milieu, with an extensive network of collection sites overseas supporting its massive headquarters at Fort Meade, Maryland. NGA has primary responsibility for the processing and dissemination of imagery (IMINT). NRO is in charge of the hardware side of the IMINT discipline, the development and operation of reconnaissance satellites. Also within DOD, DIA administers the defense attaché program at embassies overseas and provides all-source analysis on primarily military issues to the secretary of defense. The intelligence elements of the four military services focus primarily on the needs of their respective branches.

The Department of State's INR provides intelligence analysis to the secretary of state to support US diplomacy and ensures that intelligence activities are consistent with foreign policy goals. Within the US IC, therefore, the CIA's DI, DIA, and INR perform similar all-source intelligence analysis. In addition to ensuring that policymakers' needs across the executive branch are met, a somewhat competitive dynamic ensures that a spectrum of analytical viewpoints emerges on any one issue, mitigating against groupthink.

The agencies identified above constitute the foreign intelligence elements of the US IC. Although the framework for this apparatus changed with the establishment of ODNI in 2004, the roles and missions of the individual elements retain the same missions and focus. The most pronounced changes within the IC have occurred within the domestic arena, in response to the tremendous challenge to US national security represented by the 9/11 attacks and the rise of international terrorism.

The FBI has been responsible for domestic intelligence as well as law enforcement since its creation in 1908. Before 9/11, however, the bureau focused primarily on the counterintelligence aspects of this mission: thwarting the efforts of foreign intelligence services to operate against the United States. Since 9/11 the counterterrorism aspect of the FBI's intelligence mission has moved to the fore. The bureau hired hundreds of counterterrorism analysts and linguists, and shifted hundreds of personnel from criminal investigations to intelligence. It was reorganized at the headquarters level, merging its intelligence, counterintelligence, and counterterrorism divisions into the single

National Security Branch. At the field offices, field intelligence groups were established to better integrate the efforts of agents and analysts on the ground and with the intelligence function in Washington.

The Homeland Security Act of 2002 created DHS, a major new member of the IC. The Office of Intelligence Analysis at DHS employs more than five hundred personnel to coordinate intelligence from both DHS components and other elements of the community pertaining to threats to the United States. DHS also serves as an import conduit of relevant counterterrorism threat information from national-level agencies to state and local law enforcement entities.

A Diverse Team

Again, the stereotype of the secret agent plays to the lone operative in the field, and seldom dwells on the extensive team in the field and at headquarters required to support one operations officer abroad. In the NCS alone, the operations officer is backed by collection management officers, who process reporting and requirements; desk officers, who manage operations on the Washington end; specialists in logistics, security, communications, and finance; linguists; and scientists and engineers, who make the latest technology available to support collection. Yet another agency stereotype is the bookish analyst toiling alone in his cubicle late into the night. He or she is in fact backed by a team of information technologists, graphic designers, librarians, and cartographers at all points in the analytic and dissemination process. This teamwork and creativity are replicated across the INTs (HUMINT, etc.) and in all corners of the IC. Perhaps the most impressive aspect of the US IC is the breadth of talented individuals from all disciplines who have chosen to make intelligence their calling.

Obviously, this range of occupations comprises many different skill sets. Potential operations officers are evaluated for their ability to think on their feet and for their interpersonal skills. Analysts are recruited for their deep substantive expertise and their writing and briefing skills. However, intelligence professionals, no matter where they are located in the IC, share a common enthusiasm and commitment to their unique contribution to the maintenance of US national security in a complex, rapidly shifting, and at times dangerous international environment.

For potential applicants to any component of the IC, this commitment must begin before the application process. The processing is extensive and rigorous with respect to both the substance of a given position and the security-screening process that must go with the territory. Potential candidates are urged to begin the application process at least a year in advance of the possible starting date and to thoroughly understand the specific functional and security requirements of the agency to which they have applied. Nor does the emphasis on security end with an applicant's entrance of duty; a cost of employment with the IC is an explicit agreement to continuous and thorough vetting throughout one's career.

Another lingering myth of the intelligence profession is that recruitment takes place through an informal, opaque network only slightly less clandestine than the work itself. Fortunately for the IC, this is no longer the case, as the community could not find the quality or quantity of gifted candidates required through such an elitist approach. The agencies of the IC have a practical interest in attracting applicants who are as well informed as possible. There is much information out there. The first step in any decision to apply for an IC position should be a thorough review of the particular agency's website. More in-depth reading is readily available once a specific agency and career track have been identified.

As noted above, the potential applicant will find a surprising range of positions available. A look at the ODNI website captures the range of skills demanded by today's IC. Multiple agencies are looking for scientists; network operations specialists; computer, mechanical, and electronics engineers; forensic chemists; intelligence analysts; information technology specialists; and, of course, operations officers—among other occupations. In terms of skills, background, and talent, the US IC has never had the need for a more diverse workforce; nor has it ever had more to offer in terms of opportunity and challenge.

CHAPTER 4

International Organizations

The sheer breadth and depth of international organizations, coupled with their unique hiring practices, can be daunting to the job seeker. The United Nations alone has commissions, committees, funds, programs, and specialized agencies, each with its own focus, and all of which offer interesting and challenging work for professionals trained in international affairs. Whether you are a US or foreign national looking for fieldwork overseas, a headquarters position in a major international city, or a development position focusing on a specific region, you are likely to find an international organization that appeals to you. This chapter breaks the sector into three parts: the United Nations, international organizations outside the UN, and the international financial institutions. The essays do not intend to provide a comprehensive picture of all organizations, but instead give the reader a glimpse into the UN, NATO, and the World Bank, and encourage readers to think outside the box when it comes to international organizations. When researching job opportunities, applicants should pay close attention to nationality requirements. For instance, the exam for the UN Young Professionals Program is only open to nationals of participating countries, which may vary from year to year. Applicants should also pay attention to job locations, because positions may be offered in headquarters as well as field offices.

Careers in the United Nations

Izumi Nakamitsu

Izumi Nakamitsu is the director of the Asia and Middle East Division of the United Nations Department of Peacekeeping (DPKO). From 2008 to 2012 she was the director of DPKO's Division of Policy, Evaluation, and Training. From 2005 to 2008 she was professor of international relations at Hitotsubashi University, Tokyo, a member of the advisory panel to the Japanese foreign minister, and a visiting senior adviser on peace building at the Japan International Cooperation Agency. Before her return to Japan, she held a number of positions in the UN system, including head of the Office of the UN High Commissioner for Refugees in Sarajevo and in Mostar; senior humanitarian affairs officer to the special

representative of the secretary-general to the former Yugoslavia; special assistant to
the assistant high commissioner for refugees for policy and operations (Sergio Vieira
de Mello); and first officer of the UN Reform Team in the Executive Office of the
Secretary-General, Kofi Annan. She was chef de cabinet and director of planning
and coordination at the Stockholm-based intergovernmental organization the
International Institute for Democracy and Electoral Assistance (International
IDEA) between 1998 and 2004. She received a master's of science in foreign
service (MSFS) from Georgetown University and an LLB from Waseda University
in Tokyo.

The UN in Today's World

Imagine meeting an old lady in Bosnia, whose grandfathers, father, sons, and grandsons all had to fight a war—World War I, World War II, and the recent civil war in the 1990s. This old lady, living in a collective center after having been displaced from her home village, tells you that maybe there is hope for the future after all if something called the "United Nations" brings from afar young people like yourself to help the people of Bosnia. It is such a powerful experience in your early professional life to live through the real meaning of the famous first sentence of the preamble of the UN Charter, "We the peoples of the United Nations, determined to save succeeding generations from the scourge of war, which twice in our lifetime has brought untold sorrow to mankind." The UN can offer such a life-changing experience that it makes you want to fully commit to making the world a better place.

You would of course be disappointed and frustrated if you came to work for the UN only with your idealism. It is an organization that was established more than sixty years ago, and one that is struggling to adjust itself to, or find its place in, the dramatically different world today, characterized by a shifting global power balance, evolving definitions of state sovereignty and aspirations of peoples, and daunting operational needs but antiquated administrative rules and regulations. It is, however, also true that the world without the UN's multilateralism would be unthinkable today, and that the UN will play a role in most of the hardest challenges of our time, from finding ways to stop the bloodshed in Syria to helping to build peace in the newest nation of South Sudan, from taking humanitarian actions on behalf of victims of conflict and natural disasters to attempting to stop climate change on this planet. And it is true that the international community is slowly but surely making progress in some areas. It is virtually impossible today for any state to oppose the need to protect innocent civilians, and indeed many UN peacekeeping operations do protect civilians around the world, albeit with challenges. The International Criminal Court exists today as an independent international organization and has begun to enforce international humanitarian law, a development unimaginable only twenty years ago. Dag Hammarskjöld's famous quotation reminds us of a realistic role for the UN: "The UN was not created to take mankind to heaven, but to save humanity from hell."

For you to be a successful and happy professional in the UN system, you will need to have a strong passion for, and commitment to, the ideals and spirit enshrined in the UN Charter as well as the ability to think realistically and strategically to work toward the UN's goals. You will need to be a skilled communicator and negotiator, a brilliant political thinker and analyst, a competent problem solver, a dynamic and creative agent of change in a big bureaucracy, and, most important, a courageous human being with integrity who will stand up for the principles of peace, humanity, and justice.

The UN has many faces today. It is of course an important multilateral forum for 193 member states to gather, negotiate, and decide on various international affairs; set norms in international laws and human rights practices; and formulate policies on sustainable development, humanitarian actions, and environmental protection. The UN Security Council meets almost every day to discuss and decide on how to manage and resolve conflicts around the world. The UN Secretariat not only supports the work of member states in these processes but also runs field operations around the world, as well as various UN agencies, funds, and programs that have their field activities on the ground. It is worth noting that the UN Secretariat (and UN agencies, funds, and programs, for that matter) has much greater executive authority and responsibility to plan and implement operations, compared with other regional multilateral organizations. In the case of peace operations, once the Security Council decides on a mandate, it is the responsibility of the secretary-general and the Secretariat staff to develop strategies to address complex challenges and to plan and run the particular operation. This large degree of executive authority is what makes a UN career interesting and rewarding.

A Career Path in the UN

If you are interested in one of the core business areas of the UN, you are strongly encouraged to start your career in the field. In fact, more than 60 percent of UN staff work in various field duty stations around the world. A field assignment will enable you to have a first-hand experience and understanding of the real kinds of challenges the UN is trying to address in political mediation, peacekeeping and peace building, human rights, humanitarian affairs, and poverty eradication. What does it really mean for the UN to help reform and build the capacity of the military force and police of the Democratic Republic of the Congo to protect civilians? How should you negotiate access to remote villages in conflict-ridden Darfur? How do you persuade an authoritarian government fighting against rebel groups to respect human rights? What might be a coherent strategy and effective programs that will start to deliver a peace dividend soon after a peace agreement? In a peacekeeping operation, you will be confronted with these tough questions every day, negotiating with various parties on the ground, reporting back on progress, or managing activities on behalf of the UN. Without solid field experience, it will be difficult to establish later in your career a strong understanding of what is required in operational management and policy development, and therefore your professional development opportunities might become limited.

Ideally, you would want to move between the field and headquarters, as you progressively move up to more senior and managerial positions. Unlike other UN operational agencies, funds, and programs, the UN Secretariat currently does not have a staff mobility policy to move its staff members between different duty stations in a managed manner. It is hoped that there will soon be such a policy; but in the meantime, you will need to manage your mobility and career development by yourself. It is therefore very important for you to build and maintain professional networks within the organization, to know the right people, and to be known by the right people, in order to seek their advice and support.

The need to be mobile in career development will have implications for your personal life. You will be spending many years of your life in different countries away from home, often in difficult conditions. You will need to be the kind of person who finds this an exciting opportunity rather than a painful duty, and you will probably want to have a spouse with a similar attitude. It is a priority goal of the UN to increase the number of competent women in leadership positions, and therefore the organization is addressing the issue of work/life balance. Qualified women with a strong sense of determination are encouraged to pursue careers in the UN.

As the last section of this essay summarizes, there are many different job areas in the UN. It is important for you to decide earlier in your career if you want to be an expert in a particular area (e.g., an expert on justice reform, child protection, gender, or logistics) or if you want to pursue a more generalist profile to eventually become a senior manager in the organization. If it is the latter, it is important to develop versatile skills and a multifaceted knowledge of the UN's work. The organization is increasingly encouraging its staff to move across the departmental and organizational boundaries in their career development, so that they are able to acquire a more comprehensive perspective on the UN and thereby prevent various UN entities from operating as silos.

Skills and Personality Types

The required skill sets and competencies at the UN are not so dramatically different from those required in other public service organizations. Excellent analytical skills, strong communication and writing skills, the ability to find solutions to complex problems, and the ability to work well in a team are commonly sought after by hiring managers at the UN. One thing uniquely important for a UN career is an ability to work effectively in a multicultural environment. This requires a fundamental respect for diversity; a solid understanding of various cultural backgrounds; an excellent command of at least one working language of the UN (i.e., English or French), including sensitive usage of nuances; the right attitude; and patience.

It is also critical to have a strong ability to establish relationships and partnerships with people from other organizations. The UN today rarely operates in isolation from other international or regional organizations, relevant bilateral governments, or nongovernmental organizations. You will need to be able to understand the respective mandates, roles, and responsibilities of UN and non-UN organizations alike, and to establish effective partnerships with them. Needless to say, cultural sensitivity and an ability to establish strong relationships with local authorities, communities, and people is a precondition for successful work in the field.

As a young professional, you would normally be noticed and recognized in the organization through the high-quality analytical reports you have written, in addition to your hard work. Senior people will expect young officers to be able to think outside the box, be creative and innovative, and bring new perspectives into the organization. You would want to build up knowledge and expertise in your substantive area as well as to accumulate practical experiences to sharpen your judgment. As you move up, necessary skills will gradually shift more toward improving documents drafted by others, a strong verbal communication and presentation capacity, team- and consensus-building skills, and sound judgment and decision making, as well as an ability to manage performance and to inspire others to be creative and achieve a common vision.

Many UN jobs are demanding and stressful. In peacekeeping missions you often live and work in a remote field location where conditions are difficult. In the UN you might sometimes become frustrated at, or disillusioned by, the gap between what you would like to achieve and what you can actually do. It is very important that you have a strong will and dedication, and the ability to remain positive, motivated, and optimistic in difficult situations.

How to Apply for Jobs at the UN

There are currently eight substantive areas or "job networks" for UN careers:

1. political, peace. and security;
2. economic and social development;
3. management and operational support;
4. information systems and communication technology;

Notes from the Field

The UN Office on Drugs and Crime
Cheikh Ousmane Touré, MSFS 2004

Before I became a student of International Affairs at Georgetown University, my dream was to work at the roots of development and conflict issues, especially in Africa. Our class would discuss and debate theories and possible solutions to what was happening in the news on TV in Africa, the Middle East, and other conflict areas. Today, I am part of those solutions in the real world.

Starting out after graduating can be a scary and daunting process. You never know where you will end up. After graduating from MSFS in 2004, I landed my first job with the help of the Georgetown careers adviser, who put me onto an advertisement for employment with the International Foundation for Electoral Systems in Washington. I focused on democratic processes and anti-corruption issues in West Africa, especially in Nigeria and Liberia. This initial exposure to the field gave me the confidence and motivation to continue in the same vein and led me to jobs with the United Nations Development Program Chad, UN Office for the Coordination of Humanitarian Affairs Chad, the UN Office of Drugs and Crime (UNODC) South Sudan, and UNODC Democratic Republic of Congo.

My current post is as project coordinator at the UNODC in Jerusalem. As a project coordinator, I am responsible for the implementation of projects
(Continued on page 115)

5. legal;
6. public information and external relations;
7. conference management; and
8. safety and security.

Each network is divided further into several "job families." In the case of the political, peace, and security network, for example, there are six job families:

a. political affairs,
b. humanitarian affairs,
c. human rights,
d. civil affairs,
e. electoral affairs, and
f. the rule of law.

Each job network is a flexible grouping of job types and positions from departments and offices. You should determine your interest in one or more

in UNODC areas of work. In addition to ensuring project delivery, I monitor events in UNODC mandates (criminal justice, corruption, trafficking, etc.) in the region or country I am assigned to and prepare reports about developments relevant to our work. I also manage resource mobilization for future projects. The project I am implementing in Jerusalem aims at strengthening the management of the Palestinian Penitentiary System and to establish mechanisms for the effective rehabilitation of inmates in centres administered by the Palestinian National Authority, and this is a challenge that I look forward to.

I was not an expert in justice reform, corruption, or corrections or many of the things that I have worked on; however, your International Affairs degree will provide you with a solid grounding, the creativity, and the basic tools to pave your own way in the world. I believe that I have chosen a career that allows me to feel directly connected to international development in the field working with development, rule of law and governance issues around the globe. Although, it takes hard work and effort to find a rewarding job with an international organization, for those who want to work in the field you should first define what you want to achieve. It is at least a starting point, which will change and grow over the years.

In order for the field experience to be rewarding, people need to be ready to discover new sides of themselves and enjoy the ride with the aspiration that their contributions, as small they may seem, can make a difference in people's lives. The experience that you gain in the field shapes your life professionally, socially, and culturally. My wife and I met in Sudan and we now both live in Jerusalem with our two daughters. You never know where the adventure will take you until you jump right in it.

job networks and families based on your areas of interest and expertise, and apply for positions in those categories.

The UN recruitment system is complex, and there are several different ways to obtain positions at the UN. The Young Professionals Program and Associate Expert Program are most commonly used for entry-level positions, but only candidates from certain countries are eligible for these mechanisms. Internship opportunities will help you build professional networks at the UN, which might lead to finding a temporary position at the headquarters or in the field. The internship announcement and application process are decentralized. To apply to a UN high commissioner for refugees office in the field, for example, you must contact and apply to that field office directly.

Young people often start building their professional experience with nongovernmental organizations in the field, become known by their counterparts within the UN, and get recruited into UN positions. Many people enter the UN at mid-level to senior-level positions, having achieved professional success in their countries' diplomatic or other public service or private-sector or nonprofit organizations. For positions in UN agencies, funds, and programs, you will need to check the job announcements of the respective organization.

Practical information on job networks and different ways of entering the UN Secretariat can be found on the UN Careers website (https://careers .un.org/lbw/home.aspx).

A career in the UN can be incredibly rewarding, but it can also be challenging. Any organization is only as strong as the people who work for it. If you believe in the ideals of the UN, want to work in an organization that makes a difference around the world every day, and are prepared to face the challenges of working on complex problems, then you should consider a career in the UN.

Careers in International Organizations outside the UN

Ernest J. Herold

Ernest J. "E. J." Herold is a 1992 graduate of Georgetown's MSFS program. A West Point graduate with more than twenty-seven years of military service, he spent several years working for IBM before joining the North Atlantic Treaty Organization (NATO) in his current role as deputy assistant secretary general for NATO's Defense Investment Division. A French and German speaker, he has fifteen years experience in Europe as well as operational experience in the Caribbean, Middle East, and North Africa.

Working at NATO: Adventures in Diplomacy

The intrepid student of international affairs can find an excellent environment for plying their trade with NATO (www.nato.int), an organization of twenty-eight democratic nations whose shared values bind them together in a political-military alliance based on the fundamental premise that an attack on one is an attack on all. The unique co-location of all twenty-eight national missions at the Brussels headquarters immerses everyone in a multiethnic, multicultural, multilingual ambiance in which the frequent contact between nations leads to a fascinating opportunity to put all the lessons learned in academia to the test. In fact, it is frequently joked (but not without reason) that more gets done in the NATO coffee shop, thanks to the ease with which people meet there, than in most of the formal meetings conducted at headquarters.

My Story

My own interest in NATO began near the end of the Cold War, when I was a cadet at the US Military Academy at West Point, New York, studying the world I was preparing to enter as a leader of American soldiers. NATO loomed large in that universe for its place in maintaining peace and stability as well as for the synergy of its collective defense mantle. I first thought about NATO in my undergraduate courses at West Point. We were still in the Cold War, and NATO was the crown jewel of the collective Western response to external threats for an idealistic aspiring US Army officer. After graduation I went through a decade of junior assignments that included working as part of NATO forces in Germany before attending the MSFS program at Georgetown, where my intellectual horizons were expanded as I prepared to be an army foreign area officer for Western Europe.[1] An assignment to the French Staff College in Paris, followed by one year as aide-de-camp to the US military representative at NATO, only made me more eager to return to NATO work. However, the requirements of the army and career imperatives meant that I did not return to NATO in uniform. I finished my military career as chief of the Office of Defense Cooperation at the American Embassy in Paris, which opened the door to an opportunity in industry as the account manager at NATO. Despite the fabulous opportunity they gave me, I found myself on the outside looking in and longing to be a part of the NATO family when my current position came open, and I realized that the broad experience I had accumulated made me an attractive candidate for the job. Thanks to the support of the US Mission to NATO, I was competitive for the job and was lucky enough to be selected from among well-qualified, international competitors for it. Fast-forward thirty years, and I have had the pleasure of serving in NATO units and the headquarters as well as watching in admiration as the Alliance struggles with a post–Cold War identity crisis. From its initial incarnation as a Cold War defensive alliance, today NATO is emerging transformed as an Alliance prepared to face the threats of the twenty-first century, while remaining relevant in a global environment of increasing challenges.

About NATO

Like other international organizations, NATO is not a single monolithic organization in one location but forms a collection of headquarters, commands, agencies, and offices located in multiple nations on three continents, offering a wide variety of opportunities and experiences throughout an individual's working life. I have had the privilege of serving twice at NATO headquarters, once in uniform and now as a diplomat, and it is a vastly enriching experience in both roles. While in uniform, my duties revolved around the Military Committee, NATO's senior representation of the chiefs of national defense from its member nations who are charged with providing military advice to inform Alliance actions. For a young army officer this was a heady exposure to grand strategy and considerations of military efficiency in tension with diplomatic trade-offs. It was my first exposure to practicing what was preached on the Hilltop at Georgetown. My duties today on the International Staff, NATO's policy arm, place me fully in the frustrating and satisfying world of diplomacy—a world in which the lessons of the MSFS program are daily reinforced and where negotiating to find a win–win result without watering down the impact is raised to an art form. Both roles are eminently satisfying for the simple reason that you cannot escape the feeling that your work is part of making the world a safer, better place.

NATO is not the only international organization aspiring international affairs specialists should consider, though my preference may surely be understood. Commercially minded aspirants can consider global and international corporations as one route to finding rewarding work with the potential for travel and life in different places around the globe. My own time in a globally integrated enterprise before joining NATO offered incredible opportunity for rich experiences as a problem solver on several continents. Other international organizations offer opportunities to work on policy issues affecting the lives of all of us in one way or another; from peace and security and disarmament issues, to economic prosperity and settling grievances, organizations like these offer opportunities for rewarding work in exotic locales suited to almost any interest. A short list of them includes the United Nations (with UN headquarters in New York City), the Organization for Economic Cooperation and Development (Paris), the Organization for Security Cooperation in Europe (Geneva), the Organization for the Prohibition of Chemical Weapons (The Hague), the European Union (Brussels), the International Organization for Migration (Geneva), and the Association of Southeast Asian Nations (Jakarta), to name a few. Each of these organizations has some restrictions on hiring that may include a requirement to possess a passport from one of the member nations. As each is focused on different roles and functions and each has its own culture and hiring procedures, I will leave it to the reader to investigate them separately. However, no matter the organization, internships within the headquarters or satellite offices provide an excellent way to get a foot in the door for future employment consideration. Attention should be paid to the hiring criteria (even for internships), which often include language capabilities.

Career Paths in NATO

So where do you sign up to work for NATO? The answer is direct but not simple. First, a candidate for NATO employment should realize that there is no "typical" career path in NATO. In fact, that is what characterizes the experience as unique and ensures that the organization attracts and embraces new talent on a regular basis. The only prerequisite for working in NATO, or any of its agencies or commands, is that the applicant must be a citizen of a member nation of the Alliance.[2] Also, successful candidates are fluent in one of the two official languages of NATO (English and French), and most posts either require or favor ability in the second language, as well.

Broadly speaking, there are three tracks at NATO. Clearly there is the opportunity to serve as a military representative (implying that you are an active or reserve member of the armed forces of one of the member nations) in one of the NATO Commands, the International Military Staff, or as a military member of your national mission to NATO. Second, in a civil capacity you can be employed in your nation's mission to NATO or be temporarily reassigned from the national administration of a member nation (typically foreign affairs, but many other agencies, ministries, and departments are also represented in NATO) to hold a position on the International Staff. Finally, you can be employed as a freelance applicant directly from private life (whether self-employed or working in industry) in a NATO position if you have the required relevant skills and abilities. There is a fourth category, known as a voluntary national contribution, but these positions tend not to be advertised openly and are filled on an ad hoc basis based on the need for particular expertise and usually from the ranks of temporarily reassigned government officials. The environment is interestingly mixed, in that there is a large number of military posts but also several hundred civilian posts. The International Staff is predominantly civilian and comprises roughly 1,200 posts, from administrative through executive roles. Additionally, at the other locations of the Alliance (agencies, military schools, headquarters) there are opportunities to serve in a variety of positions. I offer further details on where to find information on them below. Although military service is not a requirement of employment (note that you are asked if you have completed your mandatory national military service, if any, on the application form), NATO is first and foremost a military alliance following issues related to that competency.

For first-time job seekers or those changing career fields, NATO can seem a daunting entry-level environment. The majority of jobs in NATO require a degree of experience, knowledge, expertise, and responsibility that exceeds the level most first-time applicants can claim. However, a number of internship programs, both directly through NATO and indirectly through national missions, offer experience inside the organization and its subordinate structures, which interested applicants may find helpful on several levels.[3] In addition to the experience gained from the internship, you will gain exposure to opportunities in other organizations and other fields of which you may not have even been aware. Certainly, for those who have the right passports, presence in Brussels and experience in NATO may offer a crossover opportunity to work in the European Union and its structures, for example. There are numerous paid and unpaid internship opportunities through national missions, the NATO international and international military staffs, and NATO agencies, commands, and educational institutions. The best way to find internships and open positions is through the NATO recruitment website, where most opportunities are listed (www.nato.int /wcm-asp/recruit-wide.asp).

Alternatively, all NATO opportunities are notified to each member nation and advertised nationally through government employment websites. (In the United States this is through the USAJOBS website, www.usajobs.gov). In addition, it is entirely appropriate to request information interviews with national missions, and the International Staff/International Military Staff, in order to better understand the environment and the opportunities that are or may become available. Employment at NATO is a process that can take time but is ultimately very worthwhile.

Practical Issues

Pay and benefits at NATO are based on the geographic location of the assignment as well as the pay grade of the position and are calculated to ensure a reasonable living wage for the location. Typical contracts are fixed duration (e.g., three years) and, depending on the grade, are renewable for a one- to three-year duration. A small percentage of the workforce can aspire to a permanent contract, but these are offered sparingly based on stringent criteria. The current thinking is that NATO benefits from an infusion of new ideas and experience by renewing the workforce.

Although military posts are often allocated to a particular nation or are rotated among several nations by agreement, civilian posts are more competitive, with the best-qualified candidates being selected for open posts without reference to nationality under current practice. This means that competitive candidates should seriously consider applying for any open vacancy that interests them. National missions are only too happy to support their citizen-candidates' aspirations with information, documentation, and other assistance to help them compete effectively for open posts, so be sure to contact your national mission if there is a position that interests you.

A note on work/life balance: The workday is standard in principle and long in practice. My experience is that mid-grade and senior folks are often present after hours. That said, there is a generous leave/vacation plan, and employees are encouraged to take the time off or lose it without compensation. This leads to a comfortable work rhythm, in which the employees are relatively satisfied and productive.

A Day in the Life

What is a day in the life of a NATO deputy assistant secretary-general? With the caveat that much depends on what is happening in the world, the work rhythm at NATO is conditioned by the schedule of high-level meetings planned for the Alliance. There are meetings of the defense and foreign ministers on a regular basis every few months (sometimes combined in so-called Jumbo ministerials), corresponding meetings of the Military Committee in Chiefs of Defense Session, and NATO Summits organized about every eighteen to twenty-four months (though these are also dependent on world events). The leaders of the Alliance set goals for our work at each of these meetings, and the intervening time is spent in staff and committee work to develop proposals, gain their acceptance, and negotiate their final form for adoption at the next meeting. To accomplish the work requires many meetings (both informal and formal) to discuss options and approaches and negotiate compromise. Although much of it occurs in committee rooms parsing proposals, a good deal of it takes place in smaller groups and one-to-one sessions with counterparts in the national missions, who spend almost as much time negotiating with the officials in their capitals as they do with their colleagues at NATO. My day can include acting as chairman of a committee, meeting with national representatives, holding discussions with industry, or giving a speech to visiting scholars. The beauty of the job is the variety of people I meet and the ideas we confront in a spirit of mutual respect. The specific role of our staff division, Defense Investment, is to follow issues related to the development and delivery of the capabilities NATO has identified as necessary to achieve its ambitions under the Strategic Concept. That is a mouthful to say, but we enable the successful delivery of programs managed elsewhere by creating the framework within which such programs are delivered. Examples are the current efforts to create a joint intelligence, surveillance, and reconnaissance capability to improve commanders' situational awareness or the ballistic missile defense capability to protect the Alliance's populations, territory, and forces from attack.

A complementary question from the reader might be: What can applicants expect to do as a staff officer? In short, they can expect to *write*. NATO runs on the written word and coffee (not necessarily in that order). Typical staff officers attend meetings, discuss issues, and negotiate compromise on varying levels. But in an environment where English and French are the official (but not necessarily native) languages, a premium is put on written communication. The more successful staff are strong writers, and the most successful ones can do it well in both official languages. You can find yourself writing speeches, press releases, political guidance, military assessments, white papers, and a whole host of other products for senior officials as well as personal use in daily interactions. The beauty of the work is in its variety.

The old quotation is that "the pen is mightier than the sword," and though keyboards may have replaced pens, it holds true that powerful words help demonstrate collective resolve at NATO and that good writers are well regarded. The other skill requirements are rather broad, but suffice it to

Notes from the Field

The International Organization for Migration

Shilpa Nadhan, MSFS 2011

At the beginning of 2009, I packed up all of my belongings, stuffed them into my car, and began a cross-country road trip from Los Angeles to the East Coast. I had been working in film for a couple years and had decided abruptly that I no longer wanted to dedicate myself to making next summer's popcorn flick. I needed something more to sustain me professionally, and without really knowing what foreign service or international affairs really encapsulated, other than what far-flung war correspondents reported on the news, I had decided that this was where my path would lead me.

That fall, I joined MSFS and at first was intimidated by what my classmates had to offer. Some of them worked for their governments back home, others were former military personnel or CIA analysts, and many of them had spent years in remote areas of the world. I thought I was in over my head and that survival in the program and in this line of work would be a struggle. However, I quickly learned that we were all there to learn, we were all there to listen, and we were all there to share our experience, no matter how disparate they seemed. The summer between my first and second year of graduate school, I connected with an MSFS alum working for the US Institute of Peace in Afghanistan and asked if I could come out there for a couple months to research women's access to justice. That internship gave shape to what I was learning in the classroom and demonstrated how policy and implementation do not always overlap, especially in the middle of a conflict.

That summer in Afghanistan led me to take on a full-time position after graduation as a Program Specialist at the International Organization for Migration, working on emergency and post-conflict assistance. When I was first thinking about my postgraduation plans, I always assumed I would be working for a local nongovernmental organization or for a small development consultancy, alongside beneficiaries, and as far away from Washington as possible. But, working at an international organization in Washington has taught me so much about the complexities and sheer enormity of responding to a humanitarian crisis. Just like at the beginning of grad school, I did not know what program development during an emergency actually involved. I certainly was no expert after one summer in Afghanistan, but like school, you soak it in as fast as you can and learn from your peers.

say that applicants skilled in international affairs, negotiations, language, history, culture, economics, and military affairs can likely find a matching job opportunity in the NATO orbit.

To close, I consider NATO an extremely satisfying work environment, and I would be happy to welcome you to join our team.

Careers in International Financial Institutions

Alexandra Pugachevsky

Alexandra Pugachevsky is the senior country officer for the West Bank and Gaza Country Unit at the World Bank, where she focuses on strategy development and portfolio management. Before her current assignment, she was senior mining and energy specialist in the Oil, Gas, and Mining Department of the World Bank, providing technical assistance to governments in mining- and oil-sector reform. Her work included supporting implementation of the Extractive Industries Transparency Initiative in the Central Asian countries and Yemen. During her more than ten years at the World Bank, she was fortunate to work in a number of countries, including Tajikistan, the Kyrgyz Republic, Yemen, Ethiopia, Cameroon, Nigeria, Mauritania, and Madagascar. She is a graduate of the University of Pennsylvania and received an MSFS from Georgetown University.

The World Bank is recognized as one of the leading global players in reducing poverty while promoting sustainable development. The Bank's ability to communicate directly with government authorities and decision makers helps to ensure that the policies and technical assistance provided are adopted by its clients. The Bank works in its member countries across a variety of sectors, including transportation, education, health, energy, urban development, disaster risk management, and water and sanitation. Most of the assistance is provided in the form of credits issued on varying terms, and the terms of the credits depend on the country's income and needs. Trust funds play an increasingly important role at the Bank. Some trust funds are focused on just one country or on a region or subregion. A number of trust funds are thematic. Trust fund assistance to countries is provided in the form of grants. In addition to the World Bank, the World Bank Group also includes the International Finance Corporation, which supports private-sector development; the Multilateral Investment Guarantee Agency (MIGA), which provides guarantees to promote investment; the International Bank for Reconstruction and Development, which lends to the governments of middle-income and creditworthy low-income countries; the International Development Association, which provides interest-free loans—called credits—and grants to governments of the poorest countries; and the International Centre for Settlement of Investment Disputes, which provides international facilities for conciliation and arbitration of investment disputes.

The World Bank's vast portfolio can be quite confusing, and learning how the organization functions takes time. There are country units, sector units, central units, and support units. Just to name a few: Some handle transportation issues on a policy level; some focus on transportation in East Africa. Some handle renewable energy subsidies; some handle renewable energy funds in East Asia. Dedicated staff members focus on working with donor governments, and you can find a policy specialist on just about anything, from fisheries to telecommunications to gold mining. On the most basic level, the World Bank is divided into six regions—Africa (AFR), Europe and Central Asia (ECA), Middle East and North Africa (MNA), East Asia and the Pacific (EAP), Southeast Asia (SEA), and Latin America and the Caribbean (LAC). In turn, each region is divided into country management units (CMUs) that focus on strategies for each particular subset of countries. For example, the Central Asia CMU works on Kazakhstan, the Kyrgyz Republic, Uzbekistan, Turkmenistan, and Tajikistan in the ECA region, whereas the Maghreb CMU works on Morocco, Tunisia, Libya, and Algeria in the MNA region. The regions house a number of sector units that focus on country economics, private-sector development, education, health, and transportation and energy, among others. The MNA water team will work on water-sector issues across all the various countries in that region, whereas the AFR water team will work on various water projects in that region. The CMUs are headed by country directors, who are based for the most part in the field. The country directors, in coordination with the sector units, decide what projects will be implemented in their countries each year. As this book goes to press, the World Bank's organizational structure is going through a reorganization, and the new system will be put in place in July 2014. The new structure will include fourteen global practices.

The World Bank Group is overseen by a Board of Directors that represents its member states. The World Bank Group has 188 member countries, represented by 22 executive directors. Voting is based on a weighted system.

World Bank staff are known for their diversity—the more than 10,000 staff members currently employed by the World Bank come from more than 170 countries. Additionally, the Bank's staff is supported by a large number of short-term consultants (at least 5,000). About 40 percent are based in field offices in more than 110 countries worldwide. The number of country-office-based staff has been on the rise, reflecting the push to be closer to the clients. Typically, staff members come from very strong academic and professional backgrounds. Most already have extensive international experience, including working in developing countries. Some professionals are recruited based on need, given that experience with a particular sector may be required at a particular time.

Joining the World Bank

Joining the World Bank as a staff member is a very competitive process. It helps to be in Washington when first looking for a job within the organization because most staff are based in Washington (and being in the city offers one the opportunity to learn about the organization and its mandate).

The Junior Professional Associates (JPA) program is a good option open to candidates with bachelor's degrees (or higher) under the age of twenty-eight. The program is open to all nationalities. The JPA program is highly competitive and is demand driven—departments select from a pool of available candidates based on required skills. Ideally, after applying through the general system, potential candidates will approach units directly to inquire about potential opportunities (it is here that networking can play a major role in the job search). The JPA program has been designed as an entry-level job to acquaint candidates with the development world, and it often also includes research, operational support, and administrative work. Candidates are initially given a two-year contract.

It is possible to join the World Bank in a variety of other capacities, such as operational officers, technical staff, or economists. The Young Professionals Program is another very popular program. The program is extremely competitive, accepting fewer than 1 percent of applicants, and is open to highly qualified individuals under thirty-two years of age. The program requires high academic and professional credentials—either a master's degree with five years of professional experience or a PhD with at least three years of professional experience. Direct development experience is encouraged, and the Bank looks for evidence of leadership potential. Fluency in English and at least one or two other languages is also welcome. The rigorous selection process requires several screenings and in-person interviews. Once accepted, applicants are supported during their career path to develop operational and managerial experience.

Language skills are a must—in additional to excellent English skills (both spoken and writing), fluency in one or more of the official UN languages is expected—Arabic, Chinese, French, Spanish, or Russian.

There are also a number of donor-funded staffing programs that are currently open to the nationals of Austria, Denmark, Finland, France, Germany, Italy, Japan, South Korea, Kuwait, Norway, Saudi Arabia, Spain, Sweden, and Switzerland, but these change each year depending on the particular country's need and available funding.

Some find it easier to familiarize themselves with the World Bank through a variety of short-term consultant assignments that offer greater flexibility, but these have a number of limitations. Short-term consultant contracts are limited to just 150 days per year and do not allow accrual of pension or vacation time. Consultants are rarely offered office space, but most of the time they have access to the World Bank system. Often graduates find these options attractive as they offer good exposure to World Bank projects and networking opportunities with completive compensation. Short-term consultant work varies broadly, and it is not only limited to support general staff members in their daily functions.

Working as an intern at the World Bank may also be a professionally rewarding opportunity and valuable from a networking perspective. The Bank internship offers highly motivated and successful individuals an opportunity to improve their skills while working in a diverse environment. To be eligible for the internship, candidates must possess an undergraduate degree and already be enrolled in a full-time graduate study program (pursuing a master's degree or PhD, with plans to return to school in a full-time capacity). Generally, successful candidates have completed their first year of graduate studies or are already into their PhD programs. All internships include a rewarding payment package, and at their expiry often translate into formal job offers.

I was fortunate to get two internships at the World Bank while pursuing the MSFS degree, in the ECA Region and MIGA. The two internships exposed me to various sectors of the Bank. In fact, one of the managers who supervised my work during the second internship recommended me a year later for a staff position—operations analyst in the Mining Department. That was a year after graduating from the MSFS program, and I have been at the Bank ever since.

The Nature of the Job

World Bank staff members are rarely bored; their jobs cover such a variety of subject matters—such as public expenditures review in Tunisia, investment climate assessment in Nigeria, and oil and gas law in Algeria—that it is very rare for employees to complain of lacking new challenges. There are many opportunities for traveling outside Washington.

Since I joined the World Bank more than ten years ago, I have worked on projects in a variety of countries and sectors. For example, I worked on the Extractive Industries Transparency Initiative operations, which focused on oil, gas, and mining revenue disclosure in Yemen, Kazakhstan, the Kyrgyz Republic, and Tajikistan. I also participated in mining- and oil-sector reform operations in Nigeria, Madagascar, Mauritania, Cameroon, Mozambique, and Ethiopia, as well as country assistance strategies in Mauritania and the West Bank and Gaza, and country portfolio performance reviews in the West Bank and Gaza. One of the most unique experiences I have had since

Notes from the Field

The International Finance Corporation

Thomas Pellerin, MSFS 2003

In 2008, five years after graduating from the MSFS, I joined the Paris office of the International Finance Corporation (IFC), the private-sector arm of the World Bank Group, as an investment officer. With about eight years of experience in development consulting and emerging markets banking, IFC was a perfect career match, combining my background in finance and my interest in promoting economic development.

As an investment officer in Europe, I have the unique opportunity to both conduct core investment activities and manage relationships with strategic stakeholders. My business development and investment activities focus on European companies expanding into emerging markets. Though not a majority of IFC's business, these North–South investments are nonetheless critical as they promote technology transfers and industry best practices to emerging markets. Approaching prospective clients, I have the opportunity to review project proposals and assess how an investment might meet IFC's standards for creditworthiness, development impact, and sponsor integrity among others. My interaction with clients spans from initial meetings to structuring a transaction and negotiating key terms. From an optical lens manufacturer in Laos to a wind farm developer in Uruguay, the diversity in the lines of business I cover is never boring.

In my relationship management role, I am routinely in touch with clients, business organizations, and, most importantly, IFC shareholders. As relationship manager for three European countries, my role is to interact on IFC's strategic orientations, and understand how they are affected by the shareholders' respective domestic and foreign policies.

Working for the IFC in Paris has provided me great insight into World Bank Group operations, strategies of European corporates, and challenges in emerging markets finance. With more than 50 percent of its staff in more than a hundred field offices around the world, IFC presents a multitude of opportunities to work in developing countries, and that is likely where my next position will take me.

I joined the World Bank was leading an educational exchange funded by the South–South Exchange Trust Fund that supported a trip of ten mining-sector experts from Tajikistan on a capacity-building visit to Brazil to learn about Brazil's mining-sector reform efforts.

Success in the organization requires a high level of technical competency coupled with an ability to function in a fast-pasted, diverse, multicultural—

and sometimes unpredictable—environment. Adaptability is definitely helpful.

Remuneration and Contracts

The World Bank strives to offer a competitive remuneration package to its staff members in order to attract, and retain, the best and brightest. Recent years have more or less frozen the increases in the salary scales, but the salary range remains on the higher side for the development business.

The Personal Dimension

Most World Bank staff love their jobs, but they need to sacrifice a certain part of their family lives in order to remain competitive. A heavy travel schedule is common for those in operational or technical jobs. Although this is often interesting and exciting, frequent travel is extremely disruptive to personal lives. Some missions, as they are called, last more than three weeks and could involve two to three countries to reduce costs, which interrupts the regular flow of life. The rewards are, however, very high: Staff have the opportunity to (1) interact with ministers, central bankers, and decision makers; (2) travel internationally and experience first-hand development work; and (3) influence policy dialogue and decision making.

The World Bank was conceived as democratic and "flat," so promotions are difficult to come by. Those joining from the private sector may find the Bank to be very slow to recognize talent. Even though this culture has been changing, some longer-serving staff can get frustrated with the slow pace of their careers.

Although the job environment at the World Bank is very competitive and can be stressful and involve personal sacrifice, the organization offers excellent training possibilities and exposes its employees to different cultures and customs. But perhaps most important, working at the World Bank means being at the forefront of development initiatives, contributing to the well-being of people in developing countries, and reducing poverty globally.

Notes

1. Foreign area officers are regional or country specialists who are versed in the language, culture, government, and military organization as well as the economics, history, and social issues of the nations concerned.

2. Member nations include Albania, Belgium, Bulgaria, Canada, Croatia, the Czech Republic, Denmark, Estonia, France, Germany, Greece, Hungary, Iceland, Italy, Latvia,

Lithuania, Luxembourg, the Netherlands, Norway, Poland, Portugal, Romania, Slovakia, Slovenia, Spain, Turkey, the United Kingdom, and the United States.

3. Internships can vary widely. As I write, internships listed on the NATO Recruitment website include those in the International Staff/International Military Staff, NATO Defense College (Rome), SHAPE (Supreme Headquarters Allied Powers Europe—Mons, Belgium), and the NATO Support Agency (Capellen, Luxembourg).

CHAPTER 5

Nongovernmental Organizations

In an attempt to make sense of the ever-expanding nongovernmental sector, we have broken nongovernmental organizations (NGOs) into three
broad categories by the issues they seek to address: development and humanitarian assistance, democracy and human rights, and public health and
the environment. However, these categories are merely guidelines and by
no means encompass the myriad organizations that inhabit the NGO world.

NGOs no longer—if they ever did—operate in a vacuum. Money flowing
into developing countries today comes more from private direct investment
than official development assistance, meaning that partnerships between
NGOs, private-sector entities, and public-sector organizations have become
more important than ever. These partnerships benefit both sides as they
share knowledge, expertise, and best practices. The blurred lines between
sectors also benefit job seekers; those looking to work in international development have more options than ever before, especially if their traditional
development skills are supplemented by the hard business skills needed to
effectively manage and evaluate programs. Given the traditional compensation levels and the typical living conditions of fieldwork, individuals considering the NGO career path need to believe in the mission and be dedicated
to the work. Hardships aside, as the following essays demonstrate, careers
in NGOs can be extremely rich and rewarding.

Careers in International Development
and Humanitarian Assistance NGOs

David A. Weiss

*David A. Weiss became president and CEO of Global Communities (formerly
CHF International) in 2010, having previously been a member of its board
since 2004 and chairman of the board from 2008 to 2010. Before joining Global
Communities, he was senior policy adviser at the global law firm DLA Piper for
thirteen years, advising on international trade and foreign policy matters. He
spent eighteen years with the federal government in the following roles: special*

assistant to the director of the Peace Corps, member of the US Foreign Service, economic officer in Haiti, staff aide to the secretary of state, senior special assistant to the deputy secretary of state, assistant US trade representative for North American affairs in charge of the North American Free Trade Agreement, and other senior positions in the Office of the US Trade Representative. He received the US Department of State's Superior Honor Award. He has a bachelor's degree from Hamilton College and a master's of science in foreign service (MSFS) from Georgetown University. He is a member of the Board of Directors of InterAction, the largest alliance of United States–based NGOs, and is on the Board of Advisors of New Perimeter, DLA Piper's global pro bono initiative.

Although many of the headlines today focus on the rapid and vast development of emerging markets, from Brazil and India to the growth economies of Africa, it remains a tragic fact that in the less developed parts of the world, millions are still being killed by disease, famine, malnutrition, poor water quality, and poor sanitation. HIV/AIDS, tuberculosis, and malaria, for instance, are three treatable and preventable diseases that still have a devastating impact in the world's poorest countries. The human impact of these three diseases is palpable, but their economic and social effects are also severe and measurable. Businesses are losing their labor forces, governments are losing their civil servants, and families are losing not only their loved ones but also their breadwinners.

Health issues are not the only problems that have an impact on the world's poor; from extreme weather to conflict to endemic corruption, many problems can conspire to challenge developing countries. Although many people will only read about or see these images on television, these are the environments where most of us in international development and humanitarian assistance work every day.

International development and humanitarian relief are increasingly complex fields and involve many stakeholders, including governments, NGOs, multilateral organizations such as United Nations agencies, and, increasingly, organizations in the private sector. In humanitarian relief, these organizations aim to respond simultaneously to natural disasters (e.g., earthquakes and hurricanes), and/or complex emergencies (war and other violent conflicts). These players bring life-saving skills and innovative technologies to quickly reestablish basic services, such as water and sanitation; set up shelters and schools; and provide food and medical supplies. For most development organizations, the core focus is long-term economic and civil society development, working with governments and/or grassroots communities to create sustainable programs that have a positive impact on lives and livelihoods for many years. There are many organizations that focus on each of these areas or across the whole panoply of sectors and programs in the development industry.

The development industry is dynamic, however, just as is the world around us. For example, two distinct but intertwined trends are emerging and will drastically change the way we do our work. The first is urbanization; 2008 marked the first time in history when more people lived in urban centers than outside them. According to UN Population Division projections, nearly all world population growth in the next few decades will be in urban areas in low- and middle-income countries.

The second trend is the increasing number of natural disasters and the increasing number of people affected by them. From the Indian Ocean tsunami of 2004 to the Haitian earthquake of 2010, disasters affect significantly more people now than they did fifty years ago. These disasters include droughts, earthquakes, tsunamis, hurricanes, typhoons, and floods. Although, in 1980, one hundred such disasters were reported, that number has risen to more than three hundred a year since 2000.

What these two trends tell us is this: The world's growing population is concentrating in cities; and when disaster strikes, the humanitarian response will more likely take place in a complex urban environment. This raises key questions: How do these trends change the way international development and humanitarian assistance organizations work, and what kinds of skills are they looking for when recruiting staff? These and many other changes, some of which I survey below, are also changing the kinds of staff members that development organizations are seeking.

Skills and Experience

In this day and age, the old definition of a do-gooder aid worker is outdated, to say the least. This means that the generalist who knows a little bit of everything is likely to have a more difficult time securing a position in our field. Most organizations are looking for someone who possesses the passion to change the world, but at the same time has solid technical skills that can be applied to different situations. And although there are growing numbers of opportunities for administrators, fund-raisers, grant writers, program managers, and policy analysts, expertise in a key technical area will definitely make a difference. Areas such as water management, engineering, food security, public health, nutrition, logistics, and conflict resolution are highly important, and individuals with such expertise can play a crucial role in effectively and permanently solving longer-term development problems, as well as addressing the special challenges that arise when disaster or conflict occurs.

Most recruiters in our industry are looking for a blend of idealism and pragmatism when interviewing candidates for positions in the field and at headquarters. Among the most sought-after skills are

- fluency in English and a second language (always list English on your résumé, because some candidates are not US nationals, and therefore fluency in English cannot be assumed);
- international internship or field experience (this should be listed at the top of your résumé);
- Peace Corps or similar experience (this should be listed at the top of your résumé);
- a master's degree in international development, international economics, international agriculture, or international public health; and
- excellent written and oral communication skills.

Your résumé should also indicate if you have had exposure to diverse cultures. You should list your citizenship(s), considering that different donors may have different nationality requirements.

If you choose international development as a career, make sure to get some field experience and, even if you are at headquarters, try to go to the field on short-term assignments. To succeed in our business one also needs to work well under pressure and thrive in challenging environments, as the focus and the priorities of our work are constantly changing and part of what makes our jobs interesting are their unpredictability. Cultural awareness and the capacity to work well with people from different social groups, communities, religions, and political orientations also go a long way, as does the ability to listen to others. Being a team player and at the same time being able to work independently and show leadership skills also is highly valuable. The ability to connect well with others and network can never be underestimated, given that nowadays many of us need to split our time between program implementation, program management, and business development. Individuals who need a very structured routine and are averse to change usually do not find satisfaction in our line of work.

The Broadening Array of Players

Today, there are many career options and paths in international development and humanitarian assistance. Locally and internationally, thousands of nonprofits, state and federal government agencies, and other organizations provide humanitarian or development assistance.

The *public sector* has historically been a major source of employment in our field. From large government development agencies—such as the US Agency for International Development (USAID), the UK Department for International Development, and the Deutsche Gesellschaft für Internationale Zusammenarbeit—to multilateral agencies—such as the World Bank, the International Finance Corporation, the United Nations, and the Inter-American Development Bank—these organizations mostly finance and manage projects while relying on partner organizations to implement them.

For this reason, the desirable skill set includes, for example, economics, program development, program administration, budgeting, and monitoring and evaluation.

The funding and policy landscape for development is changing rapidly. Over the past decade, there has been a greater focus on development in conflict and postconflict environments, on anticorruption and good government, and on tackling head-on the scourge of HIV/AIDS, malaria, and tuberculosis. This has given rise to newer players in the development arena, such as the vaccination-focused GAVI Alliance and new initiatives at the Department of Defense, the Millennium Challenge Corporation, and the US President's Emergency Plan for AIDS Relief. We are also seeing more collaboration and partnerships between government agencies, international foundations, and the private sector.

Most notably, globalization is bringing about profound changes and new opportunities in the field of international development. In the past thirty years, the vast majority of capital flows to the developing countries has shifted from official development assistance to foreign direct private investment. Although the main goal of international development has been poverty alleviation, there is an increasing understanding of the crucial role to be played by the private sector, especially in job creation. Many are convinced that the only path to sustainable development is through the engagement of the public and private sectors together.

USAID, for example, has put increased emphasis on *private-sector engagement* in the programs it funds, and the State Department has led a series of initiatives, such as Partners for a New Beginning, that are entirely focused on private-sector investment in developing countries. These initiatives involve multinationals, such as Coca-Cola, and smaller companies, such as the Palestine-based mobile phone service provider Souktel, which forms partnerships with development organizations in the Middle East.

Multinational corporations are beginning to see this model as the way forward because these once-distant markets are now growth markets that cannot be ignored. Haitians, Kenyans, and Indians—these are now consumers and stakeholders, not just beneficiaries of corporate charity relegated to the backs of annual reports. Corporations have recognized the need to institute higher labor standards; after all, local employees working in what were once sweatshops are now becoming consumers of the products their factories make. Combining business and social programs and targets is not only good for society; it is also good for business. More than ever before, for corporations, funding development programs is not simply social responsibility but also an integral part of corporate strategy.

Along with the private and public sectors, *foundations* continue to play an ever more important role in development. With foreign aid budgets under mounting pressure, the significance of these other flows can only grow. Indeed, the proportion of total philanthropy in the United States that goes to

Notes from the Field

Pact Inc.

Maggie Dougherty, MSFS 2010

It was the most creative use of a mosquito net that I had ever seen. The netting had been carefully rolled into a soft rope, then expertly tied together in patterns to create shin guards, arm guards, and helmets that served as the only protection for the Katchipo men who had gathered in the mountain village of Rumiit, South Sudan, for the annual stick fighting competition. In the past, the fighting was to the death, however, that year the community agreed that no one should die.

It was late July 2011, just after South Sudan's independence, and I was working as a technical assistant with the Carter Center on the South Sudan Guinea Worm Eradication Program. Based in a remote area of Jonglei State working essentially as a glorified community public health worker, I would marvel at how complicated it would be to even delve into the world of rule of law and peace building in South Sudan. Public health was challenging enough—levels of awareness and education were low and community members often ignored basic health training in favor of traditional practices that spread disease. Sitting with groups of armed, naked farmers (clothes were virtually nonexistent in Rumiit, but everyone had a gun) on the side of the mountain, surrounded by hand-sown and harvested corn fields, I would think: *What does the rule of law even matter out here?*

Six months later, after moving back to Washington, I took a job that allowed me to start thinking more strategically about that question while also building my program management skills from the headquarters side as Pact's program officer for South Sudan. In this, my current position, I support the field office on everything from new business development, grants and finance support, advocacy, research, and technical support as needed. Pact's model is to work in partnership with local organizations that implement projects in various sectors. In South Sudan, aside from access to water, our portfolio, ironically, is focused on the two sectors I always

(Continued on page 137)

international development and humanitarian relief alone is now probably about five times what the US government provides in official development assistance. Many agree that such philanthropy can provide a real source of innovation in development. Most foundations do not have the same kinds of political accountability and policy constraints that most official donors face, which makes them more likely to take on more risk and foster new approaches

thought would be incredibly messy to engage in within South Sudan: peace building and access to justice.

In February 2012 I had the opportunity to travel back to South Sudan to facilitate a number of focus group discussions on conflict, peace and justice in Upper Nile State. In July and August 2012 I returned to work with the team there to present these findings to county commissioners, partner organizations, and community representatives. My current position allows me to draw not only on my field experiences in South Sudan, but also from bits and pieces of my other previous experiences: data collection and project monitoring skills gained as the monitoring and evaluation manager based in Kandahar, Afghanistan, with Development Alternatives International; networking and database management skills gained as the community manager for the Development Practitioners Forum; focus group facilitation and capacity-building skills gained as an intern with the Ministry of Internal Affairs/United Nations Development Program in Monrovia; advocacy skills gained as an intern with Women Thrive Worldwide in Washington; and finally, community engagement and focus group facilitation skills gained as a Peace Corps volunteer in the Gambia.

Now, when I work with partner organizations on project design, I think about the challenges—in terms of both logistics and community buy-in—that they face in implementing activities like organizing peace committees, forming water management committees, holding community level paralegal trainings, introducing gender desks to county-level police, and training traditional chiefs on human rights. I think about the sheer logistics of reaching places like Rumiit—only accessible after an eight-hour hike. I have learned that yes, peace building and justice in South Sudan are, in fact, quite messy and challenging. But I have also learned that there are ways—small, small incremental ways—to start making justice accessible and understandable to community members in remote areas like Rumiit.

Much has happened in South Sudan since I watched the Katchipo stick fighting competition shortly after independence in July 2011. Sadly, the messy, challenging world of peace building and justice was highlighted—and disrupted—by the violence that spread across South Sudan in December 2013, and the widespread humanitarian needs that will now be the focus of most donor funding and programming.

and partnerships. Although foundations traditionally have been involved in key areas of international development, newer players such as the Bill & Melinda Gates Foundation have widened the scope of their portfolio and have the scale and influence to change the face of international development.

With the goal of poverty alleviation, *microfinance* began in the 1970s, when social entrepreneurs began making small loans on a large scale to the working poor. Almost forty years later, this market has served hundreds of millions of borrowers and savers, and some statistics show that 80 percent of the potential market has not yet been reached. The field of development finance is ripe for growth. Anyone looking to work in microfinance should have a financial background as well as knowledge of the social sciences and of local languages and customs. New careers are emerging to fit these unique demands. More recently, traditional career roles have been blurring as microfinance has been bringing together professionals with varied backgrounds to work in collaborative teams toward the broader aim of *financial inclusion*. In this new environment, development professionals often find themselves working side by side with venture capitalists, technology experts, and institutional investors.

NGOs and nonprofits are strategically positioned to bring all these stakeholders together and to design and implement development programs. Global Communities, for example, forms partnerships with a broad array of funding organizations, including multilateral development banks and UN organizations, bilateral government donors, foundations, and corporations. And as the line between developing and developed countries becomes more blurred, the future will include the big emerging economies—such as Brazil, China, and India—where poverty and wealth are close neighbors. Yet even as the geography of poverty is changing, our missions as international development organizations are not. NGOs, whether in the fastest-growing countries of the world or the poorest, have the role of working with the unheard voices, with those communities that are left behind. We need to be the enablers of progress, working as global citizens with creativity, care, and authenticity in the poorest communities.

Career Advice

Whether this is your first job after school or if you have recently decided to change careers and enter the field of international development, there are many possibilities and the competition is stiff. But development, and the ever-broadening array of players in what is an increasingly private-sector-led field, are changing rapidly.

Contrary to what some may say, I do not believe there is a single path to lead you to a successful career. Some people choose to follow a straight path, which may include an internship or an entry-level job with an NGO, a stint working for USAID, and some time spent in the field. Others, like me, take a more "scenic" and maybe less orthodox—although no less interesting and rewarding—route. I began with the Peace Corps staff, joined the Foreign Service early in my career, became a trade negotiator at the US Trade Representative's Office, and then, after thirteen years in the private sector, have come full circle back to my development roots, as the CEO of a large international development organization.

I am convinced that what I learned along the way has contributed immensely to who I am and where I am today. So my advice to you, as you are ready to embark on a career that is full of rewards and adventures, is to follow your passion and take every opportunity you can to challenge yourself and to improve the lives of others, whether in Washington or Timbuktu.

Careers in Democracy and Human Rights NGOs

Courtney C. Radsch

Courtney C. Radsch is a senior program specialist at UNESCO. Previously, she was the senior program manager for the Freedom of Expression Campaign at Freedom House, where she worked for three years on programming, research, and advocacy, and earlier was the assistant communications director at the Girl Scouts of the San Francisco Bay Area. She has also worked as a consultant for the Development Executive Group, Chemonics, IREX, and the Stimson Center. Before working for NGOs, she worked as a journalist, holding positions with Al Arabiya *in Dubai, the* New York Times, *and Lebanon's* Daily Star. *She conducted fieldwork in Egypt for her doctoral dissertation, "Digital Dissidence and Political Change: Cyberactivism and Citizen Journalism in Egypt," and she is frequently invited to write and speak about the nexus of media, technology, and activism in the Middle East. She received her PhD in international relations from American University, her master's of science from Georgetown University, and a bachelor's degree in mass communications from the University of California.*

The field of democracy promotion and human rights NGOs is diverse and ranges from large, well-known groups to small, specialized nonprofits focused on a particular subsection. Although Washington and New York City have the highest concentrations of these NGOs in the United States, there are also important nodes in London, Geneva, Paris, Berlin, and elsewhere, not to mention the hundreds of indigenous organizations that work on these issues in their own countries or regions.[1] Hundreds, if not thousands, of NGOs focus on a particular subset of democracy and human rights, such as governance and elections; women's rights; freedom of expression/press freedom; religious freedom; internet freedom; human trafficking; antitorture; lesbian, gay, bisexual, and transgender rights; refugees; and dozens of other themes.

If you are interested in working in this field, you must figure out whether you want to work for an international organization or a local, indigenous organization, as there are both practical and principled considerations. Most international organizations doing this work are Western, and many receive substantial portions of their budget from government sources, thus reflecting to some extent the foreign policy priorities of those states.[2] Historical interventionism in Latin America, Southeast Asia, and the former Soviet Union, along with the more recent foreign policy of the George W. Bush administration that included support for the wars in Iraq and Afghanistan and the so-called "War on Terror" under the guise of "democracy promotion" in the Middle East, have created hurdles for many Western organizations and their staffs working in this field. In Egypt, for example, several Western NGO workers and their local staffs were put on trial in 2012 for receiving illegal foreign funds and engaging in banned activities. A few months later the United Arab Emirates expelled several foreign NGOs based in the country. In the past couple of years, particularly in the wake of the 2011 Arab uprisings, new laws against accepting foreign funding and restrictive NGO laws such as those in Cambodia, Ethiopia, Russia, and elsewhere, have created even greater challenges for NGOs and activists in the country as well as those who seek to support their work.

Nonetheless, the work in this field is incredibly rewarding. The work you do makes a difference in the lives of others—whether you are helping Ugandan journalists advocate against repressive press laws, training Tunisian youth how to use social media for election monitoring, providing emergency assistance to Pakistani women's rights advocates, or training Russian activists how to monitor torture in prisons. And it is this "higher calling" that for many helps compensate for the low salaries in this field.

Career Tracks and Types of NGOs

There are three main types of democracy and human rights NGOs, distinguishable by the type of work they do:

- research,
- programming, and
- advocacy.

Most NGOs tend to focus on one or two of these general areas, although a few do some of each. There are also many new NGOs focused on technology and internet freedom, a particular growth area given the Obama administration's financial support for such programming, and Hillary Clinton's focus while she was secretary of state.

Career tracks in this field can also be broken down into three main groups: working on programs from headquarters; working in the field; and research and advocacy. The last category is the smallest and the more difficult in which to find a job because there are far fewer positions and only a few NGOs that have researchers on staff. In the United States these include Amnesty International and Human Rights Watch, both of which rely on paid staff and volunteers, and Freedom House, whose small research department of about a dozen staff is based in New York. Many groups that implement programs will conduct research as part of a given program, but they would rely on consultants or in-house expertise rather than a distinct research department. By far most people go into this field intending to work on programs.

Working in an NGO's Headquarters

The NGOs in this field differ in terms of their decentralization, with some, like Freedom House, maintaining a highly centralized approach and others, like Internews, adopting a highly decentralized structure that devolves most authority to the field offices. Working in the headquarters of an NGO typically means you will be working on program management, and will have varying levels of involvement or interaction with "beneficiaries," the term for those who are supposed to benefit from a given program.

Many positions, including junior ones, require a large amount of travel, which sounds exciting but can also be exhausting. Headquarters staff will often travel to the field for program startup and implementation, to establish or close out a field office or train field staff, or to conduct assessments or monitoring and evaluation. Trips can vary in duration, but they are always jam-packed to make the most out of a headquarters visit, particularly because donors typically monitor the international travel of headquarters staff.

Working in the Field

Working in the field is an invaluable, and I would say vital, experience for anyone interested in making a career in this arena. Whether you get this experience from studying abroad, volunteering, or working abroad in an unrelated field, it is essential that you have some firsthand experience of what it means to live in a developing country and/or one without democratic protections or respect for human rights. My experience working as a journalist in the United Arab Emirates (a country that Freedom House consistently ranks as "not free" in its annual press freedom survey), and then losing my job over an article I wrote, gave me credibility among those with whom I worked to support their efforts promoting freedom of expression in their countries. It also helped me personally understand the real economic and security risks that journalists and human rights and democracy advocates face in their countries, informing how I designed and implemented programs and advocacy initiatives. Working for a local NGO can be more fruitful than trying to get a job with an international NGO, as the latter often seek local expertise for entry- to mid-level positions while reserving the senior-level positions for international hires. In 2003 I showed up in Lebanon with a day's notice and managed to find an internship with a media development organization and a newspaper just by meeting people on the ground. You can also go through programs like the Advocacy Project, which helps place volunteers abroad for a summer or semester.

Breaking into the Field and What to Expect

Breaking into the field in Washington can require just trying to get a foot in the door as an intern, given the challenging global economic climate, which has left many professionals unemployed and college graduates searching for work; the concentration of professional programs in Washington; and the highly competitive environment for jobs with NGOs. This is not necessarily the case elsewhere, but because there is such a high concentration of democracy and human rights NGOs in Washington, internships can be a strategic first step toward a full-time paid position as new programs start and program associates rotate out. An internship can be a way to get a foot in the door of your desired organization, though it will often mean working for free or for not more than $10 to $15 an hour without benefits.

Prospective employees without an advanced degree will find they are competing for the same positions as people with advanced degrees, and that "entry level" carries with it different connotations than in many other fields. In general, a master's degree student with little or no field experience can expect to start as a program associate and spend about two years at that level. There is relatively high turnover at this level, as people leave to pursue advanced degrees or gain field experience, get promoted, or jump to other organizations. Some may also find that low salaries at this level are unsustainable given student loan debt and the high cost of living in Washington, New York, London, and other cities where NGO headquarters are clustered. In the United States starting salaries range from $28,000 to $38,000, depending on the level of education, years of experience, and languages spoken.

Depending on the organization, candidates with some relevant international experience and an advanced degree could apply at the program officer (PO) level, particularly at smaller NGOs or those with higher turnover. The title of PO varies more widely across organizations, in some cases indicating significant experience and carrying expectations of staying in that position for several years. In other NGOs a PO position requires only four or five years of relevant experience, and one would expect to remain a PO for two to five years, making a salary in the mid-30s to 50s. Higher-level positions

Table 5.1 **Typical Nongovernmental Organization Positions and Salaries**

Title	General Salary Range	Years of Experience
Program associate or assistant	$28,000–$38,000	0–3
Senior program associate or assistant	Varies	2–5
Program officer	$36,000–$50,000	4–8
Senior program officer	Varies	6–10
Project director/program manager	$50,000–$68,000	8–12
Senior program manager	$70,000–$85,000	10–15
Director	$80,000–$120,000	12–15
Vice president	$100,000–$160,000	15+

typically require extensive experience managing programs or advocacy initiatives, a proven ability to write successful funding proposals, and a network of relevant contacts.

It can be quite frustrating, however, to come out of a competitive graduate program and find that you are looking at positions that pay less than what many people made in other fields beforeo obtaining their master's. Furthermore, most entry-level positions are mostly administrative and do not necessarily put to use the substantive expertise of the program associate, which can lead to frustration and burnout, and which contributes to the high turnover rate among these positions. Another option is to seek field or other relevant experience and transfer in laterally, which was my approach. However, because many NGOs are smaller than private contractors or intergovernmental organizations working in the same field, staff members tend to have opportunities to contribute beyond the specific requirements of their position, and this is encouraged and necessary for advancement.

Although the position titles may vary, such as associate versus assistant, and there may be more or fewer rungs in the ladder, table 5.1 shows a typical outline of the types of positions from entry level upward.

A variety of degrees and experiences lend themselves to a career with a democracy promotion or human rights NGO. Although most people who go into this field have an advanced degree in international affairs or a related discipline, often from a top-tier university, it is not uncommon for someone to have a degree in law, area studies, history, journalism, or the social sciences. Significant field experience can sometimes compensate for the lack of an advanced degree. Despite the low salary levels and long hours of a career in the democracy and human rights field, a master's degree and some field experience, along with a foreign language, are typically the minimum required to even be considered for an entry-level position, much less a more mid-level position.

Skills

Demonstrated experience working in developing or repressive countries, developing and managing projects, budgeting and proposal development, and managing multicultural teams are some of the qualifications needed for a successful transfer into a mid-level or senior-level position. However, it is not necessary to have worked in the sector, as there are other fields, such as journalism or law, where the skill sets and experiences have much in common with the democracy / human rights field. Human rights monitoring and advocacy uses many of the same skills as journalism, including fact-finding and investigation, interviewing, trust building, cross cultural communication, and writing. Similarly, those with a background in law may find that many of their competencies are relevant to human rights documentation and legal reform work.

Familiarity with US government or EU funding mechanisms and compliance, in particular the subgranting process, is a definite advantage. Most democracy and human rights NGOs provide support to local groups and advocates through subgrants, and both US and EU foreign assistance agencies are increasingly interested in providing direct assistance to local groups through the subgrant mechanism, which requires extensive compliance requirements that are burdensome and challenging for international and local groups alike. Practical skills such as budgeting, financial management, logistics management, report writing, proposal development, and, above all, multitasking are also useful. In some cases familiarity with international laws and mechanisms related to human rights, such as the Universal Declaration on Human Rights, the International Covenant on Civil and Political Rights, and the various aspects of the Human Rights Council—such as the special mandate holders and the Universal Periodic Review process—would be an asset. Most positions are advertised on job sites such as those of Devex, the Foreign Policy Association, and Idealist, and the career centers of international affairs programs often circulate internship and job announcements.

Challenges of Working in the Field

Democracy and human rights NGOs tend not to be as well financed as many other sectors, and many depend primarily on program funding, meaning that there is a lack of job security. As programs wrap up, donors' priorities shift, or more competitors enter the field, staff members may find that there is no longer funding for their position. This can lead to high levels of stress along with a requirement that you fund-raise for your own position.

Another challenge of working in this field is the lack of broader institutional support systems that one would have in a private firm or international organization, like the UN. NGOs often lack the security systems, both physical and digital, organizational support services, and professional development opportunities that you may find in other sectors. For example, they make not have the resources to do a comprehensive security assessment before sending staff into the field, or to provide training and development opportunities for staff. Although management is a skill, there is little training for prospective or new managers, and the natural progression of moving up the organizational hierarchy typically necessitates moving into management (as it does in most fields). Investment in professional development opportunities is minimal because most budgets are donor-driven and overhead/ administration costs must be kept to a minimum. Most training takes place on the job, and somewhat informally, in my experience.

Trends

Choosing to work for a democracy and human rights NGO caries the benefit of doing good in the world with the trade-off of a very low salary and uncertain job security because of the ever-shifting dynamics of foreign assistance budgets. The US government is the largest funder, although other governments such as the European Union, Sweden, Canada, and the United Kingdom also support human rights work. Donors are increasingly seeking to fund local groups directly, so international and Western NGOs must figure out how to adapt, particularly as USAID and the State Department's Bureau of Democracy, Human Rights, and Labor Affairs move toward direct assistance.

International NGOs play an important normative role, however, beyond the support they give to local groups. Their reports, analysis, and advocacy form a critical part of a global strategy to empower indigenous defenders while attempting to strengthen international human rights norms and mechanisms, such as the UN Human Rights Council and the internet as a human right.

The revolutionary upheavals of 2011 that swept the Middle East caught many policymakers by surprise, but these events put democracy promotion and human rights NGOs front and center. In particular, the youth movements' innovative and strategic uses of digital networks and social media to empower previously disenfranchised people and bypass the state-run institutional media have turned information and communication technology into a central focus of programming by these NGOs. Therefore, familiarity with social media, digital innovation, and new media technology will give you a leg up in this field. Donors are increasingly interested in innovative approaches to solving the challenges in this field, which nearly always seem to equate with online and digital media platforms (even if there are traditional approaches with established success). Thus the ability to design creative programs that leverage the potential of social media platforms and

Notes from the Field

The National Democratic Institute

Sarah Moran, MSFS 2012

The office was abuzz when I arrived early on Tuesday, September 11, 2012. The Operations Team was in full swing, and it did not take long to find out why—the US Consulate in Benghazi had been attacked, and our employees in Libya were preparing to evacuate. Reports came in throughout the day that there were disturbances in and around US Embassy compounds in Egypt and Tunisia and that the State Department was instructing all nonessential staff to leave the area. My first thought? "Yeah; . . . this is complicated."

On the Governance Team at the National Democratic Institute (NDI), flexibility is the name of the game. The Benghazi attacks occurred just four days before we were scheduled to host a week-long program for visiting members of parliament and civil society leaders from the Middle East and North Africa region (Egypt, Tunisia, Morocco, Jordan, and Libya). I had been tasked with running logistics for the program, which included everything from setting the agenda to purchasing flights and ensuring that all 40 of our participants—eight from each country—were ready and able to travel by Friday, September 14.

NDI's Governance Team works primarily with legislators and representatives around the world to improve institutions of governance from the inside out. As part of a much larger effort to promote greater transparency, accountability, and openness, we often host study missions in which delegates discuss challenges and lessons learned with each other and members of the U.S. Congress and state legislators. The September program was one step in that effort, focusing on newly elected or newly empowered parliaments in the Middle East and North Africa region.

(Continued on page 147)

digital technologies for empowerment, accountability, and human rights documentation is essential to working in this field in the twenty-first century.

YouTube and other video-sharing services can be an integral part of human rights documentation and storytelling, enabling abuses to be documented and marginalized voices to be heard. In Egypt, for example, youth activists used mobile phones to document abuses by the military rulers in the wake of President Hosni Mubarak's ouster, uploaded the videos to YouTube, and set up giant screens in public squares so that those not online could see what was happening, essentially bridging the digital divide. Geotagging

On the morning of September 11 my first call was to the US consulate in Benghazi, from which I had received an urgent message that morning. I could not get in touch with my point of contact, who was in emergency meetings, so I proceeded to call each Libyan delegate personally to check in on the status of their travel. All but three that I spoke to decided that, given the circumstances, they would not be participating in the program. Next up was Egypt. NDI had been present in country since their offices were raided in early 2012, so I called the Embassy in Cairo. I was told that, unfortunately, the embassy was on reduced staff and that our participant visas, already approved, would not be printed today. Nor tomorrow. Perhaps not until Sunday, two days after the delegates were to fly. We would later hear that the participants' passports would be inaccessible until the embassy reopened to staff on Monday. Finally, in Tunisia, in anticipation of the embassy closure in Tunis, NDI's national staff immediately went to the Embassy, braving the crowd that was gathering outside, to pick up the passports and visas.

After debates with partners and funders about whether or not the program would even happen (resulting in a significant sunk cost), we made the final decision to go ahead. As a result, I spent the next four days phoning airlines, rebooking flights, negotiating with transport companies and hotels, shifting the agenda and even calling participating members of Parliament at late hours on their personal phones. (Finding flights out of Libya when the Benghazi and Tripoli airports were running alternating closures was particularly fun; if you have not spent hours listening to the hold music for Turkish airlines, you have not lived.) I knew that this program was insignificant in the bigger scheme of all that was happening in North Africa, but it was amazing to see the ripple effect play out in our Washington office. In the end, due to the remarkable efforts of our Embassy contacts overseas, our NDI field staff, and the desire of the delegates themselves to participate, we pulled it off, but barely. And while our task paled in comparison to the work of diplomats and staff overseas, I learned an important lesson: that no matter how much you think you know about your first job out of graduate school, you will inevitably be surprised.

and mapping platforms like Ushahidi can enable collaborative transparency and accountability projects related to political processes like elections or human rights abuses such as sexual assaults and prison monitoring. Social media, particularly Facebook and Twitter, have become key organizational and publicity platforms for local activists and citizen journalists around the world. In Libya, for example, young women used Facebook and Twitter to advocate for equal female representation on the ballot, and they also used these platforms to organize new NGOs and citizen initiatives, including by women who had previously been restricted from participating in the public sphere. These decentralized, individualized mass communication and organization tools have become central to the design of democracy promotion programs and human rights work vis-à-vis closed regimes, such as Iran, Belarus, and Syria; repressive regimes, such as China and Venezuela; and more open countries, such as Kenya and Mexico. Networked digital technologies and social media platforms have become an integral part of research, advocacy, and programming by NGOs in this field, although it is often the young people living in these countries who have the most innovative and creative ideas about how to harness their potential for promoting democracy and human rights. It is likely that the infatuation with what are still often termed "new media" will continue for some time, as donors and international NGOs continue to explore how to leverage the power of networks and mass individualized media for human rights and democracy promotion.

Careers in Public Health, Educational, and Environmental NGOs

Sharon Rudy and Suzanne Petroni

Sharon Rudy is the director of the Global Health Fellows Program–II at the Public Health Institute. She has more than thirty years of experience in nonprofit management and international development. She received a PhD in counseling and organizational consulting from the University of Maryland, College Park.

Suzanne Petroni is the senior director for gender, population, and development at the International Center for Research on Women. She received a PhD in public policy and public administration from George Washington University and an MSFS from Georgetown University. She has worked in foreign policy and international development for more than twenty years.

For decades, governments and others have recognized the importance of investing in public health. Combating the diseases that plague the world's poor has been a critical component of many governments' foreign policies and international assistance for years, and in many cases, decades. As people and nations realize that the 7 billion of us who inhabit planet Earth are tied together in an increasingly interdependent world, so too have we come to realize that good health is not only an outcome toward which the international community should strive but also a requirement for economic development, national security, and the enabling of basic human rights. This recognition has led to a growing field of global health, toward which professionals from a wide range of diverse background can contribute. Indeed, today's global public health professionals carry diverse skill sets, with expertise and advanced degrees in areas that can include policy, business, management, human resources, diplomacy, and education, in addition to the more traditional areas of public health, international development, and medicine.

Perhaps as important as technical knowledge and program skills, successful global health professionals today, more than ever, need the ability to identify with a particular set of values and commitment. They care about and understand the need to address the health needs of the sick—and the healthy—in an equitable and efficient manner. Eliot Freidson described the word "profession" as a special kind of occupation and as an avowal or promise. To fulfill such a promise, professionalism signifies a set of values, behaviors, and relationships that underpin the trust of the public. Working in global health is a perfect example of how such professionalism comes into play.

The Players

The Public Health Institute (PHI) has led the US Agency for International Development's (USAID) flagship global health fellowship programs for the past sixteen years. Currently, PHI's Global Health Fellows Program–II employs more than 130 junior- to senior-level global health professionals who work for USAID for two to four years across a full spectrum of technical topics and functions. The fellowship program reflects the broad range of work available and needed in the global health field, with fellows deployed across the world and in Washington to advance US interests in maternal and child health, HIV/AIDS, malaria, tuberculosis, reproductive health, and more. Because these fellows support the US government's work in these areas, they are exceptional compared with many of their colleagues in the field in at least two respects: They do not write proposals to obtain funding, and they do not provide direct health services. Instead, they provide technical assistance to government grantees and contractors, ensuring that evidence-based best practices and the most current knowledge in a variety of technical areas are used to implement USAID's global health work. They also often assist USAID in coordinating with other federal agencies and donors.

In addition to USAID, many other agencies and organizations contribute in important ways to advancing global health. In recent years the US Department of State and US Department of Health and Human Services have become major players in global health, at both the policy and programmatic levels. Internationally, at the multilateral level, among those important agencies that prioritize health are the World Health Organization, UNICEF, the UN Population Fund, the World Bank, and the Global Fund to Fight HIV/AIDS, Tuberculosis, and Malaria. Many other governments provide funding and technical support for global health activities, such as through the United Kingdom's Department for International Development, Denmark's DANIDA, the Australian Agency for International Development, the Canadian International Development Agency, the Swedish International Development Agency, and the Dutch Ministry of Foreign Affairs—just a few of the important bilateral donor agencies known for their concern with various aspects of global health. Private donor agencies—such as the Ford, David and Lucile Packard, MacArthur, Rockefeller, and William and Flora Hewlett foundations—have also long contributed to global health issues, and the Bloomberg Philanthropies and the Bill & Melinda Gates Foundation are examples of more recent and hugely important additions to this field.

Governments, foundations, and international organizations may provide the important policies, funding, and support for global health, but they often look to nongovernmental organizations for the hands-on provision of public health information and services around the world. A large number of such NGOs currently tackle global health issues, including the nonprofit organizations CARE, Save the Children, International Medical Corps, IntraHealth, International Center for Research on Women, FHI-360, International Planned Parenthood Federation, and World Vision. A growing field of for-profit companies are also engaging in global health, including Abt Associates, Chemonics, DAI, and DevTech Solutions. And increasingly, NGOs based in developing countries are becoming important players in the field. Bangladesh's BRAC, India's Public Health Foundation, Brazil's Instituto Promundo, and the Kenya-based African Medical and Research Foundation are just a few of the many country-based experts in various areas of public health.

Trends and Forecast for Global Health

Careers with these and other organizations working on global health can be exciting as well as wide-ranging. The researchers and program staff members who design, implement, monitor and evaluate, and report on programs and projects in the field cannot do their work without the business development, finance, and communications teams that identify funding sources, build relationships with donors, market their work, and craft proposals and budgets in coordination with program staff. The technical advisers and grant makers at donor agencies and foundations support their organizational leaders in identifying how and where they can add the greatest value to the global health field, and they also know how to locate and support the organizations that are doing the best work in these realms. Those who work on global health in governments and multilateral agencies provide technical guidance and policy support, and they also work with members of civil society to advance their organization's agendas on global health.

What is consistent among all these important contributors to global health is that the unprecedented pace of global change is expanding and challenging the knowledge, skills, and values of many development professionals, including those working in the health arena. Shifts in concepts of country ownership, rethinking the impact of "leave-behind" sustainability, and the always-true but now emerging priority of the impact of gender on health outcomes all present challenges to actual implementation. And though the international community has seen tremendous advances in global health outcomes over the years—such as the eradication of smallpox and guinea worm, and the leveling off of HIV infections—the tremendous challenges that still exist, such as the stubbornly slow decline of maternal mortality rates, demand that investments in and attention to the global public health sector will likely continue for the foreseeable future.

To tackle the global health challenges that we still face, the international community needs to move beyond disease-specific knowledge and siloed programs. Individuals and organizations working in global health need to become more innovative and flexible so they can address a wide range of issues, such as the following:

- *Inequities and inequality.* Poor people in developing countries face common infections, malnutrition, and maternity-related health risks, which have long been controlled in more affluent populations. Even within a country's borders, the most marginalized populations— including the very poor, minorities, displaced persons, and women, among others—often face the most significant health challenges. Globalization has brought many positive contributions to development, but it is also bringing junk food, tobacco, and environmental hazards that pose new and significant health challenges to diverse populations around the world.
- *Accelerating movement across national borders of people (including health professionals), and pathogens, new infections, and behavioral threats.* These epidemiological threats are superimposed upon rapid demographic changes that blur geographic boundaries. And they are constantly changing, forcing the global community to be on alert and continuously innovate.
- *Keeping up with demands.* Health systems struggle to keep up with the needs of the populations they serve, with donor-driven demands, and with the inadequate training and education of health professionals.
- *Increasingly complex health systems.* Such systems require a mix of different types of health professionals and community members to provide the types of information and services that are most effective and beneficial for their diverse populations. The roles that these

professionals and laypersons play are often unclear and arbitrary, reflecting the relative success of different occupational groups in mobilizing the government to award credentials specifically to establish monopolies of practice. Hyperspecialization and rigid tribalism restrict opportunities for collaboration and more porous walls between the competencies of different health professionals, which would otherwise allow for the shifting and sharing of tasks to produce those most practical and useful outputs related to health.

Skills Sought by Employers

A career in global public health offers tremendous opportunity but also great challenges. Positions in the global health field reflect the complexity of health systems and the continuous evolution of new health threats and solutions. And increasingly, they are filled by individuals who have significant experience and expertise.

At the entry level almost all employers in the field now expect an advanced degree and some kind of relevant experience. Particularly for those with less experience, it is up to the applicant to make the case, in a cover letter and résumé, and ideally through an interview, that they are a good fit for the work. Experience in and knowledge of a particular country and appropriate language skills can be extremely helpful in cases where specialized experience is not as strong. In general recruiters seek knowledge and experience in at least one of two overall areas.

The first area is technical content in the global health field. This could include experience within issues such as

- sexual, reproductive, maternal, and child health;
- infectious diseases, such as HIV / AIDS, malaria, and tuberculosis;
- nutrition, animal-to-human-borne diseases; and
- neglected tropical diseases.

Noncommunicable diseases—such as cardiovascular disease, cancer, diabetes, and lung disease—are spreading rapidly throughout the world and, surprisingly to many, are now the leading cause of death and disability globally. Just now coming to the global stage as an area of tremendous need, these diseases—which are caused by poor diet, inadequate exercise, tobacco use, alcohol abuse, environmental pollution, and other preventable factors—affect the world's poorest populations most substantially.

The second area is systems issues. Global health recruiters may seek expertise in

- policy analysis,
- program design and planning,

- logistics and supply chain management,
- behavior change communication,
- monitoring and evaluation, and
- management and leadership.

One can also specialize in addressing the needs of various target populations, such as mothers; adolescents; lesbian, gay, bisexual, and transgender people; other marginalized groups; and the special category of highly vulnerable children.

Understanding how health systems are influenced by and operate in the larger political, cultural, and socioeconomic contexts is important. For instance, traditional gender norms may contribute to early and frequent childbearing, a lack of girls' education, and restricted access to health care by women, which can all contribute to poor health outcomes. Limited access to clean water and adequate sanitation, emergencies and crises, conflict and postconflict environments, climate change, inadequate financing, and other influences in the larger governmental and private-sector systems can also affect health negatively. In other words, *broad development experience* and an understanding of the many factors that can affect health and development can be extremely helpful.

Breaking into the Field

There are many ways to break into the realm of global public health. Taking any opportunity to work in the field of health with a potential employer is a key way of increasing one's marketability. Prospective employees want to take advantage of internships and university programs that offer field-based experience. The Global Health Fellows Program–II (GHFP-II) is one of the many programs that offers both summer and year-round internships. Although GHFP-II interns work for USAID, internships that give students tremendously valuable hands-on experience can be found across the field.

As in other fields, personal networking and online access to information are critical. Attending meetings, conferences, and briefings—such as those offered by professional associations like the American Public Health Association and InterAction, and by think tanks like the Woodrow Wilson International Center for Scholars, the Center for Strategic and International Studies, the Center for Global Development, and a wide range of other organizations—are all important ways to access information and contacts. Informational interviews are common in the industry and are a great way to learn more about the various organizations working in global health.

Some of the most commonly used job hunting and related websites are

- *International Career Employment Weekly*, www.internationaljobs.org /index.html.

Notes from the Field

The Center for Clean Air Policy
Michael Comstock, MSFS 2009

As manager of international climate dialogue at an international climate change policy think tank, I work to advance the United Nations negotiations on climate change through off-the-record, roundtable dialogues of negotiators. I also bring together government officials from Latin American and Asian countries in similar dialogues to encourage renewable energy, clean transportation, or other policies that promote sustainable development and reduce emissions of greenhouse gases in their countries. My job affords me tremendous opportunity to work at the intersection of international development and climate change—arguably two of the world's most challenging and intrinsically related issues. And being at a small, independent think tank gives me the latitude to work on the cutting edge of these issues.

On a regular basis, I contribute to policy analysis and papers, facilitate roundtable discussions, and present on climate change mitigation topics at our international dialogues. I am also responsible for representing my organization and speaking at international events such as UN negotiations, energy conferences, and the Carbon Expo. Getting whisked away to Bogotá, Bangkok, Barcelona, and other exotic places on a monthly basis often makes me feel like I live out of a suitcase. But working in other countries, cultures, and languages is also the most exciting part of my job, allowing

(Continued on page 155)

- Idealist, www.idealist.org.
- Interaction, www.interaction.org.
- *Non-Profit Times*, www.nonprofittimes.com/jobs.
- Indeed, www.indeed.com.
- Devex, www.devex.com.

Experience, even internships and in-country living experience, can help get one in the door at the entry level. However, to be successful over time in the global public health environment, professionals must be able to

- access and dissect vast amounts of information, extracting and synthesizing what is necessary for decision making, whether at the level of individual services or country policies. This ability also reflects the value of lifelong learning and the ability to exploit the power of

me to develop relationships with high-level policymakers, negotiators, and ambassadors from around the world.

One of the most rewarding aspects of my position is the opportunity I have to influence these policymakers—both at the UN level and on the ground in developing countries—and to play the role of a behind-the-scenes broker to advance ambitious climate policies and international financing for these policies. For example, during a recent trip to Vietnam, I met with a group of policymakers and advised the Vietnamese government on how to approach the development of its climate policies in a way that would ensure buy-in from relevant ministries and advance development goals such as economic growth, air quality, and mobility. I also lobby European countries and financial organizations to provide financial support for these efforts in the developing world.

After completing Georgetown's MSFS program, I came into my organization thanks to a fellow MSFS alumnus who was employed there. I approached my job from the international affairs/development side, but those looking to enter the climate change field would be wise to study up on environmental economics and public policy. Many of the entry-level employees we hire—even those with graduate degrees—initially come in as interns, which gives them an opportunity to get their foot in the door and also to see whether the organization is a good fit.

Regardless of how one enters the field, a career in international climate change policy promises to be challenging. However, despite the often-gridlocked US partisan politics on climate change, most of the countries with which we work around the world recognize the threat of a changing climate to their development and well-being, and many are taking decisive action to mitigate it. Being a part of the effort to find solutions to this universal challenge is truly fulfilling.

networking and connectivity to mutually strengthen and anticipate future health threats.

- collaborate respectfully in teams that include other health disciplines and members of the community, including the target population. This competency has grown in importance because of the transformation of health systems and the role of the home and community in health. In some cases collaboration can extend to those involved in areas such as strategic communications, policymaking, philanthropy, and academia.
- optimize locally driven solutions while harnessing the benefits of transnational flows of knowledge and resources, both hallmarks of international health expertise.
- value socially responsible professionalism and ethical conduct.

Ultimately, the successful global public health professional is a global citizen with an evolving mindset that acknowledges challenges and seeks to meet them. He or she must demonstrate a consistency between professional rhetoric, stated values, and personal conduct.

To be most effective, global health professionals must understand local contexts and the contributions that can be made by local citizens. They must learn to work across professional silos and move beyond static pedagogy. And they must be committed to social justice. As Helen Keller said, "Until the great mass of the people shall be filled with a sense of responsibility for each other's welfare, social justice cannot be attained."

Notes

1. In Germany, e.g., the Friedrich Ebert, Friedrich Naumann, Heinrich Böll, and Konrad Adenauer foundations, which are affiliated with political parties.

2. The US Agency for International Development and the European Union are among the largest governmental donors, but other significant donors include the Swedish International Development Agency, the Canadian International Development Agency, the foreign ministries of several democratic countries to a lesser extent, and the United Nations indirectly through its various institutions.

CHAPTER 6

International Banking and Finance

Although career prospects in international banking and finance have ebbed and flowed since the recent global and regional financial crises, by no means have they dried up. With businesses seeking to enter emerging markets in the BRICs (Brazil, Russia, India, and China) and beyond, an ability to assess and manage risk is fundamental to one's success in the banking and finance industry. International affairs professionals will be competing with MBAs for positions in this sector. But those candidates with international affairs degrees who are armed with solid, advanced finance skills as well as a nuanced understanding of the political, economic, and policy contexts that are so essential to understanding risk can effectively differentiate themselves from those who have only been trained in a pure business curriculum. The following essay breaks down the industry and highlights areas that are particularly suitable for international affairs practitioners.

Careers in International Banking

Hernán T. Narea

Hernán T. Narea, an international investment banker, has focused his career on global emerging markets. During his more than twenty years of experience, primarily with J. P. Morgan Chase in New York, he has advised governments, companies, and banks in countries around the world on sovereign and corporate debt restructurings, infrastructure projects, mergers and acquisitions, private equity, debt trading, and syndicated finance. He is the author of various published financial articles, as well as his first novel about the financial world, The Fund *(Forge/Macmillan, 2011). He is a graduate of Georgetown University's School of Foreign Service, where he has also taught graduate courses on international finance. He holds US and Chilean citizenships, and is fluent in English, Spanish, and Portuguese. He has lived in Chile, the United States, Brazil, Venezuela, and Thailand.*

Facing a looming fiscal cliff, the finance minister had no choice but to recommend halting payments on the country's external debt. As he feared the move not only dried up the country's sources of foreign capital but also sparked a crisis of confidence in the solvency of its foreign lenders. The financial virus spread quickly, prompting scrutiny from other sovereign borrowers. Shaken senior bank managers enforced drastic measures to restore shareholder confidence, hoping to hold on to their jobs. They shored up their risk management systems to protect bank capital, cut back on lending, and instituted layoffs. Banks' CEOs pored over doomsday scenarios prepared by their risk managers. If the projections proved right, portfolio write-downs could wipe out significant chunks of their equity and they would be forced into a merger—or worse, stave off a takeover at bottom-basement pricing.

Meanwhile, government policymakers were alarmed by the rapidly expanding banking crisis and its potential impact on the overall economy. However, as much as regulators wanted to take the easy route of propping up errant borrowers and lax lenders via concessionary liquidity, they faced a clear moral hazard. If they intervened with cash Band-Aids and no strings attached, policymakers worried that the market would soon revert to the easy credit standards that had pushed them to the brink in the first place. Could they let one sovereign fall off the credit cliff, without risking that the rest would follow suit? Or were they all simply "too big to fail"?

Crisis after Crisis

All this sounds like a familiar plot line, right? Well, this true scenario that I describe above is what I encountered when I first ventured beyond the campus with an international affairs degree stuffed inside my shiny new briefcase, in search of gainful employment on Wall Street. I am now on my third decade in the financial industry, and the crisis I described, however familiar-sounding to more recent grads, is not the global financial crisis that erupted in late 2007. Rather, these events were triggered by Mexico's default on its sovereign debt in August 1982. The lesson is that the financial industry has managed its way through many crises before and will continue to do so. Cycles are the nature of the risk beast.

Although the issues faced by borrowers, lenders, and governments today have deep policy parallels with that earlier crisis, which is important to readers of this tome, the 1980s debt crisis in the less-developed countries resulted in an equally challenging job market for newly minted graduates. When revenues in any industry are down, entry-level positions are some of the first to be pulled back. Mergers are another type of event that has a negative impact on financial-sector jobs. Having survived half a dozen of these, I know that they often hinge on expense reduction (read: employee cutbacks) to get shareholder approval.

So is there any good news, you ask? Should you still be looking to join the ranks in the financial industry? The answer for an international affairs student is a resounding Yes!

Embracing Financial Risk

Each financial industry candidate will be challenged to turn the industry's current turmoil into an opportunity to create a lasting and remunerative career. The trick lies in understanding that success in the industry centers on each firm's ability to correctly assess, manage, and price risk. At its essence, the ability to balance risk across a broad spectrum of clients is the core product most banks deliver to the market. So instead of running away from risk, you should learn to embrace it using your international affairs degree as the tool to differentiate you from rest of the pack of candidates.

As part of my assignments leading various international businesses for a multinational bank, I recruited graduate students for entry-level positions from both international affairs programs and MBAs. My methodology as a recruiter scoping out potential candidates might offer hints for your approach to finding that career-making opportunity in the industry. I begin with a word of caution. With some of my industry colleagues, I witness a default preference for MBAs and what they deem to be their quantitative skills strengths, particularly when it comes to functions such as financial modeling.

In my career I have either created or reviewed hundreds of financial models for debt and equity transactions. My long-held conviction is that even the best models must rely on the quality of data inputs and assumptions. Equally, the model output must be properly analyzed and correctly understood so that it can be applied to real-life cases. In international finance any financial model that is created without deep knowledge of all the relevant country risk issues—such as economics, politics, and local regulatory and policy vagaries—will yield incorrect results, leading to financial loss.

In fact, in certain markets these country risk issues may override all other factors in a credit risk decision. This is as true today as it was during the debt crisis in the less-developed countries. There are numerous examples wherein an overreliance on modeling proved to be the Achilles heel of a firm, leading to lost revenue opportunities or, even worse, the demise of the firm. Your goal as an international affairs graduate is to demonstrate that you know how important *both* quantitative and qualitative skills are in international finance and that through your education and experience, you bring both to the table. Now let us move to your interview.

Recruiting: An Interviewer's Perspective

My first step is studying candidates' résumés, usually the night before or as I travel to on-campus interviews. Remember, the résumé will not get you the job, but it can get your qualifications pushed to the bottom of the pile. Because this book is not a guide to résumé writing, I will not go into a long exposé on the subject. However, having read several hundred résumés, I can quickly spot the carelessly prepared ones. There is a science involved in creating a succinct, well-written résumé that is error-free and presented in an unobtrusive, clear format. This is your script for an interview, so make sure it reflects the points you want to get across. Also, as an interviewer, I rely on the résumé to develop questions for face-to-face meetings with candidates. So reach out for résumé critiques from your university's career counselors and anyone else whose writing and business expertise you trust.

For the handful of stand-out résumés, I then review the candidate's coursework and, yes, his or her grade point average. In addition to the core international affairs curriculum, I also look for courses that reflect a candidate's interest in the financial industry, such as economics, accounting, and corporate finance. Beyond that, I search for any specialized courses that would indicate a

1. concentration on the language(s) and/or the political economy of a certain region of the world; and
2. more advanced finance studies, for example, spreadsheet financial modeling, financial statement analysis, corporate risk analysis, country risk analysis, capital markets instruments, syndicated loans, and project finance.

The rest of my résumé review concentrates on the candidate's experience, such as any finance-related internships and/or their international experience studying or living abroad. Rarely am I disappointed in meeting the candidates whose résumés make it to the top of my review pile. Invariably, they display a confident manner because they know where they are headed career-wise. They had been thinking about it for years, not just 10 minutes before the interview.

Industry Knowledge Is Key

Besides the ease of their presentation during an interview, the final criteria I focus on in judging a candidate's potential placement is their understanding about this industry and my institution. Therefore, it is incumbent on you to be informed. Read the financial press—the *Wall Street Journal*; the *Financial Times*; the *New York Times*, including "DealBook"; and *The Economist*—on a regular basis. Try to surface links between what you are learning in your classes and what is hitting the headlines. Here are several examples:

1. What steps could that energy multinational company have taken to avoid expropriatory action by the foreign host government against their joint project?

2. Will that European multinational company facing political pressures for higher corporate taxation in its home market be forced to move its headquarters to Asia?
3. Is that internet giant finally opening up in Asia's largest market, attempting to walk that fine line between government censorship and profit motivations?

In each of the above examples, you should ask yourself what you learned in your classes that could shape a discussion about the international issues faced by each of these companies and how these can have either a positive or negative impact on their future financial condition. Think about a particular paper you wrote or a case you analyzed that could spark that conversation in an interview. That kind of preparation underscores true interest in the industry by demonstrating how you used your coursework to prepare yourself to add to a firm's bottom line.

As I write this, the global economy continues in the throes of a seemingly never-ending crisis. The past five years of economic malaise spurred by a banking crisis will have long-lasting implications for the financial industry in both the United States and abroad for years, if not decades, to come. You must spot the coming trends in the industry in order to make judgments about where you want to focus your energies in the first few years of your career and be prepared to speak about them if you are given the opportunity during an interview. To get you started, here are a few of these trends in the current landscape:

1. *Regulation:* As governments react to the origins of the recent crisis, expect tougher regulations to be imposed on banking operations.
2. *Margins:* As banks seek to minimize risk and face higher capital requirements, expect tighter operating margins, particularly in developed markets.
3. *Emerging markets:* Fueled by their economic growth, expect more robust expansion of the financial industry in these markets versus developed countries.
4. *Technology:* Expect it to drive innovation and efficiency in the delivery of banking products around the globe.

The forces at work in these few trends alone already indicate that international affairs graduates seeking international opportunities—particularly in developing markets—should be in demand.

Finding Your Best Fit in a Firm

When I interview a candidate, I try to discern whether they have researched my firm and to uncover their specific areas of interest that they have the acumen to pursue. Therefore, you are well advised to understand the organization you are targeting. Research their business lines, always with an eye to matching your education and skill sets with their particular lines—all the better if the line you target is going through a growth phase. To guide you, figure 6.1 provides a typical organizational structure for a global financial institution.

As you look at figure 6.1, note that all the major business lines have the word "global" in the name of their division. In any large institution these product and client management lines cut across international date lines. These businesses must operate locally in each country, but with a common business culture—a strong indication that your international affairs background can have applicability in that business. The task is uncovering where. The figure is divided between

1. global regional locations,
2. business divisions, and
3. the type of function represented by each division.

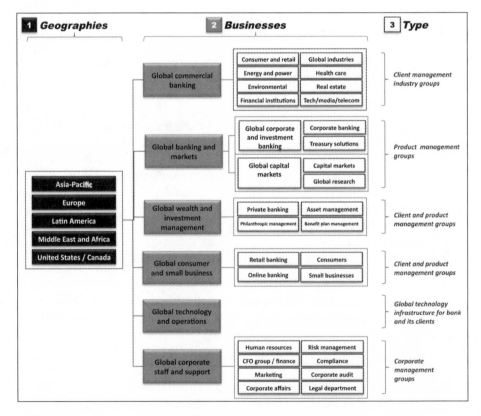

Figure 6.1

Notes from the Field

Barclays Capital

Richard Gallivan, MSFS 1992

I graduated from UC Berkeley in 1987 and spent two and a half years in Zaire (now the Democratic Republic of Congo) as a US Peace Corps volunteer. I entered Georgetown's MSFS program with the idea of a career in the Foreign Service or perhaps a multilateral development bank such as the African Development Bank, the Inter-American Development Bank, or the World Bank. While at Georgetown, I interned as a subcontractor at the World Bank and quickly determined that I did not see a career for me in a nongovernmental organization or other government institution. Several people I worked with suggested I try my luck on Wall Street to gain some critical finance skills. I spent the fall of my second year interviewing for Wall Street jobs; by the middle of the year I had landed several offers and decided to move to New York after graduation. I spent almost four years in New York where I very much enjoyed the fast paced, frenetic work environment of a Wall Street banking job. I became a corporate finance generalist coverage banker where I have continued to work with corporate clients worldwide for the last 22 years.

My wife and I moved back to our native California in 1996, where I took a job in the technology group at Salomon Brothers. Through several mergers, we became Salomon Smith Barney and then Citigroup. I rose to head up the West Coast Technology business for Citi and in 2006 decided to join Lehman Brothers to run its West Coast Technology business and global semiconductor practice from Menlo Park, California. After several years at Lehman Brothers in Menlo Park, and then after the bankruptcy of Lehman, Barclays acquired Lehman's North American operations and I then found myself working for a terrific organization in the form of Barclays Capital, the investment banking arm of Barclays, the large UK banking financial services firm. I was anxious for a new challenge and was asked to consider a move to Asia to assist in the reorganization and change of Barclays' very strong fixed-income platform into a full service investment banking business. In 2009, along with my wife and four children, I relocated to Hong Kong, where I spent three years as head of corporate finance for the Asia-Pacific region. My responsibilities in Asia were for all Barclays' investment banking corporate coverage across all industry sectors and geographies from Japan to Australia to India to Indonesia, and everywhere in between. In the summer of 2012 we returned to Silicon

(Continued on page 164)

Valley, where I now have a senior client facing role with a focus on the software and enterprise hardware sectors of the technology industry.

My career in investment banking has been a fantastic experience. I came out of Georgetown with a great worldview but limited hard finance skills. I have been constantly challenged by the diversity of clients in our business and the complexity of issues faced by both United States–based and international corporations. As a generalist investment banker, my areas of expertise include corporate finance, initial public offerings, mergers-and-acquisitions advisory, and leveraged finance. I have always pushed myself to learn all aspects of complicated financial products and I have been lucky enough to work on hundreds of corporate financing and mergers-and-acquisitions transactions over the last twenty-two years. It's been a lot of fun and very interesting along the way.

My career has taken me to many corners of the globe and I have enjoyed the challenges and opportunities working with multinational corporations both at home and abroad. I feel that my experience at Georgetown's MSFS program particularly provided me the critical thinking skills required for success in a fast-paced environment such as investment banking.

Any one of the these regional locations and business divisions can be entry points for a recent international affairs graduate. The final two business divisions shown in figure 6.1, "global technology and operations" and "global corporate staff and support," are the only support functions on the list, and therefore require more specialized skills, such as technology, legal, and other training.

In figure 6.1 the business divisions are split between "client" and "product" functions, representing the front lines of the institution in the marketplace. Client areas traditionally handle the day-to-day relationship with the bank's chosen client base, and can be organized by industry (see "global commercial banking") or the size of the client, ranging from individuals to small businesses (see "global wealth and investment management" or "global consumer and small business"). The client management teams will coordinate the client interface by the product teams, which, depending on the needs of any one client, can range from investment banking advisory services, such as debt- and/or equity-raising exercises, and mergers-and-acquisitions advisory services and funding, to capital markets solutions, such as interest rate, currency, and commodity hedging.

If you are interested in a particular industry—such as health care, transportation, or media/telecommmunications—then you should target your résumé for the client management industry groups within the global commercial banking division. If, instead, your interest lies in delivering a particular set of products—such as mergers and acquisitions, capital raising, or derivatives—to a wide swath of clients, then your focus is well placed on the global banking and markets division. And finally, if you wish to develop client and product skills at the consumer level, then you should target either the private banking or consumer banking divisions.

Although it might seem daunting to understand all these business lines before any interviews, you need to be well versed in what that institution offers its clients and where. This will allow you to understand where your interests, education, and experience can best be applied. For example, if your regional expertise lies in the Asia-Pacific region and you have taken several economics courses, you may find that your optimal entry point is global capital markets research in an institution's Hong Kong or Singapore office. Equally, if you speak Portuguese, took a more advanced, finance-related course such as credit risk analysis, and had an internship with a government development institution in Brazil, your best entry may be corporate banking, working out of a regional hub in New York or São Paulo.

For those with a specific interest in investment banking, table 6.1 shows the major business lines typically found in most global firms. Career progression at most investment banking firms will be similar, with entry-level positions being either analyst or associate—and, if successful, eventually leading to a managing director position heading up a business line. In larger firms there will be less interaction between the entry-level positions and senior managers, whereas at a smaller firm, you may have greater opportunity for such exposure, albeit with less market-leading transaction flow. Both, however, offer valid opportunities to start your investment banking career.

Table 6.1 **Investment Banking Business Lines**

Business Line	Debt Capital Markets	Equity Capital Markets	Mergers and Acquisitions
Primary function:	Advise corporates and governments on raising debt finance.	Advise corporates on raising equity finance.	Advise clients on decisions to merge, acquire other businesses, or divest business lines.
Career progression	1. Analyst 2. Associate 3. Vice president 4. Director 5. Managing director	1. Analyst 2. Associate 3. Vice president 4. Director 5. Managing director	1. Analyst 2. Associate 3. Vice president 4. Director 5. Managing director

I. **Analyst**
  a. Research companies, industry sectors, and markets.
  b. Identify industry trends and business opportunities.
  c. Assist marketing activities, such as preparing client pitch books.
  d. Assist in executing mandates.

II. **Associate**
  a. Research companies, industry sectors, and markets.
  b. Identify industry trends and business opportunities.
  c. Analyze clients' business/financial condition.
  d. Work with senior team members to create financial models.
  e. Assisting in the origination of transaction mandates.
  f. Prepare client pitch books.

III. **Vice president**
  a. Provide market intelligence and financial solutions to clients.
  b. Coordinate structuring/execution team on transactions.
  c. Maintain relationships with industry peers.
  d. Prepare and deliver client presentations.
  e. Oversee creation of financial models.
  f. Price, market, and execute transactions.

IV. **Director**
  a. Develop strategic marketing plan for financial products.
  b. Develop and maintain strong client relationships.
  c. Assist in meetings with the firm's most important clients.
  d. Manage an industry or geographic team.

V. **Managing director**
  a. Propose/win mandates from the firm's most important clients.
  b. Create target client list, based on deep industry knowledge.
  c. Provide strategic leadership, training, and guidance to business line.
  d. Develop and maintain senior-level relationships with peer firms.
  e. Approve pricing and structure of client underwriting transactions.
  f. Grow market share of chosen client base's transaction activity.
  g. Review and optimize operations and procedures for business line.
  h. Manage the profit and loss statement of group business line.

Figure 6.2 **Investment Banking Position Functions**

Figure 6.2 sets forth the typical functions of each level in an investment banking career. In a successful investment banking business, every position is contributing to the product that is delivered to the client: sound financial advice and execution. It is vitally important for you to arm yourself with this type of primary research about a firm, because it may open up other avenues for interviews or informational sessions outside the standard campus recruiting process.

I offer a final comment on perseverance, which you will need. For many, the process of finding a place in this industry is not linear. You will face rejection, setbacks, and sharp curves along your path. Expect them. In response, you will need to be resourceful and creative in finding the niche that will be your home during waking hours for a year, a decade, or more. I hope my words in these few pages can guide you in this search and that it proves successful in the end, and thus enables you to find just the right match that allows you to continuously move your career—onward and upward.

CHAPTER 7

International Business

The international business field is constantly changing, adapting to current trends and economic realities, and anticipating new ones. With an understanding of foreign cultures and norms, international economies, and government relations, students of international affairs can find important and meaningful roles in the business world in a number of areas such as emerging markets, market entry strategy, risk analysis, corporate social responsibility, and business advocacy. This chapter opens with an essay discussing trends in business since the last edition of this book was published, and it then breaks the business sector into four general areas: multinational corporations, entrepreneurship, government contracting, and government and lobbying. The value of an international affairs degree in comparison with an MBA is tackled in the essay on multinational corporations, and the government contracting and government relations essays examine the nexus of government and business. Additionally, each essay examines how the skills and knowledge unique to an international affairs professional can be successfully marketed and provide you with a competitive advantage. Although it also lies in the business sphere, consulting is treated separately, in chapter 8.

Private-Sector Changes since 2008

Barrett J. Helmer

For some readers of this book, the 2008–9 economic crash might sound like distant folklore, a convoluted collection of events that only had an impact on older generations and caused a media frenzy. Tales of failed banks, stock market convulsions, high unemployment from the loss of nearly 9 million American jobs, and annual deficits surpassing $1 trillion in the United States seem somewhat unrealistic when contrasted with more recent economic milestones. For example, in 2013 the Standard & Poor's 500 hit an all-time high and more than made up for past years' losses, corporations continue to earn record profits, and companies have stockpiles of cash ready to be spent. What is an ambitious, career-focused student of international affairs to make of this paradoxical setting at the crossroads of global economics and business? In short, even though the private sector has endured a tumultuous ride over the past few years, it remains an opportune and exciting area of employment for an international affairs graduate. However, before we take a longer look at some of the new opportunities that have emerged in the private sector since 2008, it is important to understand what has changed.

The financial services industry landscape, one of the largest and highest-paying sectors before the economic crash, now has fewer players and areas of business. Four obvious but telling examples: Lehman Brothers is gone, and what remained of Bear Stearns was acquired by J. P. Morgan. Bank of America absorbed Merrill Lynch. Wells Fargo acquired Wachovia. The list of fire-sale mergers and buyouts goes on. Jobs were lost as banks consolidated but also as firms got rid of their nonprime mortgage lending and securitization business lines and portfolios. Banks were forced to reevaluate large portions of their business model, and they are now generally more focused on profitability from sustainable business segments, both in the United States and abroad: investment banking, wealth management, project finance, fixed income, currencies, and commodities products.

Though banking had a key role in and certainly was affected by the financial crash, the economic aftermath touched all areas of the private sector. Immediately following the end of the financial crisis and related recession, many companies were forced to downsize and adjust their appetite for risk. The business market itself changed in response to consumer reactions to higher unemployment and less disposable income; spending habits changed, and we saw a shift in values concerning how money should be spent. Especially in industrialized countries such as the United States and throughout Europe, these realities have changed business.

Following the financial crisis, companies of all sizes have (and many still do) embraced the notion of the "new normal," a term coined by Mohamed El-Erian, CEO of the California-based investment house PIMCO. "New normal" views the post-financial-crash as a world defined by slower economic growth, lower investment returns, more government regulation, and increased global risk. Translated to the consumer level, individual investors and markets have relied on short-term signals for investment returns as opposed to making investment decisions based on long-term market fundamentals.

Because so much global uncertainty remains, consumers and corporations are more easily spooked, which equates to more market volatility. In such an environment companies are more likely to take a conservative approach to business and investment, which has led to reduced hiring and the term "jobless recovery." Overall, companies remain focused on doing more with less, keeping the bottom line and profit margins in good shape, stockpiling cash to invest once a more certain outlook is realized, and pursuing new markets for much-needed growth.

Many companies have ample funds to spend and realize that emerging markets are increasingly important sources of revenue and are representative of future markets. For some context, in 2012 the massive consumer goods conglomerate Proctor & Gamble generated 38 percent of its revenues from developing markets, and its product sales in the BRIC (Brazil, Russia, India, and China) markets have grown an average of 20 percent during the past decade and are growing at nearly twice the pace of sales in developed markets. In these emerging markets, new middle classes represent a consumer-focused opportunity for the private sector. These developing-country consumers, now with disposable income, have the spending power to purchase cars, home appliances, and personal technology, not to mention the ability to upgrade what they were able to pursue before their income increased: consumer goods, packaged foods, and personal care products, to name a few.

With many firms shifting attention to these emerging market consumers, the need for business support services represents a potential area of employment. It is at this convergence of international markets and business where an international affairs student is primed to benefit and contribute most; having an in-depth understanding of foreign markets and the effects of political and social developments on business is a valuable perspective that international affairs students can effectively market to business employers.

In addition to taking a closer look at emerging and frontier markets, since 2008 the private sector has also had the chance to reevaluate its value proposition, not just to financial shareholders but also to stakeholders. Stakeholders—employees, consumers, and, more broadly, anyone who has an interest in a firm and its activities—are increasingly incorporated into business models. Entire industries and individual firms have had the opportunity to ask if their business model is bringing social value to the world and to the communities in which they operate. With this long overdue shift in business practice, some notable themes have arisen since 2008. Executing public–private partnerships, focusing on social enterprise, developing bottom-of-the-pyramid strategies, and ensuring ethical supply chains are examples of practices that add to the notion that a company can "do well by doing good." Of course, how far individual companies have embraced effective corporate social responsibility (CSR) initiatives is debatable, but the public discourse, reputational considerations, and financial incentives have been raised for private-sector firms in pursuit of CSR guru John Elkington's "triple bottom line"—people, planet, profit—gains. As the business world has paid attention to and increasingly adopted these business practices, there is niche opportunity for international affairs students to help in areas such as government relations, CSR, and investor relations.

Like the world of international affairs, the private sector operates in a constantly evolving sphere of events, opportunities, and risks. It is because of this reality that business outlooks change and must be constantly monitored for new opportunities. For example, China's robust rise has been recently tempered by slower growth, and it must now try to turn to its domestic market for long-term success and regime stability. With China's appreciating currency and its related impact on the cost of exports, some manufacturing will shift to countries like Mexico that have cheaper currencies. New emerging markets such as Indonesia, Turkey, and Nigeria will be increasingly appealing for their market potential and possible influence. Energy sources such as natural gas that present alternatives to fossil fuels will have far-reaching implications for energy markets and geopolitics. It is these types of developments, among myriad others, that will have far-reaching effects on business, trade, and international affairs.

Despite the unique traits that students of international affairs bring to business, it is up to those same students to make conscious efforts to gain business acumen and fundamental skills before embarking on a job search. These capabilities, among others, include business writing, accounting, marketing, and in general having a solid grasp of how the business world works. You can gain such business knowledge through university courses, private-sector internships, and weekend seminars that boost necessary business acumen while leveraging impressive international relations skills—language, knowledge of foreign markets and cultures, insights on political and economic events—now that there are even more job possibilities available. In many ways, the private sector has indeed changed since 2008, but given the related impact on business and the search for new markets and better operating practices, international affairs students have the opportunity to find a unique and important niche that is both challenging and rewarding.

Careers in Multinational Corporations

Miguel Estien

Miguel Estien has worked for General Electric since 1998 and is currently director of mergers and acquisitions and business development at GE Capital. He holds a master's of science in foreign service (MSFS) from Georgetown University and an MBA from the Kellogg School of Management at Northwestern University. The ideas expressed in this essay are his own and do not represent the views or opinions of any of the institutions with which he has been or is currently affiliated, including General Electric.

The United Nations estimates that the world population will reach 8 billion by 2025—a 14 percent increase from today's 7 billion inhabitants.[1] The lion's share of this growth will come from Asia and Africa, and due to the transparency provided by technology today, society has a clear expectation of acceptable minimum living standards. However, the increasing demand for our natural resources risks pitting nations against each other. To a great extent the path between peace and war will be delineated by the ability of the business community to fulfill the basic human needs of consumers affordably, while being respectful of our shared resources. This goal represents both challenges and opportunities; according to the McKinsey Global Institute annual consumption in emerging markets will reach $30 trillion by 2025—the largest opportunity in the history of capitalism.[2]

This is an exciting time to pursue a career in international business. If, like me, you are mission-driven and want to be part of an organization working on tough issues, it is likely that you will enjoy the career opportunities that multinational companies offer.

My Story

After college I was recruited by General Electric's financial management training program. During my first five years with the firm, I learned the necessary skills to function effectively within a corporate setting while also expanding my global perspective through assignments in Tokyo, Mexico City, and Budapest, as well as several cities in the United States. Working overseas was an eye-opening experience, exposing me to the complexities of doing business in environments where the cultural context and the political, economic, and financial systems were unlike anything I was used to. But instead of being a stranger, I was a player in these foreign markets and, in the process, I developed close personal and professional relationships. Convinced that globalization was an irreversible trend, I decided to pursue graduate studies in international affairs and business.

So yes, I am a business guy—but I also speak the language of international affairs practitioners, which allows me to address common misconceptions about the business world and provide guidance on how others can better position themselves should they choose to pursue opportunities with a multinational corporation.

Creating Value

Let me start by addressing a prevalent misperception of what drives business leaders. In my experience the main motivation of successful leaders in this field is not power or financial remuneration but the opportunity to create value. In this regard value is not only a business concept but also a human expression of what an individual needs, wants, or treasures. The psychologist and philosopher Abraham Maslow organized our human values into a hierarchy of needs. Marketers, on the other hand, describe values as the intrinsic force that explains our needs. Nevertheless, addressing customer needs is necessary but not sufficient if economic value is ignored. Economic value is generated when someone is willing to pay more for a product or service than the costs of creating it. Innovation and productivity are the main drivers for economic value. This is the essence of what motivates business leaders—the creation of value for consumers and investors—not one or the other, but both.

You might wonder then why at times the business community is subject to so much controversy. No simple answer exists. Business leaders are constantly making tough decisions, balancing trade-offs, managing through uncertainty, and having to choose between the least harmful of several bad alternatives. But as you know, business contributions are not only valuable but also indispensable. As Warren Buffet put it, "It is in the self-interest of governments to treat capital providers in a manner that will ensure the continued flow of funds to essential projects. And it is in [the interest of businesses] to conduct operations in a manner that earns the approval of regulators and the people they represent."[3] I suspect that highly regulated sectors offer great opportunities to those with the ability to broker understanding between business and government.

Business and International Affairs

As a student, when I tried to define my professional goals given my interest in international affairs and business, I aimed to achieve clarity in three areas. First, I conducted research on an industry and a region of the world that were relevant to each other. For example, countries in Latin America and the Middle East are endowed with abundant natural resources; and as a result, the mining, oil, and infrastructure sectors are pivotal engines of economic growth. On the other hand, China and India have large populations in need of housing, health care, education, consumer goods, and entertainment.

During my time in graduate school, a friend with an interest in the energy industry conducted most of her research on the Middle East. She launched her career with an energy risk management firm, and though she had a clear command of the business and technological dynamics of the industry, what set her apart was her understanding of the region's culture, history, and political dynamics.

The second principle has to do with understanding the professional role I was inclined to play. Generally, in the ecosystem of an industry you will find *researchers* (aka thought leaders), who provide insights by highlighting macro trends, risks, and opportunities affecting the sector; *consultants*, who after gaining subject matter expertise engage with market players to guide them toward defining or achieving a strategic goal; and finally *core industry players*, who compete to fulfill the demands of the market (more on this group below). Each of these roles demands the mastery of certain professional skills. Researchers must have proficiency in synthesizing information and written communication, and consultants are expected to be creative problem solvers capable of delivering compelling presentations. Sales account executives and operations managers working for a major player in the industry are expected to be good team players capable of balancing competing priorities while adapting to change. Incidentally, all these roles offer different levels of autonomy and enable different types of lifestyles that should also influence your career decisions.

Finally, the third principle I followed to narrow my career options was to gain a clear understanding of how multinationals are organized—a concept that is particularly relevant for those aspiring to join a corporation at the heart of the industry.

The Structure of Multinational Companies

For the most part companies are made up of about six to ten teams—often called functions—but for simplicity I describe them as belonging to three groups:

1. Those functions that examine the market's needs and *determine* how to best fulfill them by creating and delivering an offering—represented by marketing, sales, research and development, and business development;
2. Functions that *operationalize, fulfill,* and *deliver* the creation of the products and services the market demands—for example, service operations, manufacturing, supply chain management, logistics, risk management, and customer services;
3. And finally, functions that *enable* the value creation across the enterprise by providing a support network of resources—for example, information technology, human resources, legal affairs, general administration, and finance.

Each of these functions is led by an executive leader (i.e., chief financial officer), who reports to a chief executive officer (CEO). Business leaders often start as functional managers and develop subject matter expertise in a particular domain before mastering general management. A practical way to understand how a multinational is organized is by identifying the leadership team via the investor relations section of the company's web page or through their financial filings and annual reports (10-K, in the case of public US companies regulated by the Securities and Exchange Commission). Social networking sites such as LinkedIn also offer a great avenue to understand how companies are organized and the skill set possessed by professionals at various seniority levels.

You might have noticed that *strategy* is not on the list of functions I highlighted above. Frequently, business strategy is the outcome of the consensus built across the executive functional heads or is developed directly by a

Notes from the Field

Target Corporation

Jill Johnson, MSFS 2011

When I entered Georgetown's MSFS program in 2009, I was a career volunteer. I had been an AmeriCorps volunteer and had served in the Peace Corps in two different countries. During those experiences, I recognized the tremendous value of governmental and nongovernmental organization work, but I had a dream to work toward international development from within the private sector. I believed the impact and speed of the work would be greater and faster.

During graduate school, I spent time learning about the intersection of development and business: the effects of free trade agreements; extractive industries; the financial sector; and ultimately export-oriented investment. Based on my experiences in developing countries with high unemployment rates and relatively informal economies, I chose to focus my career search on the sourcing and procurement divisions of large, multinational corporations. I was seeking out the international development opportunities in export-oriented investments.

I landed a job at the Target Corporation in sourcing. While the job fit my criteria from my career search, I found myself ordering little girls' headbands from our manufacturers overseas. I tried to focus on the distant connection between my orders, employment opportunities, and international development with little success.

(*Continued on page 177*)

strong, visionary CEO. Other senior professionals may also contribute to the strategy-making process, but the most effective path toward playing a valuable role in this process is to build expertise in one of the firm's core functions.

MBA versus International Affairs Degree

I am often asked about the merits of an MBA degree versus a master's in international affairs when pursuing a business career with a multinational firm. An MBA is not an absolute requirement to have a successful business career; in fact, according to *US News & World Report*, 60 percent of the CEOs of *Fortune* 500s do not hold an MBA degree.[4] MBA students are trained in marketing and finance, versus geopolitical risk in the Middle East. After two years of MBA training, students have incorporated business terms into their vocabulary and will likely prioritize reading *Bloomberg Businessweek* over *The Economist*. These all prepare the future apprentice to have an informed

By engaging in strategic internal networking and leveraging knowledge acquired at MSFS, I was able to land a global corporate social responsibility (CSR) position within nine months of starting at Target. I am on a team of two tasked with creating and implementing Target's international sustainability efforts. I work with a broad coalition of brands and retailers to create more sustainable working conditions and reduce environmental impacts in manufacturing facilities globally. Based on our team's efforts, Target has assumed a prominent position in the industrywide effort.

While in school, I continually heard that most CSR jobs are filled by internal candidates. I was frustrated with this notion because I thought that external candidates trained specifically in this domain would add unique value to a corporation. However, my time spent in my first role getting product through the supply chain to stores affords a level of business expertise where I can influence processes and decision makers at a deeper level. While this initial position was not what I had hoped for, it afforded me that elusive foot in the door you need to do CSR work.

I am not an expert in environmental science, nor may I ever be. My position today is replete with ambiguity. But my time at MSFS taught me to be comfortable with having a foundation of knowledge that can be leveraged for many different areas. MSFS introduced me to the core business and development aspects of this position—and Target has filled in the gaps.

I have learned that effecting change does take time, no matter the sector from which you approach it. It can be uncomfortable altering the status quo and influencing without authority. However, with our expansive global supply chain, the impact really can be great.

conversation about the technicalities of running a business, whereas the student of international affairs is likely to be more inclined to articulate the macro trends that will affect the business sector. Though following different approaches, both candidates are, on face value, equally attractive. Confronted with this dichotomy, the hiring manager will look for the *passion*, *potential*, and *commitment* to their line of business exhibited by the candidate through his or her demonstrated understanding of the business, research, and internships completed, along with the professional relationships cultivated. Nothing replaces *passion*.

Jobs for International Affairs Professionals

I close by sharing a few careers where I have seen a high concentration of international affairs professionals in multinational firms. Corporations today have *international business and government relations* teams whose role it is to help the company interface with the governments of the countries where they operate, in terms of either communications, managing regulations, or actually doing business with or through the government. In this environment international affairs and government expertise is extremely valuable, especially when mixed with a command of the local language and knowledge of the country's political history. A company will often bet on an external professional in this area before training an insider. These teams are often aligned with the legal, marketing, or sales functions.

In infrastructure development one of today's most exciting trends is *public–private partnerships*, whereby a government grants a company access to a privileged market in exchange for a commitment to invest and manage the development of roads, schools, airports, ports, power, and infrastructure, to name a few areas. These arrangements tend to be financially complex, but even the operational aspects of managing the relations provide exciting opportunities—particularly in the areas of sales, marketing, and business development.

The area of *corporate social responsibility* has gained great relevance during the past three decades. Professionals in this field often interact with the legal, communications, and risk management functions to set corporate policies, programs, and practices that shape how the company goes about doing business and interacting with the public. If you enjoy public policy, crisis management, and communications, this field could offer a great deal of satisfaction.

Globalization and technology have enabled companies to identify and procure resources, products, and services around the globe at the most competitive prices, and *supply chain management*, *logistics*, and *sourcing* professionals are pivotal to this goal. Fulfilling technical product specification while negotiating the best price is a big element of sourcing roles; but lately, the most challenging aspect of sourcing arrangements has been understanding the reputational, regulatory, and security risks to which companies become vulnerable when forming partnerships with players overseas. Offshoring, outsourcing, and strategic sourcing have become core capabilities of global businesses, whereby international affairs professionals bring enormous value by, for instance, examining labor standards, assessing suppliers' environmental practices, or analyzing trade tariffs.

Beyond identifying and recruiting talent, many of the day-to-day responsibilities of *human resources* professionals center on keeping employees engaged and creating a culture in which everyone feels equally accepted, respected, and motivated to perform at the highest level. Because multinational corporations employ talent from all over the world, their human resources professionals are required to comprehend global dynamics and trends while understanding the values that cut across geographic and cultural boundaries— a clear linkage with the skills of international affairs professionals.

I hope some of these ideas become helpful as you consider careers in a multinational corporation. You should define your own path with the knowledge that sometimes the road less traveled ends up being the most exciting one. I subject my career decisions to a simple truism: It is less about the destination and more about the journey. Enjoy it!

Entrepreneurship

Sloan Mann

Sloan Mann is the cofounder and managing director of Development Transformations (DT), a small business that focuses on improving the effectiveness of stability and development programming in countries in the midst of—or emerging from—conflict or political transition. Before founding DT, he held a diverse array of jobs in the military, private, and public sectors. He has worked for the US Agency for International Development for extended durations in Iraq, Sudan, and Afghanistan. He has served as a program officer and researcher at the US Institute of Peace and on a large-scale security-sector reform project with the Department of Justice. While in the military, he served as a US Army infantry officer and was a member of peacekeeping deployments to Bosnia-Herzegovina (SFOR) and Kosovo (KFOR). He received a bachelor's in international politics from West Point and an MSFS from Georgetown University.

The smell of raw sewage filled my nostrils and dust coated my face as I walked the streets of Giliani, Kosovo, in 2000. I was carrying a weapon and wearing body armor and a kevlar helmet. I probably looked frightening and surreal to the Kosovars walking the streets. As a US Army officer deployed to Kosovo as part of KFOR, I was on my way to a United Nations coordination meeting with international and nongovernmental organizations (NGOs). I was sweaty and dirty from my walk, but it was the civilians, wearing a mishmash of field clothes and semipresentable business attire, who seemed haggard and drained. Later, I learned of the long hours they put in trying to stand up the Government of Kosovo, respond to humanitarian crises, and work on myriad development programs to improve the lives of Kosovars. I was intrigued.

During my brief seven months in Kosovo, I befriended as many international aid workers as I could in an effort to learn where they went to school, the organizations for which they work, and the types of positions they hold. I was astounded—I had no idea there was an entire world of international development specialists who travel from crisis to crisis. Carrying a gun and wearing a uniform no longer interested me; I wanted to work with local citizens directly, help them if I could, and work on intellectually challenging programs in conflict and postconflict environments. Since a young age I knew I had an interest in working abroad and helping people improve their lives. But it was not until my experiences in Bosnia, Herzegovina (my first deployment), and Kosovo that I realized I wanted to turn my passion for working and connecting with people of all cultures into a career.

After five years in the army, I left to attend Georgetown's MSFS program with a concentration in international conflict management. My first post-army job was as a research assistant at the US Institute of Peace (USIP). Going from an US Army captain to a research assistant was quite a shock, but it immersed me in my chosen field, ideally placed me to continue my steep learning curve, and helped me make critical contacts. While at USIP, I was able to interact with different government agencies, meet academics and practitioners, and learn the importance of field experience. In early 2003, just as the United States was gearing up to invade Iraq, I caught a break. The US Agency for International Development (USAID) was putting together a team focused on human rights, and I was lucky enough to get a slot. They needed someone with military field experience to help translate unfamiliar human rights concepts for the military. My time in Iraq with this human rights team was the most meaningful and professionally gratifying job I have ever held.

Since 2003 I have worked on humanitarian emergencies and in conflict and postconflict environments around the world. It has been professionally challenging and fulfilling work, but it has also left me slightly frustrated. I have found US government agencies involved in international assistance to move at a glacial pace when it comes to (1) reforming the way money is appropriated; (2) training practitioners; (3) measuring programmatic impact; (4) learning from successful and failed programs; and (5) adapting methodologies to the complex and ever-evolving nature of overseas environments. I have also witnessed resistance among implementing partners—both for-profit and NGOs—to changing their programmatic approaches or to trying innovative activities. Perhaps organizations get comfortable with applying similar solutions over and over, but I also believe there is reluctance to upset donors (and potentially lose funding). I began to recognize that there was a lot of room for improvement in the way that the US government designs and implements development programs.

The tipping point came while I was in Afghanistan serving as the USAID development adviser to the US Special Forces from 2007 to 2008. Both military and civilian practitioners working on the ground were not being adequately trained or prepared to thrive in security-challenged environments. Moreover, USAID's programs, which had been designed as traditional needs-based development efforts, lacked stabilization components and the ability to adapt to the fluid nature of the highly unstable environments where we were working. After almost a decade of working in the field of conflict and transition, I had found a niche.

From an Idea to a Business

I had actually thought about starting a business for years. I wanted to wait until I had significant field experience and an ability to add value as an experienced practitioner. I also wanted a business partner with a complementary skill set who shared my entrepreneurial spirit and whom I could trust implicitly. One of my MSFS classmates, Timothy Fairbank, fit the bill, and we had been discussing starting a business for years. Being exposed to the wide variety of classes and subjects in the MSFS program introduced us to new ideas and provided fodder for thought. One of the many benefits of having a relatively small class size (there were eighty-four people in my graduating class) was the ability to get to know classmates on more than just a superficial level. I took advantage of this and developed strong and lasting relationships. It was during my time at MSFS that Tim and I first discussed the possibility of starting a business down the road.

Fast-forward four years after graduation, and Tim and I were ready to venture out on our own. Four key indicators signaled that the time was right:

1. identification of a niche where we had direct experience and substantive knowledge,
2. identification of a potential first contract (US Special Operations Forces were interested in training),
3. financial resources (savings from two years in Afghanistan), and
4. a partner 100 percent committed and willing to share in the risk.

Although we skipped the important step of conducting extensive market research, we knew there were no other companies specializing in training practitioners and improving stability and development programming in countries in the midst of—or emerging from—conflict or political transition. We felt like the timing was right for a new business. Although we envisioned our company focusing on conflict and political transitions globally, we knew that given the sizes of USAID's and the Department of Defense's (DOD's) budgets in Afghanistan, there were opportunities to start there. Finally, we both had substantial networks of people we could call upon for guidance, strategic advice, and potentially consulting services if we secured our first contract (the MSFS mantra of "Network, network, network!" is indeed useful advice).

We planned to give the business 100 percent effort for one year. If it did not work out, we thought, what would be the worst thing that could happen? Our pride would be damaged and we would lose some money—not the most important things, considering the opportunity in front of us to make a real impact both with the US government and in countries undergoing violent conflict or transition. In retrospect it was risky to leave the relative security of a government job at USAID, but I felt it was a calculated risk and the benefits far outweighed the disadvantages. Sometimes, it takes a bit of risk to have an impact, effect change, or contribute in a meaningful way.

Recognizing the need for better-trained practitioners and more effective programs during critical transition periods, Tim and I founded Development Transformations (DT) in the fall of 2008 to fill this niche. We began by sharing our own lessons learned from operating in these environments and then sought to bring together other high-caliber practitioners in an effort to add value to other organizations through training, analytical services, and program design, implementation, and evaluation. DT primarily focuses on countries in the midst of—or emerging from—conflict or political transition and works on civil society development, democracy, transitional governance, and stabilization programs. Our primary clients are USAID and the State and Defense departments. We work as subcontractors and hold prime contracts for work both domestically and abroad. In 2013 we proudly opened our first international office.

Growing the Business

The responsibility for growing a small company is challenging. Cash flow problems were our biggest headache during the early days. In some cases our invoices were not paid for six months, creating significant difficulties making payroll. We were able to secure funding from outside investors; otherwise, I am not sure how we would have made it. We also took a conservative approach to hiring new staff. Preferring to have contracts won before adding new staff, we often had to do much of the administration and project preparation ourselves.

One major factor that helped us grow was focusing our business services on a niche in high demand—stabilization and transition programming. Larger companies looking for small business subcontractors viewed us as added value. Plus, we invested resources in professional development programs for our network of consultants in an effort to keep them current on academic papers in the field, analytical methodologies, and best practices for programming technical approaches. This investment contributed to our reputation as having high-caliber staff members who provided effective and relevant training and technical services.

In this regard, here are some tips for scaling up a business:

1. *Treat staff (employees, consultants, interns, et al.) as you would want to be treated.* Since our first day in business, we have tried to go above and beyond for our staff members by getting to know them personally, making them feel like a valuable part of the team, being flexible with scheduling (e.g., allowing them to work from home), and paying them in a timely manner. Treating people with respect

and going that extra mile engenders loyalty. This is especially true when employing consultants who have options to work for different companies. Time and time again, we have found that consultants give priority to working for our company. This principle has been the most important element in the successful growth of our business.

2. *Mediocre is not good enough. Demand excellence.* For me the quality of my work, and by extension of my company, is a personal matter. I have delivered countless training sessions, written dozens of papers and proposals, and worked as a member of numerous teams. Every time, I want the results to be superb. When they are not, I take it personally and take corrective steps to improve the next iteration. I think most people are drawn to working with people and companies involved with stimulating, challenging, and high-quality work. Placing an emphasis on achieving excellence rubs off on colleagues and employees; ultimately, it will enhance the reputation of the company and increase the chances for growth.

3. *Be transparent.* Withholding information from a team, making unilateral decisions with little to no input from others, and operating in secrecy in general are not healthy for organizations. Transparency and inclusive decision-making processes help staff members identify with the business and feel like an integral part of the team. A lack of transparency can lead to staff frustration and poor morale—both recipes for retention problems. In a small business, one the keys to growing is retaining a high-quality staff.

4. *Invest in staff.* Surround yourself with intelligent and highly capable staff members. This is so critically important that in some cases I would even recommend paying them whatever it takes to get them on board. In the long run this will improve the quality of services your company provides, enhance your reputation, and contribute to growth. It is also important to intellectually challenge staff through professional development opportunities like third-party training sessions, seminars, staff retreats, and the like. Giving staff members new opportunities helps them grow with the company and creates a stimulating institutional culture. Companies that excel at this not only grow but are also enjoyable places to work.

5. *Access to financial resources.* Banks are not always easy to work with, especially for small companies. Before providing a line of credit, they like companies to have contracts or subcontracts in hand with specific dollar amounts. This can be challenging for small companies doing ad hoc work with different clients. There are many financing options, including angel investors, bank loans, financing partners, and the like. Whatever the decision, securing adequate financial resources is critical to growing a business.

Notes from the Field

CrowdHall

Jordan Menzel, MSFS 2012

I remember exactly when it happened. I was working out of the small, sign-out conference room at my public library while on a call with the Office of Legislative and Public Affairs at the US Agency for International Development, which had chosen to use an early version of CrowdHall's online town hall moderating tools for a large global forum on development and we were discussing a few final details for the upcoming event. After concluding our call, they asked if they could speak to the person in the company that handled additional business development. I paused for a moment, looked at my partner and co-founder, glanced at the lady stacking books outside and replied, "As a matter of fact, that would be me!" What she didn't know is that between my partner and me, we were everything: human resources, accounting, fund-raising, legal, sales, product development, team management, interns—you name it. It was in that moment that I realized this was no longer a side project: She thought CrowdHall was a company, and that meant it was time we started acting like one.

Entrepreneurship, like many things in life, is a combination of luck, great timing, good partners, a lot of passion, really long hours, and above all else, an impossible-to-plan trajectory. If you had told me a few years ago I would be running a social media technology start-up that spans politics, entertainment, and large consumer brands, I would have thought you were crazy. With a background in state politics and rural community develop-

(Continued on page 185)

Advice for Budding Entrepreneurs

Find something you are passionate about. It is much more enjoyable to spend long hours starting a company when you enjoy the work. Plus, there will be setbacks along the way that can be demoralizing. Having a strong belief in the services or products you provide will help keep you focused during times of adversity.

Having an MBA is not necessary to starting a successful business. I think this is especially true for people with technical skills who want to start a business within their area of expertise (like we did). Having an MBA certainly would not hurt, especially when it comes to marketing, finding investors and raising money, and developing an efficient company infrastructure. There are numerous specialty companies and individuals that can help with human

ment, along with a few years working and volunteering abroad, I enrolled in Georgetown's MSFS program intent on furthering my career in international development. I gained experience as a researcher at the US Institute of Peace, doing partnership building at the United Nations Environment Program, and finally as a teaching assistant to former secretary of state Madeleine Albright. Throughout all of it, I was constantly tossing around a number of ideas and decided it was time to sample one out. I fleshed out an idea around open government with a friend of mine, snuck into an MBA module on business planning, won a few business competitions, and the rest has been a whirlwind year of excitement, exhaustion, success, and failure.

Someone once told me they were happy to see our venture gaining momentum despite having a degree in foreign affairs and no previous background in business or entrepreneurship. The fact is, it is thanks to the cross-disciplinary nature of foreign affairs, the broad spectrum of ideas exchanged, and the diverse nature of classmates at MSFS that helped shape my perspective and inform my approach to solve the problems we aim to address. Two years ago it was an idea in a notebook, and today we are a fully funded team of eight. If my experience conveys anything, it's that at no other point in history has it been easier to identify a pressing problem, compile a passionate team, and attract the necessary resources to test out an idea, regardless of your background. Trust me, if I can do it, anyone can do it. Here are a few observations picked up along the way: You need to accept you will likely fail, but be convinced that you will not. Overpromise *and* overdeliver every chance you get. Learn to create and maintain momentum out of absolutely nothing. Surround yourself with smarter, faster, more creative people than yourself. Finally, get started now. In order to succeed you need to learn, and in order to learn, you need to fail, and great failure takes a lot of time. Have fun!

resources, contracting, insurance, taxes, payroll, accounting, and so on. The challenge is staying organized and finding individuals and companies you can trust.

Find a business partner. Having a business partner who can share the burden of responsibility and risk has worked well for me. Personalities must be a good fit, however, and above all else, you must be able to trust your partner implicitly.

Start small, do something really well, and build from there. When you exceed expectations on your work, word gets around and new work will find you. Our first company contract was designing and delivering a five-day advanced interagency skills training course for the US Special Operation Forces. We put our heart and soul into preparations, used our network of contacts to seek advice and participation, and delivered an informative and professional course. We exceeded expectations; word got around, and we began delivering the same training course to different units. Soon we were being asked to provide other types of related support, and we were able to begin working with USAID and other civilian organizations. Whenever we gain new business or work on behalf of a new client, we adhere to the same formula that has made us successful—a focus on providing exceptional services.

Find mentors. My dad is a business owner, and although it is a different industry, his mentorship and advice, especially related to finances, have been invaluable. We also have a few leading thinkers and superb writers providing us with strategic advice and reviewing the substantive papers and proposals we develop. This type of support is critical to professionalizing website content, polishing important proposals, and for getting trusted opinions on whether or not to pursue different business opportunities.

Timing is everything. My advice for budding entrepreneurs is start a business when you have a well-developed idea, time to commit to it, and the resources lined up to make it through the first year of operations. Whether these pieces come together after school or later in life, they are critical to overcoming the inevitable obstacles that test your will and resolve as business owners. As Howard Thurman said, "Don't ask yourself what the world needs. Ask yourself what makes you come alive and then go do that. Because, what the world needs is people who have come alive."

Careers in Contracting

Rich Millies

Rich Millies, who has served for most of his career at DOD, was the deputy of the Defense Security Cooperation Agency and the US Air Force's director of policy for international affairs. He has also held corporate vice president positions in international business development and international government relations at BAE Systems, Inc. He received a bachelor's degree in political science and government from Fordham University, an MSFS from Georgetown University, and an MBA from Southern Illinois University. He is a graduate of the in-residence executive development program in national security of the John F. Kennedy School of Government at Harvard University. He is now a part-time consultant.

National and international security affairs had been a long-standing interest of mine, and an educational focus during my undergraduate years. Graduate business studies while in the US Air Force subsequently exposed me to different private-sector disciplines and ways of thinking. However, it was later, when I was in Georgetown's MSFS program, that these things seemed to come together in the international business diplomacy course. Little did I realize at the time that the themes of international business diplomacy would engage me for decades. Specifically, most of my career in government and later in the private sector has been associated with issues involving the legal transfer of military equipment, technology, and information to foreign nations. I have therefore engaged in matters relating to international security, foreign policy, defense technology transfer, political-military affairs, congressional politics, and the relationships between US and foreign governmental national security organizations and the private-sector industries that support them.

Cooperation between the Government and the Private Sector

In so many areas, government and business influence one another. In the narrow sense this may take the form of government regulation of an industry, but in the best examples there is cooperation. This government–business cooperation is particularly evident in the national and international security area, in which DOD and the intelligence organizations are the major US government players, but with the Department of Homeland Security and the State Department also using industry to further national security goals. This government–business partnership traditionally involved mostly defense hardware exports (aircraft, ships, armored vehicles, etc.) from companies—contractors as they are commonly known—like Lockheed Martin, Boeing, and Northrop Grumman because private industry has the expertise to perform the research and development, design, program management, and production of items that both the United States and its international friends and allies need to establish and maintain robust defense capabilities. A newer addition to the mix, which is less visible but also important, comes in the

The Role of Government Contractors

Contractors that provide services to the US government often are criticized for performing duties that many think should be done by government workers. Derisively referred to as beltway bandits, these companies have come under criticism in the past, sometimes accused of charging the government large fees for questionable work. While there may be some instances of abuse, overall, services provided to the government fulfill a legitimate need. Contractors can fill short-term staffing gaps because it is often possible to hire and terminate their employment more quickly than that of government employees. Contractors can provide expertise not found within an agency and free up government employees to focus on core government responsibilities. Finally, contractors may actually cost less, because the agency does not have to pay benefits such as health care and retirement.

form of the softer services that private-sector companies like SAIC, Booz Allen Hamilton, and DynCorp bring to government, such as operational support, training, intelligence analysis, cultural awareness analysis and advice, and political-military analysis.

The line between the public and private sectors has become a hotly debated one, particularly since the terrorist attacks against the United States on September 11, 2001. Contractors have filled many nontraditional roles, blurring the distinction between purely governmental responsibilities and private-sector activities. Several times in my DOD career, I was asked to identify core government positions and activities, generally as a precursor for outsourcing DOD's positions to the private sector. The final decision on what is most properly a governmental activity is often in the eye of the beholder, and different administrations have different views. However, wherever that line is drawn, contractors will always play a large role supporting US national security and US government national security organizations.

The Defense and Security Sectors Are Global

Defense and related industries in intelligence and security are truly global enterprises, with companies that maintain offices around the world. The internet and other global communications have drawn business units closer together and have helped increase the pace and intensity of defense industry activities. Conference calls and webinars are the common venue for meetings, but all this instant connectivity also brings its own challenges. Sometimes the biggest challenge is choosing a time when no one must be awakened in the middle of the night to participate in a worldwide conference call.

In the defense and security areas, exports are still the most common type of international transfer. However, as a condition of purchase, recipient countries often demand offsets and technology where industry plays the major role. Foreign industries may also be part of a global supply chain for US defense and security companies. Defense companies have sometimes found that establishing subsidiaries in countries with active markets is a more effective way to address a country's needs and its demands for technology transfer. These subsidiaries generally behave and perform like a host country company.

A Nexus of Government and Industry

As I neared the conclusion of the Georgetown MSFS program, I was ambivalent about the private versus public sectors. My interest in international security affairs focused my search on DOD and the defense industry. However, the economy was in a slowdown at that time. I had offers from both private industry and DOD, but neither was related to foreign affairs, being instead based on my previous air force experience. I accepted the DOD job and learned two lessons. First, having a job that is not what you wanted is better than having no job in a mediocre economy. Second, past experiences, knowledge, and skills can be a discriminator in a job search.

Within a year of starting that job, I had moved to the Drug Enforcement Administration to serve as a foreign area intelligence analyst and then later returned to DOD to become an international technology transfer and foreign disclosure officer. It was in this position that I was able to view the government–industry partnership first hand. Because industry was the supplier of the many defense items and technologies that were transferred to other countries, I worked very closely with numerous private-sector companies. As I advanced through several positions over the next fifteen years, I assessed and authorized technology transfers from the United States to foreign countries. These transfers were generally through defense exports, license production, international research and development, or combined military operations with other countries. It was a unique opportunity to see what industry did, how industry operated, and where industry "internationalists" resided. More important for me and my career trajectory, these insights provided me with a solid, informed foundation for my departure from government to the private sector.

I learned several things very quickly that served me well in both government and the defense industry. First, the United States provides an enormous amount of defense- and security-related technologies to its international friends and allies. Therefore, the decisions regarding the types, sophistication, and quantity of these technologies have a significant impact on both international security and the companies that supply the technology. Second, these decisions occur at the intersection of policy and technology. The challenge is that policy wonks generally do not understand the significance of technology, and technologists do not understand international security policy and politics. Getting the right balance between the political and technology imperatives is difficult. Third, the ability to navigate the technological and political realms is a learned and valued skill. This ability was thus a discriminator as I moved up the ranks in DOD and a skill that was appreciated as I moved to industry.

Careers in Defense, Intelligence, Security, and Related Industries

Internationalists in the defense industry tend to fall into two general areas. First are those associated with the sale of hardware—equipment, weapons, technologies—to foreign governments. They include those doing business development, marketing, and sales; strategy; and government relations (the "Washington Office"); and offsets. Offset agreements are commitments from exporting companies to buy from, or provide additional services to, the purchasing government or its industries. By agreeing to buy components, transfer technology, provide training, establish research-and-development programs, and the like, the exporter "offsets" the foreign government purchases of defense equipment. Offsets may be a condition of purchase or an incentive offered by a particular exporter. The US government is not a party to offset agreements. Although, in the US defense industry, many business areas in the hardware realm tend to be domestically and functionally oriented, internationalists can find good fits in *international business development, marketing*, and *sales* that deal with the international customer. As such, skills in area studies and language are valuable assets. Extroverts are at an advantage because there are long and intense exchanges with the customer. A technical degree or background (military operations, requirements, acquisition) or a language skill, especially in a critical language (e.g., Arabic), can place you in demand and differentiate you from others. Internationalists with economic or other analytical skills can find a home in the strategy or long-range planning departments of defense and security contractors. As you might guess, the work is off the front lines and is more academically oriented. Internationalists in a company's government relations department will be dealing with members of both the legislative and executive branches. Those internationalists in government relations should have a practical political sense and be able to identify and promote international issues affecting the company. Most important, they must be persuasive, quick on their feet, and able to communicate the essence of an issue in simple terms.

The second area where the private sector supports national security organizations is in providing one of the softer services, which is essentially expertise, to US government departments or agencies (e.g., DOD, including each of the military departments), the intelligence agencies, and the Department of State and Department of Homeland Security. Private-sector contractors work in a variety of areas that could be attractive to those with an international interest, such as *foreign military sales country desk officer, intelligence analyst, technology transfer analyst, foreign affairs officer, counterterrorism analyst*, and *humanitarian affairs*. These contractors often work side by side with US government employees, performing like their government counterparts, but often wearing a different-colored badge and receiving their paycheck and benefits from their private-sector employer. Their reach extends beyond the Washington area. For example, the military combatant commands (based in the United States and overseas) for each geographic area of the world employ contractors providing some of these services.

The Future of Global Defense and Security Contractors

Can internationalists count on a future with internationally focused defense and security contractors? Yes, the demand for defense and security products is enormous, but there are some caveats. First, the huge post-9/11 growth in the US defense and security sector will face some contraction as the defense sector returns to peacetime norms. This has happened before—after World War II, the Korean and Vietnam conflicts, and the Cold War. However, the contraction will create winners as well as losers. Companies that are agile and provide products in high-demand areas will thrive; those that do not will disappear. High-demand products will be those based on information: intelligence, surveillance, reconnaissance, command and control, information fusion, target identification, cyberwarfare, and so on. Second, exports are growing in importance relative to total defense sales due to the anticipated contraction of US government defense purchases. This should increase the demand for internationalists with special skills such as languages, foreign area knowledge, and a technical or military background. Third, opportunities for internationalists may be even better in the adjacent security market. In this regard, a recent report on the global homeland security market estimates the 2012–22 market at $2.6 trillion, with the Asia-Pacific region leading world demand. Foreign homeland security equipment requirements are driven by terrorism, illegal border infiltration, piracy, drug trafficking, cybersecurity/espionage, and critical infrastructure security.[5] As such, those seeking employment opportunities should look beyond those supporting just the US government, as foreign governments look for the best solutions from contractors around the world to address their security requirements.

Career Planning

Purposefully, I chose to remain in internationalist-related positions the greater part of my career, even when it meant, at one point, turning down a promotion in an unrelated area. I moved into DOD's Senior Executive Service in an internationally focused position and ultimately found my dream job as the senior DOD civilian responsible for foreign military sales (similar to a chief operating officer in industry). This position involved considerable contact with senior foreign government officials procuring US defense equipment—ambassadors, Middle Eastern royalty, ministers of defense, military chiefs of staff, and defense attachés, and entailed management of an activity that operated like a business—dependent on sales revenues without government funding. All this was excellent preparation for industry. I joined a major defense company, first in international business development and then as the lead for international government relations, which brought me full circle from that international business diplomacy course at Georgetown. Looking back on my career, it was easy to identify key decision points, experiences, and lessons. Here are some thoughts that I hope might be useful as you think about your career:

Notes from the Field

CENTRA Technology, Inc.
Mathew Cahill, MSFS 2009

Working as a contractor for the federal government was completely new to me as I began my current job following graduate school at Georgetown's School of Foreign Service. As is often the case with new jobs, I was forced to learn the lingo, especially acronyms for government positions and offices. At first I thought I needed to be fully "fluent" in these acronyms, yet I soon realized that it is not necessary to memorize acronyms, as they become part of your knowledge base through continued exposure and use.

Working offsite with federal government clients can be rewarding as it can be challenging. The clients I work with are incredibly intelligent people, but they operate in an environment at times beset with bureaucracy. I do not use this term in a derogatory way, just as a matter of fact. As someone who works with government clients, I must account for some of these bureaucratic hurdles and speed bumps in planning out my workflow.

At my job I tend to shift projects every six months or so. I have worked on projects that span the intellectual spectrum—economics, humanitarian issues, finance, and security issues, among others. Graduate school prepared me well to do this. One must not be an expert in one particular field, but be able to interact with those who are, not always an easy task. One can always read up on a particular issue, but I believe graduate school provided me something more: the ability to inform myself quickly about an issue, know which questions to ask, and write concisely.

- *A plan?* Having a plan is always better than not having one, but be prepared to deviate from it. Things happen.
- *People read your résumé.* A government senior executive and friend used his stock résumé to apply for a specific position, but the résumé focused on different skills and background than what was required for the job. He should have known better! Similarly, résumés that profess a desire for a "challenging position working with people" tell the reader nothing. Research the company so that you can correlate, both in the résumé and during an interview, what you want to do and how that will provide value to the company.
- *Company size.* Think about the size of the organization where you want to work. Leaders in big business and big government would chafe at admitting how much they have in common; however, big

organizations are big organizations. Big and small ones each have their own advantages, but they are different!

- *Culture.* I once asked an industry friend how things were going following a takeover. As a former navy officer, he said, "It's like the Marines had taken over the Coast Guard." Internationalists are taught to think about foreign cultures, but companies also have their own internal cultures.
- *International.* Where does international work fit in your priorities? Someday you will be offered a position without an international focus and you will need to decide how important international work is to you.
- *Network, network.* A friend referred a young woman to me for a purely informational interview, that is, a practice interview. She was so impressive that I offered her a job nine months later when a position opened up. As a senior private-sector executive, numerous headhunters whom I had never met asked me to identify prospective candidates for job openings. Similarly, counterparts at other companies frequently asked for my assessment of job seekers. There are more behind-the-scenes discussions than you would ever imagine.
- *What do companies look for?* Companies want self-starters, problem solvers, those who can communicate, and adaptable people who work well with others—up, down, and laterally. Probably all those who are ultimately interviewed can do the job, but which person will fit best on the larger team?
- *Create value.* Always know what value you bring to the company, what differentiates you from others, and what special skills you bring to the table—and be honest with yourself. When you no longer can identify your value, either enhance your skill set or start looking for another job before it is too late.

Finally, follow your heart, but always use your head for guidance correction.

Careers in Government Relations

Lisa M. Barry

Lisa M. Barry has had a thirty-five-year career in international government relations, including most recently serving as vice president and general manager of government affairs for Chevron for ten years. Before joining Chevron, she was senior vice president for international public policy in Time Warner Inc.'s Global Policy Group. Earlier, she had a nine-year career at the Boeing Company, where she served as vice president for commercial international operations and international trade policy. She has also held a number of other positions in both the public and private sectors. She served as principal deputy assistant secretary for import administration at the Department of Commerce, and from 1987 to 1989 she served in the private sector as vice president of the Council on Competitiveness. From 1980 to 1986 she worked in the Office of the US Trade Representative. She also served as a legislative/appropriations staff member for then-congressman Silvio O. Conte. She graduated from Georgetown University's MSFS program with distinction and received a bachelor's degree from Bates College.

One of the most fundamental changes in corporate America has been the transformation of government and public affairs activities into core functions of the enterprise. Once viewed by top management as lobbying organizations designed largely to protect a company from adverse legislation and regulation, the Washington office and government and public affairs functions have evolved into strategic assets for the corporation with the potential to dramatically increase shareholder value, along with the company's reputation.

Since graduating from the MSFS program in 1979, my career has been focused on deepening my understanding of, and capabilities in, the field of government affairs and specifically global government affairs. For the last twenty-two years I have served in senior management positions in three very distinct companies—the Boeing Company, America Online (AOL), and Chevron Corporation—where I have had the ability to help shape these companies' government affairs strategic capabilities and functions. Being successful in three different industries, with very different policy agendas and corporate cultures, can be attributed to one fundamental reality: my expertise and skills as a government affairs professional. Interestingly, a successful government affairs professional today is defined not only by the traditional communications, networking, and political acumen skills; he or she now requires a broader set of corporate skills, including strategic thinking and planning, problem solving, crisis management, business acumen, and a global perspective. The MSFS program provides a strong foundation for the development of these skills.

The professionalization of the public and government affairs function opens up enormous possibilities for individuals who enter the field. Although the traditional path for many government affairs professionals, including mine, was to enter a corporation after government or related service (Congress, executive branch, trade association, or NGO) as a mid-career professional, companies such as Chevron are now establishing plans to begin recruiting public and government affairs professionals from graduate programs, much the same way the company recruits engineers, MBA students, scientists, and those with technical professional backgrounds for lifelong careers at Chevron. This is an exciting development for those of us who understand the value of the public and government affairs function and for those institutions that have focused on developing the core skills needed for success. And though the types of skills acquired in international relations degree programs provide a foundation for potential success in corporate jobs in public and government affairs organizations, they may also serve as bridges to other parts of a corporation. Opportunities in strategic planning or global security / risk management functions require a number of skills related to international relations, but traditionally success and promotion into senior-level positions in these areas may require additional training and skills in analytical areas, business, science, or engineering.

The Evolution of the Public and Government Affairs Function

I have had the privilege of working in three major companies and in helping to shape the government affairs function into a strategic asset for those companies. Although individuals in each of the companies had a very real understanding of the value of the government affairs function, in each company there were defining moments when the function's value became broadly recognized and provided the foundation for its true professionalization. The big win provided an opening; it was up to the government and public affairs professionals to leverage the opening and put in place initiatives and programs to nurture the value proposition for senior management and make the functions truly of strategic value to the corporation. In the following paragraphs I discuss three significant corporate initiatives that I managed, which I hope will provide some insights into the types of skills and attributes that are required for a successful corporate professional.

The Boeing Company's Commercial Normalization Initiative: strategic planning / business alignment / flawless execution. The Boeing Company hired me as director of international trade in 1990. This was a new position, and though I had the full support and confidence of my immediate supervisor, it would take several years—and some significant wins—before corporate management understood and welcomed the value of this function. Boeing was America's number one exporter, a fact that was not well known in government and policy circles until we began a sustained campaign, in close collaboration with the communications function, to make Boeing synonymous with international trade. But the issue that would crystallize for the company the value creation proposition of government affairs was China, and specifically Boeing's five-year plan to normalize the United States–China commercial relationship.

The Boeing plan was driven by necessity. China was emerging as a major market for commercial airplane sales, and the Chinese government was increasingly frustrated with the incoming Clinton administration's focus on human rights. China's awarding of a major commercial airplane sale to Boeing's adversary, Airbus Industrie, was a clear indication of its unhappiness with American policy. Boeing's future access to this important market was at risk.

Against this backdrop, the China Commercial Normalization Initiative was born. Boeing's goal was clear: to strengthen the fundamental economic and commercial relationship between the two countries as a foundation for the broader relationship and to prevent the traditional ups and downs where airplane sales could be at risk. In essence, Boeing's objective was to depoliticize the relationship between the two countries and to prevent Boeing's sales from being held hostage to China's concerns with broader US policy agendas.

With the support of Boeing's management, and a commitment of several million dollars to fund the campaign, Boeing launched the effort to normalize the commercial relationship with three clear goals: facilitate China's accession to the World Trade Organization (WTO) on commercially meaningful terms; secure permanent normal trade relations status for China, so that US companies could benefit from China's WTO accession; and lift the remaining sanctions imposed after the Tiananmen Square incident. Boeing engaged the support of a number of major American companies that were similarly interested in normalizing the commercial relationship and over time worked with the broader community to manage what has become a gold standard for corporate campaigns—securing permanent normal trade relations status for China.

During the five-year period when Boeing and the broader business community were working on the normalization initiative, Boeing was able to successfully position itself in the China market. With Boeing's sale of fifty airplanes during the visit of President Jiang Zemin to the United States in 1997, and clear and public indications from China's leaders of their support for Boeing ("if it's not Boeing, I'm not going" was a frequent refrain of the Chinese leadership), it was clear that Boeing had achieved its goal. To this day, Boeing remains a preferred supplier of airplanes to the Chinese market and the example of linking Boeing's commercial agenda to a broader policy goal now serves as the model for other companies.

America Online: global perspective, policy acumen/alignment with business. AOL recruited me in 1999 to help build a global government affairs function for the company. Unlike my work at the Boeing Company, which was focused around Washington initiatives to help Boeing become competitive in international markets, the AOL job required us to understand and shape the policy and regulatory environment in the countries where AOL was establishing a service. This required us to have a very deep understanding of the policy and regulatory environment in each of the countries where we were operating (issues such as intellectual property, data privacy, internet security, and content regulation) and to work with countries to help create a policy and regulatory environment that would enable development of the internet and e-commerce businesses.

I had a small team of subject matter experts on the range of policy/ regulatory issues surrounding the internet development, many of whom had been trained as lawyers in fields such as intellectual property, privacy, and First Amendment issues, and they were frequently called upon by foreign governments to provide testimony to congressional and parliamentary panels, to submit major treatises on how to shape the regulatory environment, and to convene workshops with government officials to discuss the full range of policy issues associated with internet development. AOL was the first foreign online service provider at the time to try to enter the Chinese market. Through a partnership with Legend Computer, AOL hoped to be able to develop a robust internet service in the market. Few industries required the type of policy and business model alignment that is required in developing an international internet service offering. My staff of policy and regulatory experts worked hand in glove with the AOL technical teams to develop an internet service that was attentive to the realities of internet service in China but was also grounded in AOL's fundamental principles of protecting children, data privacy, content access, and internet security.

Chevron's Unocal acquisition: campaign management/corporate alignment. I joined Chevron as the vice president and general manager of government affairs in 2004. Although it was unusual for Chevron to recruit externally for a senior position, management decided that they wanted to pursue a more aggressive external function and leadership profile for the company and I was brought in along with a new general manager of communications. Neither of us had experience working with the energy industry, but between the two of us we had worked at five major corporations—Boeing, AOL/Time Warner, Levi Strauss, IBM, and Oracle—and had developed strong business acumen and problem-solving and crisis management skills. Under the leadership of our manager and with the full support of our then-chairman and CEO, we began to reposition Chevron as the go-to company among policy influentials and external stakeholders with "The New Energy Equation," which entailed the development of the firm's human energy branding and its agenda's new focus on major initiatives in the areas of trade and investment.

The defining moment within Chevron that galvanized top executives' understanding of the value of our function was the Unocal acquisition. The government affairs and communications teams led a six-week campaign designed to showcase the benefits of Chevron's offer to acquire Unocal and to ensure that there was a clear understanding of the policy and regulatory risks inherent in China National Offshore Oil Corporation's offer. The introduction and passage of congressional legislation that mandated a six-month review of the transaction by the US Department of Energy was an important factor as Washington grappled with the idea of the first-ever subsidized financing offer that would compete with a private company offering. There was no doubt in anyone's mind—internal and external—that the public and government affairs activities were a defining factor in the success of this effort.

As in any successful organization, you are only as good as your last victory, and it was critical for Chevron to build on its Unocal success. What it did next was to capitalize on this win and build a broad base of executive support for the government and public affairs organizations through extensive plans and campaigns in order to manage critical issues for the company and develop functional processes that were based upon the same discipline used in its key capital stewardship and business decisions.

During the past five years Chevron has built out its organizational capability within government affairs by establishing formal processes for issues management, running complex issues campaigns, grassroots advocacy, stakeholder engagement, and planning for the transitions associated with major national elections. With the full support of management and the resources to get the job done, we were able to position Chevron in the eyes of the Washington community and our key global partners as a go-to company in Washington's corridors. Along with this has come the true professionalization of the function, with senior management clearly understanding the vital role of government and public affairs—both at home and increasingly in the overseas markets where Chevron operates.

Corporate Careers for International Affairs Professionals

With the growing professionalization of the government and public affairs function, there is a broader and deeper range of opportunities for individuals who want to become professionals in the field. Two of the most fundamental changes are the reality that companies are no longer focusing their hiring just on experienced mid-career professionals with government experience and the fact that there are clear skills being identified within organizations such as Chevron that are helping to guide hiring at multiple levels—entry level, mid-career, and senior level.

Within Chevron's government affairs function, there are several families of jobs, including legislative and regulatory analyst, federal relations representative (i.e., domestic lobbyist), state government affairs representative (lobbyist), international government affairs representative, and manager/analysis in the political programs and political compliance programs.

In the communications department there are positions at multiple levels in the areas of executive communications, critical issues management, external media relations, and internal communications. The senior positions are all filled by communications professionals with deep and broad experience in the field. But like the government affairs function, there are positions at multiple levels, including entry-level positions for recent graduates.

In addition to the government and public affairs function, Chevron also has a policy organization that is staffed with mid- to senior-level individuals who manage social issues for the company (voluntary principles, human rights policy, other transparency initiatives, and relationships with the NGO community), a strategic research function, and a group that manages Chevron's extensive social investment program both at home and abroad.

Apart from the core functions in policy, government, and public affairs (PGPA) at Chevron, the company also has a number of field PGPA professional positions where individuals have the opportunity to work closely with a business unit head to support the full range of PGPA activities associated with a business enterprise and management positions that organize for a business unit president the entire PGPA program for that business unit. These jobs are mainly in the United States but are also increasingly located in Chevron's operations around the world.

Although I outline below the skills that Chevron believes are important for the success of its PGPA professionals, I note that many of the individuals working in Chevron's government affairs function have technical skills along with traditional government affairs skills. In Chevron's Washington, DC office we have several individuals with engineering degrees, advanced science degrees, and law degrees. Even if an individual does not have a technical background or degree, each of us must have the ability to understand complex business issues and be conversant on those issues.

Outside the PGPA function, there are other corporate career paths that might be appropriate for an MSFS graduate, particularly those students who have structured their studies around economics, statistics, and what are referred to as the harder analytical skills. These could include strategic planning or global security functions in a corporation. In addition, there might be opportunities in corporate functions, such as the corporate secretary's office, which manages all the corporate governance functions, or the health, environment, and safety organization. In corporations such as Chevron that are largely driven by technology and engineering, a strong technical background is required for the vast majority of business functions and operations. And as noted above, the ability to deal with complex technology and business issues is fundamental to success in any positions within the company.

The Corporate World: Landing the Job and Keys to Success

A little-known fact is that in many corporations, including Chevron, hiring decisions are made through a very open and transparent selection process. Most of the jobs in Chevron's PGPA function are posted, and many are posted both internally and externally. Typically, a selection team is formed to evaluate a short list of candidates and the individuals are reviewed against criteria established for the position. Many of the positions are listed on Chevron's external website.

Chevron's PGPA function is now evaluating programs that recruit recent graduates and provide a professional career for PGPA professionals. The firm is in the early stages if this effort, but it expects over time that this will be an important route for individuals within this increasingly important function.

When I was first hired by the Boeing Company in 1990, the key factors behind my hiring were my knowledge of the executive branch, including a strong understanding of the interagency process whereby many decisions are made, an extensive network of contacts both within and outside government, effective oral and written communications skills, problem-solving skills, and an ability to deal with complex issues, including technical ones. I also had the ability to step back and think strategically about an issue and to develop an implementation plan.

I learned three very important lessons along the way at Boeing that helped me to sharpen my skills and successfully navigate this company of more than 200,000 employees. The first lesson was how to communicate with senior managers; Boeing is an engineering-driven company, and after months of being discouraged that managers had not read my multipage documents, I turned to succinct PowerPoint presentations! The second lesson was the importance of developing a robust plan; again, this engineering-driven company wanted this function to be managed like its other functions. We developed detailed plans for multiyear initiatives, such as the China Commercial Normalization Initiative, with milestones and ongoing reviews that were critical to keeping senior management engaged in the decision-making process and ensuring continued resources for the initiative. And the third lesson was how to align business challenges with public policy initiatives. Government affairs professionals can guide the business in understanding how government policy and regulatory initiatives can be used effectively to advance business goals. It requires a deep understanding by the government affairs professional of the business and its goals and confidence of the business executives that the government affairs professionals know how to navigate and leverage the inner workings of Washington and other government capitals. At Boeing, few executives initially understood the role of Washington in addressing and managing the Asian financial crisis's impact on Boeing. Again, careful development of a plan and flawless execution created an opportunity for success in helping Boeing manage the risks associated with the crisis. These three important lessons have served me well in subsequent positions.

Over the years, as both an employee and a manager, I have come to better understand what it takes to be successful at a large company. At Chevron we have begun to outline the skills that are necessary to be successful as a successful PGPA professional. These include strong written and oral communication skills, research and analysis capabilities, strategic thinking and planning, problem solving, stakeholder identification and engagement, negotiation and consensus building, business acumen, media acumen, political acumen and fluency, cultural diversity and sensitivity, project management, social impact management, crisis management, people development, and financial resource management.

These skill sets provide a good road map for success at a large company. But there are also other attributes that might not fit as nicely into a skills matrix—ethics and integrity, tenacity, good humor, generosity, tolerance— that will also serve any professional well. I would say that the most important factor behind my success has been that I always have my "A game" on. I come to work every day ready to tackle whatever challenge comes my way with excitement and interest, and it shows both in terms of my ability to lead a team and the results. As I was moving up the ladder, it is what I believe has differentiated me from others with the same or better background and training.

Final Thoughts

I never set out to become a corporate executive at a major company; however, I found that my skill set and capabilities—relationship building, communications, strategic thinking, and complex problem solving—were extremely well suited for this type of work. Equally important, I was passionate about the field of government affairs, and as often happens one becomes successful because he or she loves what they do. When I began my career more than thirty-four years ago after graduating from the MSFS program, there was no set path to become a government affairs professional at a major corporation, and in some ways I am glad of that. But even back then, there was no doubt in my mind that the Georgetown brand and the skills I had learned through the MSFS program had opened doors and provided the foundation for me to achieve success in the many exciting opportunities I have had along the way—which leads to my final thought: Take risks, and understand that every aspect of the journey—good and bad—is as important as where you end up.

Careers in Lobbying and Advocacy

Jonathan Huneke

Jonathan Huneke, a graduate of Georgetown's MSFS program, is vice president for communications and public affairs with the United States Council for International Business, a New York–based business association that represents American businesses at the multilateral level, advocates for open markets, and provides a number of services for companies doing business abroad. He previously served as a program manager in the organization, and he worked for several years as a United States–based representative of the Province of Quebec.

Notes from the Field

The US Chamber of Commerce

John Murphy, MSFS 1992

Unusually, I find myself laboring in the very field I selected as an MSFS graduate student. While at Georgetown, I concentrated in trade policy and Latin American affairs and have been pleased to pursue a career in those fields.

After graduation, I spent a year teaching economics as the first Western lecturer at the National University of Economics of Slovakia in 1993–94, and had the interesting experience of observing the peaceful dissolution of Czechoslovakia first hand. It was an excellent gig: my students were hungry for information given the dire state of Eastern European pedagogy at the time, and I enjoyed the travel.

I later worked at the Center for International Private Enterprise (CIPE) and the International Republican Institute (IRI), two core institutes of the National Endowment for Democracy. My four years or so in the "democracy industry" were very interesting. At CIPE, I worked on our communications products and learned lessons that have stuck with me about crony capitalism, the role of business associations, and free enterprise policies that foster growth. At IRI, I had fascinating experiences such as Mexico's first election of a legislature not dominated by the Partido Revolucionario Institucional (1997) and Venezuela's election of Hugo Chávez.

I took a position at the US Chamber of Commerce in 1999 as director of trade policy for the Americas and later headed our Western Hemisphere department (2001–8). Since that time I have directed international trade and investment policy as vice president for the seventy-strong International Division.

(*Continued on page 203*)

"Lobbying" is often regarded by those outside the Washington Beltway in a disparaging light—the old caricature of Gucci-wearing hotshots nefariously working to warp legislation and public policy for their corporate clients' selfish ends. But advocacy and representation—whether for one's own interests, a client's, or those of the organization for which one works—has been a defining characteristic of American democracy since its inception. The First Amendment guarantees citizens the right to petition their representatives for redress of grievances, and this has always been seen as extending to collective organizations.

It is important to note that the term "lobbying" has a very specific meaning under US federal law and the tax code. The Lobbying Disclosure Act of

I have relished the opportunity to work on trade agreements with about a dozen countries over the past decade, including South Korea, Peru, Australia, and Chile. Business organizations like the Chamber provide indispensable input to the Office of the U.S. Trade Representative on negotiating objectives and how best to frame trade disciplines to open foreign markets. Even more importantly, the Chamber, as the largest lobbying organization in Washington, has played a key role in securing congressional approval of these trade agreements through wide-ranging strategic communications campaigns, grassroots programs, and direct lobbying.

High points include my work on the US–Central America–Dominican Republic Free Trade Agreement, often called CAFTA, which the House of Representatives approved by two votes in July 2005. The good thing about a narrow vote is that it's easy to claim credit. Seriously, this vote arguably saved half a million jobs in the participating countries, so I still take great satisfaction in this legislative victory.

More recently, I had the satisfaction of directing an advocacy campaign for the US–Colombia Trade Promotion Agreement, which involved working behind the scenes at the highest levels of government. At key junctures, I can point to moments when we turned decision-making and averted the debacle of giving one of our key allies in the hemisphere the back of our hand. Instead, booming trade with Colombia since the agreement entered into force in May 2012 is creating tens of thousands of jobs in both countries.

I wanted to become a Foreign Service officer when I studied at Georgetown. In fact, I believe I have had far greater influence over public policy from my post at the chamber than I might have had in many government positions. I still take pride in how my organization operates with great integrity, railing against protectionist measures proposed by governments both foreign and domestic, and upholding the rule of trade law in a global economy that needs openness to thrive.

1995 defines the term as communication to a covered official, made *on behalf of a client*, with regard to federal legislation or rule making. This is certainly a more restrictive definition than most people would ascribe to the term, and in this chapter we look more broadly at careers in both client-based lobbying and related advocacy work.

All types of organizations lobby the government. In the 1830s Alexis de Tocqueville wrote of the American penchant for forming voluntary associations in their professional, social, civic, and political lives. Of course, today such groups are not at all unique to the United States; virtually every imaginable type of organization has some sort of representation in Washington and other major world capitals. These voluntary associations and advocacy groups—representing businesses, environmentalists, retired persons, stamp collectors, you name it—are one of the most important tools for citizens to make their views known to their elected representatives and other policymakers.

Who else lobbies? Individual companies hire both traditional lobbyists and a variety of government relations and public affairs professionals, whose job is to craft and communicate a company's views to those in power. And an array of lobbying firms, public affairs firms, public relations agencies, and law firms actively represent their clients' interests at all levels of government. In addition, though they dare not call it lobbying, government agencies themselves, along with foreign governments, employ numerous professionals who represent their interests, work to secure funding, shape public opinion, and influence the views of legislators and policymakers.

Advocacy work encompasses traditional legislative lobbying of the kind so familiar in Washington or Brussels, as well as soft lobbying—which entails convening working groups, holding conferences, commissioning research, issuing position papers and press releases, and so on. Opportunities abound in policy research organizations, which have proliferated in recent years and represent all facets of the political spectrum.

As regional and global integration has marched forward, international advocacy has grown along with it. At many UN and other multilateral diplomatic conferences and gatherings, one is confronted by an army of quasi-lobbyists and other advocates, all seeking to influence the course of negotiations. Most national advocacy organizations are part of international networks that advocate around the world and at the multilateral level, for example, the International Chamber of Commerce for business and the International Trade Union Confederation for labor. What is more, lobbying firms and the like often represent clients across borders.

There are many opportunities in lobbying and advocacy for those trained in international affairs. The international aspects of law and regulation are viewed as increasingly important, especially for companies that must operate across many borders, and as policymakers increasingly confront global challenges like environmental protection, business regulation, the impact of the internet, and the protection of human rights. The ability to communicate with people from other countries, anticipate their concerns, and represent one's organization internationally is an increasingly valued skill set. Tact and diplomacy are important no matter what the field, but they are downright essential in advocacy work.

Obviously, in traditional lobbying, it is as much about *who* you know as it is about *what* you know. Experience on Capitol Hill is essential for those working the halls of Congress, whereas experience with a federal agency is a big asset when advocating to that agency. There are many former diplomats who seek to influence the State Department and the international work of other federal agencies.

What is a typical career path in lobbying and advocacy? There is not one. Of course, many individuals may drop in or out of power through elected office or political appointments, and they often do advocacy work while on the "outside." In many corporations, government relations professionals may enter from another, operational arm of the company. There are numerous entry-level opportunities on K Street, and many use these as stepping-stones to work on Capitol Hill or in a federal agency.

Opportunities in lobbying and advocacy tend to rise and fall depending on the policy environment. In times of intense legislative action, policy development, or agency expansion (such as the post-9/11 period or following the 2010 adoption of the Obama administration's health care law), activity and hiring tend to spike upward. But even in quieter periods the US government is not going anywhere, and neither is the need for skilled, experienced, and effective advocates to influence legislation and rule making.

Notes

1. United Nations, Department of Economic and Social Affairs, Population Division, *World Population Prospects: The 2010 Revision* (New York: United Nations, 2011), http://esa.un.org/unpd/wpp/Analytical-Figures/htm/fig_1.htm.

2. McKinsey & Company, *Winning the $30 Trillion Decathlon* (New York: McKinsey & Company, 2012).

3. This is from Warren Buffett's 2012 letter to investors.

4. Menachem Wecker, "Where the *Fortune* 500 CEOs Went to School," *US News & World Report*, May 14, 2012, www.usnews.com/education/best-graduate-schools/top-business-schools/articles/2012/05/14/where-the-fortune-500-ceos-went-to-school.

5. "The Global Homeland Security Market 2012–2022," executive summary, ASD Reports, available at www.asdreports.com.

CHAPTER 8

Consulting

G iven the wide variety of jobs in consulting, treating the consulting field as a monolithic entity would be a disservice to the job seeker. Although many consulting firms perform several functions that can confound simple categorization, this book breaks down the world of consulting into the following four types of firms, based not on clients but on the unique functions performed:

- *management and strategy consulting:* classic consulting, focused on helping clients achieve better performance and productivity, and increase business;
- *risk and security consulting:* focused on advising businesses and governments on the political, economic, and social developments that could positively or negatively affect business in a country or region;
- *development consulting:* focused on helping entities execute effective plans and strategies for development initiatives, often bringing business experience and expertise to the development arena; and
- *business consulting:* outsourcing specialists on back office functions (e.g., accounting and taxes) that also includes media and the public, and marketing. This segment of consulting performs functions that are key to business success but that a company may not necessarily have in-house or that entail outside expertise that a company may occasionally need for a specific task or project.

Because some firms provide consulting as well as government contracting services (e.g., hardware and technical, operational, and analytical support), the reader may also want to consider the contracting essay in chapter 7, which is on business.

Careers in Management and Strategy Consulting

Audrey Bracey Deegan

Audrey Bracey Deegan, currently managing director at the strategy and organization advisory firm Hudson Chesapeake Ltd., has held a range of senior leadership positions, both domestically and internationally, at the OMG

*Center, Plan International USA, Deloitte Consulting, J. P. Morgan, McKinsey &
Company, Textron, and the Overseas Private Investment Corporation. An honors
graduate of Princeton University and Georgetown University's Law Center
and Master's of Science in Foreign Service (MSFS) program, she has worked
collaboratively with private-, public-, and social-sector leaders in financial
services, oil and gas, global relief, volunteerism, community engagement, and
international development to chart analytically sound strategies, build essential
capacity, and measure economic and social impact. She is on the MSFS Advisory
Board and the Georgetown University Board of Visitors. She is a board member
of the Washington Area Women's Foundation.*

When Arthur D. Little, Edwin Booz, and James O. McKinsey, some of the
reputed founding fathers of professional management consulting, created
the discipline at the turn of the twentieth century, they could hardly have
suspected the proliferation of firms and specialties that exist in the market today. Management or business management consulting is a growing industry
that has many permutations, and with each variation, the requirements for
pursuing a career in the discipline can change. Because the " it depends" factor is sure to color any essay about getting a job in management consulting,
much of what is included here are generalizations based on my more than
twenty years of experience consulting in firms of different sizes and focus.

In the next few pages, I give you my perspective on

- the range of management consulting types and career paths,
- the process for getting a position,
- the personality attributes that are best suited to consulting,
- what employers are looking for in candidates, and
- what to expect once you start work (general work hours, travel
  requirements, work/life balance).

As with any advice, it is to be taken with a grain of salt. The industry is
changing rapidly, influenced by technology and global trends. That said,
with curious inquiry, reflective self-awareness, and a healthy mix of persistence and luck, you can ride the wave, as I did, to a long, fulfilling career
in consulting.

If you had asked me when I started my career whether consulting would
have been the industry in which I would spend the majority of my working
life, I would probably have responded with a pretty basic question: "What
is consulting?" Defining management consulting can be a somewhat elusive. Because the nature of consulting can change depending on the client
focus, the size of the client, the size of the firm, and the type of issues to be
addressed, coming up with a single definition can be difficult. That said, one
common thread across the different types of firms is that the consultant is a

trusted adviser called in to provide a third eye to the issues at hand, gather data that may be difficult to get, and give those in the trenches the perspective necessary to drive important strategic or operating decisions.

The particular matters on which a consultant advises are one of the factors that account for the variety of consulting firms. The diversity of consulting specialties runs the gamut. On one side are the strategy firms like McKinsey & Company, Bain & Company, and Boston Consulting Group that give their clients big-picture strategic direction. On the other are the more technical firms, like L.E.K. Consulting and Booz Allen Hamilton, that focus on improving operations in a specific area. In between are hundreds of firms that put their own mark on the industry and the value that they bring to their clients. Another growing segment of potential interest to those with international backgrounds are firms like Dalberg, Accenture Development Partners, and FSG that meld a traditional strategy firm with a boutique development contractor. Given this diversity, the corresponding career paths vary depending on the type of consulting firm, its client focus, and its hiring philosophy.

For many strategy firms, candidates need to get on the ladder at the start of their careers. Many hire recent graduates from a core list of the top undergraduate schools and then groom them along the path to partner, often paying for the top performers to attend business school and return to the firm after receiving their MBA to launch their careers. For the more specialized firms, expertise in a given discipline or industry is the value offered to clients, in which case time working in the industry actually gaining hands-on experience is critical. The only way to really know what a firm is looking for and where it recruits is to do your research—check its website, consult your career counselor, and talk with those who have worked for it.

Once you are in the door, many firms have a similar trajectory. Depending on whether you are coming to the firm from undergraduate or graduate school, you will start as an analyst (undergraduate school) or a consultant, sometimes called associate (graduate school). In the most junior role, you are responsible for executing a discrete portion of the project research or analysis. It is here that you learn the basics of consulting, including problem solving, team coordination, and client management. As you progress through your career to senior consultant, you will be responsible for larger portions of the project, eventually leading a stream of work, before being asked to manage other's work as a manager. After building your management skills overseeing one project, in most firms, you will progress to the level of senior manager, sometimes called associate principal. This is normally the step before making partner. As senior manager, you are now responsible for managing multiple or large-scale engagements, as well as building client relationships that result in billings.

Although most strategy firms bring the majority of their talent in at the beginning of their career, the more technically oriented firms may add staff at any point in the career path. As such, the hiring is less through college recruiters than through search firms, which work with the consulting firms to capture high-quality, seasoned talent for projects in growth sectors where the firms are building depth and reputation. This experienced-hire model is much more common with consulting firms that are toward the technical end of the spectrum, because they are looking for proven skills in both designing and implementing solutions, as well as for someone who can speak the same industry language as the client.

As mentioned above, many consulting firms have recruiters who are dedicated to their target colleges and universities. If a firm in which you are interested does not recruit at your campus, consider requesting an interview. For potentially attractive candidates from nontarget schools, some firms will arrange to have them interviewed at a target school or bring them into their offices.

Most firms conduct several rounds of interviews, often mixing behavioral with case interviews. For those who have not spent the past two years being grilled in the case method, the case interview can be pretty daunting. But do not fear. What I have found, after almost twenty years of consulting, is that good old logic works pretty well at breaking a problem apart and driving you to a plausible solution. You may not have all the buzzwords and concepts at your fingertips, but most business solutions are just logic reduced to an equation or framework that makes the complex simpler. The case interview is simply a means of reducing convoluted business and operating situations down to a fairly simple example that tests how you structure your thinking to get to a solution.

Because teamwork is so vital to the consulting process, some firms will use a blitz approach, combining case and behavioral methods in both team and individual contexts. The objective here is to allow them to see your natural leadership ability, that is, how you work with your peers to drive toward a solution in a very short period without going ballistic on your teammates.

The personal attributes that most consulting firms, whether strategic or more technically inclined, seek in a candidate are

- intellectual curiosity—the inclination to keep peeling the onion until you get to the core of the problem;
- an ability to deal with ambiguity—you will get plenty of that regardless of the firm, client, or manager and must know how to make sense of it;
- high energy—this is not a job for those with low stamina whose brain fogs when they get tired;
- teamwork—almost all work and play is done in packs with a clear pack order, for all the talk about "nonhierarchy"; and

- a high level of numeracy—this does not mean you have to be a quant jock, but you do need to have considerable fluency with numbers, the same as you might have with French or Chinese.

To these are added specific technical skills (e.g., information technology, supply chain, shared services, mergers and acquisitions) or industry experience (e.g., financial services, manufacturing, consumer goods), as relevant, in the more technical consulting firms.

What consultants do for clients once they are hired can often vary by client or practice area within firms, across strategy firms with a seemingly similar client base, and at different levels of seniority within a particular firm. The analyses that you might do as a consultant can range from conducting a detailed process review of the underwriting activities of a national insurance company in order to improve loss rates, to developing an integrated global strategy for the newly merged national and international operations of a major nonprofit with the goal of increasing community impact. I have led client engagements that clarified the role of the corporate center in preparation for the merger of two large European universal banks, as well as launched a major cultural transformation, designed to improve the client experience and increase payment receipts, for the field operations of a large federal financial services agency. Although in many instances the projects were short term, between three and six months, in other cases, the engagements were conducted over twelve to eighteen months in locations away from the home office. Hence, the age-old question: What is a consultant's lifestyle like?

Although consulting does frequently require time on the road, the lifestyle can be an exciting one. Perhaps what attracts many to consulting is the rush of being in the intellectual company of some of the best and the brightest minds in the world; of being asked to help with complex business challenges by clients that have graced the front of the *Wall Street Journal* and *Forbes*; or of jetting between London, Paris, Prague, and Zurich in four days for client interviews. A consulting life is indeed fast paced and intense. Hours are often long, with 50- to 60-hour weeks being the norm. Travel is also part of the equation, and in most instances, to unglamorous locations rather than Paris and Hong Kong. Factory visits in the middle of winter in the nether reaches of the heartland, long nights of spreadsheets with numbers that refuse to square up, and cold room service at midnight can be the order of the day for some projects. But even then, the satisfaction of discovering significant levels of savings or productivity gains that allow workers to keep their jobs and small towns to be saved offsets the trials and leaves you clamoring for the next assignment. Such is a consultant's life.

Although this lifestyle is not without costs, for me consulting has had considerable benefits. The skills learned while consulting have influenced both

Notes from the Field

Management Consulting

Marc A. Sorel, JD-MSFS 2011

How does a team of consultants working with analysts from two think tanks develop in three months a viable ten-year economic growth plan that a major metropolitan city mayor can implement? I found the answer to that question on my first project as a management consultant, where we helped a steering committee comprising the city's business and civic leaders as they developed such a plan. Now, as the city government announces the creation of institutions to support its manufacturing industry and accelerate small and medium enterprise exports—initiatives drawn directly from the work we supported—I am reminded of just how much my expectations of consulting were exceeded on my first study.

My path to consulting was not linear. As a graduate student intent on working after graduation for a global private sector institution with its feet firmly planted in the United States, I thought my Georgetown JD-MSFS joint degree in law and foreign affairs would lead me to a law firm, and after that to a career in the private and public sectors. Three law firm clerkships and several rounds of consulting interviews later, my ultimate intent remained unchanged. However, I realized that the best private-sector fit for me postgraduation was in management consulting. Nowhere else

(Continued on page 213)

my professional and personal life, pervading my decision making at home as well as in the office. For one thing, I am a better thinker—more concise, able to ask more focused questions. Because I tend to be a big-picture person by nature, consulting has also been a good forcing mechanism, teaching me the importance of focusing on the details. Colleagues laugh when I tell them that even my kids have the consulting bug, preparing PowerPoints as youngsters to get the facts in front of me quickly if they really want something. Additionally, I am now most comfortable working in teams; I value the idea exchange and thought challenge that colleagues provide. Even as a CEO, where decision making could get a bit lonely, I sought the counsel and insight of my board members and fellow international development CEOs. Mostly, consulting made connecting the dots in any pattern of facts part of my DNA. As a result, I am better able to consider broader options, and hope I am more creative in my solutions.

presented me with as much of an opportunity to apply the frameworks, critical thinking, logical reasoning, research, writing, and oral presentation skills I had honed in graduate school to solve high-stakes problems for large clients in a setting that was at once collaborative, entrepreneurial, and forward looking.

The depth and breadth of my consulting experience has validated what at first felt like an uncertain choice. In eighteen months at McKinsey & Company, I have worked in telecommunications, health care, manufacturing, energy, medical devices, and the public sector. From a functional perspective, my work has touched on strategy, operations, organizational structure, and sales and marketing. I have traveled to Helsinki, Luxembourg, London, New York, Washington, Chicago, and San Antonio. I have briefed the chief financial officer of a multi-billion-dollar medical device company on efforts to restructure their sales force, spent most of an afternoon discussing the merits of gross domestic product impact calculation methodologies with a former head of a national economic advisory group, and led a day-long workshop with thirty engineers to identify opportunities for improving the profitability of their flagship product. For each study, I consistently draw upon the frameworks, reasoning, writing, research, and presentation skills honed during my graduate studies.

The question that keeps me up at night is the same one that gets me up in the morning—how do I serve my client to produce significant, positive, and enduring results that can be sustained after my work ends? Finding that answer for each client, as I did with the city economic development plan team, is what makes this work as fun as it is rewarding.

If nothing else, consulting has given me a wealth of "war stories" to share with friends over dinner and to remember fondly in my old age. Even if for a short time, consulting can be life-changing.

Careers in Risk and Security Consulting

Jackie Day

Jackie Geissinger Day is vice president for crisis and security consulting at Control Risks. She has had more than ten years of risk management, crisis, and security management experience in both the private and public sectors. Throughout her career she has worked with Fortune 500 companies across the range of industry sectors on developing and implementing global risk management programs and solutions, and she has routinely provided strategic advice to corporate leaders in response to acute crisis situations. She has lived and worked in Asia, the United States, and South America. She received a master's in law and diplomacy from Tufts University and a bachelor's in foreign service from Georgetown University. She is proficient in Mandarin Chinese and Brazilian Portuguese.

Risk consulting is becoming one of the most highly sought-after career tracks by students of international affairs, but also the least understood—in part because the different employer options vary as widely as the areas of risk they consider to be within their core competency. Unlike management consulting, risk consulting focuses on providing information, analysis, and advice to enable clients—whether public, private, or charitable—to enable them to better understand threats and risks to their organization's operations, in order to determine the most appropriate management strategy to treat or "manage" them. In this context treatment can mean mitigation of those risks deemed to present an unacceptable challenge to the successful (and profitable) achievement of an organization's strategic goals, as well as the realization of opportunities to capture the upside of risk, which could have a positive effect on the achievement of organizational objectives. This is normally done through the implementation of strategies to provide competitive advantage and enhance reputation. Risk consulting as a profession, therefore, is not one that thrives only under conditions of political and economic turmoil or decline but also during growth and prosperity.

Risks can be categorized and grouped a number of different ways, which is reflected by the complexity and number of firms in the field and therefore the number of different potential career paths one might pursue. There are a number of organizations that focus exclusively on the provision of detailed analysis and intelligence, covering a broad spectrum of political, socioeconomic, and security risks at both the micro and macro levels, ranging from the better-known firms such as the Eurasia Group, Oxford Analytica, Stratfor, and the Economist Intelligence Unit to boutique outfits like Exclusive Analysis, iJet, and many others. Then there are those risk consulting firms that are more narrowly focused on one area of risk alone, such as security risk, which are highly operational or services oriented, such as Drum Cussac, Hill & Associates, G4S, and GardaWorld, to name but a few. And finally, there are the companies that characterize themselves more as professional services firms, providing both the analytical and intelligence pieces as well as business solutions, in some cases to include audit and assessment of financial risk, such as Control Risks, Kroll, FTI Consulting, Navigant Consulting, Risk Advisory Group, and the "Big Four," PricewaterhouseCoopers, Deloitte, Ernst & Young, and KPMG. At Control Risks, we focus on the three broad categories of political, integrity, and security risks, each of which can have strategic, operational, regulatory / compliance, and / or reputational components.

Within our *political risk* department, analysts spend their time monitoring and analyzing the political, socioeconomic, and security risks prevalent in the locations where our clients operate, focusing on country-specific to global and transnational issues, and what this means for our clients. The individuals who work in this area are experts in their countries or issues of focus, have multiple higher degrees or PhDs, fluently speak the language of their country or region of focus, and have extensive networks of in-country sources to complement their own open source research. Although not exclusively so, the backgrounds of these individuals tend to be oriented toward political science, economics, and international relations, with strong academic credentials. This analytical function provides the core information and analysis—usually at a strategic level—that underpins and sets the context for the more technical areas of consulting in integrity and security.

Consulting on *integrity risk* is concerned with the issues surrounding corruption and fraud, where advice is focused on protecting clients against corrupt practices imposed by public officials, corporate malfeasance by commercial partners and competitors, and theft or fraud committed by company employees. In today's environment of increasing global regulation set against a backdrop of economic volatility and unstable regimes, damaged integrity can mean substantial fines, jail time for executives, or business failure, with substantial time and effort spent dealing with issues that could have been prevented by effective due diligence and appropriate compliance programs. Consultants who focus on integrity risk specialize in gathering and analyzing business-critical intelligence, particularly in less-than-transparent developing-country markets, and they endeavor to enable clients to operate and invest successfully, while preserving the integrity of their operations, brand, and reputation. The individuals who work in this area hail from a broad range of backgrounds and have expertise in varied sectors, including law, law enforcement, journalism, accountancy, business consultancy, investment banking, and government.

Security risk consulting is a much broader discipline than it might sound at first. Primarily focused on identifying, assessing, and mitigating operational risk, this area of consulting seeks to prevent or lessen the negative impact of loss of life, intellectual property, physical assets, and the resulting reputational damage that a lack of preparation or poor response can cause a business, along with broader business disruptions due to either human-made or natural causes. In today's complex global marketplace, multinational organizations have a broad set of imperatives to meet in order to properly secure their operations at both a corporate and local level. This includes entering and succeeding in new markets, monitoring and managing the consequences of changes in risk levels and the local security environment, resourcing and managing security operations, understanding the potential business impact of risks to ensure adequate preparations for response, and effectively responding to events when they occur.

Similar to practitioners within the integrity risk sphere, security consultants possess a range of technical and subject matter expertise, from niche areas such as information security and security engineering and design to the broader security risk and business resilience disciplines. Advice provided ranges from the strategic at the enterprise business level through to practical, on-the-ground guidance to protect people and assets in hostile and/or complex environments. The range of knowledge, skills, and backgrounds sought in potential employees therefore varies widely as well, with no single rigid profile for successful candidates. Although typical backgrounds fall within the expected categories of former military, law enforcement, and intelligence officials, those with expertise in business consultancy, academia, and government policy are also highly desirable.

Skills Sought by Risk-Consulting Employers

Moving away from specific disciplines, the core skills sought by risk consulting employers are the ability to think critically and analytically, coupled with strong listening, verbal, and written communications skills. From this foundation, language, geographic, and technical subject matter expertise are all highly desirable skills that lend themselves to the different specialty areas of risk consulting.

In many ways, the simplest way to think about the risk consulting profession is as a career in problem solving—often on the spot and without the benefit of extensive research and fact-finding to support recommendations to address the problem. Abilities to manage time, multitask, and prioritize are also key characteristics for which employers look—some of which are innate and some of which can be gained through prior experience. Thus, it is important to note that the ideal composition and mix of a good consulting team will vary from the seasoned, gray-haired subject matter expert with extensive prior experience to the bright young recruit fresh out of college.

Risk Consulting in Action

To help bring the profession to life a bit more, it is worth taking a look at a specific example involving each of the different disciplines described above addressing a client problem. In this instance, a client in the extractives sector with an extensive global footprint called our Washington office to seek crisis management advice and assistance following an incident that occurred in Africa. Although the details remained unclear, the client explained that they had an issue where one of their expatriate employees was accused of doing harm to a local national employee, possibly resulting in death, and as a result had been arrested and imprisoned indefinitely. The company had not yet been given access to their expatriate employee to verify his well-being, and did not yet understand what charges were to be levied against him.

The client called Control Risks to ask for help in understanding the political-social and legal context to inform decision making on what response actions to take, and to get an objective assessment of the degree to which the rule of law and due process would prevail in ensuring that their employee received fair treatment. In stepped our resident political risk analyst for that African country, to provide the overall intelligence and analysis of this particular situation for the client from our London headquarters office. Using her existing knowledge of the country and tapping into her well-established network of stringers, she was able to gather the requisite information in short order to provide recommendations on how best to advise the company to proceed in its dealings with both local- and national-level government representatives.

Next, the client wanted support in investigating the details of the alleged incident, to understand the facts on the ground, to differentiate them from the emotional accusations they were receiving from local national employees and the community alike, and to help ensure that the company communicated the right messages to key stakeholders to avoid inflaming the situation further. Enter our integrity risk specialist (or corporate investigator) from our local Africa office, who through interviews with employees, witnesses, community members, and other reliable in-country sources was able to determine that the expatriate employee had been attempting to prevent a crime from being committed and thus was justified in his actions—but, perhaps more important, that no harm had been done to the alleged victim. Instead, he discovered that the alleged victim had gone into hiding, which made the situation worse for the jailed expatriate employee, who by this time had been wrongfully charged with murder. Thus, the findings of the investigation meant the difference between indefinite detention and freedom for the expatriate employee.

Finally, the third leg of the client's request and our support—the security and crisis response element. In this case the client's immediate request was to engage and deploy a consultant in a response capacity to New Zealand, the home country of the expatriate employee and where his family still lived. As the consultant selected to deploy on this particular case, my primary purpose was to serve as a representative and conduit of information between the company, the family, and local government, as an extension of the company's corporate crisis management team. With the family, the dual goals were to provide regular information and assistance or support as needed while their loved one remained in jail thousands of miles away. With the government, my purpose was to serve primarily in a liaison role to advocate on behalf of company and family interests in pursuing the appropriate diplomatic channels for additional support and advice.

Each morning started with a briefing from the corporate project sponsor in North America, followed by a mid-morning update from the general manager in Africa to inform my discussions and activities for the day in New Zealand. At the end of the day I reported back to each, and repeated the cycle the next day.

The key to getting this "handholding" support right was ensuring that the family understood that the company (our client) was doing everything in its power to secure the safe and timely release of the accused individual, while also managing expectations on the duration and probable outcome, given the opacity of the situation. All this was informed by the information and analysis provided by both our political risk analyst and corporate investigator, along with our prior experience in dealing with detention situations in other countries lacking a transparent legal process.

Ultimately, this situation had a positive outcome, with both the jailed individual and company emerging unscathed by the ordeal, due in no small part to the information and advice our team provided over the course of its duration. However, the case serves to underscore the need to apply different areas of expertise in risk consulting in order to arrive at a complete solution to assist a client with a complex problem cutting across multiple geographies and technical disciplines. Although most consulting projects do not carry quite the same level of excitement, this case highlights some of the different and unexpected challenges companies or organizations with international operations can encounter in today's globalized economy.

The Way Forward

In the increasingly uncertain, regulated, and globalized economy of the twenty-first century, the challenge of establishing and maintaining successful, profitable business operations has given rise to a greater need for risk consultancies to provide objective and expert advice. As governments have increasingly sought to regulate corporate behavior through legislation such as the Foreign Corrupt Practices Act and UK Bribery Act, protecting business interests from the range of potential pitfalls has become a requirement rather than just something that is nice to have, and it yields a key driver of growth for the risk consulting industry. Private and public clients alike are now starting to see risk management as a necessary component of all business planning, whether to protect an existing investment or to enable expansion into new geographies and markets.

Notes from the Field

The Eurasia Group

Ayham Kamel, MSFS 2010

After completing my graduate degree in Foreign Service at Georgetown University, I was confident that the next step in my career needed to be a position that allowed me to leverage my experience in both the business world and politics. At the end of 2010, Eurasia Group (EG) offered me a unique opportunity to join the firm's Middle East team. EG analysts clearly possess an unparalleled ability to deliver cutting-edge political advice to hedge funds, investment banks, global corporations, and governments.

A few months into my work, a wave of political change swept the entire Middle East. Although the unprecedented events challenged all economic and political prediction models, our clients expected our advice to remain accurate, timely, and comprehensive. I was well aware that the next year of my life needed to be entirely focused on building the firm's coverage on key political transition issues. Week after week we provided our clients with accurate predictions on the potential effects of the Arab Spring on the Middle East and North Africa region, key developed economies, and global markets.

My work at EG has helped me develop my ability to integrate information from a wide range of sources, and produce business analysis that meets the expectations of our diverse client base. Very early on, risk analysts must develop an ability to delicately balance filtering information with deep analysis to provide relevant assessments that affect your client's business model. I have been able to travel to the regions EG covers and meet key stakeholders, officials, and business executives. My regular interaction with clients remains as enriching as ever. Every day I help our partners make better investment and management decisions, but I also have the unique opportunity to learn from sharp leaders in key industries.

I am confident that the market for political risk will expand in the next decade, and also become more dynamic. CEOs increasingly perceive political risk to be a critical element of their business model; bankers face a shifting global risk landscape; heads of tech companies cannot ignore risks to their technology, information, and privacy; and with rising violence and instability in emerging markets, IOCs will need to further expand their risk management programs. While I have a job that is challenging and rewarding, perhaps most important, I find myself inspired everyday; at EG I am lucky to be surrounded by kind and intelligent colleagues, the youngest owner of a political risk consultancy, and a brilliant director of a research and analysis department.

In addition to regulatory drivers, the evolution of the discourse in the field is pushing companies to realize the need to harness risk to exploit opportunities for their benefit and competitive advantage in the marketplace, as opposed to the traditional—and limited—view of defensively managing against negative threats and risks alone. This more sophisticated understanding is also contributing to growth in the field of risk consultancy, which will continue regardless of whether the next few years are characterized by further economic turmoil and possible decline or recovery.

One thing that is certain, however, is that today's business risk environment offers any number of interesting and different potential career paths within the risk consulting space. Working in the consulting world presents the opportunity for exposure to the entire range of business and industry sectors, and thus great potential to gain experience and inform a future decision to specialize in an industry as a follow-on career step. Likewise, consulting offers the ongoing opportunity to hone technical subject matter expertise, but uniquely applied to individual client circumstances in different market sectors and with vastly different appetites for risk. Though often quite demanding, the continuous challenge and intellectual stimulation of risk consulting are extremely rewarding—from providing strategic advice at corporate headquarters in the capital cities of the developed world to the grittier design of personnel protection programs in the ungoverned spaces of the developing world.

Careers in Development Consulting

Kaia Miller

Kaia Miller is founder of Aslan Global, Inc., a Boston-based consulting firm advising private- and public-sector organizations in developing economies on competitiveness and economic development. She worked with the Cambridge-based consulting firm Monitor Group as a leader in its country competitiveness practice, and she cofounded the spin-off OTF Group before founding Aslan Global in 2001. She currently serves on the president of Rwanda's Advisory Council, supporting the implementation of the country's long-term vision, and is an associate at Harvard's Institute for Strategy and Competitiveness. She chairs the New England Board for the US Fund for UNICEF. She is a member of the Leadership Council for the Public Service Center at the Massachusetts Institute of Technology and of the Advisory Board for the MSFS program at Georgetown, and she serves on the boards of the Advent School and the Maranyundo Education Initiative for girls in Rwanda. She received her bachelor's degree in international relations from Brown University and her MSFS from Georgetown University.

International development consulting is a dynamic professional field with a wide array of career paths and opportunities. There are literally thousands of international development consulting firms, and even more independent international development consultants. These firms and related independent consultants typically support projects conducted by international agencies, such as the World Bank, the United Nations Development Program, the regional development banks (e.g., Asian Development Bank, African Development Bank), bilateral aid agencies (e.g., the US Agency for International Development, the UK Department for International Development), governments in developing countries, and private organizations (e.g., nongovernmental organizations, foundations, and corporations).

The needs in the international development consulting field often reflect a continually evolving global agenda, which traditionally has been about reducing poverty and creating socioeconomic prosperity in developing countries. The field of international development grew in large part out of the post–World War II era and the need for reconstruction in affected areas; the creation of the United Nations system of organizations, including the World Bank and the International Monetary Fund; and the emergence of dozens of independent nations from the former colonial relationships.

Over time, varying emphases within the field of international development have dominated the agenda and driven the focus of the field's initiatives and projects. Some of these include the early focus on the Marshall Plan for rebuilding Europe, and the subsequent structural adjustment programs advocated by the World Bank and the International Monetary Fund during the 1970s and 1980s, which were driven by macroeconomics and top-down approaches to development. These efforts shifted toward a focus on the microeconomic drivers of growth and human development in the 1990s. In 2000 the UN Millennium Declaration, which resulted from the Millennium Summit, presented a vision for "inclusive and sustainable globalization based on human rights principles." The accompanying Millennium Development Goals (MDGs) anchored this new dialogue in concrete goals, and most international development projects became linked in some way to achieving these goals. The MDGs are eight specific international development goals, agreed to by 189 countries:

1. eradicating extreme poverty;
2. achieving universal primary education;
3. promoting gender equality and empowering women;
4. reducing child mortality;
5. improving maternal health;
6. combating HIV / AIDS, malaria, and other diseases;
7. ensuring environmental sustainability; and
8. developing a global partnership for development.

Although the MDGs provide specific targets for international development, the concepts of empowerment, particularly women's empowerment and human rights, have also been increasingly emphasized in more recent international development initiatives and projects.

The next few years in international development consulting are likely to be influenced by the post-MDG debate. In 2012 the UN secretary-general appointed a high-level panel to advise on the post-2015 development agenda. A preliminary working paper "proposes that post-2015 goals should be based on principles of equity, sustainability, and human security and address key contemporary challenges such as climate change, unemployment, inequality and global market instability."[1] The final proposal of the panel will be released in 2013. A global survey titled "My World" has been created to allow people around the world to voice their opinions. Additionally, an interactive "World We Want" platform has been created to enable broad participation in the global consultations on the emerging development agenda.

Skills and Expertise

Following the dialogue among experts about the global agenda for international development can provide anyone interested in entering the field with a sense of trends in job opportunities and of the desired skills, ideal experience, and related consulting expertise required for specific projects. But regardless of the predominant thinking, trends, and global agenda, those interested in international development consulting should also consider their own personal strengths and passions. Toward this end, it may be helpful to consider expertise along different vectors in order to home in on where one's interests and experiences might intersect with various job opportunities. For example, consulting opportunities can focus on different sectors, such as economic development, infrastructure, governance, health care, the environment, energy, education, agriculture and natural resources, water and sanitation, rural and urban development, gender equality, and human rights. Opportunities can also be focused regionally, on Latin America and the Caribbean, the Middle East, North Africa, Sub-Saharan Africa, the former Soviet Union, Asia, and specific countries, as well as subnational regions and supranational blocs.

Given the ways in which consulting opportunities are often grouped along sectoral and regional vectors, strong or unique language skills, experience working in a particular region, specific sector experience, methodological experience, and academic training aligned with the project may be attractive to organizations seeking consultants for specific projects and may help you land a consulting position. However, there are also a number of desirable skills that cut across virtually all dimensions of international development consulting. Some of these include excellent credentials (very important in developing countries), the ability to see beyond your specific expertise and understand how your piece fits into the bigger picture, strong analytical abilities, the ability to think strategically, and the ability to present ideas clearly through a variety of media, including written papers, formal presentations, in-person interviews, and daily communication. The ability to work with data sets and basic modeling is also critical. Having personally worked in a vast array of countries, sometimes speaking the language and other times not, it is clear to me that language abilities enable you to be more effective as a consultant.

In addition to skills, training, and expertise, there are also some personality types that are likely to be attracted to international development consulting. Someone who thrives on order, organization, and predictability may not enjoy this field. Because of the nature of the work, and the environments where you may find yourself, it takes someone who has a high tolerance for uncertainty, who is comfortable with unpredictability, and who can be creative in the face of challenges, such as a lack of data availability. But this does not mean that the ability to plan, design, and implement a plan is not important. In fact, it is even more important in the potentially chaotic situations where you may find yourself. The ability to design and implement a plan—including keeping people on schedule and balancing the production of deliverables with other less tangible goals such as capacity building, consensus building, and institution building—is critical.

Entering the Field

Entering the international development consulting field directly as a consultant is possible, though difficult. One can compete for one of the coveted consulting positions in a top-tier strategy consulting firm. These firms are likely to have training programs, and therefore they may be more willing to hire someone with little or no consulting experience as a consultant. These positions are highly competitive, and interested candidates should have a stellar academic record and a résumé that reflects success in chosen activities, as well as some proclivity toward the desired consulting position, demonstrated through selected courses taken, volunteer activities, or other indicators of interest. With a foundation of consulting experience at a top-tier firm, and a demonstrated fluency in international development issues, the transition to international development consulting is possible.

One can also target a consulting position with a smaller, specialized international development consulting firm, focused on a narrow slice of the field, such as economic development, the environment, health care, education, or infrastructure. Without specific expertise and experience in a given area, it will be difficult to be hired in an entry-level position, such as a research assistant or project administration assistant. However, small consulting firms often hire from within, and getting your foot in the door and excelling at the tasks you are assigned can help you advance.

In the last decade there has been a proliferation of foundations and social enterprises focused on different aspects of international development. This has created exciting job opportunities within the sector. Instead of entering the consulting field on the ground floor, it may be beneficial to work at a foundation or social enterprise to gain valuable field experience and specific expertise that can aid a future transition to consulting.

Alternately, one can follow a more academic track, as a researcher or in a teaching position at a university, and from that position take on consulting projects. One can even work directly for a large international agency—such as the World Bank, any of myriad UN agencies, or bilateral aid organizations such as the US Agency for International Development and the UK Department for International Development—gaining valuable experience that can lead to future consulting opportunities.

Finding relevant opportunities is fairly straightforward. Online searches reveal a wealth of international development consulting opportunities, as well as information about hundreds of consulting firms. Online sites such as devnetjobs.org and idealist.org list both international development jobs and consulting opportunities in the field. And the websites of international organizations such as the Asian Development Bank enable one to search consulting opportunities by country, sector, engagement period, and budget.

Landing a job in development consulting can be quite challenging. Applications can go unanswered without a personal introduction. Knowing the projects on which an international development consulting firm is bidding can help interested applicants tailor their résumés. Highlighting key words related to those projects can be helpful. In the end, however, it is more often than not one's personal network that is the most powerful driving factor in getting one's résumé read. Informational interviews are arguably the single most valuable strategy for those seeking a job in international development consulting. If you walk away from a 20- to 30-minute informational interview with the names of one or two additional people with whom to talk or of organizations to consider, you have gotten value from the interview. Informational interviewing should never stop. Be professional and impressive in your informational interviews, and follow up on suggestions, because you never know where they might lead.

Before investing valuable time and effort in a job search in international development consulting, consider whether it is conducive to the lifestyle you seek. This type of consulting can be a demanding lifestyle, with frequent travel and long-term stays in client countries. Some assignments even require temporary relocation to another country. Flexibility and a willingness to be based in a developing country can expand the opportunities available, but relationship and family considerations must ultimately be taken into consideration.

My Story

My background is in economic development consulting. I started consulting in a top-tier management consulting firm that focused primarily on strategy for *Fortune* 500 companies. After doing my share of consulting that had nothing to do with my passion for international development, I managed to get assigned to a project advising developing-country governments on economic growth strategy and competitiveness, and I subsequently continued to consult in that area. Our group spun off and created a separate firm. I was working 24/7 and had no social life.

Eventually, this became unsustainable, and I started my own economic development consulting firm. It was my strategy to achieve a better balance between personal and professional goals. I was thirty-seven years old, planning on getting married, and wanted to have children, but I needed control over my own schedule and workload to make it all happen. The heavy travel I did up to that point and the lack of control I had over my schedule became incompatible with my personal goals. By that point I had many years of experience and had developed a strong network during the course of my career, so I took the plunge. I contacted several of my former clients and asked if they would act as references for me in my new endeavor. They all said yes, a testament to strong relationships that we had formed in the course of our work together. One client said not only would he act as a reference but he also had a project for me. My firm was off and running! Depending on the size of project I take on and the skills required, I hire subcontractors to work with me, including researchers, statisticians, and other strategy consultants. I could not have done this early on in my career; having an established network and reputation is essential to building a business and bringing on effective subcontractors to deliver the work.

There are pros and cons to running your own consulting firm. On the positive side I have the freedom to select projects that are particularly interesting or challenging, and the freedom to *not* take on projects at times, for example, when I was too pregnant to travel or was trying to survive as a new mother. I have the freedom to work where and when I want. I maintain a home office, which enables me to balance the consulting work with motherhood. I was able to be with my children when they were babies. Now that both my children are in school all day, I work between 8:30 am and 3:00 pm and then turn into a mom from 3:00 to 9:00 pm when I am not traveling. I pick up again for a couple of hours after they go to bed or in the early mornings. I limit my travel to two weeks maximum per trip.

Notes from the Field

Dalberg Global Development Advisors
Shyam Sundaran, MSFS 2010

Being a consultant with Dalberg Global Development Advisors is a bit like playing global trivia with graduate school friends: You are not entirely sure what the question is going to be, or even whether you will be able to answer it immediately, but you do know you are going to arrive at an interesting answer, learn a lot on the way, and have fun doing it. The projects I have worked on at Dalberg have ranged from developing an agricultural development strategy for a leading donor in Afghanistan, to supporting the senior management team of an international organization in South Korea to improve their internal processes, and designing a nutrition intervention in Bangladesh. I have worked with small teams located in Washington and with a global team drawn from our offices in Geneva, San Francisco, and Mumbai. This is why, three years in, I still relish the idea of going to work in the morning. The diversity of the work not only dovetails directly with the skills and expertise I developed at MSFS, but continues to give me the opportunity to apply these lessons to "real life" situations. I would say that Dalberg has been a very natural extension of my time at MSFS across four dimensions:

Exposure. My time at Dalberg has exposed me to a wide set of clients, issues, and problems. I have been involved with trying to determine the optimal staffing structure for support staff for UN peacekeeping operations and identifying the need, opportunities, and challenges facing the clean cookstoves sector in India. I have worked with NGOs, multilaterals, governments, and private-sector organizations. While this might seem fragmented, for someone who is starting out in the international development space or is seeking to understand it at a deeper level, these types of engagements allow to you achieve just that. And perhaps most important, this exposure enables me to make a more educated decision around the types of issues and clients that make me most passionate and get me most excited.

(Continued on page 227)

Of course, there are also cons. I am the only one getting the consulting "gigs"; no one is doing it for me. This requires strategic networking and managing relationships, and a bit of unpredictability. Financial flows can be uneven, meaning that I may not get a paycheck every week. Furthermore, not all clients are willing to hire a lead consultant who limits travel to two weeks at a time once a quarter. In fact, I had to change my model of

Skills. A key element of any consulting engagement is strong analytic skills—in terms of research and data gathering, quantitative analysis, and presenting your findings in a clear and compelling manner. I can say that coming into the job armed with an MSFS degree, I had the fundamentals required for success, but the rigor and quality that Dalberg projects demand forced me to hone these skills further and deeper than I might have otherwise. These types of skills are critical in creating and sustaining change for any organization, and are portable well beyond the consulting world.

Entrepreneurialism. One of the elements I have appreciated most about Dalberg is that entrepreneurship is in the company's DNA. This not only applies to how we approach our projects, but also in how we build our firm. Each employee is empowered to find ways to develop new areas of expertise within the firm, improve the working culture of the offices, and identify new platforms we should be engaging—be it by authoring an op-ed or identifying volunteer opportunities for the team to commit to. The spirit of independence and drive is evident every day at Dalberg.

Team. Arguably, my favorite part about working at Dalberg is the people. We have people from a variety of backgrounds—from traditional engineering and emerging markets finance, to fieldwork in fragile states and corporate strategy consulting. Despite the variety in background, everyone is bound together by a desire to make change in the world and a passion to do it in an inclusive and fun manner.

While there are clear upsides to the work that Dalberg does, there are some disadvantages too. Primary among them is that we traditionally do not "implement" the ideas that we develop—as strategic advisers, we help others think through the issues and design the most effective program/initiative possible, but at the end of the day, they are the ones to implement it. My previous experience with the World Bank was very instrumental in teaching me about the challenges of execution and implementation, and I am eager to get back to that world one day. Nevertheless, Dalberg, and consulting in general, has offered me a wealth of opportunities in terms of content, people, skills, and problems that I would likely not have been exposed to in such a short period of time working anywhere else. For that, I remain grateful and I feel incredibly lucky to have found a job that in many ways is a natural extension of my time at MSFS.

consulting to one that involves building particularly strong relationships with those on the ground, because I cannot be there all the time. Additionally, in my case, it can be challenging to work alone most of the time. To manage this I make a point of getting together with others in similar or related fields on a regular basis. Proximity to universities, think tanks, international organizations, and other consulting firms helps tremendously in this regard. I maintain ties with a professor at a local university with whom I have worked in the past, and we occasionally work together and have an ongoing dialogue about economic development. Technology that makes video conferencing easy and inexpensive also helps to maintain an active network and dialogue with colleagues in the field.

International development consulting can be an extremely rewarding field. You are at the forefront of the global development agenda, and you can have a tremendous impact on improving socioeconomic prosperity around the world. There are many paths that can lead you there. Your path may be circuitous, and you may find yourself doing things completely unrelated to your ultimate goal. But by keeping your eyes focused on this goal and making the most of every position you have in the interim, you can get there.

Careers in Business Consulting

Rebecca Bou Chebel-Macmillan

Rebecca Bou Chebel-MacMillan is the vice president for the Middle East at Qorvis GeoPolitical Solutions. She manages Qorvis's operations in the Middle East and develops and implements the firm's strategic plan for growth in the region. She has worked in Iraq twice, as the senior media relations officer for USAID in Baghdad, and as a RAND Corporation senior communications consultant to US Task Force 134—which handled all the US detention facilities in Iraq after the Abu Ghraib incident. She worked for Grey Worldwide in Qatar as a public relations manager handling the 2006 Doha Asian Games accounts and Qatar Telecom, among other clients. She has also served in the office of Her Highness Sheikha Mozah Bint Nasser Al Misned, first lady of Qatar, as her media adviser. Ms. Bou Chebel-MacMillan is fluent in three languages— English, French, and Arabic. She received an MSFS from Georgetown University.

When Tiger Woods crashed his SUV into a fire hydrant at 2:25 am outside his Florida home he could not have anticipated the consequences—within days, his life would be turned upside down and his public image would be damaged, possibly forever. By the time his managers came up with a strategy, it was too late; a sporting icon and international household name had become damaged goods. A good public relations (PR) campaign could have spared him the worst of the media onslaught, but his team members were too slow to act—they lost the golden hour, and damage control became impossible.

The international free flow of information, globalization, and the speed at which news is being disseminated via social media have made the fields of PR and marketing imperative for any government or corporation. From world-leading nations to small islands, global corporations to local businesses, all are finding themselves exposed and vulnerable to the speed of communication and the power of unchecked narratives channeled through the Web. Today more than ever, they are vulnerable to a crisis, as they are constantly being put under the microscope. It is within this new media world order that the need for constant "engagement" and "relationship building" has become the bread and butter of PR and marketing professionals. This essay discusses the various career paths that newcomers to the global hiring market can pursue in marketing and PR, viewed from the perspective of international relations, ranging from independent careers with PR agencies and firms to corporate in-house jobs. It shares insights about the best ways to get these jobs, the specific personality types and lifestyle challenges young professionals must consider, and the skill sets required to succeed. Observations about the outlook for this sector, highlighting the current events that have helped shape this viewpoint, conclude this analysis.

Where the Jobs Are

Today, marketing and PR jobs are no longer restricted to Madison Avenue and K Street. Given the massive expansion in global communication with the internet and the rise of social media in recent years, those two fields have become an integral part of international organizations and governments. Job descriptions and concentrations abound, depending on level and years of experience. They vary from entry-level associates to mid-career managers and from directors to senior-level positions as high as managing director or partner in a firm.

The typical route for a young professional seeking a job in marketing or PR is with an agency servicing a range of clients. When international affairs is your niche, a PR firm that specializes in crisis communications, public affairs, and reputation management for sovereign nations such as the US government, or government contractors such as Halliburton or Boeing, could be the right fit for you. You would most likely start as a basic news analyst handling press clippings and media analysis or as an entry-level speechwriter drafting blog entries and press releases. You could also start as a social media associate monitoring target sites, placing content, and advising on best strategies for the client's social media issues. Individuals with more experience are hired to manage clients' accounts, with lower- to mid-level positions and a broader scope of work than entry-level associates. The job may include servicing federal clients and government contractors, drafting proposals, leading small teams, providing strategies, and having daily contact with your counterpart at the client's offices. For specific accounts you will be expected to navigate the US Congress or service high-level foreign government representatives seeking advice on how to mitigate bad press or how to best promote policies.

From another perspective the global financial turmoil of 2008 resulted in the downfall of previously well-regarded companies and governments facing significant fiscal issues. All had sought the services of PR experts to help mitigate their crises and provide strategic support. From Wall Street to Dubai, clients called on marketing and PR firms to fight the trouble, doubling their budgets and workload. Therefore, if your forte is finance and international affairs, you can easily marry these two fields, using your knowledge of international affairs and politics with your financial expertise to effectively communicate with the world on behalf of your client as a finance communication consultant. And if media relations are of interest to you, then focus on press outreach and interview pitching, while building solid relations with journalists for your client. It is not uncommon for former journalists switching to consulting to give media training to clients and coach them on public speaking. You could be part of that unit.

All the above-mentioned positions can be found in-house, within an organization's communications' department, working to secure solid PR and marketing processes to protect their stakeholders' best interests and to ensure mutually beneficial relationships internally and externally. The most coveted and trendy in-house jobs are with companies such as Google and Facebook. They are highly specialized, technical, and competitive, and are considered niche communication and PR consulting positions. The United Nations and international nongovernmental organizations, depending on funding and size of programs, also recruit public affairs and communications consultants at various levels with job descriptions similar to those found in the independent firms, but the scope is limited and contracts are usually shorter term, based on specific assignments.

Landing a Position

Having discussed positions, the pertinent question is: How do you get them? PR and marketing jobs are posted online daily, at websites ranging from LinkedIn to Career Builder, to more targeted sites such as PR News and PRSA, or via private headhunters and the career section on corporate sites. The most straightforward way to land a position is to go through these sites and submit your résumé. We have all spent hours crafting our biographies and retouching our résumés to match the exact requirements of each vacancy, and from my experience, those hours were lost and had only minimal positive results. They may be helpful sometimes for entry-level positions but harder as you gain more experience. For new entrants, internships can be an excellent tool to entering the field; based on your performance, you may get noticed by the employer who then offers you a permanent job.

What I found most effective is the power of personal and direct contact with a potential employer or a decision maker at the organization where you want to work. Key to success is strategizing your move and positioning yourself to get noticed. By "noticed," I do not mean wear bright clothes or be pushy, but to actually impress your audience with a subtle approach, confidence—not arrogance—and commitment. That should shine through. Also, network with crowds that allow you to connect with people in high places. Do not go to every networking event armed with your 60-second pitch and your best suit. You can do that, of course; but it would be more useful to select your venues and ask your professors or professional friends how to craft your résumé—because it must catch the eye of a reader who is often too busy to go through something generic or dull. You want to market yourself correctly for the job you want. Ask to whom to send your résumé and how to secure one-to-one meetings. The rest is up to you to make a solid connection. If the people you meet with are impressed by your personality and your work, they will remember you, not your résumé. Often, without you knowing, these same people will refer you for a job or better position elsewhere. The key is not to expect immediate results but to stay discreetly in touch and keep them informed of your accomplishments, because you never know when you will need them or when they will come through for you.

In my twelve-year career in PR—working in war-torn Baghdad, for Qatari royalty, and in Washington politics—I never once got a job from a résumé posted online. I got them all via personal connections I made along the way where strong referrals led to successful interviews. A job well done with high performance was noticed, leading clients or firms to contact me directly and ask me to work for them. This has been the case for my most rewarding, well-paid, and career-boosting moves.

What Is Necessary for Success?

The PR and marketing world is fast paced, intense, and at times unforgiving. You are paid to manage your client's reputation and perception by the world, and you often operate behind the scenes while managing your client's character quirks and demands. How a news headline reads is often tied directly to what you say or advise your client to say and do. If it is positive, the client is the hero of the day; if it is negative, it is your mistake. With this comes responsibility and pressure not made for the fainthearted. This is not your 9-to-5, five-days-a-week gig. You are on call, with you suitcase packed to go wherever you are needed, and you are expected to arrive fully briefed, ready to deliver. This routine can be taxing, both physically and mentally. You must love and be fully convinced of what you are doing, or else you will struggle. Life/work balance may seem hard at times, but if you manage your time and expectations well, you will be able to enjoy both. If you have a family, this gets harder, especially for women. That is why it is important for some

Notes from the Field

APCO Worldwide

Anna Tunkel, MSFS 2006

I came to Georgetown's MSFS program with an undergraduate degree in political science and East Asian studies in Tel Aviv University and experience with a number of nongovernmental organizations in Israel, focusing on migrant workers and human rights. My dream career path at the time was in the field of diplomacy, ideally with the UN or another multilateral organizations. During my two years at Georgetown, I took classes focusing on both foreign policy and business government relations. In retrospect, it was invaluable training—both in theory and in practice of international affairs. The workshops, negotiations stimulations, memos and assignments, and projects such as presenting in front of seasoned practitioners and distinguished statesmen like Dennis Ross, Tarik Yousef, George Tenet, and Madeleine Albright helped cultivate the skills that I am using daily in my job.

At the end of my first year at MSFS, a couple of classmates and I had the privilege of representing the program at the Academy of Achievement Summit in New York City. The three-day summit brought together distinguished leaders from the policy, private, and nonprofit sectors and student scholars from various prestigious programs around the world for dialogue and debate. In a fortuitous turn of events, at a luncheon hosted by Mayor Michael Bloomberg at Gracie Mansion, I found myself sitting next to the founder and chief executive officer (CEO) of APCO Worldwide—a global public affairs, communication, and business strategy consulting firm. I was familiar with APCO from my internships search and she apparently had looked at my resume from the participants pull. She was interested in my Russian-Israeli background, given APCO's extensive work in Russia, and coincidently, the opening of its Israeli office that very month.

Following that encounter, I joined APCO's Washington headquarters as an intern in my second year at MSFS, and have stayed with the company since then, for almost eight years. APCO's work focuses on business, public affairs and communication strategy that helps our clients—whether they are private-sector firms, governments, foundations, or nonprofits—build successful brands and a global reputation. Currently, I am a vice president

(Continued on page 233)

and director, leading strategic initiatives for the office of the CEO and managing a number of APCO's global seven-figure accounts.

The last eight years have been a true roller-coaster journey for me, taking me across the world to almost every one of APCO's thirty-three global offices in twenty-nine countries, participating in negotiations in Kazakhstan and at the deputy prime minister's office in Vietnam, meeting with some of the world's most fascinating entrepreneurs and philanthropists in Davos, and much more. After my internship I joined full time as a special assistant and chief of staff to APCO's founder and CEO, effectively building the function of office of the CEO and focusing on global business development, strategic partnerships, and a number of special projects. I prepared and advanced the CEO's trips to more than a dozen markets, working closely with the company's senior management and APCO's diverse global team of over six hundred consultants. I had the opportunity to participate in negotiations and witness strategy development at the highest levels.

After four and a half years in that position, I accepted an exciting offer to move to Shanghai to manage a number of our projects in the region, including several initiatives around Shanghai World Expo 2010. I always had a special interest in China (having studied Mandarin for my undergraduate degree) and jumped at the opportunity to work in one of the world's fastest-growing markets. In Shanghai, I managed a number of teams and projects, and worked with fascinating clients, including Chinese corporations that were rapidly expanding overseas and multinational firms seeking to succeed in China. My clients included the world's second-largest telecom company, an emerging market sovereign wealth fund, and a number of global firms actively involved in the Shanghai 2010 World Expo.

Two years later, I returned to the United States, and have been promoted to a vice president position, where I am responsible for managing several global client accounts for the firm and leading a number of external initiatives and partnerships with organizations like the World Economic Forum and the Clinton Global Initiative. My work touches on all the aspects of diplomacy I was striving for when I first started graduate school. It is truly global in nature—even when I am not on the road, I find myself on conference calls to Beijing, Tel Aviv, London, or Mexico City on a daily basis. I work on issues ranging from energy and water security to women's empowerment, global health, and development. MSFS provided me with a unique skill set and experience that proved invaluable in my job today.

of us women to expect and accept slowing the pace at times, to reassess our priorities, and to be prepared to get back in the grind, full throttle, when ready.

Creativity, patience, courage, speed, and assertiveness are some of the most important character traits needed to succeed in this business. You need creativity to masterfully navigate the various personalities and crises with which you must deal on a day-to-day basis, patience to understand your clients' frustrations, and a sense of the urgency of their needs without flinching so you do not lose sight of the solution you are asked to provide. You also need courage to embrace your clients' cause and constantly venture outside your comfort zone. And you need stamina to keep up with the global 24-hour news cycle where problems never sleep. You must be quick on your feet, fast to come up with a solution, and ready to provide answers and communicate them, often all at once. Most times, your deadline is yesterday. As for assertiveness in this cutthroat industry, if you are not bold enough to take the bull by the horns and tackle the problems with confidence while continuously showing initiative, you will sink.

Every job is different, but across the board the most important skills needed are stellar analytical thinking, solid writing skills, and the ability to communicate powerfully—to listen and be heard. Analytical thinking is paramount, because you are expected to have in-depth understanding and be able to advise on any issue, international news, or event affecting your client. Writing skills are crucial to craft artful strategic messaging and content that might end up on the front page of the *New York Times*. And finally, you should aim to communicate powerfully because your job is mostly to connect with audiences, to convincingly sell words and narratives while remaining approachable. When hiring, employers look for these skills, for years of experience, for areas of expertise, and for degrees that vary from international affairs and communications to economic and financial studies. Language skills and international experience are always a big plus. You are more likely to thrive in Shanghai if you speak Chinese and understand the culture, or to succeed in Latin America if your Spanish is up to scratch.

The outlook for the communication industry is looking good for decades to come—as long as the information sphere keeps shrinking; as long as wars, financial crises, scandals, and human interest stories continue to unfold on Twitter and Facebook; and as long as amateurish, unedited videos of anything and everything go viral on YouTube. With sector growth and technological advances come new types of jobs; and with these new jobs, various opportunities arise continuously. More and more, governments and corporations are appreciating the importance of PR and marketing consultants while constantly placing their public image and reputation in the hands of these consultants. One person's misfortune is another person's opportunity.

Note

1. Sakiko Fukuda-Parr, *Should Global Goal-Setting Continue, and How, in the Post-2015 Era?* DESA Working Paper 117 (New York: United Nations Department of Economic and Social Affairs, 2012), abstract.

CHAPTER 9

Universities, Research Institutes, and Think Tanks

The world of academia and think tanks draws more PhDs than any other field discussed in this book. Although this chapter examines teaching and research positions, it also discusses other areas—particularly in universities—where an international affairs professional (with or without PhD credentials) can successfully apply his or her skills. Though these essays focus on opportunities in the United States, one should recognize that similar opportunities focused on education and informing the public and policy discourse exist in institutes and universities throughout the world. In evaluating opportunities both here and abroad, job seekers may wish to pay attention to an organization's mission, board members, and sources of funding to help determine where the organization falls on the political spectrum.

Careers in Universities

Laura J. Mitchell

Laura J. Mitchell, a graduate of the Master's of Science in Foreign Service (MSFS) program at Georgetown University, is associate professor of history at the University of California, Irvine, where she was acting director of the Center for Global Peace and Conflict Studies for 2012. She is the author of Belongings: Property, Family and Identity in Colonial South Africa *(Columbia University Press, 2009) and, with Ross Dunn, of* Panorama: A World History *(McGraw-Hill, 2014). She received her bachelor's degree from the University of California, Berkeley, and a PhD in African history from the University of California, Los Angeles.*

College and university campuses are home to some of the most polyglot, multinational, and culturally diverse communities on the planet. In both the United States and in other countries, a working life on campus can be a direct connection to a broad spectrum of international opportunities and globally minded colleagues. Academic settings also tend to be dynamic, challenging, and collegial places to work—energized and regularly reinvigorated by the students whose education is central to the university's mission. Few people end up working in academia by chance, so if you pursue a job in academia, you are very likely to work among people who also really want to be there.

At colleges and universities in the United States, there are four general employment categories on campus where an interest in international affairs would be rewarded and an advanced degree would serve you well: research centers, institutes, and specialized degree programs; student affairs, including study abroad and international exchange programs; teaching; and faculty positions that have both teaching and research components. There is a wide range of options within each category, and different paths to employment in the administrative, research, and teaching spheres. Before working through those specifics in turn, it is worth considering some general campus characteristics.

Reflecting on your experiences at your undergraduate and graduate institutions gives you a starting point for thinking about the kind of working environment where you would thrive. You can find unique challenges and rewards in the hustle and bustle of a large, urban campus; at a smaller college that facilitates more sustained personal connections with students and staff; at a research-focused institution that may involve more solo work projects; or at teaching-focused programs that prioritize collaboration with students. The type of campus will also affect whether the work is hands-on or more theoretical, connected to the policy community, aimed at other researchers, or structured to create opportunities for students. In all cases, schools where a strong international affairs background is a good fit are likely to have robust visitors' programs, an active events calendar, and frequent occasions to use your language skills. It is particularly important to note that college campuses tend to be one of the few places to pursue internationally inclined careers away from the Atlantic seaboard and Pacific Rim. So if you have a geographic target for your job search, look carefully at opportunities in the local higher education sector.

Research Centers and Specialized Programs

Most universities and some liberal arts colleges support research centers that are a natural fit for a graduate of an international affairs program. Whether devoted to topics such as diplomacy, international economics, security studies, peace and justice, or conflict resolution, campus-based research centers typically combine long-term studies, coverage of emerging issues, connections to current courses, and some public visibility—such as presentations by resident scholars or visiting researchers that are open to the general public. The best-known of these centers are in regular dialogue with the policy community, and senior practitioners move from campus appointments to government service and back again. For example, Condoleezza Rice served as national security adviser and secretary of state in George W. Bush's administrations between appointments at Stanford University. After serving as assistant secretary-general of the United Nations and special adviser for policy planning to Secretary-General Kofi Annan, Michael Doyle went on to co-direct the Center on Global Governance at Columbia Law School. Of course, not all who move in and out of campus jobs engage in such high-profile public service. Legions of others have transitioned from both political appointments and career employment in the State Department and other government agencies. The path in both directions is well worn.

To find out about specific employment opportunities, start by investigating center websites in order to understand the range of research, teaching, and public programming they support. Cornell, Harvard, Massachusetts Institute of Technology, Princeton, the University of Maryland, and the University of Washington are among many universities with robust international studies centers that oversee a multitude of specific research groups, including many area studies programs. Your interest in a particular country or region could be an entrée to a Latin American or Asian studies center. Another option lies in administrative work in specialized degree programs, such as Georgetown's MSFS or sister programs on other campuses. Consider conventional international affairs programs as well as allied specializations, such as conflict resolution and human rights. In addition, there is a demand for expertise coordinating joint-degree programs with law, public health, or other academic units. Because international and area studies centers are not the only points of global engagement on campus, you should also take a careful look at other topical research centers. Your international perspective could find a home in a program focused on women's studies, development policies, the environment, human rights, wealth and poverty, or interdisciplinary endeavors such as the recently founded Institute for Money, Technology, and Finance at the University of California, Irvine.

Most senior positions and full-time research jobs in campus-based centers are linked to full-time faculty appointments, and thus require a PhD and a publication record (more on the PhD track below). But typically there are opportunities for part-time, entry-level work available to students. Larger centers also employ full-time directors, administrative staff, junior researchers, and/or research assistants. Entry-level staff or research positions can be a useful stopping point early in your career. There is rarely a clear path from entry-level staff to senior researcher within a center or program. Moving up the ladder likely means making moves, either to other units on campus or to other employers, to expand your management experience—or for more schooling. Consequently, a first or early-career job in this field is often relatively short term (two to three years), and a way to explore your options and prepare to apply for other employment or further study. Such work helps you build expertise in the field and gives you insight about how you want to direct your career. After experience in a research-based environment, do you want to cultivate your academic skills and pursue a PhD, or do you want to move into more hands-on policy work? Regardless of your next step, working in a research center provides you with opportunities to make contacts, engage regularly with senior figures in the field, and benefit from mentoring relationships that develop in a campus setting.

Student Affairs

Another set of internationally oriented campus-based careers focus on the undergraduate student experience. From helping American students prepare for study abroad to welcoming international students to the United States, colleges need administrative staff with language skills, awareness of social and cultural differences, and experience overseas. The website for the United States–based professional organization for international educators provides a helpful introduction to issues in the field, including a comprehensive link to exploring careers (www.nafsa.org). Other aspects of student life—including housing management, event planning, service learning, internships, and volunteer experiences—are all increasingly globally aware and provide meaningful opportunities to engage in international dialogue, build cross-cultural experience, and develop community in the United States.

Teaching in Higher Education

The opportunities for teaching both international affairs and international topics—broadly construed—to post-high-school students in the United States are simultaneously dizzying and Byzantine. From community colleges to research universities, from the occasional class through regular part-time contracts to full-time appointments, there are many ways to teach in higher education.

For professionals engaged in policy work—whether in government, nongovernmental organizations, businesses, or think tanks—part-time teaching related to your work provides opportunities to reflect on your practice, to read and discuss the most recent analysis and commentary, to mentor those new to the field, and (quite frankly) to scout for new talent for your organization. Many international affairs programs in the major hubs of Washington and New York regularly draw on the ranks of local practitioners to give their students a combination of academic specialization from the permanent faculty and up-to-date, real-world experience from experts currently working in the field. Networks to the revolving door between campus-based research centers and public service are the principal connection for such part-time offers. Colleagues who have made this transition in their full-time employment rely on their contacts to recruit able professionals as teachers. If you are currently working and would like to share your expertise with students, arrange to talk with research center directors and academic program coordinators to discuss your interests and qualifications. Academic course planning is often quite long term, so anticipate a delay between making initial contacts and being able to find the right match in a course schedule.

For community college teaching, whether in preprofessional courses or on more conventional academic topics such as introduction to international politics or economics, a master's degree in an appropriate, relevant field is the usual prerequisite. But structural changes in higher education employment patterns have meant that for at least the last two decades, there has been an oversupply of PhDs in the social sciences and the humanities—qualified scholars who have not found full-time employment at four-year colleges. Consequently, deans and hiring committees prefer to hire applicants with more advanced credentials. Community colleges can now staff most of their classes with PhDs, so if you hold a master's degree, you should be prepared to make a case for your particular professional expertise or previous teaching experience in order to be competitive.

A PhD and Tenure-Track Employment

Earning a PhD is the threshold for the great majority of higher education teaching and research positions. However, excelling in a PhD program—let alone simply finishing—is no longer a secure path to college or university employment. So you should not consider a PhD as a lengthy and expensive preparation for a specific career but rather as an opportunity to develop your research skills, grow as a thinker, and get some experience as a college teacher—in preparation for a range of possible jobs, both in academia and beyond.

For individuals interested in international affairs, long-held conventional wisdom still prevails: A discipline-specific PhD (in history, political science, sociology, or economics) is the most secure route because you are then eligible for jobs in academic departments and interdisciplinary programs, including international studies, development studies, area studies, and women's studies, for example. If you are coming from an interdisciplinary background, carefully consider the kinds of books and articles you most enjoy reading and the kinds of research questions that interest you as you focus on a subject. In most international fields a PhD will take between five and eight years to complete, with at least three of those years devoted to your individual, loosely supervised research project. To succeed, you need to be

Considering a PhD

Laura J. Mitchell

A PhD program is not the best place to wait out an economic downturn or take some more classes while you figure out what else you might do. Just because you are a good student is not reason enough to stay in school. But if there is a topic you are passionate about, and you want to spend the next five to seven years posing questions and looking for answers, the professional and intellectual formation of a PhD program might suit you well.

Admission to top-tier PhD programs is highly selective (and a degree from an institution without a national reputation is unlikely to offer the research support or post-degree employment opportunities that would make your effort worthwhile). In the social science and humanities, the most competitive applicants present a coherent (if still open-ended) research interest, a strong sense of the field (why history, economics, or anthropology is the best framework for approaching your research question), and a compelling reason to work in a specific department (faculty expertise, library resources, exceptional language training, or other area studies support). Being able to put a competitive application together takes motivation, research, a wide range of advice, and some long-range planning. Applications are typically due during the fall term for admission a year later. If you are starting from absolute scratch, gearing up in August or September may not leave you enough time to do the necessary research, make contacts, and secure helpful letters of recommendation.

General admissions criteria vary greatly across programs. Outside the laboratory sciences, a master's degree is generally not required to apply

(Continued on page 243)

self-disciplined and highly motivated to purse a set of research questions for its own end, not simply to complete an assignment or fulfill a requirement necessary for future employment.

For those who want a full-time faculty appointment, there is a structured hiring process for the transition from PhD to faculty. The job cycle follows the academic calendar; vacancies are nationally (and internationally) advertised, and application closing dates are strict. The hiring process, from posting a job to making an offer, can take nine months; it is typically complete by late spring, so that the successful applicant can wrap up his or her current year's teaching obligations and move in time for the start of the next academic year.

The path for a newly hired assistant professor working toward tenure is also quite clearly marked. The specific requirements vary by campus, but

for PhD programs. However, students who transition directly from finishing a bachelor's degree in the spring to a PhD program the next fall are a minority. Applicants with some relevant professional experience, time living outside the United States, long-term language study, or evidence of success in other graduate programs are simply more competitive. Most programs publish minimally acceptable undergraduate grade point average and Graduate Record Examination scores; many have profiles of their current students on the web. Logging hours on the Internet will give you a good idea of how your interests and experience fit in various departments.

Ask faculty members you know for advice about programs to consider. You will need personalized, detailed letters of recommendation in your application. It is helpful to start that process well ahead of time by having conversations with as many professors as you can, asking them about their grad school experiences and where they think grad students are currently doing the most exciting work. You will want to follow those conversations up with more web-based research to learn which faculty members in those programs would be potential advisors for you. It is a good idea to write to those individuals to ask if they are currently accepting PhD students, and whether or not they are interested in supervising your proposed topic.

The process just to apply to a top school is admittedly daunting. If that puts you off, then maybe the PhD route is not for you. Pursuing a PhD demands exceptional self-discipline and motivation. You have to want to do the research on your own, without deadlines or close supervision. If you are not spurred by curiosity and internally compelled to complete a big project, then being in a PhD program becomes a burden, rather than an opportunity.

in general consist of a record of scholarly publications, positive teaching evaluations, and evidence of participation in faculty self-governance and campus life (serving on committees). Tenure affords lifetime employment security, so the evaluation of a tenure application after a five- or six-year probationary period is quite rigorous—and stressful for the candidate. But the rewards of academic life are great. Faculty members teach courses on topics that interest them and pursue research that is entirely self-directed. Working hours can be long, but offer a higher degree of flexibility than most other professions. Outside scheduled classes, faculty can arrange time for research, grading student papers, and meeting with students around family and civic commitments. The downside of such flex time is that work can often encroach on evenings and weekends. But I find the trade-off to be hugely beneficial. I will grade papers (on a topic I set) in the evening, in

Notes from the Field

Georgetown University
Nicole Bibbins Sedaca, MSFS 1997

After a decade of democracy, human rights, and security work at the State Department and three years in Ecuador running a democracy project and teaching at the Universidad de San Francisco de Quito, returning to Georgetown to teach graduate students was a perfect next step for me. My work in the public and nongovernmental organization sectors provided me with tremendous hands-on experience in democracy and human right policy and programming, which allow me to approach my teaching from both practical and academic perspectives. Georgetown has a strong reputation for providing students with the academic framework, global perspective, and practical understanding to prepare them for professional success, and I am delighted to be part of that effort. With courses on religion and international affairs, policy innovation, and new global security challenges, I am able to explore the academic and applied outlooks on issues central to foreign policy challenges.

I find academia tremendously enriching for many reasons. This time has allowed me to delve deeper into the theoretical underpinnings of the issues I have worked on for years, and challenges me to think more creatively about foreign policy prescriptions. Additionally, being part of a diverse community of academicians and practitioners is a rich and rewarding experience that brings even greater depth to my learning and teaching. But the absolute best and most important part is contributing to the exciting educational process of a talented, motivated, and inquisitive group of students. Their energy, curiosity, and passion are motivating, and I am privileged to participate in their educational and professional development, and to see them launch into amazing international careers.

The flexibility of academia has allowed me to be able to serve on boards of two nongovernmental organizations—one promoting religious freedom, and the other combating human trafficking and violence against the poor—as well as undertake writing projects on democracy and human rights issues. And equally important, these flexible opportunities allow me to dedicate time to my family and personal undertakings as well.

exchange for having some daytime hours free to participate in events at my child's school. Few jobs consistently offer this kind of flexibility and the luxury of setting your own intellectual agenda. I am never bored, and the work is never routine.

The Range of Academic Life

Whether you are responding to media requests for interviews at a center for global cooperation and security, editing a journal of European studies, teaching a night class on arms control, preparing a group of students in Nebraska for a trip to central Africa, or introducing a group of freshmen to the challenges of world history, working life on campus affords you an unlimited extension of the best aspects of student life: exploration, new learning, and steady contact with intelligent, motivated, and engaged people. It also offers perks that student life does not: a steady paycheck, a good benefits package, and the opportunity to forge long-term connections with people working toward a shared goal.

Careers within Think Tanks and Research Institutes

Kevin Massy

Kevin Massy, a graduate of the Master of Science in Foreign Service program at Georgetown University, was the associate director of the Energy Security Initiative in the Foreign Policy Program at the Brookings Institution in Washington between 2010 and 2013.

Between the profit-driven frenzy of the private sector and the political treadmill of life in the government sits the nonprofit research sector, which comprises think tanks and research institutes. The value of this sector lies in its ability to bring to public policy discussions considered analysis that is independent of business or political interests and that, unlike research conducted by private-sector consulting firms or government departments, is shared in the public domain to improve the quality of policymaking. In comparison with other democracies, the United States has a large number of such think tanks and nongovernmental organizations, and the output from some of these institutions has a significant impact on the way that governments and businesses interact and make decisions. In an age of fragmented and partisan news media, such organizations also provide an increasingly important role as arbiters of information both domestically and internationally.

Work in the think tank sector can be diverse, intellectually stimulating, substantive, and rewarding. It often involves tackling some of the world's most difficult policy problems without the distraction of commercial or political deadlines. It is a sector that attracts some of the most intelligent, creative people in the knowledge economy, and many think tanks comprise clusters of smart, motivated employees working on a dizzying range of inter-connected issues. Removed from many commercial and political pressures, employment in the think tank sector can offer the opportunity for a healthy work/life balance. In many think tanks based in Washington, work plans and projects correspond roughly to the academic year, meaning that the summer season sees a reduction in the number of events and meetings and a less-demanding schedule. Even during other times of year, work in the think tank sector does not typically demand the long working days and weekend shifts required in the private sector. In addition to having a meaningful impact on public policy and public opinion and relatively humane working hours, think tanks also provide their employees with a longer-term platform for starting or advancing their careers in the public and private sectors. Many of the senior employees in the sector have worked at the highest level of government, and they can provide junior staff with the connections and recommendations necessary to enter the State Department and other areas of the federal government.

With such a large number of potential benefits, it is no surprise that the sector is very popular among young foreign policy professionals. However, before resolving on a move to a think tank, it is important to know what to expect when you get there, including some of the sector's potential limita-tions. First, very few people make a career in the think tank sector. Although many organizations in the public and private sectors provide scope for ad-vancement within a specific field, think tanks are different. In many think tanks it is impossible for an employee to join in a junior position—such as a research assistant—and progress upward through the organization. Even for people joining with many years of sector-specific experience and advanced degrees, the options for advancement within certain areas of the think tank sector are limited without a doctorate. The second consideration is that very few people become rich in the sector; given the high level of demand for positions at many levels and think tanks' nonprofit status, the salaries they are able to pay are low relative to the private sector, and, in many cases, rela-tive to positions requiring comparable skills and qualifications in the public sector. Finally, think tanks can feel highly structured and bureaucratic—in the words of one my colleagues, they provide all the administrative efficiency of the federal government combined with the creative flexibility of academia; in other words, not much of either.

The engine of the academic research community are fellows and senior fellows, who conduct self-directed research to produce books, papers, journal articles, newspaper opinion pieces, and give presentations to policymakers, public- and private-sector stakeholders (often at conferences), and media interviews. The definition of fellows and senior fellows and the requirements for entry into such positions vary by institution. Some think tanks—especially older, more academically focused institutions or those dealing with highly technical or quantitative subject matter—require fellows to be educated to the PhD level at a minimum. The work of the Brookings Institution, for example, is based on professional scholars, the vast majority of whom have doctorates and postdoctorates from the world's leading schools of international affairs and political science. In a minority of cases fellows and senior fellows do not hold doctorates; in such cases they have other advanced degrees (mostly law degrees) or come with distinguished careers in the public sector. In other research organizations the requirements for appointment as a fellow or senior fellow do not include a PhD. The Center for Strategic and International Studies, the Carnegie Endowment for International Peace, the Pew Research Center, and the Atlantic Council are all examples of well-respected research organizations that hire a significant proportion of fellows without doctorates. In most cases, irrespective of the formal academic requirement, fellows and senior fellows are candidates who have proven themselves to be authorities in certain subjects before their arrival, in the public, private, or nonprofit sectors. It is very rare that fellows are hired directly out of graduate school.

Between fellows and junior staff (see below), the think tank world offers a few middle-tier positions. Such positions, often at the assistant director level, range from being wholly administrative, with responsibilities for budgeting, management of staff, events, and communications, to being predominantly substantive, with responsibilities similar to those of fellows and senior fellows. Entry requirements for such positions often include an advanced degree from a leading school and several years of proven professional experience in the sector, often in a public-facing role and with a demonstrated publications record.

For people graduating with masters' degrees looking to directly enter the world of think tanks and academia, the more likely entry point is as a research assistant or project coordinator. Research assistant positions involve the provision of research and administrative support to senior scholars. Project coordinators typically have less of a substantive focus and more administrative responsibilities. The competitive landscape for junior positions within think tanks is changing. Such positions provide an excellent opportunity for young, ambitious professionals to gain the contacts and the visibility (often through articles copublished with senior scholars) to advance their careers in either the public or private sectors. Given the high level of competition, some think tanks are beginning to regard a graduate degree in international affairs from a leading school (e.g., Georgetown, the Paul H. Nitze School of

Advanced International Studies at Johns Hopkins, Columbia, or Harvard) as table stakes; that is, as a necessary but not sufficient requirement for consideration.

To succeed as candidates for such positions, both undergraduate and graduate students need to differentiate themselves with relevant experience, either from their academic programs or from previous employment. Work in the foreign policy think tank world requires strong qualitative and quantitative skill sets. Irrespective of which area of foreign policy in which you work, a fundamental grasp of economics, and its interrelationship with politics, is essential. The ability to analyze, synthesize, and distill a large amount of complex information is a critical component of life at a research-focused organization, as is the ability to communicate verbally. Strong interpersonal skills—such as verbal communication, teamwork, and multitasking—are also important. However, the single skill that is probably the most important in the research institute sector is the ability to write clearly and effectively. The product of think tanks and similar organizations is written output, in the form of books, studies, white papers, policy briefs, and newspaper articles. The ability to write to a standard that enables your work to be published with minimal editing or modification is one that will appeal to hiring managers in the sector.

The most effective way to demonstrate your writing ability is to come bearing gifts: to show the hiring manager one or more examples of your analytical writing—preferably published in a third-party journal or the like—on a subject relevant to the department's research agenda. A couple of such articles (providing they are written to a high standard) will work far more effectively in proving your suitability for a position in the research world than the most impressive abstract qualifications.

Another effective way of breaking into the international affairs research sector is through an internship. Internships provide invaluable perspective on the broader goals and culture of the institution, as well as the specific research interests of the department for which you are interested in working. The challenge with internships in the think tank world is that, given the nonprofit nature of the institutions and the high level of demand, they are usually unpaid. For those who can afford to take an unpaid internship, they are an excellent way of gaining visibility among senior staff, getting something published (depending on the requirements of the institution), and taking advantage of any openings that become available at the time or in the future. Another benefit of internships is that they provide brand recognition for your résumé. Like all hiring managers, those at think tanks and research organizations have limited time when short-listing candidates either for internships or jobs. Those candidates that have interned at organizations that hiring managers will recognize automatically differentiate themselves, creating a virtuous circle of associations and opportunity.

A final recommendation for those looking to enter the world of think tanks and research organizations: Start early, persevere, and be creative. Do not wait for internship vacancy announcements to appear at your ideal place of work: Be proactive and make inquiries. If you have applied and have not heard anything back, contact the hiring manager. If you did not get the position, follow up and suggest that the institution keep your information on file. In the meantime, seek out current employees for informal coffee discussions and get acquainted with the department's research agenda; most important, turn yourself into the supply for the institution's demands.

There are very few professional opportunities that give you the chance to directly apply the skills and experience of graduate school and to do meaningful, independent work on a wide array of important issues above the commercial and political fray. Although the competition for entry is fierce and the prospects for upward progression are limited, the rewards of working in the think tank world are worth the effort.

CHAPTER 10

The Media

The field of media and journalism is in a state of flux as the use of new media rises and the number of news outlets increases. But with change comes opportunity, and those job seekers with international affairs backgrounds have many options in the media field, as illustrated by the contributors to this chapter: a television producer, an economic reporter, and a war correspondent. Career paths today may be less traditional, but the skills needed to succeed are familiar; strong research abilities and concise writing skills are paramount. As the essays in this chapter note, expertise in a particular area—such as finance, policy, or area studies—can be extremely useful, but in and of themselves will not land you the job. The creative use of social and new media can help you build and promote your brand, and assist in the job application process. Interest in media can also lead to a career in media relations and public affairs, an area covered in the business consulting essay in chapter 8.

Careers in the Media

Sujata Thomas

Sujata Thomas is an editorial producer for Fareed Zakaria GPS *on CNN. Before joining CNN in 2007, she worked on* Foreign Exchange with Fareed Zakaria, *which aired on the Public Broadcasting Service, and* America Abroad, *which aired on NPR. She has held other positions, including with the National Football League Players Association and Share Our Strength. She received a master's of science in foreign service (MSFS) from Georgetown University and a bachelor's degree from Mount Holyoke College in politics and economics.*

Over the past ten years, the media industry has undergone a remarkable transformation. Traditional news networks and newspapers have faced increased competition from cable television, satellite radio, and online sources.

Blogs, Twitter, and social media outlets have not only become sources for information but also agents of change in their own right. This ever-changing media landscape can be daunting, but at the same time it offers a vast array of options for those seeking to build a career informing and educating the public on international affairs issues.

The media are an important player in the foreign policy arena. In this increasingly connected world, people need to understand how an economic crisis halfway around the world or a coup in an obscure, oil-rich country can affect our daily life. Some take popular media to task for dumbing down issues for public consumption, but this misses the broader point. International issues are complex, often steeped in years, decades, or even centuries of history. Although there is a place for an in-depth analysis of these issues, there is also a role for reporting that can convey them simply to the broad public, providing context for the issues of the day. To help translate these issues for a broader audience, there is a need for people who understand the details of international security issues, can speak the language of international finance, and are familiar with the players in the field of international development.

When people ask me about the typical career path for someone in the media industry, I often hesitate when answering, given that my career has been so atypical. I have had the good fortune of being in the right place at the right time and of meeting people who have helped me along the way.

My career path is unusual; I have worked in a law firm, for a National Basketball Association team, on antihunger campaigns, in the office of a CEO, and for the National Football League Players Association. The common denominator, however, was that I sought new challenges—the last thing I wanted was to be bored. In addition, everywhere I worked I built strong relationships and networks, and worked hard to connect people with others. This skill has been invaluable in my current position as an editorial producer for *Fareed Zakaria GPS* on CNN.

As an editorial producer I am responsible for the guests who appear on the international affairs show. That includes working with the executive producer and Fareed on determining the content and balance of the show each week. Basically, anything associated with a guest that appears on the show is my responsibility. I confirm their appearance on our show and handle all the logistical matters associated with their appearance—from making sure the guests gets to a studio to ensuring that the satellite feeds are operational. Making a connection with a guest is important, but maintaining relationships with them is just as crucial. It is this relationship building, coupled with the international components of our show, that make my work truly enjoyable. The constantly changing nature of my job (we focus on a new issue for every weekly show) also keeps my job exciting and interesting—and prevents boredom.

I have a real interest in international issues, and this position enables me to marry these interests with my skill in bringing people together. For instance, gathering former US secretaries of state for a show on foreign policy advice for the newly elected president of the United States was a task I really enjoyed. I get to talk with the people who have made history.

Working on international issues, often with high-level officials from around the world, adds a different and challenging element to my job. No matter who your counterpart is, you must be cognizant of their cultural norms and understand the most effective way of operating in their culture.

One program of which I am particularly proud is our interview with now-former Iranian president Mahmoud Ahmadinejad. Along with most journalists in the United States, we wanted an interview with the Iranian president. However, this was not something that was going to develop overnight. I understood that it was imperative that we establish trust and build good faith with the Iranian administration. I worked with their press people at their UN mission in New York, and we interviewed their finance minister and foreign minister when they came to New York. Throughout these interactions, we developed a level of trust. The Iranians knew that we would not avoid difficult issues, but they also had confidence that we were looking to understand their positions and share that knowledge with our audience, not to trick them into making a mistake that would then be aired to gin up ratings.

One evening while out with friends, I received a text message from the Iranian mission's press official asking if we wanted to interview President Ahmadinejad the following week. Four days later we were traveling to Iran for the interview. Although it only took 48 hours to nail down the interview and deal with the logistics, it was possible only because of the two years we had spent developing the relationship and laying the groundwork.

I went to graduate school to focus my diverse interests. Unlike many of my classmates I did not concentrate on one subject area but instead took courses in everything that interested me, from development to microfinance to conflict resolution. I could never claim that I was an expert in any one area, but I could talk on a range of issues such as the euro zone crisis, nuclear weapons in Pakistan, and leadership dynamics in Russia. I was a true generalist. I was comfortable talking across the spectrum of issues, as one learns to do in graduate school, but I also could dig deep when needed, and I knew where to go to get more detail and get experts who knew the issues backward and forward. Perhaps most important, I could translate my academic knowledge in these areas into something that was easily understood by the layperson. This led me to a job with a radio show that was aired on National Public Radio, and then to television with Fareed Zakaria at PBS. Admittedly, at the time I did not have the deep rolodex that one usually

Notes from the Field

Bloomberg News

Allen Wan, MSFS 2000

After working for several years as a journalist overseas, I felt I needed a change and wanted to pursue a career in foreign policy. As a political science major in college, I had always fancied myself being a diplomat and thought entering a top-notch international affairs program would give me that opportunity. During the summer of my first year at MSFS, I was offered several internships with the government. The position I chose required a high-level security clearance, which unfortunately did not come through in time. Luckily, I was offered an internship with the Japan desk of the US Treasury Department during my second year and spent several months gaining valuable unpaid government experience writing analytical reports using Bloomberg data. This experience would prove useful in subsequent jobs with the government, as Asia Bureau Chief of CBS MarketWatch, and my current position as Deputy Bureau Chief for Bloomberg News in Shanghai. My favorite class was a small seminar on national security taught by Tony Lake, President Bill Clinton's former National Security Advisor. I also found courses in Statistics (regression analysis), Chinese history, and an MBA class in African economic development very useful in my future work. Many of my MSFS classmates joined the Foreign Service, or took

(Continued on page 255)

needs in such a position. But I could reach back to my Georgetown MSFS graduate professors, such as Chester Crocker and Anthony Lake, and use their connections to get more information on specific issues and find guests for our show.

Getting Started in the Media

The mass media form such a diverse—and constantly changing—field that it can seem overwhelming for those trying to break in. The opportunities are quite wide-ranging, from the job function to the type of media. For instance, one could pursue work in print, radio, cable, or network TV, or Web media. Job functions range from reporting and writing to filming, editing audiovisual pieces, producing programs, and even performing business functions for a media organization. Those interested in print journalism will also want to

jobs working for international banks. I chose to return to journalism because I realized I enjoyed making a living traveling and meeting people from all walks of life. I just needed a break from the job to realize that. Looking back, I am glad I went to Georgetown, though that is mostly for the friendships that endure to this day.

At Bloomberg in Shanghai, I write and edit stories about anything from Bitcoin to pollution, though my focus is on the nation's financial markets and economy. Even though China is the world's second-biggest economy and has one of the largest stock markets, very few people truly understand what is going on because of its lack of transparency and accountability. Part of the problem is that economic data is very unreliable and the stock market is used by the state to boost its coffers rather than to reward investors. My job is to help clients determine whether China is an investible country or the world's biggest Ponzi scheme, as some critics have argued. There is always a risk of retribution from the government when it does not like what you write. Al Jazeera's China correspondent was forced to leave the country after her visa was not renewed. Bloomberg's web site in China was attacked by hackers and eventually blocked after we wrote award-winning investigative stories on the nation's new leadership. Reporting on China has its risks but there are plenty of rewards as well. I was recruited to teach an eMBA class to executives at Shanghai Jiaotong University about China's markets and economy, and find myself constantly challenged by the level of inquiry from students and the need to change the material to keep up with what's happening in the country. China is the best story around and where it ends up will have global ramifications for a long time.

consider whether writing for a daily, weekly, or monthly publication is most appealing, given the different rhythms of their publication cycles. Internships can be helpful for making contacts, developing skills, and gaining a better perspective on the industry and the type of media or job functions that one enjoys. Similarly, doing freelance or working as a stringer for a newspaper or other media outlet is also a great way to develop a body of work, or clips, that can later be used in job applications, or for getting one's foot in the door at a larger media outlet. Some aspiring journalists start out at small media outlets covering local news and try to work their way up to larger metropolitan outlets. Others try to get internships or lower-level positions at the bigger-name publications or programs. There are pluses and minuses to both approaches. At small outlets one may be able to get more hands-on, interesting, and varied work experience and responsibility. At larger outlets one gets the benefit of having the brand name on their résumé and

Notes from the Field

The Wall Street Journal's *Beirut Bureau*

Rima Abushakra, MSFS 2006

Being a journalist feels personal and can drift into routine. I had run a big relief effort in northern Lebanon in 2007 during the battles in the Nahr el-Bared camp. After that incredible experience, I felt constricted at a desk job at a government office in Beirut, and journalism really appealed to me. Journalism gives you the opportunity to look at how big—sometimes foreign—decisions impact the average person. You get to experience history in small ways and portray them for the reader. These historic events become more than just the background to your life; they become part of your own memories.

In my year working with Agence France-Presse in Beirut, I covered everything from a political crisis, to Hezbollah's armed takeover of Beirut, to the construction of modern high rises at the expense of the country's antiquities. There is a sense of duty in getting the story right. But you also have to rationalize that the events are happening to you and others living in your midst. Journalism allows you to look at a society from a variety of angles.

(Continued on page 257)

the opportunity to network with some of the leading professionals in the industry. It depends on the personality type of the individual to determine the path that is best for them. There is not one best way to get to your dream job.

Regardless of which path you follow, networking with your colleagues is important. It will not just help you build relationships that could bear fruit in the future; it will also allow you to gather as much information as you can about the industry to enable you to make informed decisions about your career path. I have often found that most people are very approachable and happy to talk with students or interns who express an interest in their job or industry. Be proactive, flexible, and willing to take on additional tasks, and try to meet as many people at the station as you can. Take them to coffee and ask them questions.

Like networking, the value of internships cannot be overstated. Pick a couple of areas that interest you and try them out through internships. Seek out internship positions with local TV stations, newspapers, or journals. Work for your university's international affairs journal. No matter what it

I left journalism for a little while and have now returned to the field working as an independently contracted reporter with the *Wall Street Journal*'s Beirut Bureau. The biggest part of my job is covering Syria, a country I had only visited once and knew little about, but a country whose uprising and subsequent devastating civil war will have such far-reaching repercussions that we are only beginning to understand. I feel lucky, but as I said, it feels personal. So while it can be a really difficult experience, it is certainly exciting.

The industry is definitely changing with time. I have always wanted to work for a newspaper and feel fortunate to have this opportunity. It is amazing to see how much research goes into a story and how newspapers package the stories in order to differentiate their product from breaking news. It is also fascinating to see how mundane factors like word count, space on the foreign page that day, and personal assessments about how significant something is determine what news the consumer gets.

Working for a wire is a great stepping-stone for a career in journalism. It teaches you to build a story with the most accurate detail in the shortest amount of time possible. You can get bogged down in the details and events, but wires are on the ground and they produce quality work.

There is not one clear trajectory to making it as a journalist. Sometimes all it takes is being in the right place at the right time and proving yourself. The key is to keep things in perspective and not get too caught up in the excitement: keep focused on being safe while remaining true to your craft.

is, you need to gain experience not only to build your résumé but also to test the waters and make sure that you like the particular area of media. One of the advantages of this field is that there are no specific boxes that one needs to check in order to qualify for an entry-level position—although learning the computer programs associated with your field is very helpful and an example of how internships can be valuable.

Whether you are an undergraduate or graduate student, take advantage of the access you have to university resources (e.g., film departments and equipment) and to people. If you are interested in being on the air, check out a camera (or use your iPhone) and interview people for school projects or for the campus or local newspaper. You will be surprised how willing people are to be interviewed by students for school papers, projects, or news articles. If you are interested in writing, write press pieces for the university's press office or website, or start a blog on your own. Likewise, use this opportunity to network. Take people in the industry out for coffee to learn about their jobs and positions to help you decide if this is an area in which you would be interested working.

It is important to realize that this field is very hierarchical. When going into television, most people start as a production assistant (performing tasks such as logging in tapes and looking for video), then rise to the position of associate producer, producer, and eventually executive producer. My field—production—is not typically internationally oriented. Shows such as PBS's *The Charlie Rose Show*, CNN's *Amanpour*, and CBS's *60 Minutes* all cover a mixture of domestic and international issues, so it is possible to find a position with an international component. Many of those with similar positions eventually end up in public relations, either within a government doing press relations; for large organizations, focusing on getting their top officials into the media; or for public relations firms, helping clients manage crises or the public perception of their brand.

The Value of an International Affairs Degree

Although many students interested in media careers will consider attending journalism school, the reality is that the industry does not reward students for gaining extra academic credentials. A person's ability to rise in the field is typically based on the quality of his or her work, past experience, and connections. Your degree will not translate into a job or higher salary. Still, I have found that my degree in international affairs has been extremely helpful in developing my broad base of knowledge and contacts, and my ability to talk about international issues, which has helped me to succeed in this field. If you have a degree in international affairs, you will need to be able to articulate the skills that you bring to the table that set you apart from other applicants: an understanding of the political, economic, and social aspects of international affairs; the ability to identify the key points in complex issues and communicate them to a broader lay audience; and strong writing and research skills. These abilities, coupled with relevant internships and experiences, will make you a compelling candidate.

The Media's Future

The media industry is not without its challenges. Like so many other sectors, media outlets face budget issues and cutbacks, which often lead to a reduction in full-time employees. International bureaus of US media organizations increasingly are targeted for reduction or closure, which complicates the job search for those interested in international issues. Freelance war and field reporters are now more the norm than the exception. When I asked Thomas Friedman of the *New York Times* what advice he would have for those entering the industry, he said he would encourage people to go into the field—to Cairo, Islamabad, and the like—and write and submit freelance pieces. Take the opportunity to get to know people who are in the field reporting; you will gain legitimacy.

With the changing media landscape, it is difficult to predict where the industry will be in ten years. However, no matter how the field shifts, if you are good at what you do and are flexible and able to adapt to a changing environment, you will succeed. It is important to find something that speaks to you, about which you are passionate, and that plays to your strengths. If your job involves something that you like, you are more likely to excel. You should not enter the field of journalism for fame and fortune, but rather because of the intellectual challenge, the rush you get when you are in the field, and the importance you place on influencing the public discourse.

PART III

Directory of Organizations

Directory of Organizations

Barrett J. Helmer and Jennifer E. Steffensen

The *Careers in International Affairs* Directory of Organizations is a resource to help you explore the great diversity of international affairs career opportunities available in the United States and throughout the world. The directory lists more than 250 organizations that we believe are especially relevant to those seeking careers in the international affairs arena. Although this directory is not an exhaustive list of all relevant international affairs organizations, the agencies, businesses, firms, nongovernmental organizations (NGOs), think tanks, and media outlets that follow were carefully selected based on their past history of employing and offering internships to students with international affairs degrees from universities that belong to the Association of Professional Schools in International Affairs.

As you explore the following organizations, please note that the directory is organized in the same order as this book's chapters themselves—beginning with US government agencies and ending with careers in media outlets. Each entry starts with the organization's name, headquarters location, and website URL, followed by a general description of the organization, which typically includes details about its size, function, and office locations in the United States and around the world.

In preparation for including the individual organization overviews, we visited each organization's website, evaluated summaries of the organization written by independent sources such as Bloomberg and Reuters, and reviewed publicly available company information such as stock filings and company reports. Additionally, in some cases we reviewed business and trade magazines that had special features and rankings, such as the *Fortune* 500.

Where possible, we included information about the types of jobs or internship opportunities offered and desirable qualities of applicants. However, this information is subject to change, as organizations, and their goals and needs, continually change and evolve. The prudent career seeker thus should view this directory as a starting rather than ending point for their research on international affairs–related organizations. Additionally, we encourage you to be open to considering other organizations that may not have been included in the directory as potentially viable employers. Finally, we advise you to consider the organization listings in tandem with the earlier chapters of this book. The book's international affairs career essays and "Notes from the Field" pieces provide more details about career opportunities and trajectories in these organizations, about how to break into the field, and, in general, a more comprehensive picture of the attributes and experiences desired by employers within individual organizations and across industry sectors.

We hope you will find the organization directory to be a useful resource as you navigate through opportunities in the international affairs arena, and that you continue to consult its pages as you explore the twists, turns, and many exciting possibilities that lie ahead in your career.

The US Government

Executive Branch Agencies

Agriculture, US Department of
Washington, DC
www.usda.gov

The US Department of Agriculture (USDA) is responsible for developing and executing US federal government policy on agriculture, farming, forestry, and food. USDA's key functions are to expand markets for agricultural products, enhance food safety by addressing foodborne hazards, provide food assistance and education, and to serve as a key player between the US public and private sectors. USDA also represents US agriculture and its related interests abroad, and pursues these efforts through the **Foreign Agriculture Service (FAS)**. The FAS works to build and improve foreign market access for US food and agricultural products, build new markets, and improve the competitiveness of US agriculture in global markets. The FAS also administers the USDA's export-financing programs designed to expand and maintain foreign markets for US products. The FAS carries out a broad array of international training, technical assistance, and other collaborative activities with developing and transitional countries to facilitate trade and promote food security. The FAS has a competitive testing and application process, somewhat similar to State Department's recruiting process for Foreign Service officers.

Commerce, US Department of
Washington, DC
www.commerce.gov

The Department of Commerce promotes US international trade, economic growth, and technological advancement. Commerce works to strengthen the international economic position of the United States and facilitates trade by opening up new markets for US goods and services. Commerce is made up of nine broad divisions—Bureau of Industry and Security, Economics and Statistics Administration, Economic Development Administration, International Trade Administration, Minority Business Development Administration, National Oceanic and Atmospheric Administration, National Telecommunications and Information Administration, Patent and Trademark Office, and National Institute of Standards and Technology—each of which has international opportunities. One of the most relevant areas of international opportunity is the **Foreign Commercial Service** (FCS). Like the USDA's Foreign Agriculture Service and Department of State's Foreign Service officer paths, the FCS is the US Commercial Service's international service corps, which represents American trade and investment interests abroad, particularly in export expansion. Other elements of the International Trade Administration also help US organizations compete at home and abroad: manufacturing and services, market access and compliance, and import administration. Whereas the International Trade Commission is studying the effects of unfair trade practices that have an impact on US products and markets, the International Trade Administration is working to ensure that US products find their way to foreign markets.

Defense, US Department of
Washington, DC
www.defense.gov

The Department of Defense (DOD) is responsible for providing the United States with the military forces it needs for its security, and it does so by coordinating and supervising all agencies and functions of the US government related to the nation's security and its armed forces. DOD is the largest and oldest US government agency, and it includes the military services (Air Force, Army, Marines, Navy), National Guard, the Joint Chiefs of Staff, nine combatant commands (the Africa, Central, European, Northern, Pacific, Southern, Special Operations, Strategic, and Transportation), and seventeen defense agencies (including the Defense Intelligence Agency, Defense Threat Reduction Agency, and Defense Security Cooperation Agency). In addition to the more than 1 million active duty service members, DOD employs more than 600,000 civilians. Offices of potential interest to international affairs professionals include the Office of the Under Secretary of Defense for Policy

(OUSDP), which develops and coordinates US national security and defense policies, and provides advice to the secretary of defense on the integration and oversight of DOD policy and plans to achieve national security objectives. The OUSDP covers a wide range of issues, such as counternarcotics, counterproliferation, counterterrorism, cyber policy, international security, special operations, stability operations, and strategy and force planning. Other DOD offices with significant international responsibilities include the Office of the Under Secretary of Defense for Intelligence and the Office of the Under Secretary of Defense for Acquisitions, Technology, and Logistics. Students of international affairs may also be interested in defense agencies such as the Defense Threat Reduction Agency, which focuses on safeguarding the United States and its allies from weapons of mass destruction by providing capabilities to reduce, eliminate, and counter the threat and mitigate its effects. DOD hires individuals with a wide variety of backgrounds. Information about jobs and internships with DOD can be found on its website.

Energy, US Department of
Washington, DC
www.energy.gov

The Department of Energy's (DOE's) fundamental objective is to ensure the United States' security by addressing its energy, environmental, and nuclear challenges through science and technology solutions. As the primary agency focused on securing US energy needs and markets, DOE promotes innovation and science education, and advances new biofuel technologies for energy generation and energy-efficient products and buildings. DOE also works on US nuclear efforts and enhances nuclear security through defense, nonproliferation, and environmental initiatives. DOE is increasingly integrated with the United States' fundamental strategy to reduce its dependence on foreign oil, address climate change, and develop domestic and international markets for new energies and products. DOE also has a small intelligence section that works on the nuclear-focused capabilities of foreign states.

Environmental Protection Agency
Washington, DC
www.epa.gov

The Environmental Protection Agency (EPA) is responsible for executing federal laws for the protection of the environment. EPA's mandate covers water quality, air quality, waste, pesticides, toxic substances, and radiation. Within these broad areas of responsibility, EPA program efforts include research and development and the development, implementation, and enforcement of environmental regulations. EPA is involved in many policy and technical aspects of transnational, regional, and global environmental and health-related issues. These international activities also include information sharing with many international organizations and directly with other countries on common issues, problems, and solutions.

Export-Import Bank
Washington, DC
www.exim.gov

The US Export-Import Bank (Ex-Im Bank) is the main US government agency responsible for boosting exports of US goods and services. With this focus, the mission of Ex-Im Bank is to create US jobs through the financing of exports to international markets and buyers. Ex-Im Bank achieves this effort through a host of loan, guarantee, funding, and insurance programs. A main difference between Ex-Im Bank and other US government trade-focused agencies is that Ex-Im Bank's expertise applies to small businesses, and states that "no transaction is too small," as 87 percent of Ex-Im Bank's transactions benefit small business exporters of American-made goods and services. Ex-Im Bank's products include risk protection, buyer credit, working capital, and term financing. Ex-Im Bank takes full-time and part-time interns throughout the year.

Federal Bureau of Investigation
Washington, DC
www.fbi.gov

The responsibility for investigating violations of most federal laws and civil matters of interest to the US government rests with the Federal Bureau of Investigation (FBI). In addition to these duties, the FBI provides the executive branch with information related to national security and interacts with cooperating foreign police and security services. Because the FBI is an intelligence-driven and threat-focused national security organization with both intelligence and law enforcement responsibilities, its mission is to protect and defend the United States against terrorist and foreign intelligence threats, to uphold and enforce US criminal laws, and to provide leadership and criminal justice services to federal, state, municipal, and international agencies and partners. The FBI is part of the Department of Justice.

Board of Governors of the Federal Reserve System
Washington, DC
www.federalreserve.gov

As the central bank of the United States, the Federal Reserve Board sets monetary policy to foster stable economic conditions and long-term economic growth. The Fed's responsibilities include creating monetary policy, supervising and regulating banks, maintaining the stability of the financial system, conducting economic research, and providing financial services to the United States and foreign governments and depository institutions. The Fed is made up of twelve regional Federal Reserve banks that, along with the Federal Open Market Committee, constitute the Federal Reserve System. The regional Federal Reserve banks include the Federal Reserve Bank of New York, which independently executes open market operations, serves as an agent in foreign exchange and financial markets, and stores gold reserves on behalf of foreign central banks.

Homeland Security, US Department of
Washington, DC
www.dhs.gov

The Department of Homeland Security (DHS) was created by the Homeland Security Act of 2002 to coordinate and provide a base for the key US national security efforts of various institutions. With nearly 240,000 employees, DHS's fundamental mission is to monitor and mitigate threats to the United States, including preventing terrorism and enhancing security, managing borders, administering immigration laws, securing cyberspace, and ensuring disaster resilience. DHS has four main directorates (Border and Transportation Security, Emergency Preparedness and Response, Science and Technology, and Information Analysis and Infrastructure Protection) and oversees a number of agencies and administrations such as the Coast Guard, Transportation Security Administration, and the US Secret Service. Elements of particular interest to students of international affairs may include the Office of Intelligence and Analysis; the Office of Policy, Immigration, and Customs Enforcement; Customs and Border Protection; Citizenship and Immigration Services; and the Secret Service (which has field offices across the United States and in sixteen foreign countries).

International Trade Commission
Washington, DC
www.usitc.gov

Considered a quasi-independent agency, the mission of the US International Trade Commission (ITC) is to administer US trade laws in a fair and objective manner; provide the president, the Office of the US Trade Representative, and Congress with independent analysis, data, and support on matters relating to tariffs and international trade; and maintain the US Tariff schedule. In essence, ITC's primary objective is to ensure sound and accurate US trade policy. ITC's five major operations include import injury investigations, intellectual property–based import investigations, industry and economic analysis, tariff and trade information services, and trade policy support. In all these efforts, ITC is working to determine the impact of imports on US industries, and subsequently calls for action against unfair trade practices.

Justice, US Department of
Washington, DC
www.justice.gov

The Department of Justice (DOJ) is the primary federal criminal investigation and enforcement agency. DOJ is made up of divisions, offices, and law enforcement agencies. For students of international affairs, the Criminal Division is especially relevant because it participates in criminal justice activities involving foreign parties. The Criminal Division's Office of International Affairs supports the department's legal divisions, US attorneys, and state and local prosecutors regarding questions of foreign and international law, including issues related to extradition and mutual legal assistance treaties. Office attorneys also participate in a number of committees established under the auspices of the United Nations and other international organizations that are directed at resolving a variety of international law enforcement problems such as narcotics trafficking and money laundering. Although many DOJ employees have legal degrees, there are paralegal, support, and research positions that work on a variety of interesting and important cases. Of special note is the inclusion in DOJ of the Drug Enforcement Administration, which is the top agency for the domestic enforcement of federal drug laws, and for coordinating and pursuing US drug investigations abroad.

Labor, US Department of
Washington, DC
www.dol.gov

The Department of Labor (DOL) is responsible for occupational safety, wage and hour standards, unemployment insurance benefits, reemployment services, and some economic statistics. The purpose of DOL is to promote the welfare of US wage earners, job seekers, and retirees. The agency accomplishes this by improving working conditions, advancing opportunities for profitable employment, and assuring work-related benefits and rights. DOL's international activities are concentrated in the Bureau of International Labor Affairs. The bureau's major duties are in the areas of trade, combating child labor, trafficking and forced labor, and representing the United States in international organizations. The bureau also conducts research on international labor issues and monitors international labor developments.

National Security Council
Washington, DC
www.whitehouse.gov/administration/eop/nsc

The National Security Council (NSC) is the president's primary forum for evaluating national security and foreign policy matters with appointed senior national security advisers and cabinet officials. The NSC's function is to advise and assist the president on national security and foreign policies. The NSC also serves as the president's principal arm for coordinating these policies with other US government agencies. Given the high-level nature of the executive branch, the NSC deals with issues of the highest national importance. A large percentage of the NSC's professional staff members are temporarily loaned from other US government agencies.

Nuclear Regulatory Commission
Rockville, Maryland
www.nrc.gov

The Nuclear Regulatory Commission (NRC) was developed to ensure the safe use of radioactive materials for beneficial civilian purposes while protecting people and the environment. NRC regulates commercial nuclear power plants and other uses of nuclear materials through licensing, inspection, and the enforcement of key governmental requirements. NRC's efforts are focused on operating and monitoring nuclear reactors, developing and properly managing nuclear materials, appropriately disposing of nuclear waste, and ensuring nuclear safeguards and security. NRC's Office of International Programs supports US international interests in the promotion of the safe and secure use of nuclear materials and in guarding against the proliferation of nuclear weapons. NRC provides assistance to international organizations and countries in developing effective regulatory mechanisms and rigorous safety standards for nuclear materials.

Office of Management and Budget
Washington, DC
www.whitehouse.gov/omb

The Office of Management and Budget (OMB) is the largest office within the Executive Office of the President of the United States. OMB performs a wide variety of functions, including developing and executing the federal budget; overseeing performance of government agencies; reviewing and coordinating all federal regulations and executive orders; and analyzing all legislative correspondence with Congress, including reviewing testimony and draft bills. OMB also assesses the quality of agency programs, policies, and procedures and ensures their adherence with presidential policies. The

National Security Programs Office, which is divided into two divisions (International Affairs and National Security), is responsible for OMB's review of international programs.

Overseas Private Investment Corporation
Washington, DC
www.opic.gov

The Overseas Private Investment Corporation (OPIC) provides political risk insurance, financing, and a variety of investor services to encourage US private investment in emerging and frontier markets around the world to promote US foreign policy interests, address development challenges, and support job and economic growth in the US and abroad. Although wholly owned by the US government, OPIC is organized along the lines of a private corporation. OPIC works to encourage and transfer private-sector funds from the United States into investment in developing countries and countries transitioning from nonmarket to market economies. OPIC's principal activities include insuring US overseas investment against political risk and violence, and financing businesses overseas through loans and private investment funds.

State, US Department of
Washington, DC
www.state.gov

With both Foreign Service officer (FSO) and Civil Service positions, the Department of State is a top employer of international affairs students. State operates the diplomatic missions of the United States abroad and is responsible for implementing US foreign policy and diplomacy. FSOs and Civil Service personnel work together in the United States and in US embassies, consulates, and diplomatic missions around the world to accomplish the foreign policy goals of the United States. FSOs (numbering more than 12,000) can be deployed to any embassy or mission throughout the world to serve the diplomatic needs of the United States. Becoming an FSO is a rigorous, multistep, highly competitive examination process (for details, see the essay "Careers in the US Foreign Service" in chapter 3). Applicants select one of five "cones" in which they will work throughout their FSO career: consular affairs, economic affairs, management affairs, political affairs, and public diplomacy. State also employs more than 9,000 civil servants, most of whom work in Washington, formulating, representing, and implementing US foreign policy. Positions in the Civil Service include foreign affairs specialists, intelligence analysts, security specialists, economists, financial management and budget specialists, attorneys, and public affairs specialists. Offices within State are divided into regional and functional bureaus and cover a wide range of issues, including arms control and nonproliferation; conflict and stabilization; consular affairs; counterterrorism; democracy and human rights; economics, energy, and the environment; multilateral affairs; political and political-military affairs; public diplomacy; refugees and humanitarian affairs; and regional affairs. Internships are available year round in Washington and in embassies around the world. Application details are on the State Department's website.

Treasury, US Department of
Washington, DC
www.treasury.gov

The Department of the Treasury is the primary federal agency responsible for the economic and financial prosperity and security of the United States. In the international arena, Treasury works with other federal agencies, the governments of other nations, and the international financial institutions to encourage economic growth, raise standards of living, and predict and prevent, to the greatest extent possible, economic and financial crises. Treasury's Office of International Affairs protects and supports economic prosperity at home by encouraging financial stability and sound economic policies abroad. This office performs in-depth analyses of global economic and financial developments and engages with financial market participants, foreign governments, the international financial institutions, and multilateral forums to formulate and promote appropriate policies. The Office of Terrorism and Financial Intelligence develops and implements strategies to address terrorist financing both domestically and internationally. The office also seeks to prevent terrorists, weapons of mass destruction proliferators, money launderers, and drug-related individuals and organizations from illicitly using the financial system.

US Trade and Development Agency
Arlington, Virginia
www.ustda.gov

The US Trade and Development Agency (USTDA) helps companies create US jobs through the exporting of US goods and services for development projects in emerging economies. USTDA links US businesses to export opportunities by funding project planning activities, pilot projects, and reverse trade missions while creating sustainable infrastructure and economic growth in partner countries. USTDA assists US firms by identifying high-priority development projects that can be met by US commercial goods and services. USTDA's activities serve as a catalyst to encourage US private-sector involvement in infrastructure projects. USTDA accomplishes its goals by providing grants for feasibility studies, training programs, and other project planning services for public-sector development projects that can be assisted by US company expertise.

Office of the US Trade Representative
Washington, DC
www.ustr.gov

The Office of the US Trade Representative (USTR) develops and coordinates US international trade, commodity, and direct investment policy as well as overseeing trade negotiations with other countries. USTR negotiates directly with foreign governments to create trade agreements, resolve trade and commercial disputes, and participate in global trade policy organizations. USTR also meets with governments, business groups, legislators, and public interest groups to gather input on trade issues and explain the president's trade policy positions. USTR works closely with Congress and Congress's relevant committees on developing and executing appropriate trade initiatives.

Capitol Hill

Congressional Research Service
Washington, DC
www.loc.gov/crsinfo

The Congressional Research Service (CRS) is the independent, public policy research arm of the US Congress. As a legislative branch agency within the Library of Congress, CRS works primarily and directly for members of Congress and their committees and staffs on a confidential, nonpartisan basis. CRS is divided into five areas of research: US law, domestic social policy, foreign affairs, defense and trade, government and finance resources, and science and industry. The Foreign Affairs Defense and Trade Division is broken down into seven regional and functional areas, which analyze security, political, and economic developments around the world. Analysis is wide ranging and includes issues such as foreign aid effectiveness, global economic institutions, human trafficking, international arms trade, religious freedom, and weapons systems.

Government Accountability Office
Washington, DC
www.gao.gov

The Government Accountability Office (GAO) is an independent agency in the legislative branch of the federal government. Commonly known as the "investigative arm of Congress" or the "congressional watchdog," the

GAO examines how taxpayer dollars are spent and advises lawmakers and agency heads on ways to make the government work better. This agency has a mission to provide Congress with timely information that is professional, objective, fact-based, nonpartisan, nonideological, fair, and balanced. GAO has several units that are relevant to international affairs, including the International Affairs and Trade Team, which analyzes the effectiveness of US foreign aid programs and assesses how trade agreements further US interests, and the Defense Capabilities and Management and Information Technology teams, which are often involved with international issues.

House of Representatives
Washington, DC (and US state capitals)
www.house.gov

The House of Representatives is one of Congress's two chambers (the other is the Senate), and is part of the US federal government's legislative branch. The House has a total of 435 members from all fifty states, and each individual House members has his or her own staff, both in Washington and in their home state district. In addition to members of Congress's staffs, some individuals work directly for the House, primarily on its various committees and subcommittees, whose main purpose is to review existing and proposed bills and to provide oversight for the executive branch. Among others, committees of interest for international affairs students include Armed Services, Foreign Affairs, Homeland Security, and Intelligence.

Senate
Washington, DC (and US state capitals)
www.senate.gov

The Senate is one of Congress's two chambers (the other is the House of Representatives), and is part of the federal government's legislative branch. The Senate has one hundred total members, with two Senators from each state. Each individual senator has his or her own staff, both in Washington and in their home state. The Senate has the responsibility for confirming appointments of cabinet secretaries, regulatory body officials, federal judges, military officers, and ambassadors. In addition to senators' staffs, individuals work for the Senate on the various committees and subcommittees, whose main purpose is to review existing and proposed bills and the oversight of the executive branch. Among others, committees of primary interest to international affairs students include the Armed Services Committee, the Homeland Security and Government Affairs Committee, the Select Committee on Intelligence, and the Committee on Foreign Affairs.

Development Agencies

Millennium Challenge Corporation
Washington, DC
www.mcc.gov

Launched in 2004, Millennium Challenge Corporate (MCC) is an independent US foreign aid agency that delivers development assistance by forming partnerships with countries that promote good governance, economic freedom, and investment in their home populations. Under these premises, MCC offers grant-recipient countries funds to execute country-led programs for reducing poverty by promoting sustainable economic growth. MCC grants are separate from other US aid programs and donations, and support country-led initiatives in health services, agriculture, infrastructure, water supply and sanitation, finance, land rights, anticorruption programs, and educational programs.

Peace Corps
Washington, DC
www.peacecorps.gov

President John F. Kennedy established the Peace Corps in 1961 with three goals in mind: to help the people of interested countries meet their need for trained men and women, to help promote a better understanding of Americans on the part of the peoples served, and to help promote a better understanding of other peoples on the part of Americans. The Peace Corps trains US volunteers in local languages, the technical skills necessary for the particular task they will be performing, and the cross-cultural skills needed to work with peoples of a different culture. Following successful completion of training, volunteers are sent to various sites within foreign countries, where they spend a period of two years aiding the country's economic and social development. There are more than 7,749 Peace Corps volunteers in seventy-three countries. Assignments vary according to volunteers' qualifications and host country needs. Volunteers work primarily in the fields of agriculture, forestry, fisheries, education, health, business, and community development–related activities. Peace Corps employees are also stationed in Washington and other US cities for recruiting purposes.

US Agency for International Development
Washington, DC
www.usaid.gov

The US Agency for International Development (USAID) is the US government's primary international development agency. Launched in 1961,

USAID works throughout the world to help the developing nations acquire the knowledge and resources to build the economic, political, and social institutions needed to promote and maintain national development. USAID often works to provide this assistance in conjunction with other US government agencies, including the Department of State and the Peace Corps. The assistance covers many diverse sectors, including but not limited to the environment, agriculture, economic growth, democracy strengthening, health and family planning, education, disaster preparedness, and humanitarian assistance. The USAID administrator reports to the secretary of state.

Intelligence Agencies

Central Intelligence Agency
Langley, Virginia
www.cia.gov

Created in 1947 upon President Harry Truman's signing of the National Security Act, the Central Intelligence Agency (CIA) serves as an independent source of analysis on topics of national security concern and also works closely with the other organizations in the US intelligence community, ultimately reporting to the director of national intelligence (DNI). The CIA's responsibilities include collecting intelligence through human sources; correlating, evaluating, and disseminating intelligence; coordinating and providing overall direction for the collection of intelligence outside the United States by human sources; and performing other functions and duties related to intelligence as directed by the president or the DNI. The CIA has four basic components: the National Clandestine Service, the Directorate of Intelligence, the Directorate of Science and Technology, and the Directorate of Support. In addition, the director of the CIA has several staffs that deal with public affairs, human resources, mission innovation, protocol, congressional affairs, legal issues, information management, and internal oversight. The CIA engages in research, development, and the deployment of high-leverage technology for US intelligence purposes. CIA operatives conduct varied activities, ranging from research, translations, and obtaining and vetting foreign intelligence sources to assisting with certain elements of US military operations and conducting CIA-led tactical operations overseas. With these varied objectives and capabilities, staff members of the CIA work in the following roles: analysts, Clandestine Service operatives, operations officers, and collection management officers. Internship and career opportunities are posted on the CIA website.

Defense Intelligence Agency
Washington, DC
www.dia.mil

As a member of the US intelligence community, the Defense Intelligence Agency (DIA) is a dual military and civilian US government agency that provides military intelligence to war fighters, defense policymakers, and force planners in DOD and the intelligence community. With more than 16,500 military and civilian employees worldwide, DIA is a major producer and manager of foreign military intelligence in support of US military planning and operations. DIA employs civilian and military personnel with a wide range of expertise, who work domestically and overseas, including in US defense attaché offices in US embassies worldwide.

Office of the Director of National Intelligence
Washington, DC
www.dni.gov

The director of national intelligence is the head of the intelligence community, directing the implementation of the National Intelligence Program and acting as the principal adviser to the president, NSC, and the Homeland Security Council for intelligence matters related to national security. The Office of the Director of National Intelligence (ODNI) oversees the sixteen-member US intelligence community (Air Force intelligence, Army intelligence, CIA, Coast Guard intelligence, DIA, DOE–intelligence, DHS, Department of State–intelligence, Department of the Treasury–intelligence, Drug Enforcement Administration, FBI, Marine Corps intelligence, National Geospatial-Intelligence Agency, National Reconnaissance Office, National Security Agency, and Navy intelligence), as well as six ODNI centers, including the National Counterterrorism Center, the National Counterproliferation Center, and the National Intelligence Council. The ODNI also operates the Open Source Center, which collects foreign open source intelligence. The ODNI has a number of responsibilities, including ensuring that timely and objective national intelligence is provided to the president, the heads of departments and agencies in the executive branch, the chairman of the Joint Chiefs of Staff and senior military commanders and Congress; establishing objectives and priorities for the collection, analysis, production, and dissemination of national intelligence; and overseeing the coordination of relationships with the intelligence or security services of foreign governments and international organizations. Individuals interested in intelligence should look at each of the sixteen members of the US intelligence community and the intelligence centers, in addition to ODNI. Although some agencies have traditionally hired more international relations students than others, there are relevant and important intelligence opportunities in each of these agencies and centers, even if they do not have an individual entry in this directory.

National Geospatial-Intelligence Agency
Bethesda, Maryland
www.nga.mil

The National Geospatial-Intelligence Agency (NGA) is a major intelligence and combat support agency of DOD. NGA supports national policymakers and military forces by providing timely, relevant, and accurate geospatial intelligence derived from the exploitation and analysis of imagery and geospatial information to describe, assess, and visually depict physical features and geographically referenced activities throughout the world. As the intelligence community's functional manager for baseline geospatial intelligence, NGA provides critical support to the national decision-making process and the operational readiness of US military forces. The NGA's workforce is in fields such as cartography, imagery analysis, the physical sciences, computer and telecommunication engineering, and photogrammetry.

National Security Agency
Fort Meade, Maryland
www.nsa.gov

The National Security Agency (NSA) coordinates, directs, and performs highly specialized activities to protect US government information systems and produce intelligence information on foreign signals. A high-technology organization, NSA is on the frontiers of communications and data processing. NSA is also one of the most important centers of foreign language analysis and research within the US government. With its technological reach, NSA is a key player in the US intelligence community. NSA carries out technology-intensive activities related to the collection and analysis of foreign e-mails, telephone calls, and other types of electronic-based communications that could transmit intelligence intended to harm the United States.

International Organizations

The United Nations

International Labor Organization
Geneva, Switzerland
www.ilo.org

The International Labor Organization (ILO) is a United Nations agency promoting labor rights. The ILO was the first specialized agency of the United

Nations when it was established in 1946. Through the creation of international policies and labor standards and the provision of technical support, the ILO encourages workers' rights, job creation, social protection, and social dialogue. The agency has a special focus on forming partnerships with governments and civil society organizations to address youth unemployment.

United Nations Children's Fund
New York, New York
www.unicef.org

The United Nations Children's Fund (UNICEF) is a UN agency that promotes the development of children by advocating for their health, equality, education, and protection. The agency engages in providing emergency assistance to children in conflict and long-term developmental support for children in developing countries. UNICEF's activities are wide-ranging but include promoting basic education and gender equality, providing immunizations, distributing food aid, preventing the spread of HIV/AIDS, and advocating for the rights of children. The agency is active in more than 190 countries.

United Nations Conference on Trade and Development
Geneva, Switzerland
www.unctad.org

The United Nations Conference on Trade and Development (UNCTAD) is the primary organization working on trade, investment, and development issues within the United Nations General Assembly. Founded in 1964, UNCTAD provides an intergovernmental forum for member states to share ideas and technical assistance in the areas of trade, investment, finance, and technology. Additionally, UNCTAD conducts research and policy analysis on emerging economic issues. UNCTAD has 194 active member countries.

United Nations Department of Economic and Social Affairs
New York, New York
www.un.org/en/development/desa

The United Nations Department of Economic and Social Affairs (DESA) is a body of the **United Nations Secretariat** that works on a range of development issues. DESA forms partnerships with NGOs, civil society, the private sector, research and academic organizations, intergovernmental organizations, and other members of the UN to address economic and social challenges. Based in New York City, DESA primarily collects and analyzes data on development issues, arranges conferences and summits, works with member states to formulate development policies, and builds the capacities of member states.

United Nations Department of Peacekeeping Operations
New York, New York
www.un.org/en/peacekeeping

The United Nations Department of Peacekeeping Operations (DPKO) co-ordinates all UN peacekeeping operations. DPKO provides policy and operational guidance for all peacekeeping missions conducted in member states around the globe. Because the UN does not have its own military or police force, member states contribute the peacekeepers who serve worldwide to promote international peace and security. DPKO hires civilians, police officers, and military personnel.

United Nations Development Program
New York, New York
www.undp.org

The United Nations Development Program (UNDP) is the main UN agency focusing on international development. UNDP works in the areas of poverty reduction, democratic governance, crisis prevention and recovery, and energy to help nations build resilience and improve living standards. The agency has offices in more than 170 countries, where it works with local staff members to build capacity and address pressing development issues. In addition, UNDP commissions the annual *Human Development Report*, which examines topics in development and policy proposals for member states.

United Nations Educational, Scientific, and Cultural Organization
Paris, France
www.unesco.org

The United Nations Educational, Scientific, and Cultural Organization (UNESCO) is a United Nations body that promotes education, science, and culture to build peace and security. Founded in 1945, UNESCO is headquartered in Paris and has more than sixty field offices worldwide. Information on UNESCO's current vacancies and its Young Professionals' Program, which is available to eligible young professionals from nonrepresented and underrepresented member states, can be found on its website.

United Nations Office for the Coordination of Humanitarian Affairs
Geneva, Switzerland
www.unocha.org

The United Nations Office for the Coordination of Humanitarian Affairs (OCHA) is a body under the **United Nations Secretariat** that coordinates humanitarian actors during emergency response efforts. In addition to mobilizing humanitarian action, OCHA advocates for rights and promotes disaster preparedness and prevention. OCHA has thirty offices located in countries around the world. Vacancies at OCHA's headquarters in Geneva and its global offices are listed on its website.

The Office of the United Nations High Commissioner for Refugees
Geneva, Switzerland
www.unhcr.org

The Office of the United Nations High Commissioner for Refugees (UNHCR) protects the rights and well-being of refugees. UNHCR provides support to refugees by assisting in asylum processes, voluntary returns, local integration, and third-country resettlement. Full-time positions and internships are advertised on the UNHCR's website. UNHCR also offers a Junior Professional Officer Program, which gives qualified young professionals the opportunity to gain two to four years of field or headquarters experience.

United Nations Population Fund
New York, New York
www.unfpa.org

The United Nations Population Fund (UNFPA) is a UN agency that focuses on reproductive health and rights. The organization promotes sexual and reproductive health care, family planning, and gender equality. UNFPA also forms partnerships with governments, other agencies, and civil society to analyze population demographics by conducting research and censuses. Information about current vacancies and UNFPA's Junior Professional Officer Program is posted on its website.

United Nations Secretariat
New York, New York
www.un.org/en/mainbodies/secretariat

The United Nations Secretariat is a principal body of the United Nations that administers the programs and policies established by other UN principals. The UN secretary-general is the Secretariat's chief administrative officer and heads it. The Secretariat has a diverse portfolio of work that varies based on the needs of the UN's other principal organs that the Secretariat services. Secretariat staff members are citizens of UN member countries and work in duty stations around the globe.

United Nations Security Council
New York, New York
www.un.org/en/sc

The United Nations Security Council is a principal organ of the United Nations that maintains international peace and security. The Security Council has fifteen members, five permanent and ten nonpermanent. The five permanent members are China, France, Russia, the United Kingdom, and the United States. The ten nonpermanent members are selected for two-year terms. Each member is allotted one vote during Security Council voting sessions. The Security Council determines threats to peace, and it encourages UN nations to settle disputes peacefully before deciding to impose sanctions or use force to restore international peace and security.

United Nations World Food Program
Rome, Italy
www.wfp.org

The United Nations World Food Program (WFP) is a humanitarian agency working to fight hunger. By forming partnerships with the Food and Agriculture Organization, the International Fund for Agricultural Development, governments, NGOs, and other UN agencies, the WFP reaches more than 90 million people in more than seventy countries with food assistance. The WFP has a main office in Rome and more than eighty country offices. International vacancies are posted on the organization's website. The WFP participates in the Junior Professional Officer Program, which provides work and training opportunities to young, motivated professionals.

International Organizations outside the UN

Council of Europe
Strasbourg, France
www.coe.int

The Council of Europe is an international organization promoting human rights, democracy, and the rule of law throughout Europe. The Council of Europe encourages cooperation among its forty-seven member countries in these key areas in order to build tolerant and civilized societies. The European Court of Human Rights and the European Pharmacopoeia Commission are bodies of the Council of Europe. The Council of Europe is a separate entity from the European Council and the European Union.

The Global Fund to Fight AIDS, Tuberculosis, and Malaria
Geneva, Switzerland
www.theglobalfund.org

The Global Fund to Fight AIDS, Tuberculosis, and Malaria is a public–private partnership that collects and disburses funding to prevent and treat HIV and AIDS, tuberculosis, and malaria. The Global Fund provides grants to governments, NGOs, the United Nations, private-sector actors, and civil society organizations to implement anti-AIDS, tuberculosis, and malaria programs. Since it was founded in 2002, the Global Fund has supported programs in more than one hundred fifty countries.

International Organization for Migration
Geneva, Switzerland
www.iom.int

The International Organization for Migration (IOM) is an intergovernmental organization that manages migration. IOM was founded in 1951, and it has offices in more than 100 countries. It forms partnerships with governments, NGOs, and the United Nations to provide humanitarian assistance to migrants and address migration issues. It specializes in migration and development, facilitating migration, regulating migration, and forced migration.

Organization of American States
Washington, DC
www.oas.org

The Organization of American States (OAS) is a regional organization representing the thirty-five independent states of the Americas. It is the region's premier forum for multilateral dialogue and concerted action. The organization aims to promote solidarity and collaboration in the Western Hemisphere, establish peace in the region, and defend the sovereignty and independence of its member states. The OAS's activities are structured around the four main pillars of democracy, human rights, security, and development. Employment preference is given to nationals from OAS member states for permanent positions and consultancies.

Organization for Economic Cooperation and Development
Paris, France
www.oecd.org

The Organization for Economic Cooperation and Development (OECD) is an international economic organization that works with governments to foster economic growth and financial stability. The OECD monitors trade, economic, and financial events in its member countries, and it collects data to analyze and subsequently make policy recommendations. It has thirty-four member countries in North and South America, Europe, and the Asia-Pacific region. With some exceptions, professionals seeking careers at the OECD must be citizens of its member countries.

World Economic Forum
Geneva, Switzerland
www.weforum.org

The World Economic Forum is an international organization that engages world leaders in shaping global agendas. Most notably, the World Economic Forum organizes an annual meeting in Davos, Switzerland, where business leaders, politicians, academics and journalists convene to discuss pressing development and economic issues. The organization also arranges regional meetings that take place in various locations around the world. In addition to organizing meetings, the World Economic Forum produces reports on global issues, and it works with businesses, governments, and civil society to address key development challenges.

World Trade Organization
Geneva, Switzerland
www.wto.org

The World Trade Organization (WTO) is an international organization working on international trade. The WTO is managed by its 159 member governments, which collectively make all decisions. The WTO serves as the managing body for the enforcement of trade agreements, implements and monitors trade policies, provides a forum for dispute settlement, and builds the capacities of its member states to engage in trade. Its current vacancies are advertised on its website. It only hires nationals of its member countries.

International Financial Institutions

African Development Bank
Abidjan, Côte d'Ivoire
www.afdb.org

The African Development Bank (AfDB) is a development finance institution founded to advance the economic and social development of African countries. Established in 1964, the AfDB comprises three constituent institutions: the AfDB itself, the African Development Fund, and the Nigeria Trust Fund. By providing funding to African governments and private companies interested in investing in its fifty-three African regional member countries, the AfDB assists in reducing poverty and improving the living conditions of African citizens. It posts current openings on its website, and it also has a Young Professionals Program that attracts individuals under the age of thirty-two years from its member countries for rotational assignments and on-the-job training.

Asian Development Bank
Manila, Philippines
www.adb.org

The Asian Development Bank (ADB) invests in the Asia-Pacific region in order to alleviate poverty. Through loans, grants, policy dialogues, technical assistance, and equity investments, ADB assists its forty-eight regional member countries in promoting economic growth and development. It was founded in 1966, and has a headquarters in Manila, twenty-seven resident missions, and three representative offices in Tokyo, Frankfurt, and Washington.

Inter-American Development Bank
Washington, DC
www.iadb.org

The Inter-American Development Bank (IDB) provides development financing for countries in Latin America and the Caribbean. Established in 1959, the bank offers loans, grants, technical assistance, and knowledge generation for its twenty-six Latin American and Caribbean borrowing members. The IDB lends to autonomous public institutions, civil society organizations, private-sector companies, and national, provincial, state, and municipal governments to promote sustainable economic growth and eliminate poverty and inequality. In addition to offering fixed-term and consulting contracts, the IDB has a Young Professionals Program, a Research Fellowship Program, and an Internship Program.

International Finance Corporation
Washington, DC
www.ifc.org

The International Finance Corporation (IFC) is a global development institution that supports private-sector development. Established in 1956, the IFC is a member of the World Bank Group. The corporation is owned by its 184 member countries, which collectively determine its policies. The IFC invests in for-profit and commercial projects in more than a hundred developing countries that reduce poverty and promote development. The IFC supports companies and financial institutions in emerging markets to create jobs, generate tax revenues, improve corporate governance and environmental performance, and contribute to their local economies.

International Monetary Fund
Washington, DC
www.imf.org

The International Monetary Fund (IMF) is an international organization that fosters macroeconomic stability. Since its founding at the Bretton Woods Conference in 1944, the IMF's membership has grown from 45 to 188 countries. The IMF conducts economic surveillance for each of its member countries to alert them to macroeconomic risks. Additionally, the organization provides policy advice, gives technical assistance and training to member states, and lends to countries facing acute economic challenges.

World Bank Group
Washington, DC
www.worldbank.org

The World Bank Group is the largest development bank in the world. It is composed of five organizations: the International Bank for Reconstruction and Development, the International Development Association, the International Finance Corporation, the Multilateral Investment Guarantee Agency, and the International Centre for Settlement of Investment Disputes. These five institutions work to reduce poverty and support development through technical and financial assistance. Established in 1944, the World Bank Group has 188 member countries. The World Bank Group has a Young Professional Program for people thirty-two years of age or younger who have a master's degree and at least three years of relevant experience or continued academic study at the doctoral level.

Nongovernmental Organizations

International Development and Humanitarian Assistance NGOs

AmeriCares
Stamford, Connecticut
www.americares.org

AmeriCares is a nonprofit disaster relief and humanitarian aid organization that works to provide immediate emergency medical response and long-term humanitarian assistance. AmeriCares has offices and/or clinics in India, Sri Lanka, El Salvador, and Haiti. The organization is dedicated to supporting all people regardless of race, creed, or political persuasion. A variety of job, internship, and volunteer opportunities are posted throughout the year on the AmeriCares website.

Ashoka
Arlington, Virginia
www.ashoka.org

Ashoka is a nonprofit organization that supports societal transformation through a global network of social entrepreneurs pursuing sustainable social solutions. Ashoka has established programs in more than sixty countries and employs two hundred staff members in twenty-five regional offices across Africa, the Americas, Asia, Europe, the Middle East, and North Africa.

Bank Information Center
Washington, DC
www.bicusa.org

The Bank Information Center (BIC) is an independent, nonprofit NGO that seeks to influence the World Bank Group and the other international financial insitutions through partnerships with civil society groups in developing and transition countries. The organization aims to promote social and economic justice and ecological sustainability by promoting the protection of rights, participation, transparency, and public accountability in the governance and operations of the World Bank and the regional development banks. BIC supports local communities and civil society organizations through information dissemination and capacity-building activities, coalition building, project and policy monitoring, and advocacy support services. BIC has offices in Washington, New Delhi, Jakarta, and Bangkok.

CARE International
Geneva, Switzerland
www.care-international.org

CARE International is a global federation of fourteen member organizations dedicated to fighting global poverty through programs in HIV / AIDS, clean water and sanitation, economic development, and natural resource protection. CARE places a special focus on working alongside poor women, guided by the belief that women have the power to help whole families and entire communities escape poverty. The organization operates more than a thousand relief and development projects in more than eighty-eight countries. Although CARE employs roughly eleven thousand employees worldwide, 97 percent of its staff are nationals of the CARE program countries. CARE has member offices in Europe, Australia, Asia, and the Americas.

Catholic Relief Services
Baltimore, Maryland
www.crs.org

Catholic Relief Services (CRS) is the official international relief and development agency of the United States Conference of Catholic Bishops. From its origin as a response to the call to help rebuild a shattered Europe during World War II, CRS has expanded its programming to provide relief in times of disaster, while also laying the foundation for developing stronger communities for the future. CRS operates programs in nearly a hundred countries in emergency response, agriculture, education, food security, health, HIV/ AIDS, microfinance, peace building, water/sanitation, and policy change. The standard qualifications for many positions with CRS include a master's degree in international development or an equivalent field and at least two to three years experience working in development programs overseas. CRS also offers a one-year fellowship program that places twenty to thirty candidates overseas with various country programs.

Clinton Global Initiative
New York, New York
www.clintonglobalinitiative.org

The Clinton Global Initiative (CGI), established by President Bill Clinton in 2005, is a nonpartisan forum that brings together global leaders to develop solutions to global problems. Leaders participating in CGI come from a variety of political, ethnic, religious, and geographic backgrounds, and the organization's initiatives cover issues related to the environment, education, energy, women and girls, global health, entrepreneurship, technology, and disaster preparedness and relief. A variety of job, internship, volunteer, and occasional fellowship opportunities are available throughout the year. The CGI website also has links to job boards with the **Clinton Foundation**, the **Clinton Global Health Initiative**, and the **Alliance for a Healthier Generation**.

Eurasia Foundation
Washington, DC
www.eurasia.org

The Eurasia Foundation supports the development of open, just, and progressive societies through its programs in local economic development, youth engagement, cross-border cooperation, independent media and public policy, and institution building in the Eurasia region. The organization has transitioned from a United States–based foundation with multiple field offices into a network of affiliated, locally registered foundations across

Russia, Central Asia, the South Caucasus, Ukraine, and Moldova that work in partnership with the United States–based Eurasia Foundation. The Eurasia Foundation also has programs in China supporting local community development.

FINCA International
Washington, DC
www.finca.org

FINCA International—or the Foundation for International Community Assistance—is a global charitable financial organization that offers financial services to the world's lowest-income entrepreneurs. FINCA's financial services aim to create jobs, build assets, and improve living standards, while operating on commercial principles of performance and sustainability. The organization is best known for pioneering the Village Banking Method. FINCA operates in twenty-one countries around the world, with primary operations in Africa, the greater Middle East, Eurasia, and Latin America. Positions with FINCA are available around the world and are advertised on its website.

Ford Foundation
New York, New York
www.fordfoundation.org

The Ford Foundation is an independent, nonprofit, grant-making global organization dedicated to advancing human welfare by strengthening democratic values, reducing poverty and injustice, promoting international cooperation, and advancing human achievement. The foundation makes grants through its ten regional offices in Asia, Africa, and Latin America that support programs in more than fifty countries. Its website posts information on US and global career opportunities. About half its staff members are in New York, and the rest are overseas. Summer internships are also available in Ford's three grant-making programs: Economic Opportunity and Advancement; Democracy, Rights, and Justice; and Education, Creativity, and Free Expression.

Global Communities
Silver Spring, Maryland
www.globalcommunities.org

Global Communities, formerly CHF International, is an international development and humanitarian aid nonprofit organization with a mission to bring about sustainable changes to improve the lives of livelihoods of low- and moderate-income communities around the world. The organization was founded in 1952 as the Foundation for Cooperative Housing, initially focused on rural and urban America, and today works on a variety of social, economic, and environmental issues in more than twenty countries in Africa, Asia, Europe and the Caucasus, Latin America and the Caribbean, and the Middle East. Global Communities works to forge partnerships between local communities, governments, the private sector, and NGOs. Its projects are focused on microenterprises and small and medium-sized enterprises, housing finance, infrastructure and construction, governance and urban development, civil society and capacity development, global health, and emergency response.

Grameen Foundation
Washington, DC
www.grameenfoundation.org

Grameen Foundation is a nonprofit organization that works to apply the **Grameen Bank's** microfinance model around the world through a global network of microfinance institutions. The Grameen Bank model was created by the bank's founder and managing director, Muhammad Yunus, who developed a small-scale loan credit delivery system to provide banking services to the rural poor in Bangladesh. The Grameen Foundation has a headquarters in Washington and offices in Seattle, Medellín, Accra, Hong Kong, Jakarta, Nairobi, Metro Manila, and Kampala; a wholly owned subsidiary in India; and a joint venture company with offices based in Dubai.

Innovations for Poverty Action
New Haven, Connecticut
www.poverty-action.org

Founded in 2002 by the Yale University economist Dean Karlan, Innovations for Poverty Action (IPA) is an American nonprofit that conducts randomized controlled trials and other quantitative research to measure the effects of development programs. IPA's research covers a range of sectors, including microfinance, education, health, governance, agriculture, charitable giving, and community development. The organization works with nonprofits, governments, and for-profit companies. IPA staff receive rigorous training in implementing randomized controlled trials in the field. Country offices are located in Ghana, Bangladesh, Kenya, Liberia, Malawi, Mali, Mexico, Mongolia, Peru, the Philippines, Sierra Leone, Uganda, and Zambia.

International Committee of the Red Cross
Geneva, Switzerland
www.icrc.org

Founded in 1863, the International Committee of the Red Cross (ICRC) is a private, humanitarian organization solely focused on protecting and assisting victims of armed conflict and strife. ICRC accomplishes its mission through direct action around the world and by encouraging the development of and respect for international humanitarian law by governments and all weapon bearers. The ICRC recruits staff, trains them, and develops their skills. ICRC's 1,400 employees include both specialized staff and delegates in field missions around the globe. Jobs in international programs generally require at least three to five years of experience and very specific expertise. The ability to work in different languages is not essential but is desirable. ICRC staff are supported by 11,000 local employees and 800 staff housed at the organization's Geneva headquarters. ICRC is part of the **International Red Cross and Red Crescent Movement**, along with the **International Federation of Red Cross and Red Crescent Societies** and 186 national societies.

International Crisis Group
Brussels, Belgium
www.crisisgroup.org

International Crisis Group (ICG) is an independent, nonprofit NGO committed to preventing and resolving deadly conflicts. ICG influences the policy debate on international conflicts through the publication of reports, briefings, and opinion pieces, and by communicating its research and policy recommendations through a variety of channels, including advocacy meetings and the publication of its monthly bulletin, *CrisisWatch*. ICG has a diverse, permanent staff of more than a hundred fifty people worldwide. Employment opportunities with ICG are available in Washington and in its field and advocacy offices.

International Rescue Committee
New York, New York
www.rescue.org

International Rescue Committee (IRC) is a United States–based nonsectarian, international relief and development NGO whose mission is to provide emergency relief, postconflict development, and resettlement services. Since its founding in 1933 at the request of Albert Einstein, the organization has assisted millions of people affected by conflict, natural disasters, and oppression. IRC's staff of eight thousand includes first responders, humanitarian relief workers, international development experts, health care providers, and educators. Jobs and a limited number of internship opportunities are available in IRC's US and international offices. Volunteers are also invited to support IRC's refugee resettlement offices in the United States.

Kiva
San Francisco, California
www.kiva.org

Kiva is a nonprofit organization focused on alleviating global poverty by connecting people through global lending. By leveraging the internet and a worldwide network of microfinance institutions, Kiva enables individuals to help end global poverty with contributions as low as $25. Headquartered in San Francisco, Kiva also has an office in Nairobi. A variety of internship and job opportunities are posted throughout the year on the Kiva website.

Mercy Corps
Portland, Oregon, and Edinburgh, United Kingdom
www.mercycorps.org

Mercy Corps is an international development organization that helps people around the world to survive and thrive after conflict, economic collapse, and natural disaster. Mercy Corps supports immediate relief in the aftermath of a crisis and also works for extended periods with communities to support local entrepreneurship, boost food security, rebuild social capital, and stimulate the market through "cash for work" programs and a variety of lending models. With headquarters offices in Europe and North America, the agency's unified global programs reach people in forty countries. Mercy Corps also has offices in Cambridge, Massachusetts, Seattle, and Washington.

Microsave
Lucknow, India
www.microsave.org

Microsave is an international financial inclusion nonprofit that promotes market-led approaches to achieving poverty relief. The organization works with financial institutions to develop sustainable and viable products and delivery systems to serve the low-income market in Africa and Asia. With a staff of a hundred working in ten global offices, Microsave manages projects across twenty-five countries. Microsave works with a variety of investors and donors implementing rapid institutional assessments and conducting due diligence and strategy business planning exercises. Its work areas include financial service delivery, electronic and mobile banking, small and medium-sized enterprises, microfinance, responsible finance, and private-sector development.

MIX Market
Washington, DC
www.mixmarket.org

MIX Market provides objective, qualified, and relevant financial performance data and analysis on microfinance institutions, funders, networks, and service providers to serve the financial-sector needs of low-income clients. MIX has regional offices in Azerbaijan, India, Morocco, and Peru. It publishes the *MicroBanking Bulletin* and *Mix Microfinance World*. Its work is strengthened through cooperation with the Bill & Melinda Gates Foundation, CGAP, Omidyar Network, the MasterCard Foundation, the International Fund for Agricultural Development, the Michael & Susan Dell Foundation, and the Citi Foundation. Applicants for analyst positions may be required to take tests to demonstrate their quantitative and reasoning and writing abilities.

Oxfam International
Oxford, United Kingdom
www.oxfam.org

Oxfam International is an international confederation of seventeen organizations working together in more than ninety countries to combat poverty, hunger, and injustice. Oxfam works directly with communities to give poor people a voice in the decisions that affect their lives through policy research, advocacy, campaigning, emergency systems, and long-term development programs. Oxfam's programmatic areas include agriculture, aid effectiveness, climate change, education, emergency response, HIV/AIDS, minority rights, youth outreach, and more. The Oxfam International Secretariat is located in the United Kingdom, and Oxfam affiliates are located across Europe and North America as well as in India and Hong Kong.

Plan International
Woking, United Kingdom
www.plan-international.org

Plan International is one of the oldest and largest children's development organizations dedicated to promoting children's rights as a path to reducing poverty. Originally founded in 1937 with a mission to provide food, accommodations, and education to children whose lives were disrupted by the Spanish Civil War, Plan now works to support children in fifty developing countries across Africa, Asia, and the Americas. Plan has worked with more than 84 million children. The organization is independent, with no religious, political, or governmental affiliations.

Rockefeller Foundation
New York, New York
www.rockefellerfoundation.org

The Rockefeller Foundation was founded in 1913 to promote the well-being of humanity by addressing the root causes of serious problems. This approach has produced such breakthrough work as the professionalization of public health; the development of a vaccine against yellow fever; the Green Revolution in Latin American, Asian, and Indian agriculture; and the creation of public–private partnerships to develop promising new vaccines. The foundation's Innovation for Development initiative is of particular interest to students of international affairs.

TechnoServe
Washington, DC
www.technoserve.org

TechnoServe is a nonprofit organization that believes in the power of private enterprise to reduce poverty in the developing world. By linking people to information, capital, and markets, TechnoServe uses business solutions to generate income, jobs, and wealth for families and communities in Africa, Latin America, and India. TechnoServe hires professionals in areas including program development, finance, fund-raising, communications, and human resources. Senior country staff typically hold an MBA or equivalent degree and have senior management experience in developing countries and/or the private sector.

World Vision International
London, United Kingdom
www.worldvision.org

World Vision is a Christian relief, development, and advocacy organization that works with children, families, and communities to combat poverty and injustice. The organization focuses on emergency relief, education, health care, economic development, and justice promotion for the world's most vulnerable people, regardless of religion, race, ethnicity, or gender. World Vision has consultative status with UNESCO and partnerships with UNICEF, the World Health Organization, UNHCR, and the ILO. Its international offices are located in London and Los Angeles, and it has affiliate and regional offices around the world.

Democracy and Human Rights NGOs

Amnesty International
London, United Kingdom
www.amnesty.org

Amnesty International (AI) is an NGO dedicated to the defense of human rights throughout the world. AI's mission is to undertake research and action focused on preventing and ending grave abuses of the rights to physical and mental integrity, freedom of conscience and expression, and freedom from discrimination, within the context of its work to promote all human rights. The organization's International Secretariat is based in London, and its national organizations, called "sections," have offices in an additional eighty countries. The Secretariat is AI's global center for research, campaigning, legal, lobbying, and membership work.

American Bar Association Rule of Law Initiative
Washington, DC
www.americanbar.org/advocacy/rule_of_law.html

The American Bar Association Rule of Law Initiative (ABA ROLI) works to advance the rule of law around the world through cooperation with in-country partners. Working in more than forty countries in Africa, Asia, Europe and Eurasia, Latin America and the Caribbean, and the Middle East and North Africa, ABA ROLI implements programs in several key areas: access to justice and human rights, anticorruption and public integrity, criminal law reform and anti–human trafficking, judicial reform, legal education reform and civil education, legal profession reform, and women's rights. ABA ROLI has a staff of more than four hundred professionals, including short- and long-term expatriate volunteers. Desirable qualities for applicants for US and global positions include relevant language skills, international experience, and familiarity with the US government's funding requirements.

Carter Center
Atlanta, Georgia
www.cartercenter.org

The Carter Center is a nonprofit NGO devoted to advancing peace and human rights worldwide. Founded in 1982 by former US president Jimmy Carter and his wife Rosalynn, the organization has a staff of 175 who work to prevent and resolve conflict, enhance freedom and democracy, and improve public health. The Carter Center has a partnership with Emory University, and its staff members are hired through the Emory University's Human Resources Department. A strong academic background, experience addressing real-world problems, foreign language proficiency, and strong communications skills are desired. In the global health programs, many staff members have medical or public health training. In addition, staff work in fund-raising, administration, public information, and conferencing.

Human Rights Watch
New York, New York
www.hrw.org

Human Rights Watch is a United States–based, independent nonprofit that promotes human rights worldwide. The organization conducts regular systematic investigations of human rights abuses in approximately seventy countries and implements advocacy campaigns to raise awareness of human rights abuses and to affect the policies of the United States and other influential governments toward abusive regimes. Human Rights Watch maintains offices in Washington, Los Angeles, London, Brussels, Berlin, and Moscow, and its staff members are based in various locations around the world.

International Republican Institute
Washington, DC
www.iri.org

The International Republican Institute (IRI) is a private, nonprofit, nonpartisan organization dedicated to advancing democracy worldwide. In its infancy, the IRI focused on planting the seeds of democracy in Latin America. Since the end of the Cold War, IRI has broadened its reach to support democracy and freedom around the globe. It has conducted programs in more than one hundred countries and is currently active in more than sixty-five countries.

IREX
Washington, DC
www.irex.org

IREX is an international nonprofit organization that works to build three key elements of a vibrant society: high-quality education, independent media, and strong communities. Founded in 1968, its program activities include conflict resolution, technology for development, and gender and youth. IREX has a staff of more than five hundred professionals worldwide and works to develop practical and locally driven solutions with partners in more than a hundred countries. Positions are available at its headquarters and field offices around the world. Many of the field positions require technical expertise and prior work experience in a developing country, as well as proficiency in the relevant foreign languages.

National Democratic Institute
Washington, DC
www.ndi.org

The National Democratic Institute for International Affairs (NDI) is a nonprofit organization working to strengthen and expand democracy worldwide. Calling on a global network of volunteer experts, NDI provides practical assistance to civic and political leaders advancing democratic values, practices, and institutions. The NDI works with democrats in every region of the world to build political and civic organizations, to safeguard elections, and to promote citizen participation, openness, and accountability in government.

National Endowment for Democracy
Washington, DC
www.ned.org

The National Endowment for Democracy (NED) is a private, nonprofit organization created in 1983 to strengthen democratic institutions around the world through nongovernmental efforts. NED is governed by an independent, nonpartisan board of directors. With its annual congressional appropriation, it delivers hundreds of grants each year to support prodemocracy groups in Africa, Asia, Central and Eastern Europe, Latin America, the Middle East, and the countries of the former Soviet Union. The NED website lists both internships and positions at headquarters and in the field. Education, experience, and language skills are critical for most positions.

Open Society Foundation
New York, New York
www.opensocietyfoundation.org

The Open Society Foundation (OSF) works to build vibrant and tolerant democracies whose governments are accountable and open to the participation of all people. Founded by the investor and philanthropist George Soros, the organization initially supported a network of foundations in Central and Eastern Europe and the countries of the former Soviet Union. Today, OSF has expanded to encompass the United States and more than sixty countries in Europe, Asia, Africa, and Latin America. OSF implements a range of initiatives to advance justice, education, public health, and independent media. In addition to the network of Soros foundations, OSF has offices in New York, Baltimore, Brussels, Budapest, London, Paris, and Washington. OSF's offices, particularly the larger ones in New York and Budapest, typically offer program assistant, program associate, program coordinator, program officer, and associate director positions.

PACT
Washington, DC
www.pactworld.org

PACT is an NGO that delivers technical assistance in HIV/AIDS, economic opportunity, the environment, democracy/governance, and peace building. Founded in 1971 as a membership organization of US private and voluntary organizations working in relief and development to facilitate the distribution of small USAID grants to these organizations, PACT now assists more than twelve thousand organizations in sixty-two countries. Its programs include the Impact Alliance, a global partnership for capacity development, and WORTH, a women's empowerment program. Pact has offices in more than twenty countries in Asia, Europe, and Africa.

Save the Children
Westport, Connecticut
www.savethechildren.org

Save the Children is a leading independent nonprofit organization that works to create lasting change in the lives of children in need around the world. Save the Children works in more than fifty countries, including the United States, and serves more than 33 million children and 32 million others working to save and improve children's lives, including parents, community members, local organizations, and government agencies. Save the Children hires professionals with a minimum of three to five years' experience, especially gained in the field or overseas, in health, education, microfinance, and areas of crisis.

Search for Common Ground
Washington, DC
www.sfcg.org

Since its founding in 1982, Search for Common Ground has been dedicated to transforming the way the world deals with conflict. The organization promotes a collaborative, multifaceted approach to problem solving through media initiatives and engagement with local partners in government and civil society. The organization works to find culturally appropriate means to strengthen a society's ability to deal with conflicts constructively. Search for Common Ground's European office is located in Brussels.

Social Accountability International
New York, New York
www.sa-intl.org

Social Accountability International (SAI) is an international, multistakeholder organization with headquarters in New York City. By promoting ethical working conditions, labor rights, corporate social responsibility, and social dialogue, SAI works with partners to advance human rights around the world. The organization engages with companies, trade unions, NGOs, and governments to encourage greater compliance with labor laws. Positions range from internships in Bangalore to senior manager positions at headquarters in New York. SAI representatives are also located in Brazil, China, Costa Rica, the Netherlands, the Philippines, Switzerland, and the United Arab Emirates. Positions typically require familiarity with ILO conventions and other labor and human rights standards in addition to other educational and skill-related qualifications.

Public Health, Educational, and Environmental NGOs

American Councils for International Education
Washington, DC
www.americancouncils.org

The American Councils for International Education is a US education and international training organization with expertise in academic exchange, professional training, distance learning, curriculum and test development, delivery of technical assistance, research, evaluation, and institution building. American Councils operates US government programs and non-US national fellowship programs, as well as partnership programs between the United States and the countries of Eastern Europe and Asia. Its full-time professional staff of more than 370 works in the United States and forty cities in Eastern Europe, Asia, and the Middle East.

ARC Finance
New York, New York
www.arcfinance.org

ARC Finance is a global nonprofit that strives to develop solutions for access to finance for clean energy and water. ARC Finance provides innovation funding, or seed capital, to microfinance institutions and energy/water enterprises to develop new products, business models, and delivery and payment mechanisms to increase access to clean energy and water. This innovation funding is aimed at developing and testing new approaches that have the potential for rapid scaling up and that are replicable.

Bill & Melinda Gates Foundation
Seattle, Washington
www.gatesfoundation.org

The Bill & Melinda Gates Foundation is the world's largest transparently operated private foundation. Founded by Bill and Melinda Gates, the

Seattle-based foundation is primarily focused on enhancing health care, reducing extreme poverty, and expanding educational opportunities and access to technology. The foundation hires candidates with a solid education, relevant experience, humility, and dedication to the greater good. It also has offices in Washington, Delhi, Beijing, and London.

Center for Clean Air Policy
Washington, DC
www.ccap.org

The Center for Clean Air Policy (CCAP) is an independent, nonprofit think tank that focuses on climate and air quality policy issues at the local, national, and international levels. CCAP promotes innovative, market-based solutions to major climate, air quality, and energy problems that take both environmental and economic interests into account. CCAP conducts multistakeholder dialogues, education and outreach, qualitative and quantitative research, and technical analyses, and it presents policy solutions. CCAP works on five continents. Talented individuals from diverse backgrounds are encouraged to apply. Staff work in the following sections: US and international climate programs, finance and administration, and communications.

Clinton Foundation
New York, New York
www.clintonfoundation.org

The Clinton Foundation was established by former US president Bill Clinton with a mission to improve global health, strengthen economies, promote healthier childhoods, and protect the environment. The foundation's key focus areas are economic inequality, climate change, global health, and childhood obesity. It accomplishes its mission through partnerships with governments, businesses, NGOs, and private citizens. The organization offers job, internship, and volunteer opportunities as well as occasional fellowships. See also **Clinton Global Initiative.**

Institute of International Education
New York, New York
www.iie.org

An independent nonprofit founded in 1919, the Institute of International Education (IIE) is among the world's largest international education and training organizations. Its mission is to promote closer educational relations between the people of the United States and those of other countries, to strengthen and link institutions of higher learning globally, to rescue threatened scholars and advance academic freedom, and to build leadership skills and enhance the capacity of individuals and organizations to address local and global challenges. A total of 18,000 men and women from 175 nations participate in IIE's programs each year. IIE has offices in New York, Washington, Chicago, Denver, Houston, and San Francisco, as well as eleven international locations.

International Medical Corps
Santa Monica, California and London, United Kingdom
www.internationalmedicalcorps.org

The International Medical Corps is an international humanitarian nonprofit that works to save lives and relieve suffering through health care training and relief and development programs that benefit underserved communities in twenty countries around the world. The organization is private, voluntary, nonpolitical, and nonsectarian. It looks for highly trained medical staff for its emergency response roster. There are also opportunities available for nonmedical international volunteers and domestic volunteers, who may assist with a variety of administrative and programmatic tasks based on their work experience and background. Volunteers receive a daily food allowance, shared housing, emergency medical evacuation insurance, and, in some cases, a monthly stipend. International Medical Corps also offers a highly competitive graduate internship program.

Médecins Sans Frontières
Geneva, Switzerland
www.msf.org

Médecins Sans Frontières (MSF) is an international humanitarian aid organization that provides emergency medical assistance to populations in danger in more than seventy countries. In countries where health structures are insufficient or even nonexistent, MSF collaborates with authorities such as ministries of health to provide assistance. MSF works on the rehabilitation of hospitals and dispensaries, on vaccination programs, and on water and sanitation projects. It also works in remote health care centers and slum areas and provides training for local personnel. All this is done with the objective of rebuilding health structures to acceptable levels. Most employment opportunities are posted on MSF's specific national websites.

Natural Resources Defense Council
New York, New York
www.nrdc.org

The Natural Resources Defense Council (NRDC) is an international environmental advocacy group with a broad agenda for promoting environmental protection. NRDC has a staff of more than four hundred lawyers, scientists, and policy experts, as well as 1.3 million members and online activists in the United States who support its program and advocacy efforts related to curbing global warming, reviving the world's oceans, defending endangered species and wildlife, preventing pollution, ensuring safe and sufficient waters, and fostering sustainable communities. NRDC's offices are located in Washington, San Francisco, Los Angeles, Chicago, and Beijing.

Partners in Health
Boston, Massachusetts
www.pih.org

Partners in Health (PIH) is a humanitarian NGO affiliated with Harvard University that pursues a mission to provide preferential health care for the poor, with a focus on preventing diseases before they occur. Founded in 1987 by Dr. Paul Farmer, Ophelia Dahl, Thomas J. White, Todd McCormack, and Dr. Jim Yong Kim, the organization brings modern medical science to those most in need around the world by establishing long-term partnerships with local sister organizations. PIH works closely with Harvard's School of Public Health and the Brigham and Women's Hospital. PIH's research and advocacy arm is the Institute for Health and Social Justice. A defining feature of PIH is its commitment to hiring and training people in the communities where it works.

Population Services International
Washington, DC
www.psi.org

Population Services International (PSI) is a Washington-based nonprofit organization that harnesses the vitality of the private sector to address the health problems of low-income and vulnerable populations in nearly seventy developing countries. With programs in malaria, safe water, tuberculosis, reproductive health, and HIV/AIDS, PSI promotes products, services, and healthy behavior that enable low-income and vulnerable people to lead healthier lives. Products and services are sold at subsidized prices rather than given away in order to motivate commercial-sector involvement. PSI employs a staff of eight thousand in its offices and affiliates based throughout Africa, the Americas, Asia, and Eastern Europe. Support services and advocacy are provided by its staff in Washington and its European office in Amsterdam. Most overseas positions require experience in the field and fluency in a relevant second language.

United Nations Foundation
Washington, DC
www.unfoundation.org

The United Nations Foundation is a public charity that connects the United Nations with businesses and NGOs worldwide. Ted Turner established the foundation in 1998, and he currently serves as its chairman. The foundation focuses on energy and climate issues, global health, women, and populations, and on supporting the United Nations. Employment opportunities are advertised on the foundation's website.

World Resources Institute
Washington, DC
www.wri.org

The World Resources Institute (WRI) was launched in 1982 as a center for policy research and analysis for global resource and environmental issues. WRI aims to move beyond research to put ideas into action, working globally with governments, business, and civil society to build transformative solutions that protect the Earth and improve people's lives. WRI focuses its work on four key programmatic goals: climate protection, governance, markets and enterprises, and peoples and ecosystems. The work of WRI is carried out by an interdisciplinary and international staff of approximately two hundred twenty people that is augmented by a network of partner institutions in more than fifty countries. WRI also has an office in Beijing and has recently opened a Brazil office.

International Banking and Finance

American International Group, Inc.
New York, New York
www.aig.com

American International Group, Inc. (AIG), is an international insurance organization. AIG has a network of offices located in more than ninety countries worldwide. It provides property casualty insurance, life insurance, retirement services, mortgage insurance, and aircraft leasing. Career opportunities are available for recent graduates and experienced professionals. The firm offers a Summer Internship Program and a Full-Time Development Program for students and recent graduates.

Bank of America Corporation
Charlotte, North Carolina
www.corp.bankofamerica.com

A global firm, Bank of America is the largest commercial and investment bank in the world by revenue, per *Fortune* magazine, and ranks number thirteen on the 2012 *Fortune* 500. Bank of America is commonly referred to as Bank of America Merrill Lynch, following the 2008 acquisition of New York–based Merrill Lynch. Bank of America operates in every US state and in forty countries around the world, and it has activities in consumer banking, corporate banking, and investment management. A large portion of its revenues comes from its consumer sector, and the acquisition of Merrill Lynch gave it a stronger position in wealth management. Its global operations include consumer and small business banking, corporate and investment banking, risk management, wealth and investment management, and technology operations. At the end of 2012 Bank of America had $2.2 trillion in assets and more than 267,000 employees around the world.

Barclays
London, United Kingdom
www.group.barclays.com

Barclays is a British multinational and financial services company engaged in personal banking, credit cards, corporate and investment banking, and wealth and investment management. Headquartered in London, Barclays has international operations in more than fifty countries and territories, employing approximately 140,000 people worldwide. Candidates with a strong background in finance, solid communication skills, and fluency in more than one language are desired for positions in operations, corporate communications, facilities management, wealth management, finance, global financial risk management, investment banking, and debt capital management, research, sales, trading, and related fields. Candidates for associate positions are expected to have or be studying toward a master's degree in finance or an MBA with relevant professorial work experience. Barclays also offers summer internships at both the analyst (undergraduate) and associate (typically graduate) levels.

BNP Paribas
Paris, France
www.bnpparibas.com

BNP Paribas is a Paris-based global banking group formed through the merger of Banque Nationale de Paris (BNP) and Paribas in 2000. BNP was ranked by Bloomberg and *Forbes* in 2012 as the third-largest bank globally, as measured by total assets. With its 200,000 employees worldwide, BNP

Paribas is engaged in three strategic business units: retail banking, corporate and investment banking, and investment solutions, which includes asset management, custodial banking, and real estate services.

Citigroup
New York, New York
www.citigroup.com

Citigroup is a US multinational financial services corporation that provides financial services in more than 1,000 cities and 160 countries. Headquartered in New York City, Citigroup has 16,000 offices worldwide and a staff of roughly 260,000. It offers analyst programs for those in their final year of undergraduate or graduate school. Those in their final year of an MBA, JD, or PhD program can apply for Citi's associate program. Summer analyst and summer associate opportunities are also available for those seeking to explore careers at Citigroup.

Credit Suisse
Zürich, Switzerland
www.credit-suisse.com

Credit Suisse Group is a global financial services group based in Zürich that provides advisory services and professional products to companies, institutional clients, and high-net-worth private clients. Operating in fifty countries on five continents worldwide, Credit Suisse employs more than 48,000 people from roughly a hundred different countries. Its businesses include sales and trading, investment banking, alternative investments and private equity, financial advising, securities underwriting, asset management, and private banking. The group's clients include businesses, governments, and wealthy individuals. Graduate students finishing MBAs or other postgraduate programs can apply for associate positions within the investment banking, fixed income, equity, and private banking units as well as analyst positions within equity research. Undergraduates can apply for analyst positions within investment banking, equity, and fixed income and for associate positions within equity research and information technology.

Deutsche Bank
Frankfurt, Germany
www.db.com

Deutsche Bank is a leading global investment bank with a strong and profitable private client franchise. A leader in Germany and Europe, the bank is also growing in North America, Asia, and emerging markets. Deutsche Bank offers financial services throughout the world. The bank seeks highly motivated candidates with a proven work ethic who have demonstrated outstanding academic and extracurricular achievement, leadership, and community involvement. It offers analyst internship and training programs for both graduates and undergraduates. MBAs are invited to participate in its associate programs, which include both summer and full-time training.

Goldman Sachs
New York, New York
www.goldmansachs.com

Goldman Sachs is an international investment banking and securities firm that provides a range of investment and financing services to corporations, governments, institutions, and individuals worldwide. Founded in 1869, Goldman Sachs is among the oldest and largest of the United States–based international investment banks. Its areas of work include debt and equity trading and underwriting, mergers-and-acquisitions advice, privatizations, currencies, commodities, bank loans, corporate banking, asset management, and fundamental and quantitative research. The firm has more than forty offices throughout the world. It seeks to hire a diverse group of individuals with various skills and professional orientations.

HSBC Holdings PLC
London, United Kingdom
www.us.hsbc.com

HSBC Holdings PLC is a bank and multinational corporation. It was founded in London in 1992 by the Hongkong and Shanghai Banking Corporation; hence the name HSBC. It offers banking, borrowing, investing, retirement, and insurance services for customers. These services are distributed among the bank's four main business groups: Commercial Banking, Global Banking and Markets, Retail Banking and Wealth Management, and Global Private Banking. HSBC has 7,200 offices in eighty-five countries worldwide.

J. P. Morgan Chase & Co.
New York, New York
www.jpmorganchase.com

J. P. Morgan Chase & Co. is a leading global financial services firm with operations in more than fifty countries. The firm specializes in consumer and community banking, corporate and investment banking, asset management, private banking, and commercial banking. J. P. Morgan Chase was formed through a merger between J. P. Morgan and the Chase Manhattan Group in 2000. The firm acquired the Bear Stearns Companies in 2008. A component of J. P. Morgan Chase serves US consumers and corporate, institutional, and government clients globally. Undergraduates and graduates can choose from a range of opportunities within the firm in corporate, wholesale financial services, and consumer financial services.

MicroVest Capital Management
Bethesda, Maryland
www.microvestfund.com

MicroVest Capital is a financial investment advisory firm focused on providing financing to low-income financial institutions in developing countries. A for-profit venture that is majority owned by four nonprofits, MicroVest Capital manages a family of investment funds that make debt and equity investments in microfinance and other bottom-of-the-pyramid financial institutions around the world. The firm seeks to provide capital to microfinance institutions, help build capital markets for the microenterprise system, and support self-sustaining financial institutions that serve the poor. With an estimated $149 million in assets under management, it provided $403 million in total financing from 2004 through 2012.

Moody's Corporation
New York, New York
www.moodys.com

Moody's Corporation is a publicly traded firm that provides credit ratings, research, tools, and analysis utilized by the global financial system. It is divided into Moody's Investor Service and Moody's Analytics, and it has operations in twenty-eight countries and nearly seven thousand employees. Moody's Investor Service offers credit ratings and research, and covers thousands of corporate, public, and structured finance obligations in more than 115 countries. Moody's Analytics focuses on serving capital markets teams by identifying, measuring, and managing risk through constant analysis, economic research, and financial risk management.

Morgan Stanley
New York, New York
www.morganstanley.com

Morgan Stanley is a US multinational financial services firm with 1,300 offices in forty-two countries. Its operations cover asset management credit services, securities business, and international financial services. The firm is organized into three main divisions: Institutional Securities, Global Wealth Management Group, and Asset Management. Programs for candidates with graduate degrees are available in investment banking, investment management, private wealth management, research, sales and trading, and strategy and execution.

Standard & Poor's
New York, New York
www.standardandpoors.com

Standard & Poor's (S&P), a division of the McGraw-Hill Companies, is a key provider of financial market intelligence, independent credit ratings, indices, risk evaluations, and investment research and data. The S&P Indices Group—which offers the widely known S&P 500, S&P Global BMI, and S&P GSCI—provides a variety of benchmark indices that the financial services industry utilizes for investment decisions and overall operations. S&P, a credit rating agency, also issues credit ratings for the debt of public and private corporations, as well as the investment grades of countries.

Swiss Re
Zürich, Switzerland
www.swissre.com

Swiss Reinsurance Company Ltd. is the world's second-largest reinsurance company and provider of insurance and other insurance-based forms of risk transfer. Swiss Re's global client base of insurance companies, midsized to large corporations, and public-sector organizations receives services from three company business units: Reinsurance, Corporate Solutions, and Admin Re. Reinsurance provides property and casualty insurance and life and health insurance. Corporate Solutions offers risk transfer policies to midsized and multinational corporations. Admin Re provides risk and capital management solutions. Swiss Re also offers credit and political risk insurance, which is useful for companies operating in regions of the world susceptible to political upheaval and instability. A publicly traded global firm, Swiss Re has offices in twenty-five countries.

Taylor-DeJongh
Washington, DC
www.taylor-dejongh.com

Taylor-DeJongh is a private investment banking firm that provides corporate and project finance advisory services; mergers-and-acquisitions advisory services; and strategic advisory and consulting services for oil and gas, conventional, and renewable power, industrial, and infrastructure clients. With involvement in projects through the world, Taylor-DeJongh has especially robust and specialized experience in advising on the development, structuring, negotiations, and financing of billions of dollars worth of debt and equity investments in more than a hundred countries.

UBS
Basel and Zürich, Switzerland
www.ubs.com

A global investment bank, UBS has operations in all major financial centers worldwide. Its four primary businesses are investment banking and securities, wealth management, asset management, and Swiss market retail and corporate banking. The investment bank provides securities and research in equities, fixed income, rates, foreign exchange, precious metals, and derivatives. UBS's wealth management segment offers high-net-worth individuals a range of advisory and investment products and services. The UBS asset management business line offers investment products, including equities, fixed income, alternative investments, real estate, and infrastructure for private clients and institutional investors. UBS's private wealth management division is considered especially strong on a global scale. Finally, UBS offers a consumer banking segment within its home country of Switzerland. UBS operates in more than fifty countries and has about 63,500 employees.

Zurich Insurance Group
Zürich, Switzerland
www.zurich.com

Zurich Insurance Group is a global insurance company organized into three business segments: General Insurance, Global Life, and Farmers. Zurich offers its services to individuals, small and midsized businesses, multinational corporations, and insurance brokers and dealers. Zurich Insurance also provides political risk insurance, which insures companies against issues such as riots, coups, revolts, and political upheaval. As a publicly traded company and Switzerland's largest insurer, Zurich Insurance employs about 60,000 people serving customers in more than 170 countries around the world.

International Business

Multinational Corporations

BP
London, United Kingdom
www.bp.com

BP, formerly British Petroleum, is the world's fourth-largest company and third-largest energy company, per the 2012 *Fortune* 500. BP operates in all areas of the oil and gas industry, including exploration and production, refining, petrochemicals, trading, and consumer energies. BP also has activities in renewable energies, biofuels, and wind power. The firm has operations in more than eighty countries, and in 2012 it produced approximately 3.3 million barrels of oil per day, and had nearly twenty-one thousand gas stations worldwide, the bulk of which are located in the United States. As a publicly traded multinational company, BP has a variety of staff positions available, ranging from engineers to risk analysts to futures traders.

Chevron Corporation
San Ramon, California
www.chevron.com

Chevron Corporation is the third-largest company in the United States, per the *Fortune* 500. Chevron's business includes energy exploration and production, and manufacturing, products, and transportation, all focused on the energy sector. Chevron also has smaller interests in mining, chemicals, power grids, and technology. As the fifth-most-profitable company in the world in 2012, Chevron develops traditional oil resources such as oil and natural gas, renewables such as geothermal and solar, and emerging fuel sources such as biofuels and fuel cells. It operates in more than 180 countries worldwide.

Coca-Cola Company
Atlanta, Georgia
The Coca-Cola Company is best known for its top product, Coca-Cola. In addition to this iconic soft drink, the firm currently offers more than five hundred brands in more than two hundred countries or territories and makes more than 1.7 billion servings each day. Coca-Cola's products include other well-known soft drinks, juices, waters, and sports drinks, as well as local international soft drink brands that are generally unknown in the United States. Coca-Cola receives the bulk of its sales from the United States, but an increasing amount comes from emerging markets such as Mexico, Brazil, India, and China.

ExxonMobil Corporation
Irving, Texas
www.exxonmobil.com

ExxonMobil, the global energy firm, is the largest company in the United States and the world's largest publicly traded international oil and gas company, per *Fortune*. ExxonMobil is also the world's largest refiner and marketer of petroleum products, and its chemical company ranks among the world's largest. The ExxonMobil Corporation comprises ten separate companies, making up upstream, downstream, and chemical businesses. The upstream segment provides the majority of ExxonMobil's revenues. As a publicly traded firm in the development, refinement, and transportation of energy, ExxonMobil works throughout the world.

General Electric
Fairfield, Connecticut
www.ge.com

General Electric is a global conglomerate with products in technology, manufacturing, and financial services. GE operates in four segments: energy, technology infrastructure, capital finance, and consumer and industrial. Each segment includes a host of businesses and operations, ranging from jet engines to power generation, water processing, appliances, medical imaging, and consumer finance. GE has operations in more than a hundred countries, and its main areas of business are energy infrastructure, aviation, health care, transportation, home and business solutions, and GE Capital. A publicly traded company, GE is consistently one of *Fortune*'s most profitable and largest US companies.

Google
Menlo Park, California
www.google.com

Google has stated that its mission "is to organize the world's information and make it universally accessible and useful." Its more than thirty thousand employees work in offices throughout the world, and they develop and manage products such as Gmail, Chrome, YouTube, mobile devices, Picasa, and many more. Google has grown to be a top player in the internet segment. The firm also has business functions in social responsibility, finance, marketing, and it is constantly working on new products in the technology space.

IBM
Armonk, New York
www.ibm.com

International Business Machines Corporation is an information technology company that manufactures and markets computer hardware and software, and offers infrastructure, hosting, and consulting services. IBM has five business segments: global technology services, global business services, software, systems and technology, and global financing. In 2012, per *Fortune*, IBM was ranked the second-largest US firm in number of employees, fourth in market capitalization, and nineteenth in revenue.

Johnson & Johnson
New Brunswick, New Jersey
www.jnj.com

Johnson & Johnson is a multinational manufacturer of pharmaceutical, diagnostic, therapeutic, surgical, biotechnology, and personal hygiene products. Some of J&J's many products include Tylenol, Visine, Neutrogena, and Listerine. J&J was ranked the world's most respected company by *Barron's* magazine, and it was the first corporation awarded the Benjamin Franklin Award for Public Diplomacy by the US State Department for its funding of international education programs. J&J's growth comes from markets in both developed and developing countries, with its varied product lines leading to $25.4 billion in revenue in 2012.

Mitsubishi International Corp.
New York, New York
www.mitsubishicorp.com/us/en

Mitsubishi International Corporation (MIC) is a US subsidiary of Mitsubishi Corporation (MC), the Japanese multinational firm. MC is a global business enterprise that develops and operates businesses in various industries, including industrial finance, energy, metals, machinery, chemicals, foods, and environmental business. MIC promotes and sells MC's trade and marketing services worldwide, and offers consulting services in risk management, financial resource development, project development, logistics, and other business operations. Other important functions of MIC include marketing, distribution, materials procurement, technology transfer, product sourcing, and supply chain management.

Nestlé S.A.
Vevey, Switzerland
www.nestle.com

Nestlé S.A. is a multinational nutritional, snack food, and health-related consumer goods conglomerate. Nestlé is the largest food company in the world measured by revenue, per *CNNMoney*. Nestlé's products include baby food, bottled water, breakfast cereals, coffee, confectionery, dairy products, ice cream, pet foods, and snacks. Nestlé organizes its business under the categories of food and beverages, Nestlé waters, Nestlé professional, Nespresso, Nestlé health science, and joint ventures in both the food and beverage and pharmaceutical categories. A sample of Nestlé's brands includes NesCafe, Gerber, Hot Pockets, Purina, and Lean Cuisines; however, there are also numerous others.

Novo Nordisk
Bagsvaerd, Denmark
www.novonordisk.com

Novo Nordisk is a pharmaceutical and health care company that does significant work in diabetes care. The company also has positions within hemophilia care, growth hormone therapy, and hormone replacement therapy. Its four product areas are diabetes care, haemostasis management, growth hormone therapy, and hormone replacement therapy. It also has substantial research-and-development initiatives. A publicly traded company, Novo Nordisk employs approximately 34,700 employees in 75 countries, and markets its products in more than 180 countries. In January 2012 Novo Nordisk was named the most sustainable company in the world by *Corporate Knights*, the magazine about socially responsible businesses.

Pfizer
New York, New York
www.pfizer.com

Pfizer is the world's largest pharmaceutical company by revenues, according to Bloomberg. Pfizer is known as a leader in research and development in the pharmaceutical industry, and it produces products such as Advil, Celebrex, Xanex, and Viagra. It also has a smaller consumer unit that makes goods such as Chapstick and Robitussin. Pfizer manages its operations through five segments: primary care, specialty care and oncology, established products and emerging markets, animal health and consumer health care, and nutrition. Its massive international footprint makes it a major global player with diverse international operations and initiatives.

Procter & Gamble
Cincinnati, Ohio
www.pg.com

Procter & Gamble is a consumer goods company. It sells brand-name products—primarily beauty and grooming and household care products— that are among the best-known ones in the United States. The company has offices around the world. Domestic and international career opportunities are advertised on its website.

Royal Dutch Shell
The Hague, Netherlands
www.shell.com

Royal Dutch Shell is a group of energy and petrochemical companies that operate worldwide. Shell strives to meet global energy demands and provide returns to its shareholders by investing in new projects and generating profits from existing assets. The company has offices in more than eighty countries and territories. Information regarding international positions can be found on the Royal Dutch Shell website.

Samsung Group
Seoul, South Korea
www.samsung.com

Samsung Group is a South Korean multinational conglomerate in the semicomponent and electronics manufacturing industry. Samsung is South Korea's largest *chaebol*, or family-owned conglomerate, and the company has played an important role in South Korea's economic development. Samsung is renowned for its electronics components, including LCD panels, DVD players, and wireless telephones. Its flagship unit, Samsung Electronics, is one of the top global manufacturers of DRAMs, or dynamic random-action memory, and other memory chips. Samsung SDS, Samsung Card, Samsung Life Insurance, Samsung Engineering, Samsung Securities, and Samsung C&T Corporation are all Samsung Group affiliates. Samsung has six design laboratories staffed by 450 people, and the company invests $6 billion in research per year.

Target Corporation
Minneapolis, Minnesota
www.target.com

Target Corporation is a US retailer that sells general merchandise and limited food assortments through its discount merchandise stores located in forty-nine US states and the District of Columbia. Founded in 1902 under the name Dayton Dry Goods Company, Target is now the second-largest US discount retailer after Walmart. In 2011 Target expanded its operations into Canada through its purchase of leaseholds from the Canadian chain Zellers. The company has three segments: US retail, US credit cards, and Canadian. Target offers career opportunities in the United States, Canada, and India.

Contracting

BAE Systems
Arlington, Virginia
www.baesystems.com

BAE Systems PLC is a global defense and aerospace company, or defense contractor, that offers a range of products and services for air, land, and naval forces, and customer services in advanced electronics, security, and information technology, including intelligence gathering and cybersecurity. About 43,000 employees work for BAE Systems in the United States, United Kingdom, Sweden, Israel, Mexico, and South Africa. BAE Systems, Inc., is the US subsidiary of BAE Systems PLC.

BAI Inc.
Alexandria, Virginia
www.bai-inc.net

BAI Inc. is a professional service provider serving the US government. BAI Inc., a service-disabled veteran–owned business, provides arms control, non-proliferation, national security, information technology support, security administrative support, and intelligence analysis services. The company has offices in Alexandria, Virginia, and Glynco, Georgia. Employment opportunities are advertised on the company's website.

Ball Aerospace & Technologies Corporation
Boulder, Colorado
www.ballaerospace.com

Founded in 1956, Ball Aerospace & Technologies Corporation designs, develops, and manufactures innovative aerospace systems. With a staff of 2,800, Ball Aerospace has a reputation for expertise in support of space and Earth science, exploration, national security, and intelligence programs. The company also has pioneered the development of the commercial remote-sensing market and has spurred market demand for imaging systems for spacecraft. Ball Aerospace offers a paid ten-week summer internship program. In addition to its Colorado locations, Ball Aerospace has offices in Ohio, New Mexico, Georgia, Virginia, and Washington.

Boeing Company
Chicago, Illinois
www.boeing.com

The Boeing Company is an international leader in aerospace technology and defense contractor. Boeing is the primary contractor for the International Space Station and is the largest manufacturer, by sales, of commercial jetliners and military aircraft. Boeing was ranked the second-largest defense contractor on the list of the largest one hundred US federal contractors in 2012, after Lockheed Martin.

CENTRA Technology, Inc.
Burlington, Massachusetts, and Arlington, Virginia
www.centratechnology.com

Centra Technology provides security analysis and support to the US government and private sectors. Centra offers security, analytic, technical, engineering, and management services to clients primarily in the security and defense industries. The company was founded in 1985 and has a staff of more than 560 professionals. A wide range of positions are available for intelligence analysts, systems engineers, and linguists. Immediate job openings are posted on the Centra website.

Dyncorp International
Falls Church, Virginia
www.dyn-intl.com

Dyncorp International is a government services provider. The company offers support for defense, diplomacy, and international development work. Five strategic business groups make up Dyncorp's work: aviation, contingency operations, global logistics and development solutions, security services, and training and intelligence services. Dyncorp International provides employment resources on its website, and it also lists upcoming job fairs and events where staff members can meet with prospective applicants.

General Dynamics Corporation
Washington, DC
www.generaldynamics.com

General Dynamics Corporation is an aerospace and defense company headquartered in Washington. The company has four business groups: aerospace, combat systems, information systems and technology, and marine systems. Founded in 1952, General Dynamics Corporation has acquired more than sixty businesses, and has grown significantly since the company was created. The company advertises available positions on its website.

Halliburton
Dubai, United Arab Emirates
www.halliburton.com

Halliburton, founded in 1919, is an oilfield services company and defense contractor. The company provides products and services to the energy industry, serving the upstream oil and gas industry through thirteen product service lines in two divisions: drilling and evaluation, and completion and production. Halliburton moved its headquarters to Dubai in 2007; however, it maintains a corporate office at its old headquarters in Houston. Halliburton has a staff of 72,000 employees from one hundred forty nationalities in eighty countries.

L-3 Communications
New York, New York
www.l-3com.com

L-3 Communications is a services contractor that works with US government agencies, foreign governments, and domestic and international businesses to provide national security solutions. It offers a range of services related to electronic systems, aviation modernization and maintenance, national security, and command, control, communications, intelligence, surveillance, and reconnaissance. L-3 has offices in the United States and Canada.

Lockheed Martin
Bethesda, Maryland
www.lockheedmartin.com

Lockheed Martin is a global security, aerospace, and information technology company with a special focus on researching, designing, developing, manufacturing, integrating, and ensuring the sustainability of advanced technology systems, products, and services. The majority of the firm's business is with DOD and other US federal government agencies. For instance, Lockheed Martin manages Sandia National Laboratory for DOE's National Nuclear Security Administration. Lockheed Martin employs 120,000 people worldwide and has several offices in the United States and the United Kingdom.

Mitre Corporation
Bedford, Massachusetts, and McLean, Virginia
www.mitre.org

The Mitre Corporation is a nonprofit firm that provides systems engineering, acquisition, and advanced technology expertise. Mitre was established in 1958 to create new technology for DOD. In 1963 the US Federal Aviation Administration charged Mitre with responsibility for the projected National Airspace System. Mitre operates several federally funded research-and-development centers that focus on developing a safe, efficient worldwide air traffic management system; modernizing enterprise systems; protecting the nation from terrorist threats; aiding the flow of legal immigration and commerce; and recovering from natural disasters and other national emergencies. Mitre employs top-notch engineers and scientists with experience in diverse technologies. Roughly two-thirds of Mitre's staff have a master's degree or a PhD.

Northrop Grumman
London, United Kingdom
www.northropgrumman.com

Northrop Grumman is a global security company that supports government and commercial customers around the world with systems, products, and advisory services in the areas of unmanned systems; cybersecurity; command, control, communications, computers, intelligence, surveillance, and reconnaissance; and logistics and modernization. Career opportunities are available in business, cybersecurity, engineering, health information technology, human resources and administration, and production and manufacturing. Northrop Grumman welcomes applications from students and recent graduates, military veterans, and experienced professionals.

Raytheon Company
Waltham, Massachusetts
www.raytheon.com

Raytheon Company is an international aerospace and defense firm that works with a range of commercial and government clients. Its operations cover four key areas: integrated defense systems, intelligence, military systems, and space and airborne systems. It provides products and services in eighty countries and maintains offices in nineteen countries. Raytheon International pursues business overseas and coordinates the operations of its global locations. Raytheon employees 68,000 people worldwide, and its sales reached $24 billion in 2012.

Science Applications International Corporation
McLean, Virginia
www.saic.com

Science Applications International Corporation (SAIC) is a science and technology company and defense contractor that provides scientific products, technology, and expertise in the areas of national security; health; engineering; cybersecurity; intelligence, surveillance, and reconnaissance; and logistics, readiness, and sustainment. SAIC has about 40,000 employees worldwide and offices in numerous locations across North America, Europe, Asia, and the Middle East.

SRA International
Fairfax, Virginia
www.sra.com

SRA International is an information technology consulting company. It provides services for government clients working in civil administration, defense, health, intelligence, homeland security, and law enforcement. SRA International's areas of expertise include information technology lifecycle services, solutions development and integration, management consulting, and mission-specific domain expertise. The company posts job opportunities on its website, and it also has a VIP community that candidates can join to learn more about upcoming openings.

Business Advocacy and Lobbying

Business Council for International Understanding
New York, New York
www.bciu.org

The Business Council for International Understanding (BCIU) is a nonprofit organization that connects businesses to political leaders worldwide. The organization hosts galas, conferences, roundtable discussions, and private meetings to encourage the promotion of business opportunities and the resolution of disputes. Additionally, BCIU is a certified government contractor that focuses on implementing trade projects. BCIU offers permanent positions and internships.

Emerging Markets Private Equity Association
Washington, DC
www.empea.org

The Emerging Markets Private Equity Association (EMPEA) is a membership organization that develops private equity and venture capital industries in emerging markets. EMPEA has more than three hundred members who believe that private equity can assist emerging markets by providing returns on investment and creating value for companies. The association focuses its work on three areas: education and advocacy, research, and networking. EMPEA advertises available positions on its website.

US Chamber of Commerce
Washington, DC
www.uschamber.com

The US Chamber of Commerce is a lobbying group that represents American businesses and trade associations. The chamber lobbies on behalf of more than 3 million businesses of all sizes, making it the largest business organization in the world. It aims to develop and implement policy on business issues. The chamber advertises employment opportunities on its website, where potential candidates can also apply directly online.

US–China Business Council
Washington, DC
www.uschina.org

The US–China Business Council is a private, nonprofit organization of approximately 240 US companies that conduct business with China. The council has offices in Washington, Beijing, and Shanghai, through which it provides information, advice, advocacy, and program services to its membership. Internships and job opportunities are posted on the organization's website.

United States Council for International Business
New York, New York
www.uscib.org

The United States Council for International Business (USCIB) is a protrade and promarket organization that promotes economic liberalization. USCIB provides services in the areas of policy advocacy, dispute resolution, and trade. It works with more than three hundred members, which include multinational companies, law firms, and business associations. USCIB has an office in Washington and sister organizations operating worldwide.

Consulting

Management and Strategy Consulting

Accenture
Dublin, Ireland
www.accenture.com

Accenture is a global management consulting, technology services, and outsourcing company. By identifying business and technology trends, the company helps clients enter new markets, increase revenues, improve operational performance, and deliver their products more effectively and efficiently. Accenture consults with both companies and governments worldwide. With a staff of 259,000 people, the company serves clients in more than 120 countries. Technical, engineering, management, legal, mathematical, financial, and communications backgrounds are all desirable.

Albright Stonebridge Group
Washington, DC
www.albrightstonebridge.com

Albright Stonebridge Group is a global strategy firm founded in 2001 by former US secretary of state Madeleine Albright. The company advises corporations, associations, and nonprofit organizations on how to achieve their overarching goals. By providing services in the areas of government relations, market risks, regulatory strategies, growth, partnerships, and corporate citizenship, Albright Stonebridge Group has assisted clients in more than ninety-five countries. The group is headquartered in Washington, with offices or staff in Bangkok, Beijing, Berlin, Kampala, Madrid, Moscow, New Delhi, São Paulo, Shanghai, Stockholm, and Sydney.

A.T. Kearney
Chicago, Illinois
www.atkearney.com

A.T. Kearney is a global management consulting firm that consults on strategic and operational issues. The firm works across a wide number of industries, including aerospace and defense, automotive, chemicals, communications and media technology, consumer products and retail, financial institutions, health, metals and mining, oil and gas, private equity, the public sector, transportation, travel and infrastructure, and utilities. A.T. Kearney has fifty-seven offices in thirty-nine countries, with three thousand staff members possessing broad industry experience.

Avascent Group
Washington, DC
www.avascent.com

Avascent Group is a strategy and management consulting firm that works with clients from government agencies. Avascent provides strategy, growth, marketing, and organizational services to its clients. The firm's Paris office serves as the base for its European operations. In addition to posting positions on its website, Avascent frequently hires for entry- and mid-level positions during campus recruiting sessions at universities.

Bain & Company
Boston, Massachusetts
www.bain.com

Bain & Company is a global management consulting firm founded in 1973. The firm advises global leaders on strategy, marketing, organization, operations, technology, and mergers and acquisitions across all industries. Bain works with clients including large multinational corporations, private equity firms, mid-sized companies, small start-ups, and nonprofit organizations. Bain has forty-eight offices in thirty-one countries worldwide.

BearingPoint
Amsterdam, the Netherlands
www.bearingpoint.com

BearingPoint is a management and technology consulting firm headquartered in Amsterdam. BearingPoint is organized into three industry business units: public services, commercial services, and financial services. The firm works with clients in commerce, finance, and government across a wide range of industries, tailoring solutions to each client. BearingPoint has operations in seventeen countries in Europe, North and South America, Africa, and Asia.

Booz Allen Hamilton
Washington, DC
www.boozallen.com

Booz Allen Hamilton is a strategy and technology consulting firm that provides consulting and advisory services to US government clients. The firm has expertise in strategy and technology consulting, organization, change, and process improvement, program management, human capital, learning, and communications, systems engineering and integration, public infrastructure, supply chain and logistics, and cybersecurity solutions. Booz Allen Hamilton Inc. was acquired by the private equity firm Carlyle Group in 2008, at which point **Booz & Company**, the firm's commercial arm, was spun off as a separate firm. Booz Allen employs more than 25,000 people worldwide and has offices in the United States, Azerbaijan, Georgia, Kazakhstan, Russia, Qatar, and the United Arab Emirates. Booz Allen recruits undergraduate and graduate students, transitioning military, experienced professionals, and individuals with active security clearances.

Booz & Company
New York, New York
www.booz.com

Booz & Company serves commercial and international businesses and government ministries by providing a wide array of consulting services to build organizational capabilities. The firm has offices in more than thirty countries in North America, Europe, Asia, Latin America, and Australia. Before 2008 Booz & Company was part of **Booz Allen Hamilton**. Booz & Company posts openings for experienced professionals online and recruits at US and international campuses.

Boston Consulting Group
Boston, Massachusetts
www.bcg.com

The Boston Consulting Group is a global management consulting firm that advises clients on business strategy. The group works with clients including organizations from the private, public, and nonprofit sectors. The group assists clients in identifying opportunities, addressing challenges, transforming their enterprises, building capabilities, and achieving sustainable impact. The group is a private company with more than seventy-five offices in forty-three countries.

The Cohen Group
Washington, DC
www.cohengroup.net

The Cohen Group is a global business and strategy consultancy founded by former secretary of defense William S. Cohen. The group advises multinational companies to compete in global markets. It provides strategic advice in marketing and regulatory affairs, and it also assists clients with transactional services. The group has offices in Washington, Beijing, and Tianjin, China.

Deloitte LLP
New York, New York
www.deloitte.com

Deloitte LLP is an organization of member firms around the world that provide audit, tax, consulting, and financial advisory services to twenty industries and sectors, such as oil and gas, state and federal governments, banking and securities, and aerospace and defense. As the world's largest management consulting firm, Deloitte provides talent and capabilities in the areas of human capital, strategy and operations, and technology. It has 193,000 employees in more than 150 countries. Student opportunities include the Deloitte Global Internship program, which places interns in a host country for four weeks. Global interns have the opportunity to work in teams on business cases, develop cross-cultural awareness, and build their network. Deloitte also hosts an annual invitation-only International Student Business Forum. Interested candidates should complete an online application.

Frontier Strategy Group
Washington, DC
www.frontierstrategygroup.com

Frontier Strategy Group (FSG) is a strategy consulting firm specializing in emerging market clients. Founded in 2007, the firm provides information services to executives of more than two hundred multinational companies in emerging markets. FSG provides market intelligence, best practice research, analytical tools, events, and networks, among other services, to assist clients in successfully performing in emerging markets. The firm has regional offices in Singapore, London, Miami, and New York.

McKinsey & Company
New York, New York
www.mckinsey.com

McKinsey & Company is a global management consulting firm that advises businesses, governments, and institutions worldwide. McKinsey works with clients to expand their growth opportunities, help them explore entry into new markets, and capitalize on new technology. Additionally, McKinsey provides a range of other services on request. The firm has more than a hundred offices in more than fifty countries. More than half of McKinsey's consultants possess a PhD, JD, MD, or nonbusiness master's degree. Undergraduates typically enter the firm as business analysts. Those entering with advanced professional degrees typically have an accelerated career path.

Risk Consulting

Business Monitor International
London, United Kingdom
www.businessmonitor.com

Business Monitor International (BMI) is a risk consulting firm. BMI assimilates data on country risks, financial markets, and industry research to advise clients on managing risks and utilizing business opportunities. The firm has a range of clients, including multinational companies, financial institutions, multilaterals, and governments. BMI posts current vacancies on its website.

Center for Intelligence Research and Analysis
Washington, DC
www.defensegroupinc.com

The Center for Intelligence Research and Analysis (CIRA), a division of Defense Group Inc. (DGI), provides open source and cultural intelligence services to clients throughout the US government and business community. Staffed by an experienced team of security-cleared analysts with advanced language skills, CIRA's mission is to provide cutting-edge open source and cultural intelligence support to its clients. CIRA accomplishes its mission through the conduct of objective, independent, and relevant research and analysis, under strict quality guidelines. DGI seeks talented people from a variety of disciplines. Those with active security clearances are highly encouraged to apply. All applicants selected are subject to a government security investigation and must meet eligibility requirements for access to classified information.

Control Risks
London, United Kingdom
www.controlrisks.com

Control Risks is a global risk consultancy that specializes in advising organizations on managing political, integrity, and security risks. The firm assists clients by consulting on strategy, providing in-depth analysis and investigations, advising on political issues, and giving support and protection on the ground in complex or hostile environments. Control Risks has offices in Africa, the Americas, Asia, Europe, and the Middle East.

Diligence
London, United Kingdom
www.diligence.com

Diligence is a risk consultancy that assists clients in confronting business challenges. Diligence uses business intelligence and analysis to inform clients of the potential risks originating from regular business operations or unforeseen occurrences. The consultancy works primarily in the finance and banking sectors, but it also provides support to extractive industries. It has offices in London, New York, Geneva, Moscow, and São Paulo.

Ergo
New York, New York
www.ergo.net

Ergo is an intelligence and advisory firm that collects and analyzes data to help clients identify new opportunities, make decisions, and protect assets. Ergo has clients operating in a wide range of industries, and it has conducted projects in more than ninety countries. Ergo has regional offices in Washington, Chicago, Abu Dhabi, and Beijing.

Eurasia Group
New York, New York
www.eurasiagroup.net

Eurasia Group is a political risk research and consulting company. Founded in 1998, it originally focused on the Soviet Union and Eastern Europe, but it now monitors political, economic, social, and security developments in Africa, Asia, Europe, Latin America, the Middle East, and North America.

The company also examines cross-border issues such as trade, energy and other commodities, financial regulation, climate change, and global health. Eurasia Group works with clients—including financial institutions, multinational corporations, and government agencies—to identify risks in their operating environments.

Exclusive Analysis
London, United Kingdom
www.exclusive-analysis.com

Exclusive Analysis is an intelligence company that forecasts business-related risks. Using intelligence tools, the firm forecasts political risks in order to inform business leaders worldwide of potential risks to their work. Forecasts are classified by region on the company's website, where viewers can also register for intelligence updates. Immediate job openings are posted on the career section of the company's website.

iJET Intelligent Risk Systems
Annapolis, Maryland
www.ijet.com

iJET Intelligent Risk Systems provides operational risk management solutions. The company utilizes intelligence to inform multinational corporations and government organizations of potential risks to their operations. iJET also customizes preparedness and response solutions for clients. Current employment opportunities are advertised on the company's website.

Information Handling Services, Inc.
Douglas County, Colorado
www.ihs.com

Information Handling Services, Inc. (IHS), is a global information company that serves international clients in the areas of energy, economics, geopolitical risk, sustainability, and supply chain management. The company specializes in data-supported solutions that help clients plan market and investment strategies, improve operational efficiencies, and reduce costs and supply chain risk in global markets. IHS brands include **IHS Jane's**, a global defense and security company; **IHS Cambridge Research Associates, Inc.**, which provides advisory services on energy markets to clients; and **IHS Herold**, an independent research firm that analyzes companies, transactions, and trends in the global energy industry. IHS has more than 5,500 employees in more than thirty countries.

Kroll
New York, New York
www.kroll.com

Kroll is a risk and security consulting firm founded in 1972. Kroll provides advisory services in the areas of corporate investigations, business intelligence, due diligence, cybersecurity, and physical security. The company has offices in the Americas, Europe, the Middle East, and Asia. Kroll posts internship and full-time positions on its website.

McLarty Associates
Washington, DC
www.maglobal.com

McLarty Associates is an international strategic advisory firm that advises established corporations, emerging companies, and nonprofits on strategic planning, government issues, market access, and risk issues, among other services. Additionally, the firm has specialized practices in the areas of financial markets, film and entertainment, and food and agriculture.

Oxford Analytica
Oxford, United Kingdom
www.oxan.com

Oxford Analytica is a strategic advisory and analysis consultancy. The firm researches and analyzes macroeconomic shifts and global politics in order to advise clients on strategy and performance. It has regional offices in New York, Washington, Paris, and Hong Kong. It offers summer internships in Oxford and year-round internships in Washington.

PFC Energy
Washington, DC
www.pfcenergy.com

PFC Energy is a global consulting firm specializing in the oil and gas industry. By providing oil and gas consulting, risk analysis, and forward-looking scenarios, PFC Energy assists clients in strategy development, investment evaluations, and commercial decisions. The company has offices in Beijing, Houston, Kuala Lumpur, Moscow, Paris, Singapore, and Washington. PFC Energy has been serving oil and gas operators, national oil companies, service companies, investors, governments and other stakeholders since 1984.

Stratfor
Austin, Texas
www.stratfor.com

Stratfor is a global intelligence company that publishes daily geopolitical analysis that clients can access by subscribing through its website. Using open-source monitoring and a network of contacts, Stratfor collects and analyzes intelligence and publishes the results. Stratfor has professional positions available, as well as a three-month analyst development program held in Austin.

Development Consulting

Abt Associates
Cambridge, Massachusetts
www.abtassociates.com

Abt Associates is a global research and program implementation firm. The firm addresses challenges in the fields of social, economic, and health policy, and international development. It consults with governments, businesses, and private organizations, and it offers technical assistance, research, information technology, and data collection services to clients. Abt Associates has program offices in more than thirty countries.

Bankable Frontier Associates
Somerville, Massachusetts
www.bankablefrontier.com

Bankable Frontier Associates (BFA) is a consulting firm that provides financial services and promotes financial inclusion. BFA concentrates its work in developing countries where access to financial services is limited. It connects development agencies, donors, financial regulators, and government social transfer programs with banks, payment service providers, payment system operators, insurers, and investors to improve access to financial services for unserved populations. BFA has staff members located in Africa, Latin America, Europe, and the United States.

The Bridgespan Group
Boston, Massachusetts
www.bridgespan.org

The Bridgespan Group advises nonprofit organizations and philanthropies. It works with clients in three primary areas: opportunities for disadvantaged populations, environmental sustainability, and civic engagement. It provides services in strategy consulting, leadership development, and philanthropy advising, and it also offers a nonprofit job board where users can search for jobs in nonprofit organizations around the world. This job board and information about working for the group can be found on the company's website.

Business for Social Responsibility
San Francisco, California
www.bsr.org

Business for Social Responsibility (BSR) is a sustainability consulting and research firm. BSR provides sustainability strategy services for a global network of three hundred member companies to assist them in maintaining a competitive advantage in global markets. The firm offers consulting, research, and cross-sector collaboration services to its members to encourage corporate responsibility and collective action. BSR has offices in Beijing, Guangzhou, Hong Kong, New York, Paris, San Francisco, and São Paulo.

CARANA Corporation
Arlington, Virginia
www.carana.com

CARANA Corporation is a consulting firm that works on economic growth strategies. CARANA has managed more than 250 projects for government, business, and donor clients, particularly USAID. The firm designs and directs strategies for enterprise development, agribusiness, trade policy and support, labor markets, and financial-sector development. CARANA supports projects around the globe.

Castalia Strategic Advisors
Washington, DC
www.castalia-advisors.com

Castalia Strategic Advisors is a public service delivery advisory firm. Founded in 1980, Castalia adapted French models for public service delivery to situations in Europe, Asia, Africa, Latin America, and the Caribbean. The firm advises clients on strategy, public policy, regulation, and governance. Castalia also has offices in Paris, Sydney, and Wellington.

Chemonics International Inc.
Washington, DC
www.chemonics.com

Chemonics International is an international development consulting firm that has formed partnerships with local and international organizations to promote social and economic change around the world. Chemonics manages projects in 145 countries in the areas of agriculture, conflict and disaster management, democracy and governance, education, energy, environmental services, financial services, gender, health, development management services, and private-sector development. The company offers an entry-level professional program that recruits and develops professionals for a career in international development.

DAI
Bethesda, Maryland
www.dai.com

Development Alternatives Inc. (DAI) is a private development company providing consulting services in the fields of economic growth, governance, corporate services, health, stability, and environment and energy. DAI serves government and private-sector clients in more than 150 countries. DAI has regional offices in Jordan, Mexico, Pakistan, Palestine, South Africa, and the United Kingdom.

Dalberg Global Development Advisors
New York, New York
www.dalberg.com

Dalberg is a strategic advisory firm that addresses global challenges and aims to raise living standards in developing countries. Since the company was founded in 2001, it has worked on more than eight hundred projects in more than ninety countries in all regions of the world. Its clients include both corporations, foundations, and NGOs working in developing markets and also national governments. The firm has offices worldwide, including in Copenhagen, Dakar, Geneva, Johannesburg, Mumbai, Nairobi, New York, San Francisco, and Washington.

Development Transformations
Washington, DC
www.developmenttransformations.com

Development Transformations (DT) is a consultancy focused on development projects in conflict and postconflict areas. DT utilizes best practices from its experience working in countries in conflict or transition to inform programs that contribute to stabilization. Its main clients are USAID, DOD, nonprofit organizations, development firms, and foreign governments.

Financial Markets International, Inc.
Washington, DC
www.fmi-inc.net

Financial Markets International, Inc. (FMI), is an international law and economics consulting firm headquartered in Washington. It works with international donor agencies and private commercial clients to promote economic growth in emerging markets. FMI has worked in more than thirty countries. Current job opportunities are advertised on its website.

Global Emergency Group
Middleburg, Virginia
www.globalemergencygroup.com

The Global Emergency Group consults on humanitarian response, with the goal of improving humanitarian coordination worldwide. The group specializes in humanitarian response consulting, operations support, humanitarian response and coordination training, disaster risk reduction, logistics and supply chain consulting, and evaluations. It has an office in London.

Management Systems International
Washington, DC
www.msiworldwide.com

Management Systems International (MSI) is an international development firm. MSI provides technical assistance for international development programs, particularly in conflict-prone and fragile states. The firm has expertise in democracy and governance, economic growth, strategic planning, organizational capacity building, health, and the justice sector. The firm currently manages more than seventy projects worldwide. In 2008 Coffey International Development, a development firm, acquired MSI.

Business Consulting

American Continental Group, Inc.
Washington, DC
www.acg-consultants.com

American Continental Group, Inc. (ACG), is a government affairs and strategic consulting firm. ACG advises businesses, states and municipalities, and nonprofit organizations. The firm offers strategy consulting services, such as counsel and advocacy, as well as business services that analyze how policy decisions will affect business portfolios. The ACG website provides information regarding careers and internships with the firm.

APCO Worldwide
Washington, DC
www.apcoworldwide.com

APCO Worldwide is an independent, global communication and business strategy consultancy that serves clients including multinational companies, trade associations, governments, NGOs, and educational institutions. Its team of more than six hundred employees works in thirty offices across major business and media capitals in the United States and globally across five continents. APCO is a women-owned business that is certified under the Women Presidents' Educational Organization. It offers student internships as well as global career opportunities at the entry level, mid level, associate consultant/consultant level, managerial level, and director level.

BroadReach Healthcare
Arlington, Virginia
www.broadreachhealthcare.com

BroadReach Healthcare is a health care consulting company that strives to improve access to health care by providing implementation and program management services to a wide range of clients. The firm works with large donors and life sciences companies to increase access to health care, treatment, and medicines in the developing world. BroadReach operates in more than thirty countries and has main offices in South Africa, Kenya, Switzerland, and China.

Corporate Executive Board
Arlington, Virginia
www.executiveboard.com

Corporate Executive Board (CEB) is a member-based company that provides research and advisory services to businesses. It advises clients on best practices and decision making, talent management and measurement, and tools and solutions to improve business impact. CEB has offices in the United States, Canada, the United Kingdom, Germany, India, Singapore, and Australia. Positions are available for research analysts and associates, sales associates, and managers, among others.

DCI Group
Washington, DC
www.dcigroup.com

DCI Group is a public affairs consulting firm that assists its clients with public relations, communications, government affairs, and business. The firm specializes in helping clients shape their messages and establish strategic partnerships. DCI Group has offices in Washington, Brussels, and Houston.

Environmental Resources Management Group, Inc.
London, United Kingdom
www.erm.com

The Environmental Resources Management Group, Inc. (ERM), is a sustainability consultancy founded in 1971. It provides environmental, health, safety, risk, and social consulting services to business and government clients. In addition to the consultancy, ERM staff contribute pro bono time and funding to the ERM Foundation, which supports environmental initiatives worldwide. ERM has more than 140 offices in thirty-nine countries.

Ernst & Young
Wilmington, Delaware
www.ey.com

Ernst & Young is an international professional services and accounting firm. Ernst & Young is a global organization of member firms located in more than 140 countries with headquarters in Wilmington, Delaware. The company assists its clients by offering advisory, assurance, tax, transactions, and strategic growth markets services. It has developed global industry centers around the world that serve as virtual hubs for sharing industry-focused knowledge and experience, and it has a global network of 167,000 professionals who work across a number of industries. Ernst & Young is one of the "Big Four" auditors, along with **Deloitte**, **KPMG International**, and **PricewaterhouseCoopers** (see the separate listing for each firm).

Grant Thornton LLP
Chicago, Illinois
www.grantthornton.com

Grant Thornton LLP is a professional services firm that offers assistance to clients in the areas of audits, taxes, and advisory services. The company is part of the global network of Grant Thornton International, which has partner organizations in more than a hundred countries. Grant Thornton provides information about career opportunities for recent graduates and experienced professionals on its website.

KPMG LLP
Amstelveen, Netherlands
www.kpmg.com

KPMG LLP is a professional services company offering audit, tax, and advisory services. It works across a number of industries spanning both the public and private sectors. KPMG LLP is the US member firm of KPMG International Cooperative, which has partners in 152 countries. KPMG is one of the "Big Four" auditors, along with **Deloitte**, **Ernst & Young**, and **PricewaterhouseCoopers** (see the separate listing for each firm).

Marsh & McLennan Companies, Inc.
New York, New York
www.mmc.com

Marsh & McLennan Companies is a professional services and insurance brokerage firm. The company is composed of four subsidiaries: Marsh, a risk and insurance company; Guy Carpenter, which advises clients on risk management and reinsurance; Mercer, a talent, health, retirement, and investments consulting firm; and the Oliver Wyman Group, a global management consulting firm. Marsh & McLennan has employees located in more than a hundred countries worldwide.

Navigant Consulting
Chicago, Illinois
www.navigant.com

Navigant Consulting is a dispute consulting and business advisory consulting firm. Founded in 1999, the firm offers services in the areas of disputes and investigations, economic and financial advisory and analysis, management consulting, and research. Navigant has offices in North America, Europe, the Middle East, and Asia.

PricewaterhouseCoopers
London, United Kingdom
www.pwc.com

PricewaterhouseCoopers (PwC) is a multinational professional services firm formed in 1998. PwC offers audit and assurance, tax, and consulting services to clients. The company's US office provides additional services in the areas of human resources, deals, forensics, and other services. PwC has offices in 159 countries. PwC is one of the "Big Four" auditors, along with **Deloitte**, **Ernst & Young**, and **KPMG International** (see the separate listing for each firm).

Qorvis Communications
Washington, DC
www.qorvis.com

Qorvis Communications is a digital and public relations agency that advises governments, trade associations, nonprofits, and corporations on communications and marketing strategies. The agency specializes in public relations, advertising, media relations, and crisis communications.

Vista International, LLC
Vienna, Virginia
www.vistaintl.com

Vista International LLC is a consulting firm providing business entry and market analysis services. Vista International conducts research and decision-making analysis in order to advise clients on business facilitation. The firm has offices on the East and West coasts of the United States, but it also works on projects in East and Central Asia, Southeast Asia, Europe, the Middle East, Africa, and South America.

Weber Shandwick
New York, New York
www.webershandwick.com

Weber Shandwick is a public relations firm started in 2001. The firm offers public relations and communications services to companies operating in a variety of industries. It has seventy-three offices in thirty-one countries, as well as a network of partner companies throughout the world. It offers internships and full-time positions, and more information regarding career opportunities can be found on its website.

Universities, Research Institutes, and Think Tanks

American Enterprise Institute
Washington, DC
www.aei.org

The American Enterprise Institute (AEI) is a private, nonpartisan, nonprofit institution dedicated to research and education on issues of government policies, economics, politics, and social welfare. Through inquiry, debate, and writing, AEI supports the principles of limited government, competitive private enterprise, individual liberty and responsibility, vital cultural and political institutions, and vigilant and effective defense and foreign policies. Entry-level opportunities include research assistant positions in all of

AEI's policy areas. Positions ranging from the entry to executive levels are regularly available in development, event planning, government relations, communications, human resources, accounting, information technology, public relations, and other business departments. Internships are also available year-round for undergraduate and graduate students.

Aspen Institute
Washington, DC
www.aspeninstitute.org

The Aspen Institute is an international nonprofit organization dedicated to fostering enlightened leadership and open-minded dialogue through seminars, policy programs, conferences, and leadership development initiatives. The institute has campuses in Aspen, Colorado, and on the Wye River on Maryland's Eastern Shore. Its international network includes partner Aspen Institutes in Berlin, Rome, Lyon, Tokyo, New Delhi, and Bucharest, as well as leadership programs in Africa, Central America, and India. Full-time employment opportunities are listed on the Aspen Institute website. The institute also offers a variety of internship and fellowship opportunities.

Atlantic Council of the United States
Washington, DC
www.acus.org

The Atlantic Council of the United States promotes constructive US leadership and engagement in international affairs based on the central role of the Atlantic community in tacking twenty-first-century challenges. The council seeks to stimulate dialogue on critical international issues and promote consensus on appropriate responses of the US administration, Congress, the corporate and nonprofit sectors, and the media, as well as among leaders in Europe, Asia, and the Americas. The council also conducts educational and exchange programs for successive generations of US leaders. It offers fall, spring, and summer internship opportunities as well as career opportunities, including entry-level research assistant positions.

Battelle Memorial Institute
Columbus, Ohio
www.battelle.org

Battelle Memorial Institute is the world's largest nonprofit research-and-development organization with a mission to bring business and scientific interests together to achieve positive change. As a 501(c)(3) tax-exempt charitable trust, Battelle's work includes managing the world's leading national laboratories and maintaining a contract research portfolio that includes national security, health and life sciences, energy, the environment, material sciences, and education. With a staff of more than twenty thousand employees across more than a hundred locations globally, Battelle provides resources and talents for a broad range of clients—from large government agencies and multinational corporations to small start-ups and incubator projects.

Brookings Institution
Washington, DC
www.brookings.edu

The Brookings Institution is a private, nonprofit organization devoted to independent research and innovative policy solutions that inform the public debate rather than advance a political agenda. More than 140 resident and nonresident scholars research issues; write books, papers, articles, and opinion pieces; testify before congressional committees; and participate in dozens of public events each year. More than 200 research assistants and support staff contribute to the institution's research, publishing, communications, fund-raising, and information technology operations. Brookings maintains an employment page on its website for career and internship opportunities.

Carnegie Endowment for International Peace
Washington, DC
www.carnegieendowment.org

The Carnegie Endowment for International Peace is a private, nonprofit organization dedicated to advancing cooperation between nations and promoting active international engagement by the United States. It was founded in 1910, and its work is nonpartisan and dedicated to achieving practical results. The endowment has offices in Washington, Moscow, Beijing, Beirut, and Brussels—five locations that the endowment believes will determine the near-term possibilities for international peace and economic advancement. The endowment offers a variety of job and internship opportunities in its Washington and global locations.

Center for New American Security
Washington, DC
www.cnas.org

The mission of the Center for a New American Security (CNAS) is to develop strong, pragmatic, and principled national security and defense policies. CNAS was founded in 2007 by Michele Flournoy and Kurt M. Campbell. Building on the expertise and experience of its staff and advisers, CNAS engages policymakers, experts, and the public with innovative, fact-based research, ideas, and analysis to shape and elevate the national security debate.

A key part of CNAS's mission is to inform and prepare the national security leaders of today and tomorrow. Its research is independent and nonpartisan. CNAS does not take institutional positions on policy issues.

Center for Economic and Policy Research
Washington, DC
www.cepr.net

The Center for Economic and Policy Research (CEPR) was established in 1999 to promote democratic debate on critical social and economic issues. CEPR is committed to presenting issues in an accurate and clear manner, through professional research and public education. CEPR was cofounded by the economists Dean Baker and Mark Weisbrot, and the CEPR Advisory Board includes the Nobel laureate economists Robert Solow and Joseph Stiglitz; Janet Gornick, a professor at the City University of New York's Graduate School and director of the Luxembourg Income Study; and Richard Freeman, a professor of economics at Harvard University. Apart from the senior economist and director levels, positions are offered for interns, research assistants, program assistants, research associates, and senior research associates, among others.

Center for Strategic and International Studies
Washington, DC
www.csis.org

The Center for Strategic and International Studies (CSIS) is a bipartisan, nonprofit research organization that strives to advance global security and prosperity by providing strategic insights and practical policy solutions to decision makers. Founded in 1962, CSIS is guided by a board of trustees chaired by former senator Sam Nunn and consisting of prominent individuals from both the public and private sectors. The nearly two hundred researchers and support staff at CSIS focus on three main subject areas: (1) defense and security; (2) regional stability; and (3) transnational challenges, ranging from energy and climate to global development and economic integration. A variety of internship and career opportunities are available for talented individuals with interest and experience in CSIS's regional and functional policy areas.

Council on Foreign Relations
New York, New York
www.crf.org

The Council on Foreign Relations (CFR) is a leading nonprofit membership organization, research center, and publisher dedicated to increasing America's understanding of the world and contributing ideas to US foreign policy. CFR has an office in Washington and programs nationwide, and its more than four thousand members are prominent leaders in international affairs and foreign policy. It publishes *Foreign Affairs*, a prominent journal on global issues, and it provides up-to-date information about the world and US foreign policy on its website. Graduates are typically hired as research associates or program associates, whose responsibilities include research, writing, editing, program development and coordination, budget management, and administration. CFR also sponsors a professional development training program to enhance and build skills for associates' current and future work in the field.

Henry L. Stimson Center
Washington, DC
www.stimson.org

The Stimson Center is a nonprofit, nonpartisan institution dedicated to offering practical solutions to problems of national and international security. Since its founding in 1989 by Barry Blechman and Michael Krepon, the Stimson Center has been engaged with key international security issues—from eliminating weapons of mass destruction to confidence-building measures for the Korean Peninsula. The Stimson Center offers a variety of job and internship opportunities throughout the year.

Heritage Foundation
Washington D.C.
www.heritage.org

The Heritage Foundation is a think tank dedicated to formulating and promoting conservative public policies based on the principles of free enterprise, limited government, individual freedom, traditional American values, and a strong national defense. The foundation's staff pursues this mission by producing research, generating solutions consistent with their beliefs, and marketing these findings to Congress, the executive branch, the news media, and others. Several professional positions are filled annually, and openings are listed on the careers page of the foundation's website. The Heritage Foundation also maintains a job bank that places qualified applicants in policymaking positions throughout the administration and Congress.

International Institute for Sustainable Development
Winnipeg, Canada
www.iiss.org

The International Institute for Sustainable Development (IISD) is a Canadian-based international public policy research institute for sustainable development with offices in Winnipeg, Ottawa, Geneva, and New York. IISD believes sustainable development must be promoted not only by generating wealth but also by advancing social justice, combating poverty, and promoting a healthy and resilient ecosystem. Through its research and the communication of its findings, IISD engages decision makers in government, business, NGOs, and other sectors to develop and implement policies that are simultaneously beneficial to the global economy, to the global environment, and to social well-being. IISD runs an international internship program for young Canadian professionals seeking to gain experience in sustainable international development.

National Bureau of Asian Research
Seattle, Washington
www.nbr.org

The National Bureau of Asian Research (NBR) conducts advanced independent research on strategic, political, economic, health, and energy issues affecting US relations with Asia. Drawing upon an extensive network of the world's leading specialists, NBR disseminates its research through briefings, publications, conferences, congressional testimony, and e-mail forums, as well as through collaboration with leading institutions worldwide. NBR provides internship opportunities for graduate and undergraduate students aimed at attracting and training the next generation of Asia specialists. With offices in Seattle and Washington, NBR offers temporary positions, including internships, fellowships, and a variety of positions in research, project management, and administrative or business functions.

Peterson Institute for International Economics
Washington, DC
www.iie.com

The Peterson Institute for International Economics is a private, nonprofit, nonpartisan research institution devoted to the study of international economic policy. The institute's staff of about fifty includes more than two dozen researchers. Its agenda emphasizes global macroeconomic topics, international money and finance, trade and related social issues, investment, and the international implications of new technologies. Current priority is given to China, globalization and the backlash against it, outsourcing, the reform of the international financial architecture, and new trade negotiations at the multilateral, regional, and bilateral levels. Institute staff cover all key regions—especially Asia, Europe, the Middle East, and Latin America, as well as the United States itself.

RAND Corporation
Santa Monica, California
www.rand.org

The RAND Corporation is a broad-based think tank with a mission to help policymakers around the world find solutions in the areas of defense, health care, education, criminal and civil justice, and other issues. RAND employs more than 1,500 full and part-time staff. Eighty-five percent of RAND's research staff hold advanced degrees. Most researchers work in RAND's Santa Monica headquarters, and several hundred are also based in Washington, Pittsburgh, Cambridge, and Doha.

US Institute of Peace
Washington, DC
www.usip.org

The US Institute for Peace (USIP) is an independent, nonpartisan conflict management center created by the US Congress to prevent and mitigate international conflict without resorting to violence. USIP works to save lives, increase the government's ability to deal with conflicts before they escalate, reduce government costs, and enhance US national security. USIP offers a variety of staff and contractor positions and paid part-time research assistant student positions. Graduates are typically hired as program assistants. Ideal candidates should have a record of high academic achievement, a degree in international relations or a related field, and work and/or internship experience, including strong administrative, research, writing, and computer skills. Language skills and regional expertise may be required for some positions.

Woodrow Wilson International Center for Scholars
Washington, DC
www.wilsoncenter.org

The Woodrow Wilson International Center for Scholars is a research institute dedicated to independent research, open dialogue, and actionable ideas. Based in Washington, the Wilson Center hosts approximately 160 scholars who conduct independent research on national and/or international issues addressing key public policy challenges. The center hosts scholars in residence through a variety of programs, including its flagship international Fellowship Program, its Public Policy Scholar Program, and through individual Center Scholars Programs. The center also offers a variety of other job, internship, and fellowship opportunities throughout the year.

The Media

Agence France-Presse
Paris, France
www.afp.com (French-language site); www.afp.com / en / home
  (English-language site)

Agence France-Presse (AFP) is the largest French news agency, and one of
the three large wire services in the world alongside the Associated Press
and Reuters (see the **AP** and **Reuters** entries below). AFP is headquartered
in Paris and has regional offices in Nicosia, Montevideo, Hong Kong, and
Washington and bureaus in 150 countries. AFP transmits news in French,
English, Arabic, Spanish, German, and Portuguese. AFP is a government-
chartered public corporation, but it is officially a commercial business independent of the French government.

Al Jazeera
Doha, Qatar
www.aljazeera.net / portal (Arabia-language site); www.aljazeera.com
  (English-language site)

Al Jazeera is a broadcaster owned by the privately held Al Jazeera Media
Network. Initially launched as an Arabic news and current affairs satellite
TV channel, Al Jazeera now encompasses several outlets, including the internet and specialty TV channels, broadcasting in multiple languages around
the world. Until 2011 Al Jazeera was owned by the Government of Qatar,
although its present editorial independence is disputed. The Al Jazeera Network has received acclaim for its coverage of the war in Afghanistan and the
Arab uprisings in 2011. Al Jazeera operates through more than sixty bureaus
across six continents.

Asahi Shimbun
Osaka, Japan
www.asahi.com (Japanese-language site); www.asahi.com /english
  (English-language site)

Asahi Shimbun, or *Morning Sun Newspaper*, is one of the oldest and largest
national daily newspapers in Japan. The newspaper has a circulation of 7.96
million for its morning edition and 3.1 million for its evening edition. The
newspaper has both Japanese- and English-language websites. The *Asahi
Shimbun* has offices in several cities throughout Japan and representative
offices worldwide.

Associated Press
www.ap.org
New York, New York

The Associated Press is a nonprofit cooperative owned by its contributing news, radio, and television stations in the United States. Many newspapers and broadcasters outside the United States are AP subscribers and pay a fee to use AP material. In 2005 news collected by AP was used by more than 1,700 newspapers and 5,000 television and radio broadcasters. The Associated Press has an international staff working at bureaus in more than 120 countries.

BBC
London, United Kingdom
www.bbc.com

The BBC is a semiautonomous British public service broadcasting corporation. Its primary mission is to provide impartial public service broadcasting in the United Kingdom, the Channel Islands, and the Isle of Man. The BBC is the largest broadcaster in the world, with a staff of about 23,000. Outside the United Kingdom, the BBC World Service has provided services by direct broadcasting and retransmission contracts by sound radio since the inauguration of the BBC Empire Service in December 19, 1932, and more recently by television and online.

Bloomberg
New York, New York
www.bloomberg.com

Bloomberg is a global business and financial information provider and news agency. Bloomberg delivers global news via television, radio, mobile devices, the internet, and two magazines, *Bloomberg Businessweek* and *Bloomberg Markets*. The company delivers data, news, and analytics to more than 300,000 subscribers globally as part of its professional services. In addition to Bloomberg's global headquarters in New York City, it has regional headquarters in London and Hong Kong. With a staff of more than 15,000 people globally, it employs people in 192 locations around the world.

CNN
Atlanta, Georgia
www.cnn.com

CNN is a global news agency with more than two dozen news and information services transmitted via cable, satellite, radio, wireless devices, and the internet across two hundred countries. CNN's US cable network broadcasts primarily from its headquarters in Atlanta, the Time Warner Center in New York City, and its stations in Washington and Los Angeles. CNN International is the most-watched global 24-hour news network, and it encompasses several regional services: CNN International Europe, the Middle East, Africa, Asia Pacific, South Asia, Latin America, and North America. CNN offers an hourly, nonsalaried video journalist program for entry-level employees in addition to other job and internship opportunities.

Economist Group
London, United Kingdom
www.economistgroup.com

The Economist Group provides analysis on international business and world affairs through publications in a range of formats, from newspapers and magazines to conferences and electronic services. Its publications and services include *The Economist* newspaper, the Economist Intelligence Unit, *CQ Roll Call*, and *European Voice*, among others. The Economist has a staff of 1,500 throughout the world, with offices in London, Beijing, Brussels, Frankfurt, Geneva, Paris, Dubai, Johannesburg, New Delhi, New York, Washington, Hong Kong, Shanghai, Singapore, and Tokyo. The Economist Group offers job and internship opportunities in its offices in the Americas, United Kingdom, Continental Europe, the Middle East and Africa, and Asia.

Foreign Policy
Washington, DC
www.foreignpolicy.com

Foreign Policy is a daily online magazine and monthly US print magazine founded by Samuel P. Huntington and Warren Demian Manshel. Contributors to *Foreign Policy* include former diplomats, speechwriters, foreign policy advisers, award-winning journalists, scholars, and authors. The magazine aims to strike a balance between providing content for international relations specialists and engaging the general-interest reader. *Foreign Policy* publishes in English and Spanish, and the magazine accepts submissions for publication. Job and internship opportunities are available throughout the year.

NPR
Washington, DC
www.npr.org

NPR, formerly National Public Radio, is a nonprofit membership media organization that broadcasts across the United States through a network of nine hundred public radio stations. NPR receives both public and private funding and is well known for its two flagship news broadcasts, *Morning Edition* and *All Things Considered*. Its content is available via the Web, mobile devices, and podcasts. NPR offers a fall, spring, and summer internship program for students and recent graduates in Washington and its affiliates throughout the United States.

Reuters
London, United Kingdom
www.reuters.com

Reuters, an international news agency, is a division of Thomson Reuters, a New York City–based multimedia and information firm dedicated to delivering intelligent information for businesses and professionals. The world's largest international news agency, Reuters operates two hundred bureaus around the world and employs nearly three thousand journalists. Reuters offers a trainee program for aspiring journalists, who are given the opportunity to work in newsrooms in Europe, the United States, Latin America, and Asia. Internships are considered crash courses in political, business, and general news reporting, and advanced language skills are considered an asset. The training portion of the program covers writing skills, journalism ethics, and basic financial knowledge. If journalistic standards are met, the nine-month training program can lead to a staff job.

Voice of America
Washington, DC
www.voanews.com

Voice of America (VOA) is the official external broadcast institution of the US federal government. It is one of five civilian US international broadcasters under the umbrella of the Broadcasting Board of Governors, the others being Radio and TV Matri, Middle East Broadcasting Networks (which include Radio Sawa, Al Hurra, and Radio Farda), Radio Free Europe / Radio Liberty, and Radio Free Asia. VOA provides a range of programming for radio, TV, and the Web in more than forty languages, reaching an estimated global audience of more than 123 million people. The mission of the organization is to promote freedom and democracy, and to enhance understanding through multimedia communication of accurate, objective, and balanced news, information, and other programming about America and the world to audiences overseas. Jobs with VOA are advertised on the USAJOBS website (www.usajobs.gov). Strong writing, editing, multimedia production, and foreign language abilities are desired skills for positions with VOA.

Wall Street Journal
New York, New York
www.wsj.com

The *Wall Street Journal* is a US English-language international daily newspaper that specializes in business and economic news. Founded in 1889, the *Journal* has the largest circulation of any newspaper in the United States. Its online website was launched in 1996 and operates as a paid subscription news site. The *Journal* has US, Asian, and European versions in various languages, and it is published by Dow Jones & Company.

Index